The Last Generation of Jews in Poland

Efraim Shmueli

Cherry
Orchard
Books

The Last Generation of Jews in Poland

Efraim
Shmueli

Edited and Translated
by Gila Shmueli

BOSTON
2021

Originally published in Hebrew as *Bador ha-yehudi ha-aḥaron be-Polin*
by Aleph Publishers Ltd., Tel Aviv, 1986

Library of Congress Cataloging-in-Publication Data

Names: Shmueli, Ephraim, 1908-1988, author. | Shmueli, Gila, 1946- translator.
Title: The last generation of Jews in Poland / Efraim Shmueli; edited and translated from the Hebrew by Gila Shmueli.
Other titles: Ba-dor ha-Yehudi ha-aḥaron be-Polin. English
Description: Brookline, MA: Cherry Orchard Books, 2021. | "Originally published in Hebrew as Bador ha-yehudi ha-aḥaron be-Polin by Aleph Publishers Ltd., Tel Aviv, 1986." | Includes bibliographical references and index.
Identifiers: LCCN 2021033455 (print) | LCCN 2021033456 (ebook) | ISBN 9781644695975 (hardback) | ISBN 9781644695982 (paperback) | ISBN 9781644695999 (adobe pdf) | ISBN 9781644696002 (epub)
Subjects: LCSH: Shmueli, Ephraim, 1908-1988. | Jews--Poland--History--20th century. | Jews--Identity. | Hasidim--Poland--Łódź--Biography. | Łódź (Poland)--History--20th century. | Łódź (Poland)--Social life and custorms. | Łódź (Poland)--Ethnic relations. | Łódź (Poland)--Biography.
Classification: LCC DS134.53 S52813 2021 (print) | LCC DS134.53 (ebook) | DDC 943.8/47 [B]--dc23
LC record available at https://lccn.loc.gov/2021033455
LC ebook record available at https://lccn.loc.gov/2021033456

Book design by PHi Business Solutions
Cover design by Ivan Grave. On the cover: *Torso II*, by Ardyn Halter.
Reproduced by permission.

Published by Cherry Orchard Books, an imprint of Academic Studies Press
1577 Beacon Street
Brookline, MA 02446, USA
press@academicstudiespress.com
www.academicstudiespress.com

In memory of my parents, הי"ד, may God avenge their blood.

Contents

Editor's Preface ix
Author's Introduction xvii

Chapter 1. The World of Polish Jews 1
Chapter 2. Pilgrimage to the Rebbe 12
Chapter 3. Holiness and its Heirs 17
Chapter 4. Inside Lodz 25
Chapter 5. Lodz Economy and Politics 39
Chapter 6. Sanctity and Sin 60
Chapter 7. A Town and its Ẓaddik 70
Chapter 8. Portrait of a Ḥasidic Rebbe (Admor) 85
Chapter 9. Farewell to Aleksander 102
Chapter 10. A Hebrew High School in its Heyday 114
Chapter 11. My Teachers 132
Chapter 12. With the Poet Yiẓḥak Katzenelson 172
Chapter 13. The Holocaust Poet 192
Chapter 14. A Small Town in Poland 215
Chapter 15. Return to Poland 227
Chapter 16. Poland's Five Great Changes—and One Fixation 275

Notes 281
Glossary 299
About the Author 307
List of Photographs 309
Index 313

Editor's Preface

A bright young man, barely 20 years old. All spiritual and mental powers are alert and receptive to take on life and his world: Jewish Poland of the 1920s—in many ways a truly heroic age.

In the last decade of his life, the author, my father, reflects back on his youth in those years. Acutely attuned to the fundamental conflict governing his life and that of his generation, he examines it from different angles of his personal experience. For him, it was a conflict played out between tradition, experienced as the solace and richness of the Ḥasidic world in which he was raised, and modernity and activism in the form of Zionism and its chief agents—the Hebrew high school he attended and the modern literature that nourished his soul. He knew that Ḥasidism could not be dismissed with the ridicule of assimilationists or of "enlightened" modernists, as the satirical novelist Mendele the Book Peddler and his fellow writers had begun to do a half century earlier. As evidenced by his own eyes, the faithful Ḥasidic Jews he saw all around him did not warrant such belittling. On the contrary, he saw them as hardworking, life-loving, God-seeking people, whose faith inculcated noble ethics and much courage.

He saw in Ḥasidism something else as well. In the Ḥasidic rebbe's charismatic leadership, he sensed tremendously invigorating spiritual strength, a precious quality in leaders, then and now. He understood something profound about the power of religious faith and the access it afforded to "an enhancement which lies beyond the reach of our rational consciousness and our overt will, far above any realistic reasoning ... rooted in wondering and in wonder, beyond the visible and its comprehensible symbols" (Chapter 9).

Affinity for the Ḥasidic world does not of course mean acceptance, and the author views it with the requisite critique. His chief interest, however, is in understanding where its "redeeming" power succeeded or failed. He seeks an explanation for the magnetic attraction exercised by a Ḥasidic rebbe on his adherents, transcending frontiers of time and space. When he lived in the U.S.

(1963–1976) and taught philosophy at the Cleveland State University, he published an article intriguingly titled *The Appeal of Ḥasidism to American Jewry Today* (1969). Here he analyzed why, in post-World War II America, Ḥasidism had gained considerable recognition as a serious, life-enhancing response to dilemmas of the modern era, how certain of its aspects had come to appeal also to intellectuals.

In contrast perhaps to the Ḥasidic rebbe, the author then draws the portrait of the Hebrew poet and educator Yiẓḥak Katzenelson, the first famous literary figure he met in person. Examining the life and work of a man whose first art blossomed under the sign of love and joy, sunshine and youth, and whose last works earned him the dark epithet "Poet of the Holocaust," the author meditates upon this tragic transformation. With deep emotion, he cites the poet's courageous humanist-Zionist message of consolation and transcendence, continuity and rebirth, delivered in the Warsaw Ghetto, in the face of absolute evil (Chapters 12–13).

In 1928, the year that serves as his vantage point for the events described in this book, the author did not simply leave Poland as a young man eagerly looking forward to education in superior German universities; he felt he was, literally, *escaping* Poland. He experienced Jewish life there in its misery—degrading poverty, unemployment, relentless anti-Semitism, a dead end that offered no prospects for a young Jew. In notes he jotted in preparation for this memoir, I found details that go unmentioned in the book. For example, when playing soccer in Targova Square (Chapter 3), Polish boys would pelt him and his Jewish friends with gravel. The colorful school caps he describes (Chapter 10) identified him and his classmates as Jewish boys, thereby making them easy targets for Polish taunts. Jewish parents of boys whom he tutored occasionally refused to pay him. How hard it must have been to provide for the family, how hard to be the "responsible adult" at such a young age, to witness the humiliation of an unemployed, vanquished father, who in 1928 was no older than 42 years old.

Much of this is elided, or suppressed, in the memoir-study-reflection he brought to print. This was not going to be an autobiography, and he was not going to dwell primarily on the deprivations of Jewish life in interwar Poland. He was going to focus on the spiritual, inner life of his contemporaries, as he had experienced it and as he had reflected upon it later. In other words, he would write about that sphere of life where the Jewish spirit could transcend its severe environment. It is for this all-important endeavor—and achievement—that he wished to gain the reader's sympathy.

The definition of a generation has always challenged historians. These days, we talk of generation X, Y, or Z—a terminology produced, I suspect, largely by marketing-driven interests, ever anxious to keep a finger on the pulse of whatever may become the next hot trend. Here, however, the author is not looking at biological age, at a "demographic cohort," let alone at what young people consume, but at the tensions, distresses and problems—real or imagined—that preoccupy them. This criterion is always pertinent, for the simple reason that, as he wrote elsewhere, there is no societal life without tension between the real and the desirable.

If a generation's problems are its characteristic features and define its boundaries, how do we explain the *variety* of opinions and beliefs, tastes and styles among the members of the same generation? We can identify and explain the source of something new blowing in the wind, there may be a certain unity in a generation's style, for example, all demonstrators around the globe may be wearing frayed jeans and message-bearing tee shirts. The messages, however, are not the same; the reactions and solutions to the same distresses are diverse. Members of a generation decide how to interpret the conditions, facts and situations which surround them, how to define them and what to do with them. Each person, the author reminds us, constitutes his or her world.

The author's keen awareness that the world is not out there, outside of us, as something separate from our understanding or from our "constitution" of it, may explain his attitude to the writing of history, sociology and philosophy. In describing his history teacher Dr. Filip Friedman (Chapter 11), we catch his reservations about the attempt to write "objectively," "neutrally," "non-judgmentally" in the humanities and the social sciences, the kind of writing that came to predominate in twentieth century scholarship.

No, he seems to have decided early on that he would not be devoting his scholarly life to an accumulation of data aspiring to neutrality, to non-judgment; rather, he would study the burning issues that challenged his generation, and not only in the Jewish context. This he did throughout his career, beginning with his first major article on education, published in Poland in 1932, until his last posthumously published Hebrew book *Judaism between Authority and Inspiration*, nearly six decades later. He never became, never aspired to become, an expert in any narrow field of erudition. His ambition was to be an inspiring teacher and a thought-provoking scholar, such as he had known in his high school in Lodz.

This high school experience, as described in Chapters 10 and 11, was indeed deeply formative. The school's conscious effort not to compartmentalize knowledge (Jewish learning versus Polish literature, or Jewish versus Roman ethics, etc.), gave him, or reinforced in him, the sensibility for integrating fields of knowledge—from diverse cultures and languages, from different times and places. Integrating history, philosophy, literature, sociology, psychology, he pursued his own, rather solitary, scholarly path. If there is a unifying thread that connects his decades-long studies of heretics and skeptics (Spinoza, Giordano Bruno, Uriel d'Acosta), various men of the Renaissance (Machiavelli, Thomas More, Montaigne, Cervantes), Existentialism and Ḥasidism, it is perhaps the unfolding of individualism in European culture and in Judaism.

Another intellectual tendency embedded in him in youth was a resistance to the tyranny of modern science and technology. Not, of course, in the sense of refuting its undeniable, breath-taking achievements, but in the sense of rejecting a simplistic dichotomy between facts and values, the assumption that science can be free of values. This explains, if I understand correctly, his openness to that "sphere of wonder" beyond the visible, mentioned earlier. This is what his early religious faith implanted in him.

Chapter 14 is devoted to some reminiscences of his earliest years in a small *shtetl*, Zdunska Wola, a shrine of warm childhood memories. However, beyond some inevitable nostalgia, he evokes a ferocious internecine dispute that ripped apart the town's Jewish community. This painful illustration of failed Jewish leadership was another theme that preoccupied him throughout life, both in historic studies and in the excessive factionalism that continues to bedevil political life in the independent Jewish state to this day.

The book's final chapters relate his impressions of Poland as he saw it during a one-week visit in the turbulent autumn of 1982. Like most Jews who visited Poland, certainly in the Communist period, his overwhelming experience is of the great Jewish void, of everything that is no more, of non-being itself. However, he knew this in advance and seems to have braced himself not to allow this feeling to get the better of him. Rather, keeping his eyes open and his ears alert to the new Poland, he spoke with as many people as he could, taking notes. Today, of course, this chapter no longer tells us as much about "contemporary" Poland as the author had intended; now it is a sort of time capsule of what a traveler saw during one moment in time, on the cusp of the Solidarity revolution.

Among his observations scattered in the book about Poland and the Polish people, some may be surprising. Although he had experienced Poland as an intensely nationalistic, anti-Semitic country, he was well aware of its sufferings as a nation, admired its great poets and writers, felt the beauty of its language, and believed in its potential. With all the pain he experienced during this visit in 1982, he shows keen interest in the new Poland and its people.

It is inevitable that a writer's personality be disclosed in his writing, no matter how discreet he wishes to remain. The reader will readily see that the young man of this memoir became a deep-thinking and broad-minded scholar, a philosopher and historian, a gifted teacher, a tolerant soul who creatively mastered and blended the contradictions that made up his early life as described in this book.

ABOUT THIS TRANSLATION

My father felt no need to equip his memoir with more than a handful of footnotes and references. He assumed that his Hebrew reader was familiar with the "echo chamber" of biblical, Talmudic, and the vast post-Talmudic literature and poetry. For this translation, however, I believe additional footnotes are needed. In the age of Wikipedia, I did not footnote well-known names in Hebrew or other cultures, but limited myself to the lesser known names or subjects. In other words, where there is no footnote, the subject may be at least somewhat familiar to the reader, and if not, there is a lot of information on the internet.

As for the author's use of quotes from the classical Hebrew repertoire as an organic element of his style, that "echo chamber," I have left them without references. *Hamevin yavin*—readers who hear the echoes will savor them and those who do not may appreciate a lighter text, one that was never meant to be burdened with a scholarly "apparatus."

All quotations from literary works cited by the author are my free translation from his Hebrew, unless otherwise noted. Where I was fortunate to find on the internet what seemed to be more professional translations than mine, I used those sources. Working under Covid-19 restrictions through most of 2020, I did not have access to the Hebrew National Library for checking out the references as thoroughly as might have been necessary had this been a standard work of research rather than a memoir.

Biblical citations are generally, though not always, from the King James Version.

Transliteration has given me quite a headache. Generally, though, not always:

1) Most of the Hebrew words used appear in the transliteration established by the Encyclopedia Judaica, as requested by the publisher.

Some of the names, however, appear as they have become generally recognizable in the West.

2) In most cases I have used the modern Sephardic pronunciation of Hebrew words, names and titles, rather than the Ashkenazi Yiddish pronunciation used in the Polish diaspora.
3) I have given the names of places in Poland as they were pronounced by Jews. The Polish name appears in brackets if the Yiddish spelling might otherwise be unrecognizable to a Polish reader.

The Microsoft Word software occasionally prompts the user to consider changing words to be gender neutral. I have chosen not to follow this cue. It seemed to me unnatural to inject an element of contemporary awareness into the consciousness of a century ago. The author's world—the Ḥasidic life, the Second Boys' Hebrew High School—was a man's world.

The author's frequently used terms "Israel" or the "House of Israel" are the ancient Hebrew names for designating the Jewish people. Likewise, when referring to the ancient homeland he uses the term Ereẓ Israel (Land of Israel), and when speaking of the modern State of Israel, he specifically names it thus.

The word Torah, or studying Torah, traditionally refers not only to the Pentateuch but to the entire rabbinic-halakhic literature, chiefly the Talmud and its commentaries.

Finally, I recall with some qualms my father's description of the immense joy with which, as a teenager in 1925, he first saw his name in print in a Lodz newspaper, followed by dismay at seeing how the editor had truncated it. He cryptically notes there that he "learned his lesson" from this unpleasant experience, but does not elaborate what it was. Probably, never trust an editor!

Yet here am I taking similar liberties with his personal memoir. He self-published this book without an editor, with the almost inevitable result of some repetitiveness. I have abridged here and there, have moved some paragraphs around, and created shorter chapters. Where my interference is minor, merely for the purpose of elucidating or giving a date or a source, I have not made a note of it. Only where I have stepped in more aggressively, i.e., actually added a phrase that was not in the text, I use square brackets.

I thank the readers of my manuscript for their great help: Arlene Aviram, Gabriela Goliger, Ardyn Halter, Ellen Shnidman, and Dr. Barbara M. Pendzich of Wroclaw, who helped with the Polish. It's always embarrassing to think what one's manuscript would look like without the eyes and brains of one's kind, patient proofreaders.

I also thank Dr. Kamila Klauzinska of Zdunska Wola, Poland, and Nobel Laureate Prof. Ada Yonath of the Weizmann Institute of Science in Israel (granddaughter of Rabbi Eliezer Lipszyc mentioned repeatedly in this book) for photos of the Zdunska Wola cemetery.

Gila Shmueli
Tel Aviv, December 2020

Author's Introduction

The book seeks to describe the Jewry of Poland between the two world wars, mainly in the 1920s. The author wishes to focus not on his own life story but on deeds and events, life conditions and struggles for their improvement, typical behavior patterns of Jews in the diverse camps, livelihoods and social classes, education of sons and daughters, in brief—a variegated web of life as he saw it shortly before the destruction. The descriptions, memories, and experiences and their retroactive elucidations are accompanied by factual-historic details that have been researched and checked. Although few footnotes and references are offered, the reader will quickly realize that the author did not rely solely on his memory. Memory, however, vivifies and refreshes the narrative with personal observations, intimate hopes and deliberations from those days.

At the heart of the first chapters is the description of Ḥasidism, the guardian of the "old *niggun* of Poland," and the "court" of the Rebbe of Aleksander, a town near Lodz, that speaks for itself and serves as an illustration of the large Ḥasidic courts in Poland. The profile of the Rebbe *Yismaḥ Yisroel* is a portrait of a specific, distinct individual, but also illustrative of the Ḥasidic rebbes in those last generations before the Holocaust.

There are descriptions of the city of Lodz, its population, its livelihoods and businesses. There is also a description of a small town, a *shtetl*, in Congress Poland—Zdunska Wola, in times of change produced by the establishment of the new Polish state, and the struggle with the authorities for the rights of the Jewish minority. This struggle is illustrated by the example of the Hebrew *gymnasia* in Lodz founded by Dr. Markus Braude with a teaching staff of superb educators and scholars. The Jewish educational system in Poland always had to struggle to ensure its existence and its individuality according to the lights of each ideological camp in the Jewish polity; Lodz's complex school network was among the best in the country.

The transformations in that generation, especially the passage from traditional to secular-modern modes of life and creativity, are highlighted in the description of some of the city's writers and publicists, foremost of whom was Yiẓḥak Katzenelson, before the Holocaust and in it.

The last chapters tell of the Polish state in recent days, based on a visit in October 1982. The cities and small towns described in the book as they had been between the two wars—how do they look now?

This general outline wishes only to direct the reader and to hint how and where the author tried to set a memorial to the last generation of Jews in Poland, in the era of its great awakening to its own creative powers, the likes of which had never been seen in the history of the Jewish polity in that country.

Mt. Carmel, Haifa
1986

CHAPTER 1

The World of Polish Jews

Three conflicts in maturation. The great awakening of Polish Jews in the 1920s and an appeal for sympathy for an insufficiently known and appreciated community.

THE WORLD IN WHICH WE ARE BORN, THE WORLD WE CREATE

I was born into the world of Polish Jews. When I reached the age of mental maturity during my youth in the newly liberated sovereign Polish state, it was, of course, not I who had shaped the character of this world. Deeds and events predating me had already fashioned my generation's fate—World War I had dismantled empires and established new nation-states. Transforming the political map, the war had convulsed and destroyed, confounded old views, and turned beautiful hopes into nightmares. It had also germinated new dreams. The Communist revolution of Lenin and Trotsky, the Russian civil war, the pogroms in the Ukraine, the shedding of Jewish blood during the war, the aftermath of revolution, the inflation in Germany and Eastern Europe—all were facts of my life when I came of age and began to look at the world around me. Among these were also the resurgence of the Polish state with its multiple ethnic minorities, the hopes it inspired in the hearts of Poles and minorities alike, as well as the pogroms against Jews in Lvov and elsewhere in Poland.

Other formative landmarks were the Balfour Declaration (1917) and the expectations it engendered; the third (1919–1923) migratory wave—*aliyah*—to *Ereẓ Israel,* the Land of Israel; Grabski's[1] economic decrees which triggered the fourth *aliyah*—the mass migration of Jewish artisans, traders, and industrialists from Poland to Ereẓ Israel in the mid to late twenties. These and similar realities constituted the world in which I had to find my way. They awaited my evaluation or indifference, my dissent or adjustment. When eventually I began consciously deciphering the meanings of deeds and events, the commitments and expectations whose horizons formed the boundaries of my life, I realized that they were beyond my control. Yet neither could I ignore them or evade attempting to understand them properly and to influence them to the best of my ability.

I was born into certain conditions of health care when women still died at childbirth and infants often did not survive their first year. Scant medical knowledge, filth, and poor infant nutrition took their toll. It was considered a miracle when, as a child, I survived severe pneumonia. I had already been wrapped in a prayer shawl, a *tallit*,[2] a last resort for my distraught parents. The community into which I was born was still quick to seek medical advice from the holy *ẓaddik* rather than from the physician and indeed the Rebbe of Aleksander[3] included children's diseases in his prayer, in the same breath as other afflictions: "And let not diphtheria and the evil spirits that roam the earth have rule over them … rather, may they be healthy and sound to perform their work and to fear Thee all their life."

Among the principal events that impacted my early life were the Fourteen Points presented by U.S. President Woodrow Wilson in his address to Congress in 1918, wherein Point Thirteen stated: "An independent Polish state should be established which should include the territories inhabited by indisputably Polish populations, assured with free and secure access to the sea, and whose political and economic independence and territorial integrity should be guaranteed by international covenant." The treaty, however, also guaranteed minority rights in the new state, which Poland vowed to respect.

In those days, when I was ten years old, I was not yet capable of reading a single character of the Latin alphabet since I was busy studying the Talmud and its late Medieval *halakhic* additions, the *tosafot*, in the *ḥeder*. However, I did already know that in addition to the peoples of antiquity—the Egyptians, the Assyrians and the Babylonians, the seven nations of Canaan, the Ammonites and Moabites, the Edomites and Amalekites—there were also Russians and Germans who had waged war against each other, had alternately ruled our city of Lodz, and had retreated from it. In the barracks at the end of our street, flags and armies had come and gone until one day I saw new banners and different uniforms. From our apartment window, I could see soldiers carrying stretchers with the wounded: first Russians, then Germans, finally, Poles. Poland's flags and its troops paraded in formation into the barracks and marched out of its gates again to the sound of military drums and rowdy singing.

From early youth I felt my life was governed by a threefold tension, although it was not one that I could articulate properly and even less interpret or resolve. The first and principal conflict pitted docility, imitation, and passivity—and all the blessings and hardships these entailed in the process of

The author as a *ḥeder* boy, c. five years old

growth and maturation, study and practice, during which I was kneaded by many hands—against action by my own exertions of body and mind.

The second conflict was between necessity and accident, the eternal and permanent versus the mutable and ephemeral. Patterns of life were permanently encased in a tradition of commandments and customs, the ineluctability of a Jew's life decreed from on high, unquestioned, an eternal Torah which implanted in us eternal life by the will of the "Eternal One of Israel." On the other side stood everyday occurrences, the passing plights of time, the adventures of youth, fleeting things, impressions and experiences, acts and opinions, imprinted by their very nature with the mark of transience and insignificance.

The third conflict was between the opaque, or the nebulous, between lacunae of intention or meaning, and that which was intelligible by virtue of the illumination of meaning. The resolution of this conflict via comprehension of meanings of things and deeds, or the conferral of meaning upon things and deeds in one form or another, whether in speech or in writing, has throughout my life given me cause for wonder; I have especially admired action performed with intention and knowledge, for which full responsibility is assumed.

In brief, my youth and early adulthood, the years in which I came of age, were characterized by emergence from a world into which I had been thrust, given over to its deeds and events and destined by chance to inhabit, to the efforts of constituting—with the beneficent aid of my teachers and comrades—a personal world endowed with meaning and purpose. In the course of this awakening, many transient matters and events were later revealed to me as appertaining to the very order of the world and its designs, while many things that had been imprinted with the mark of permanence, and even eternity, were revealed as frail, brittle, fragmented, ephemeral and bound for oblivion.

I learned from a young age that the totality of "objective" conditions, things, facts and situations, in the sense in which they existed in Poland and presented themselves to me, were not yet my world, for we constitute our world through choices, by attraction and rejection, evaluation and decision. It is not merely an amalgam of known and unknown objects, nor even the combination of all conditions, facts and situations in which we live within our environment. Although the world may be known and familiar, it is not an object posited across from us and it is not "objective." The world ignores us, and it falls on us to discover and interpret it. Only through evaluations and choices do we open peepholes into it, transforming that which is our environment into our world. Man alone has a world, or, at least, has the possibility of creating his world. He alone is capable of constituting or not constituting that world in partnership with many other members of his generation.

Much to my astonishment and joy, I came to realize that in my awakening to the polarities within and in my attempts to dissolve or resolve them in the process of building my world, I was not alone. Many of my contemporaries were similarly laboring to reinvent their world, each in the light of understanding the anguishes afflicting the individual and the troubles besetting the community. Polish Jews in the period between the two World Wars were in the throes of a great awakening to right the wrongs of centuries, to rise and take action to put one's house in order in all spheres of life. While this memoir bears witness mainly to the first decade of the Polish state (the 1920s), these efforts did not diminish in its second decade. Jews split into many camps wrangling about political blueprints and spiritual directions, about historical principles of faith and over lesser tactical issues, in struggles with the authorities and with internal adversaries. I hope my memoir renders obvious my intention of not revolving on my own axis but of expressing the predicaments of many of my generation, who surely embodied one of the most intensive periods in the history of Polish Jews, in all areas of endeavor and achievement.

In Jewish history, Polish Jewry was one of its greatest centers in terms of number and importance. A unique mode of Jewish ethnic-religious existence—perhaps one of the most beautiful modes of Jewish life in the diaspora—came into being in this country. However, already in my youth, well before the Holocaust, the foundations of this existence had begun to weaken and disintegrate. Internal and external upheavals changed our attitudes to life and to ourselves; spiritual and social revolutions, especially World War I and its aftermath of tremors, brought down old barriers, yet the sense of a mighty, profound pulsation of national life still animated Polish Jews, irrespective of affiliation. This sense developed into a sharp awareness that it was impossible to continue in the old ways, that a change in Jewish corporate status and life was imperative, that both its physical and spiritual existence were in danger. Moreover, many Jews began to believe that the Jewish corporate body indeed had the power to change the conditions of its life. Many felt that it was urgent to devise appropriate methods and means for creating a new life, either in the Polish exile itself, or across the ocean, or through *aliyah* and settlement of the Land of Israel. However, the difficult conditions of Jews in Poland, especially their economic impoverishment, did not permit all of these vital forces—and they were many—to attain their full expression.

ABOUT THIS MEMOIR

The generation whose story I wish to recount was—as it later became evident to the anguish of those of us who survived—the last Jewish generation in Poland. The concept "generation" refers here not only to a demographic cohort, but also to a commonality of experiences, emotions, ideas and especially, shared problems and distresses from which one seeks to be relieved—deliverance for the individual soul and for the community. It is with this last Jewish generation that the memoir is concerned, and my role is to observe, contemplate, and reflect rather than to play an active role in the cast of characters. The year of my departure from Poland for studies at German universities in 1928 serves as a vantage point from which to survey both the past and the future of those Jewish communities at a time when they were still ebullient and vibrant. Each in its own way was combating, with dynamism and deftness, with the ardor of total commitment and in wise industry, the stresses of life under difficult conditions imposed by a hostile nationalistic Polish polity. The flowering of Polish Jewry occurred close upon its withering and death.

My memory, aided by reading and research, is the basis for the description of Polish Jewry as I saw it in those days. How was this generation reflected in the stream of my life? Reflection is an image used here metaphorically, for I am referring to more than the mere passivity of a reflecting surface, a mirror. The creative imagination fashions an image, and memory, as we know, is selective, forever sifting and winnowing. Our world is gone forever, and yet it continues to exist in memory, in musings, where it returns to us and stretches before us in its full stature, in all its vitality and radiance, as it appeared to us in its own day. Those deeds and events that are well known have already been recorded in history books; it is to their pages that I return from time to time to corroborate what I have preserved in the archives of memory.

Unlike our cultures of faith, which were enjoined to "observe and remember," to "remember the days of old," and which themselves instructed that "remembering leads to action," our contemporaries no longer place trust in memory. They suspect memory of unconsciously confounding the real with the imaginary in response to its own requirements of disclosure or concealment. The distrust in which recent generations hold transmission based on memory is relatively new, an outcome of the revolution with which historical awareness jolted the nineteenth century. This school of historiography wished to establish credibility based on documents and in accordance with verifiable methods of acquiring objective certitude. Increasingly, the goal of critical historical research was to present deeds and events "as they really were," rather than based on attenuating or inflating "biases," or on repressed and veiled desires of religious or secular ideologies.

This book is not a work of historical research, although it avails itself of research and its output to bolster memory. Essentially, it seeks to infer from the particular to the general, but also from the public to the private, and I would like to think it is free of the characteristic narcissism of autobiographies which Thomas Mann, in his essay *Goethe and Tolstoy*, described as "a definite claim on the love of the world—an absolute claim, indeed."[4] The writer of memoirs and confessions, Mann argued, wishes his readers to identify with him, and just as he thinks highly of himself when he commits to paper his feats and foibles as deeds that merit the attention of future generations, so he claims his readers' sympathy and appreciation. However, in these pages, I plan, as I have said, to describe the members of my generation, to bear witness to the fabric of their life, a life still experienced to the tune of the "old *niggun*," but already exposed to change in the small towns of Poland and in the bustle of the large, industrial, already capitalistic city of Lodz, where new evaluations came to the fore and new relationships were being spun. Tradition became problematic in the new fabric of life ordained by Lodz. As a member of this last Jewish generation, one who, by the grace of the

Great Disposer of all events, escaped the fate that struck most of them, I observed the tensions and the changes.

If an appeal for sympathy and appreciation exists in these pages, it is addressed to the reader's attitude toward the Jews of Poland who did not succeed in their lifetime in making themselves properly understood—not their so spiritually exhilarating hopes of renewal, nor their disappointments that a prodigious exertion of effort endured in courage and suffering came to naught.

Perhaps these reflections will somewhat contribute toward an understanding of the conditions governing Jewish life, especially of the quandaries of young people like myself during this period of relative calm. I wish thereby to add a modest memorial to the largest of all Jewish graveyards, a private epitaph, written in deep affinity, affection, and appreciation.

A number of chapters deal with the fabric of popular Ḥasidic life and naive faith, which characterized the Jewish multitudes in Poland, and with the internal and external breakdown of these molds. The Ḥasidic movement originated in Poland, in Galician[5] Podolia, whence it spread throughout Poland's extended boundaries of that period and into Romania. It did not reach beyond these boundaries and its attempts to penetrate Western Europe failed. It is, therefore, a distinctly Polish phenomenon, Polish Jewry's gift to the Jewish people, its attempt to overcome the widespread popular confusion after the collapse of the Sabbatean movement and the Frankist devastation.[6]

The Jews in Poland's historical pre-partition boundaries constituted the majority of European Jewry. Toward the end of the nineteenth century, Jewish immigrants streamed in masses across the oceans, establishing important new communities elsewhere. In its heyday from the sixteenth to the eighteenth centuries, Polish Jewry was also the nation's cultural bulwark, and the Ḥasidic movement—one of its very influential elements.

Of the three major Ḥasidic centers of Poland, Belz, Gur (or Ger),[7] and Aleksander, I have chosen to describe the latter, to which I was close both by virtue of my upbringing and because of its geographical proximity to Lodz. However, as a youngster growing up in a large city and studying at the Hebrew *gymnasia*, I already saw clearly how the new life in Poland, especially the one crystallizing between the two wars, was gnawing at the underpinnings of the Ḥasidic movement, institutions and modes of life. Many of its former adherents turned toward Zionism, toward the Labor movements, and to ideologies that opposed the Ḥasidic worldview. Politically, the Ger Ḥasidim, most of whom joined the Agudat Israel party, generally supported the Polish government, and at any rate, confronted it with only minimal demands. The Aleksander Ḥasidim formed a bloc of "unaffiliated *ḥaredim*,"[8] which frequently went along with the Zionists, and especially with the Mizraḥi[9] movement and its offshoots, but they were a minority.

My interest then lies largely in prototypes: how did Jews behave in the historical situation in which they found themselves? How was their spiritual and material status enhanced, and how was it destroyed? What were the forces that undermined the ramparts of a tradition still faithfully observed at the end of the nineteenth century, during my father's childhood, by 90 percent of all Jews in Congress Poland,[10] most of them Ḥasidim? How did members of these last generations adapt to an environment transformed by industrialization and urbanization, by the breakdown of authority, the spread of Western culture, and all the other complex and rapid processes that accelerated change in opinions and beliefs? What role did the Ḥasidic movement play at that period, and why did multitudes still cling to it, regardless of the opposition voiced by most rebbes to Zionism, to migration to America and, in general, to any change in the fabric of life legated by their forefathers?

JEWS AND POLES—PERCEPTIONS

I believe that the large Jewish community of more than three million in inter-war Poland has not received the attention it merits in research and scholarship. It was during this period that institutes for historic research (notably YIVO) were founded, and journalists, economists, and historians began publishing in numerous new Jewish periodicals and newspapers. Yet members of this generation did not really have sufficient time to look at themselves, to reflect upon their own powerful spiritual and material exploits and accomplishments, certainly not with any historical perspective.

Much was written in those days about pre-World War I Jewish Poland and, as we know, a detailed literature developed after the Holocaust on its horrors and victims. The members of this generation believed there was still time. Only after the Holocaust was a move made to collect and save from oblivion Yiddish and Hebrew works of Jewish authors from that inter-war period, in response to the special appeal of depictions of Jewish life. For example, after the Holocaust the central organization of Polish Jews in Argentina published a Yiddish series, edited by Mark Turkow, encompassing dozens of volumes of descriptions and stories, which, in retrospect, express a harrowing lament over the destruction of the Polish diaspora.

Let us take a moment to consider the background of Jewish life in Poland. I recall that in that same year which I have chosen for this memoir, 1928, I read in Polish *The Jewish City in Lublin*[11] by Majer Balaban, the eminent historian of Polish Jewry who perished in the Holocaust. The opening lines of this excellent history wished to reveal to the reader what Jewish existence had been like in the generations considered to have been the "golden age" of the Jewry of Po-lin[12]:

> Tall and erect rise the spires and towers of Lublin's ancient churches, while deep, deep below, at the bottom of the hill, the old Lublin synagogue crouches at the foot of the castle mount. Above, on the broad shoulders of the hill, rises the old city of Lublin; its ancient gates, narrow alleys, remnants of citadels and towers, venerable churches, cloisters, noble mansions and burghers' homes can be seen from afar, and down below, in the depths, in dampness and in filth, in puddles and mire, encircling the palace mount, lies the Jewish city of Lublin.

This description is surely simplistic, a poetic metaphor. Israel's dwellings in the Polish diaspora are to be found in the shadow of a hill, bent and crowded, lacking fresh air, surrounded by the Gentiles' hostility and persistent resentment, and living in anticipation of plunder, even of bloody violence. A somber, albeit over-generalized, picture. I knew from my own experience that times had changed. There were Jews living in large and spacious homes, and there was no small number of Poles residing in poor tenements. However, the hostility was still pervasive. For countless generations two populations had dwelt side-by-side, working with each other at making a living, yet spiritually at the antipodes, separated and insulated by enormous chasms. I had already read in my history books about the privileges accorded to the Jews and about those periods of relief and rapprochement that historian Ben-Zion Dinur called "periods of consolidation." I also learned that the Romantic poet Adam Mickiewicz, Poland's great "bard,"[13] had been influenced by Jews and had referred to Israel as "our elder brother." The Frankists infused a great deal of Jewish blood into the veins of the Polish nobility and the bard's mother was herself the daughter of Frankists. Berek Joselewicz organized a unit of Jewish soldiers to fight for Poland's independence during the Kosciuszko Uprising of 1794 and fell in the Napoleonic wars. His son Joseph participated in the Polish uprising of 1831. A number of important Jews supported the Polish nobles who rebelled against Russia in 1836.

Colonel Berek Joselewicz wearing Duchy of Warsaw mounted riflemen uniform, painted by Juliusz Fortunat Kossak (1824–1899).

Polish poets exercised tremendous influence on young Jewish men and women. They strengthened our yearning for national freedom, love of our homeland, defiance at the suffering inflicted on a persecuted nation.[14] We were thrilled by their writings. About this time, a young poet from Galicia, Shimshon Meltzer, my contemporary and later my friend in Israel, translated into Hebrew the poem *Anhelli* by Juliusz Słowacki, Poland's second bard. The Polish exiles in Siberia reminded young Meltzer in Galicia, as they reminded me in Poland, of our own sufferings in exile. A number of contemporary Jewish poets and writers became part of Polish literature. In Lodz, people were familiar with the poetry of our townsman, Julian Tuwim, and proud of it.

The story of the beneficial influence exercised by Poles on Jews has not yet been told, how significantly they fructified the Jewish community, what good qualities and important values were acquired by grace of the sovereign-denizen nation. Much has been written on their baneful influence, which led to assimilation and apostasy. And, of course, Poland in the last generation became for us the principal vale of slaughter, the "Promised Land" for the location of crematoria.

Before I begin my recollections and discussion of these changes, I shall first describe the experience of Ḥasidim traveling in earlier generations to visit the *ẓaddik*. Although the means of transportation had changed in my day, the pilgrimage experience was still largely preserved in that last generation when I myself traveled to the court of the Rebbe of Aleksander on the day of the annual memorial, the *hillulah*.[15]

CHAPTER 2

Pilgrimage to the Rebbe

A Ḥasidic pilgrimage to a holy spiritual leader at the end of the nineteenth century—an experience of comradeship and freedom, of God's might and goodness, of yearning and happiness.

Should you deem yourself unlikely to see reward for performing God's commandment, you are certainly assured reward for the journey toward it—the journey to perform a *miẓvah*. The journey on foot to the rebbe's court, the endless processions of Ḥasidim in the early generations, and later the departure by train, was a journey to fulfill a commandment, a spiritual awakening to go forth and behold the serenity of the *ẓaddik*'s countenance, to approach the holy man, to bask in his light, and delight in his wisdom.

The nature of the experience of journeying to the *ẓaddik* deserves to be looked at more closely. I refer to the generations of my grandfather and my father, basing myself on stories I heard from Father and conversations with my uncles and with old Ḥasidim.

The journey itself was a treat, especially in the spring and summer months, at the time of the Passover or Shavuot festivals. During the rainy and snowy season one traveled in canvas-covered wagons, crouching under the coverings when it rained, or in open peasant carts. From time to time it was necessary to coax the horse by hauling the wagon and pushing the wheels. A group of bearded youths and recently married young men (*avrekhim*) could assist the driver and ease the burden on the horses. There was little luggage: *tallit* and *tefillin*, clothes for the Sabbath and festival day, a clean shirt, stockings, a *shtreimel*—not a large bundle, but when thirty Ḥasidim joined a wagon, the cargo got heavy. Much of the time, one walked on foot alongside the wagon. Sometimes the excursion would be entirely on foot. There is a well-known Ḥasidic tune about Kotzk: "To Kotzk we do not ride, to Kotzk we do not journey, to Kotzk we make pilgrimage on foot." This folk song was sung with great gusto.

Great pleasure was had in meeting old friends. Ḥasidim from diverse and distant towns would meet on the road and delight in small talk and Torah talk, in stories about the *ẓaddik*'s wonders and tales about his sainted ancestors. The journey was usually somewhat of an adventure, with some good things happening on the way, and some mishaps—a cart breaking down, overturning, or getting stuck in the mud, people catching cold. My grandfather (after whom I was named some years after his death) was making his way in the fall or winter season to Vurka,[1] to Reb Mendel,[2] anxious to reach the holy man for Simḥat Torah or Ḥanuka. Running alongside the cart, he caught cold and fatally contracted pneumonia.

The journey to the rebbe was also enjoyed for the sights of the road: fields and forests, meadows, hills, and valleys. There was leisure to contemplate God's work, to behold the acts of Creation. One could see Him spreading out the heavens like a tent and taking the clouds for His chariot, riding on the wings of the wind. One could hear the trees of the forest whisper His praises, the birds of the air sing among the leaves, while creatures large and small found sustenance in His bounty. The verses of Psalm 104 "Bless the Lord, my soul," psalms from *psukei dezimra* and the Sabbath eve liturgy took on palpable reality. "Let us then go forth and sing, for He is good, let us sing to our Lord, for He is pleasant, glory be unto the Lord." Singing and chanting accompanied the journey. That same psalm, however, also speaks of "wine to gladden men's hearts"—drinking contributed to the merriment, to the joy of *miẓvah* and, it need hardly be said, warmed the bones on chilly days.

Moreover, the journey to see the rebbe was also a going out, a departure from the daily routine and the rigid mold of small town *shtetl* life. A young *avrekh* would leave his in-laws' home and his studies at the *beit midrash* and, though doubtlessly saddened to have parted from his young wife and small children, he would immediately join up with a group of peers, acquaintances, and friends. Many Ḥasidim looked forward in this journey to renewal which would elevate them from the drabness of life's tedious routine. They were leaving home for the chance of drawing upon themselves the ineffable light of the life to come. The rebbe's wisdom implanted in them eternal life. In brief, this was a journey toward light, spiritual perfection, and a mended world. From mire and mundaneness, from distress and perplexity, they were departing for the wondrous: this was their journey to "distant isles, exalted worlds, / in our dreams beheld/… the gold isles for which we thirsted/ as to a homeland."[3] In expectation of something recondite, both nebulous and brilliant, distant yet very near, as a yearning for happiness, even the endless toil over Talmudic minutiae took a back seat.

Sometimes this itinerant celebration lasted two or three days. The travelers stopped for prayer, stayed overnight at inns, drank at taverns. If they received no hospitality from fellow Jews, they ate whatever they had brought with them from home. I imagine they were in no hurry. There was time. They may have sung their *zemirot* to the tune of brisk military marches, but the journey was enjoyed for itself and there was no particular hurry to expedite its end. A well-known anecdote tells of a *ẓaddik* who, when told that the steam train could bring his Ḥasidim to him in no time, asked: "Why rush?" There was still plenty of time in those days, an abundance of non-physical, unmeasured, time and, of course, there was even more reason not to be stingy with it when it was well spent. For on the road they witnessed that the Lord was great and mighty and His wisdom without end. The road was also a place to learn that He had distinguished those who were on it from those who had strayed from the path.

In those days, the world was still very much as it had been in the time of their fathers and forefathers. To them, Copernicus had not yet demonstrated that the earth revolved around the sun. There may have been some distant rumors of this discovery, trickling down from David Gans's book *Ẓemah David* (*Offspring of David*, 1592), or from the writings of Joseph Solomon Delmedigo, a student of Galileo, but these rumors had not reached the Ḥasidim of the "Seer of Lublin,"[4] the "Holy Yood,"[5] Rabbi Simḥa Bunim of Pshyscha,[6] the Rabbi of Kotzk,[7] or the Ḥasidim of Vurka, Biale, Ger, or Aleksander. The earth stood firm, while the sun and moon followed their course, as stated in the Book of Joshua, "Sun, stand thou still upon Gibeon; and thou, Moon, in the valley of Ayalon."

Indeed these processions of travelers had more affinity to Gibeon and to the valley of Ayalon in ancient Israel than to the expanses of the stratosphere in which the earth was only one of many planets. Certainly, the Holy One, Blessed be He, had previously created 310 worlds for each of his *ẓaddikim*, and many others that He had destroyed. But what did any of this have to do with the molecular mechanisms of life or with the modern chemical sciences that explained life's secrets in ways unmentioned in the Torah? But then again, who knows, perhaps allusions to molecules were to be found in the Torah? And if the universal laws of gravitation were operative on these roads, were not these strange sounding laws just as much God's counsel? To what avail, then, were the Gentile scholars and their calculations?

Just as Ḥasidim yearned to journey to the rebbes, the latter were sometimes prompted by affection for their flock to hurry out to greet them. At least, this is what I heard from my granduncle, Reb Yidl, of whom I shall say more later. One winter, so he related, he traveled with my grandfather, his brother-in-law, to the Young Rebbe of Vurka, Reb Mendel.[8] When they reached the inn, a few miles outside Vurka, pausing to rest and ready themselves for the encounter with the *ẓaddik*, they were suddenly informed that the rebbe was about to arrive in person, he and none other, in his carriage, accompanied by an entourage of local Ḥasidim in their carts. "We were astounded at the news," said Reb Yidl, "our hearts filled with great joy and with admiration for the rebbe." And indeed Reb Mendel arrived, greeted his Ḥasidim, all drank a toast, received his blessing, and rejoiced together. The Ḥasidim's yearning for their rebbe seems to have been reciprocated by his longing for them, in the spirit of the Song of Songs: "My beloved is mine, and I am his," and "draw me, we shall run after thee."

From time to time, *ẓaddikim* traveled to nearby and even distant towns on their way to renowned doctors, to health spas, or to family gatherings—weddings, circumcisions or, God forbid, funerals of notable deceased. The rebbe would be accommodated in a spacious house belonging to one of his prominent Ḥasidim. There they prayed and held *Tish*,[9] and to this house local Ḥasidim and non-Ḥasidim would flock. The rebbe would more frequently visit a town where one of his sons resided, as we shall soon hear about the Rebbe of Aleksander, who used to visit the town of Radom.

The Ḥasidic community was not confined to a single dwelling place and its boundaries. This community stressed the "expressive" (in the sense of self-expression and self-realization) and the "non-formal" dimension in interpersonal relations, in contrast to "instrumental" and "formal" relations—if I may borrow sociological jargon. The link between the Ḥasid and the rebbe transcended the boundaries of geography and practical utility, adding mobility, social as well as geographic. Certain Ḥasidim followed their rebbe even across the ocean after the Holocaust, and the rebbe sought out and found his Ḥasidim in difficult periods of emotional-spiritual and socio-political stress. The renewal of the Ḥasidic movement and the rebbes' courts in the State of Israel and in the United States is both an example and decisive proof of those forces of *eros* exemplified by "draw me, we shall run after thee," that is, of the special nature of the bond expressed in those days in the journey to the courts of the East European *ẓaddikim*.

I regret to conclude my description of the journey to the rebbe with a disappointing admission, one, however, that should not dissipate the charm of that pilgrimage. The Aleksander Ḥasidim of whom I shall speak, i.e., those who lived in Lodz, did not walk on foot to their rebbe; they did not even take the train. A tram, apparently introduced at the beginning of the twentieth century, conveyed them in about three-quarters of an hour to the rebbe's court in the town of Aleksander. I myself was not privileged to see people walking there. However, for me too, even as a high-school student, there was still novelty in journeying to the rebbe. I put on the long black coat, the *kapota,* the wide sash, and donned a "Jewish" hat: I was in masquerade, or perhaps it was merely a return to an earlier state of existence.

CHAPTER 3

Holiness and its Heirs

Remembering the first two rebbes of the Aleksander dynasty. How was a new rebbe chosen? The author's soul is torn between traditional faith and modernity.

THE EARLY *ẒADDIKIM* OF ALEKSANDER

My father used to journey to Aleksander on days of a *hillulah*, possibly because on those days there was a better chance of being received by the rebbe. On regular Sabbaths and Holy Days there was a large throng, multitudes

Father Mordekhai Dovid Szmulewicz, Lodz, 1937, 50 years old

of devotees arriving from outside Lodz. At that time the number of "active" Aleksander Ḥasidim who made regular appearances at the rebbe's court was estimated at 50,000.

Initially, we had planned on going to Aleksander on the first day in the month of Shevat (January), on the anniversary of the death of the second Rebbe of Aleksander, the author of *Yismaḥ Yisroel*—Reb Yeraḥmiel Yisroel Yiẓḥak Dancyger, presiding from 1894 to 1910, and the rebbe of my father's youth. My father held him in the highest esteem, loved and feared him. He never tired of extolling the rebbe's perspicacity and the subtlety of his intelligence. My father was eighteen when he first met the rebbe. He was about to marry my mother, a native of the town of Zdunska Wola, whose father (the runner in the snow from Chapter 2, no longer alive at the time of the betrothal) and two brothers were Aleksander devotees. When the marriage contract was drawn up (1907), and perhaps even earlier, the brothers-in-law brought the prospective groom to their rebbe. Zdunska Wola was still in the grip of the great schism between the devotees of Ger and those of Aleksander, a ferocious and bitter dispute (described in Chapter 14) and it was important to my mother's brothers that their future brother-in-law be like them and like the bride's late father, an Aleksander Ḥasid. When my father returned to his native Lodz from studies at a *yeshiva*, he used to pray with his father in the small prayer-room, the *shtibel*, of the Ger Ḥasidim, simply because it was the nearest *shtibel* to their home at 3 Ogrodowa Street. In fact, my father was not a Ḥasid in those days, nor was my grandfather Moses Szmulewicz.

The *Yismaḥ Yisroel* (so called, as was customary, after the title of a rabbinic author's major book) was his first rebbe. He was drawn to him by filaments of inexplicable enchantment and spent every Sabbath studying his writings. Father knew the then fifty-four year old rebbe during the last three years of the latter's life. The Wise Rebbe's reputation was widespread and drew thousands from far and near. Further on, I shall elaborate upon the precious qualities of this rebbe and on the impact that he had on his devotees. In my day, he was still mentioned in every conversation about Aleksander. Thinking of him, my father's heart would "fear and be enlarged," and the word fear is no hyperbole. There was an element of the *tremendum*[1] in this rebbe.

I believe it was because of a snowstorm that we delayed our journey to the fourteenth of Shevat, date of the second *hillulah* of that month, which was the anniversary of the death (1894) of the much-revered Old Rebbe, Reb Yeḥiel, father of the *Yismaḥ Yisroel*. The Old Rebbe was held to be a saint whose prayer, uttered in tears and intense devotion, wrenched hearts and made a profound impression "up there." On a blank page in his Yom Kippur prayer book, a handwritten notation was found to the effect that a man must pray for "the name of Your beloved saints" more than for himself, and that one who pours his soul before God in supplication and tears moves others to tears, "and this was of great benefit."

Reb Yeḥiel was known for his loud and lachrymose prayer. He would call to his Maker: "Shome'a tefila, Herer, kehr sich zu di nakte tefilos shel amcha Yisroel!" ("Hearer of prayer, Listener, bend to the naked prayers of Your people Israel"), to prayers, that is, that were simple and unadorned. This type of tear-drenched prayer in which the whole congregation took part remained thereafter the Aleksander hallmark. This rebbe held his stewardship for eighteen years.

In my day, one still heard stories of the rebbe's great humility—he would humble himself before every person, and although his devotees included great rabbis, outstanding scholars and righteous men, men of the highest distinction, all of whom venerated him, the rebbe deemed himself the "worst of the worst." It was recounted that he used to say, with just a slight twist of the verse in the Song of Songs: "They made me the keeper of the vineyards because [instead of 'but' as in the Bible] mine own vineyard have I not kept," i.e., his responsibilities were a punishment for his own failings. He also said, "Our Ḥasidim have the attribute of truth, and one third of them are rebbes in every respect" ("senen alle rebbes"). It was toward his gravesite in Aleksander that Father and I were heading.

ACCEPTANCE OR REJECTION OF A ḤASIDIC REBBE

It is worthwhile to consider for a moment how a rebbe became accepted as such, and the disputes this engendered. Reb Yeraḥmiel Yisroel Dancyger, author of *Yismaḥ Yisroel,* had seen himself as his father's servant and assistant in leading the community and after the Old Rebbe's death, as a mouthpiece for his teachings. Many of the latter subsequently appeared in the book *Yismaḥ Yisroel.* When the Old Rebbe fell ill, he asked this son, his eldest, to compose a prayer. It was natural that after his father's death the Ḥasidim would accept his leadership, but this was not self-evident. His appearance was not too pleasing, or at the very least, unusual: a smooth face with no moustache or beard. And he was childless. However, as he had tremendous spiritual powers, great Torah learning and piety and was very smart, he succeeded in appealing to multitudes of Ḥasidim and became more famous than his father had been. After his death, however, many Ḥasidim were reluctant to accept the authority of his younger brother, Reb Shmuel Ẓvi. They preferred to return to their origins, to the legacy of Vurka and Biale, and chose as their rebbe Reb Aharon Bialir, a disciple and devotee of *Yismaḥ Yisroel.* Reb Aharon and his brother, Reb Mendele, sons of the old Rebbe of Biale, had traveled after their father's death to Aleksander and accepted the authority of the *Yismaḥ Yisroel,* but they did not want his brother, Shmuel Ẓvi. Thus, upon the death of the *Yismaḥ Yisroel,* Reb Aharon went back to officiate in Biale, and Reb Mendele (who resided many years in Zdunska Wola, where my grandfather and his sons were his friends) finally settled in Zgierz near Lodz and called himself the Rebbe of Strykow.

It was, apparently, during these days of rebellion that the tune spread: "Lamir sich halten banander / Lamir furen noch Aleksander!" ("Let us stick together, let us go to Aleksander!"), an appeal for unity and for allegiance to the new rebbe. This was in 1910. It was only a few weeks after the death of the *Yismaḥ Yisroel* that his brother Reb Shmuel Ẓvi assumed the leadership of the congregation on a Sabbath eve, Torah section *Mishpatim.*

When Reb Shmuel Ẓvi died, it was his son, Reb Yiẓhak Menaḥem, and not his younger brother, Reb Beẓalel Yair, who became Rebbe of Aleksander. The charisma now passed in succession and became institutionalized, as the sociologists would say. I have read a letter of Reb Beẓalel Yair from 1932, which he signed as son of the Old Rebbe and as brother of the two rebbes of Aleksander who succeeded their father, but omitted mention of his nephew, the Rebbe Yiẓhak Menaḥem, who was his junior.

Reb Beẓalel Yair came to Lodz in the difficult days of World War I, when his brother the third rebbe also lived in town. At the *beit midrash* that his Ḥasidim erected for him he prayed, like his father and his brother, in a lachrymose, pleasant, pleading voice, which infused the heart with warmth and sweetness. His face spoke of remoteness from this world, of one who lives in a sphere entirely spiritual, as if he were a sort of materialization of the incorporeal, immersed in divine light. It was recounted that he was a great kabbalist and that he prayed according to kabbalah. In order to counteract the barrier that separates man from the Holy One, he used—through mystical meditations and single-minded concentration on "unifications"—the power of the holy letters of the alphabet, which become pure when the soul disrobes itself of the body and is enveloped in pure and holy thoughts. However, Reb Beẓalel Yair, son of a rebbe and brother of two rebbes, did not attain the status of a rebbe and did not receive petitions (*kvitlach*) scribbled on little notes by believers. Nonetheless, he published letters of guidance and instruction, wherein, for example, he appealed: "When it is known that an impurity has spread among certain Jewish homes through publications, which are full of obscene language and profanities that abase the brain and the heart, God forbid, and especially among youths, I request this of my brethren: have mercy on your souls and on your dear sons, may they live," etc. A rebbe's epistle in every respect, an interdiction on newspapers and periodicals in Lodz, in 1932!

People said of him that he "worked salvation" and Ḥasidim who despaired of salvation from Aleksander came to him. They said that once his elder brother, author of *Yismaḥ Yisroel*, admonished him severely: "How could you have promised to the merchant so and so that he will win his case in court? On what basis did you draw that?" To which Reb Beẓalel Yair replied that he had learned from their father never to lie, "for this reason I am certain that if I promise, the man will win his case. The Holy One will not turn my promise into a lie."

A YOUNG PERSON'S QUANDARIES ABOUT ḤASIDISM AND HIGH SCHOOL

I returned from school earlier than usual. The days were short, and we had to hurry. Mother prepared sandwiches for our supper. As I put on the black coat, the *kapota*, borrowed by my father from one of the Ḥasidim, and replaced my high-school cap with the "Jewish" hat, I felt that with the new costume I had assumed a new role. I was not really a stranger to the Ḥasidic youth whom I was about to impersonate. In those days, I observed the commandments, prayed with devotion and diligently studied Torah. I was preparing myself for the rabbinate, albeit of the modern *Doktor Rabbiner* variety, in the famous Jewish Theological Seminary of Breslau, a bastion of West European Science of Judaism.[2] Nonetheless, my attire was a dramatic change. I was, after all, a student in the largely secular Hebrew high school, where teachers were not observant of the Sabbath and *kashrut*. I was an ardent Zionist and a voracious reader of Hebrew and non-Jewish books expressive of an attitude that was, to put it mildly, unsympathetic to Ḥasidism. In Aleksander, all secular studies for boys were opposed.

I wished to weld together two worlds, as if to hold the stick by both ends and to derive benefit and blessing from each of the warring camps, in keeping with the nature and purpose of each. And not only these polarities did I wish to fuse in me, but also other opposing and contradictory opinions and beliefs, the proponents of which deemed themselves each other's foes. Communal disputes were at their height in those days in Poland, and Jews splintered into camps and sects that turned public discourse into a daily battleground. The struggles focused on issues of the highest consequence, not only in matters of livelihood, economics, and communal leadership, but also in matters relating to one's philosophy and the meaning of life.

Psychologists tell us that every child learns to regard those who surround him with ambivalence: Other people are good, but sometimes also bad. Mama is loving, Papa is kind, but sometimes they are angry and they punish. Thus, the loved one is also hated. This dualistic attitude ("respect him and suspect him" as the Talmud cautions) acquired in childhood developed in me as I grew older and became more complex. I experienced contradictory modes of behavior, such as the ultra-Orthodox mode and the secular mode, and I could not bring myself to conclude that one was entirely good and the other wholly bad. My dilemmas were common to many young people at that time, and probably still trouble some young people today.

Although my side locks were quite short, I looked like one of the faithful. Is there not in each one of us more than one persona, each wishing to live its life under a different mask, playing a different role? To all appearances, I had changed my identity, but perhaps precisely through this masquerade I was hoping to be true to myself? At an age beset by doubts and perplexities, when I was still largely uncertain and unformed, malleable and capable of interchanging reality with make-believe at a whim, I wanted to take on a durable,

The author at age 18

typical form, untroubled by internal or external questioning. I yearned to be transformed, at least for a short time, to escape from a complicated, multiform, problematic, variegated and endlessly contradictory existence into the clarity of a life whose answers were firm, unequivocal and definitive.

On the other hand, it was impossible to refrain from mischievous, skeptical thoughts that perhaps others too were masquerading. The *maskil* in me, suspecting and critical, was curious to uncover what might be lurking behind the masks. The previous rebbe, author of *Tif'eret Shmuel,* who held the Aleksander leadership from 1910 to 1924, used to say, as the story went among the Ḥasidim, "Ḥasidim who live far from Aleksander think me a great *ẓaddik,* and the farther away they live, the more they praise and revere me. Whereas my assistant, the *gabbai,* and my sexton know that I am simply a charlatan, a deceiver." Later, I read that Goethe and Hegel had said something similar: The *Kammerdiener* (valet) who serves his employer most intimately can find in his master little majesty. No such statement, however, had ever been heard before from a rebbe. Only in Aleksander, where the humility of Reb Yeḥiel had set a new norm, was such an utterance possible.

The house of Aleksander had absorbed from Kotzk and Vurka something of the importance that the latter two dynasties attached to the dichotomy between the hidden and the manifest, between the external appearance, a mask or an ornament, and the truth of real intention. It was obvious to me in those days that in the Aleksander rebbes there was much more of the hidden than of the manifest. It was said of the Old Rebbe, Reb Yeḥiel, that even though he was famous for his teaching, sanctity, purity, and for his prayers, which, like those of Reb Levy Yiẓḥak of Berditchev, pierced the heavens, no man knew his hidden, true essence. Only the angels created from his Kabbalistic formulas for unifications truly knew it. The rebbe's talk about the *gabbai* and the sexton, who considered him a charlatan, only enhanced his credibility, one assumes, for the rebbe surely intended it as a joke.

The Dancyger Dynasty—the Rebbes of Aleksander

Rebbe **Shraga Fayvel Dancyger** of Gritsa (d. 1848), disciple of Rebbe Israel Yiẓḥak Kalish of Vurka, served as the rebbe of the Vurka Ḥasidim in the final six months of his life.

1 Rebbe **Yeḥiel Dancyger, the Old Rebbe** (1828–1894), first rebbe of the Aleksander dynasty, son of Rabbi Shraga Fayvel.

2a Rebbe **Yeraḥmiel Yisroel Yiẓḥak Dancyger** (1853–1910), author of *Yismaḥ Yisroel*, son of Rebbe Yeḥiel.

2b Rebbe **Shmuel Zvi Dancyger** (1860–1923), author of *Tiferet Shmuel*, son of Rebbe Yeḥiel.

2c R. **Beẓalel Yair Dancyger** of Lodz (1861–1934), son of Rebbe Yeḥiel.

3 Rebbe **Yiẓḥak Menaḥem Mendel Dancyger** (1880–1943), author of *Akeidat Yiẓḥak*, son of the *Tiferet Shmuel*, murdered in Treblinka with his family.

4 Rebbe **Yehudah Moshe Tyberg** (1892–1973), author of *Emunat Moshe*, son-in-law of R. Beẓalel Yair, became Rebbe of Aleksander following the Second World War.

5 Rebbe **Avrohom Menaḥem Dancyger** (1921–2005), son of Yehuda Moshe Tyberg, author of *Imrei Menachem*.

6a Rebbe **Yisroel Zvi Yair Dancyger**, oldest son of Avrohom Menaḥem Dancyger, is the current Aleksander Rebbe in Israel.

6b Rebbe **Shneur Zalman Dancyger**, younger son of Avrohom Menaḥem Dancyger, is a Rebbe in Cleveland, OH.

CHAPTER 4
Inside Lodz

As the tram threads its way through the city streets, the author recollects sights and sounds, including speeches by prominent Jewish leaders who contributed to his political education.

ON THE TRAM THROUGH THE STREETS OF LODZ

Father said that the rebbe and his entourage would be leaving for the cemetery at about three o'clock and if we caught the tram going to Balut (Polish Bałuty)—the poor Jewish section of town from which one departed for Aleksander—we would surely arrive on time. The air was brisk and clear. A winter sun was shining, gently melting the snow on the pavements and one had to beware of skidding. We stepped out onto our small Skladowa Street, located near the Warsaw-Vienna train station, turned left, and passed along the barracks to the tram stop. At the end of our street and on its left were walled and fenced army barracks dating back to the Russian occupation, probably from the end of the nineteenth century. On each side of the gate, a sentry stood guard, each next to his little sentry box. Only once, when the Germans fled Lodz in 1918, were we privileged to step inside this gate. The new Polish regime, still struggling to establish its authority, allowed citizens to help themselves to cans of kerosene and other necessities in a kind of organized looting of the looters, to gladden the populace celebrating Poland's liberation and the establishment of its state. On this single occasion I saw the large drill square, the buildings and grounds, which included a pond and meadows for the horses. After this occasion, the gate closed to the public, but whenever I passed by there, I always strained to peek inside. Soldiers, sometimes in drunken song, would pass through our street to and from the barracks on foot or on horseback.

The tram arrived from the Lodz terminus where the trains returned at night, a distance of two stops from where we were waiting. This was already the town periphery, an area of factories, few streets and many empty plots, fields and a municipal garden, Staszic Garden. The tram would take us from the eastern end of town to its southern edge, [where we would catch the suburban tram to Aleksander].

Lodz was in that first post-World War I decade a city of 600,000 people—Poland's second largest after Warsaw in terms of its total population and of its Jewish community. Jews made up over one-third of its population, and about one tenth of all Polish Jewry.

Most worked in industry or in artisanship. Everywhere in the city, as also near the stop where we were standing, were textile workshops. The city dealt in all branches of the textile industry: wool, cotton, silk, linen, jute, cotton wool, knitwear, laces and ribbons, vicuna, gloves, various garments, and millinery. The factories and dye-works spewed out soot and smoke, the air was filthy, but who, except those whose lungs were affected, cared? On May Day people assembled near the station in Targova Square, later renamed Dombrowski Square, for protest demonstrations. The demonstrators included members of the Jewish labor parties—the Bund and the Po'aley Zion, internationalist and Zionist socialists, respectively. There would be passionate and grandiloquent speeches against the subjugation of the workers, against exploitation and oppression, but air-pollution was certainly not on their agenda. In the years 1927–28, industry in

The great manufacturing City of Lodz, often called "The Polish Manchester,"
through which the Red Army swept in their drive to the West.

Lodz skyline

the "Polish Manchester" (as Lodz was called) was making a recovery and production reached the levels prevailing prior to the devastation of World War I, but this recovery was short-lived. The demonstrations were mainly occasions to let off steam with complaints and demands. The authorities took a dim view of the May Day protests, especially when the outlawed Communists displayed their banners and sang their anthems. The police would disperse the demonstrations and marches issuing from this square, reserving its roughest treatment for the Jewish workers. So our newspapers would report the following day. There were always a few injuries from club blows. On weekdays we played soccer on these grounds, but as the square was paved with stones, body and shoes took a beating. Once a week an open market was held there when housewives would emerge to shop for vegetables, fruit and poultry. In later years, the markets ceased, and only boys played in the square.

The tram taking Father and me to Aleksander was nearly empty. I would have felt very uncomfortable if any of my schoolfellows from the Hebrew *gymnasia* had been on board. They would not have understood, and at any rate, they would have been embarrassed and would have caused me embarrassment. We passed by beautiful buildings, four or five stories high, mostly inhabited by Jews. On the right stood the house of Wiślicki, a wealthy Jewish industrialist, who, after retiring from business, had donated two spacious rooms on the ground floor of his apartment building as a hall of prayer. Both Ḥasidim and non-Ḥasidim worshiped there. To this prayer house I came every dawn that year for morning service. From there I ran home for a light and hasty breakfast and then straight to school. Generally, I prayed there also on Saturdays. My father frequented the *shtibel* of the Aleksander Ḥasidim on Voschodnia Street, but I, who was dressed in the school uniform of a *gymnasia* student, would not have been favorably regarded there, and my father hated friction.

The tram passed the pharmacy, which was open on Saturdays, even though its owner was Jewish. He forbade entry into his pharmacy with one's head covered.[1] I remember my confusion upon entering into that antiseptic cleanness and its strange smells when I was perhaps twelve years old, a Ḥasidic boy, ignorant of the shape of a Latin character and incapable of one sentence in Polish. The pharmacist ordered me to take off my hat and hand over the prescription.

Life for the Jews in Lodz had changed a great deal between the wars, although it remained largely within the boundaries set by tradition. The common people still kept the commandments, in varying degrees of observance, although not with the same fervor as their forefathers. Most Jewish shops were closed on Saturdays and festival days. Some of the Jewish factories also closed,

Newsstand displaying the *Haynt* (Today), *Vort* (Word), *Folks-tsaytung* (People's Newspaper), *Moment, Shpilki* (Barbs), *Nasz Przegląd* (Our Review), and *Letste nayes* (Latest News), Łódź, 1930s

i.e., a portion of half of the city's textile mills, especially the small ones. The state imposed upon Jews cessation of labor and trade on Sundays and on Catholic holy days. Nonetheless, most Jews resisted temptation and did not desecrate their Sabbaths and festival days. In the smaller towns, particularly those with a Jewish majority, hardly anyone opened a shop. In a city like Lodz, mostly in the streets where non-Jews lived, ten percent of Jewish shops were already open on Saturday immediately after the war, and the number kept growing. World War I, with its decrees, hunger, unemployment, and immoral practices in trade and manufacturing, wrought havoc to tradition. Compulsory education in Polish in public and private schools also took its toll. Western culture spread rapidly in Lodz due to the constant influx of Jews from elsewhere, enlightened "Litvaks" from the border regions of Russia, as well as immigrants from Galicia, where Jews had been awarded rights even before the war and where Viennese influence predominated. It must be said to the pharmacist's credit that he did close his shop on the High Holy Days.

On the right stood the newspaper vendor's kiosk, which sold papers in Polish, Yiddish, and Hebrew. (The renewed *Ha-ẓefirah*[2] appeared that year, also *Ha-olam*[3] and *Ketuvim*[4]). There for the first time, in the summer of 1925, I saw my own name in print at the head of an article in the *Lodzer Tageblatt,* edited by Lazar Kahn. Despite my initial joy, the printed article caused me deep disappointment. Someone had abbreviated and altered it. "There was no space," the editor apologized, because another contributor, Dr. A. Mukdoni, had also expounded on the same topic—the feuilletons of Theodore Herzl. Years later, Ẓvi Kroy, by then on the editorial staff of *Davar,*[5] told me that it was he who had truncated my article, moved paragraphs about, at the editor's command. I accepted his apology, though with chagrin. Already in those days I learned my lesson, indeed a number of lessons.

On the left was the Station Garden—about four or five blocks enclosed within a square of trees and lawn, through which I would zip on my hurried way to town and on my return home. In general, I was always in a rush, as were most Lodzers. If you saw a person walking unhurriedly you could immediately tell that he was a villager who just arrived in town, one who had not yet learned how to walk-run through it. In my childhood, I was very interested in the children who played in the garden's sandbox with their nannies or mothers. Sometimes there were also boys and girls of my age, but it was unseemly for a "*ḥeder* boy" like me to play with them. Besides, no boys there were dressed as I was.

The next stop was near the large Hotel Polonia, which always looked to me extremely lavish, especially then when the Christmas and New Year's decorations had not yet been removed from the windows and the main entrance. Because of the shortage of flats, a number of bachelors lived there permanently, among them Yeḥiel Rosenzweig, a teacher in the girls' Hebrew high school, who had made a name for himself among us with some poems published in *Ha-tekufah* and by his Hebrew translation there of Juliusz Słowacki's love poem *In Switzerland.* On Saturday mornings, barely out of bed before my arrival, he would receive me in his room for a literary conversation and a reading of my poems. I already had returned from prayer and from the *kiddush* while he was still sleepy from a Friday night party, usually at the home of the poet Yiẓḥak Katzenelson. Rosenzweig composed our school's anthem: "Our strength is not yet spent, we have not tired on the road—behold our banner high, waving overhead." Even though the poet promises in this long anthem, "Our prophets' vision is fulfilled, and every man is our brother," he continues, as befits a teacher in a Zionist school, "For the beauty of Israel's land, our eyes still yearn. From the east there shines upon us the light of an eternal sun." The song's main thrust was to stimulate joy: "Burst forth in song, burst forth, and every heart shall rejoice!" I dare say this was also the tenor of most of his other poems. However, I needed an advisor in poetics, and he was a young beginner trying to establish himself,

Yeḥiel Rosenzweig, teacher and poet

only eight or ten years older than I was,[6] I believe. What happened to Yeḥiel Rosenzweig, I do not know. Most likely, his fate was like that of all our townsmen, who did not reach the "beauty of Israel's land" in time.

We saw a few more streets on either side of Zielna Street on which we were coursing straight onto Piotrkowska Street, our town's main thoroughfare. We still called it Zielna, although formally its name was now Narutowicza, named for Poland's President, assassinated just a few years earlier. On one of the side streets on the right stood the girls' Hebrew high school founded by Dr. Braude. About this school and other educational institutions that he established in our town and elsewhere, more in Chapter 10. At that period of my life, I had my eye on a certain girl in the school, who was one year younger than I was, but she did not reciprocate my feelings, to my great heartache.

Even though most of the city was fairly new, only seventy years old, and the streets that we passed were at most only fifty years old, the sidewalks were not cleared of snow, and drainage was inadequate. Cleanliness was not exemplary and at night street lighting was poor. But of course, as a young man on the tram that day the city's maintenance problems did not really bother me.

GREAT ORATORS OF THE DAY

On the right side of Zielna Street stood the theater, popularly known as the concert hall. Indeed it contained a spacious hall for concerts and all manner of artistic performances. I heard there a number of great cantors, such as Gershon Sirota. Here one could hear key speakers of Poland's Jewish community and renowned guests from abroad: politicians, literary figures, and artists. I remember a survey held that year in the Zionist paper *Nasz Przegląd* (Our Review), which asked readers to list the world's most famous Jews. The readers' responses ranked them in the following order: Weizmann, Sokolov, Einstein, Jabotinsky, Bialik, Sholem Asch, Yiẓḥak Gruenbaum, Herbert Samuel, and the Baron Edmond de Rothschild. Of these, I heard in the concert hall Sokolov, Gruenbaum, and Jabotinsky. Weizmann did not travel in Eastern Europe. If I am not mistaken, he never appeared in Warsaw or Lodz.

Naḥum Sokolov, who played a major role in securing the Balfour Declaration, in the confirmation of the British mandate over Palestine, and in all the Zionist endeavors, was not a particularly effective public speaker. His strength

Naḥum Sokolov in the 1920s

lay rather in personal negotiations with non-Jewish political and spiritual leaders. However, his address was a rich fabric of ideas with one topic leading into and interposing on another. A short time previously he had eulogized the scholar and Zionist leader Rabbi Ẓvi Hirsch Pereẓ Chajes (died December 1927) in Vienna in an address replete with historical detail, reflection and Torah-learning, which was immediately published in *Ha-olam*. To his contemporary Hebrew readers, author and journalist Naḥum Sokolov served as a mentor, an interpreter of the phenomena of life, thought, and art. He was a towering political figure, a roving diplomat, an emissary to the nations of the world and to the congregations in the Jewish diaspora. Polish Jews saw in him a noble expression of their own quintessential popular genius, of the shrewdness and acumen symbolic of Jewish spiritual resourcefulness, which had penetrated into the wide expanses of foreign cultures thanks to an extraordinary natural gift for fusing and bridging between the Jewish heritage and the spiritual culture of the nations. I no longer recall his words in that address at our concert hall, but its tone, the special Jewish *niggun* of Polish Jews, was dear to me. N.S., as he would sign his articles, was indeed a *nes* (both a banner and a miracle in Hebrew), a symbol attesting to the wealth of Jewish creativity and its untold potential.

Yiẓḥak Gruenbaum was quite a different type. I often heard him speak quietly to a huge crowd, with logical, well-reasoned arguments like a lawyer, about the purpose and status of Zionism, and debating leaders of other parties. He was an energetic polemicist, but lacked philosophical depth or the verve of popular wit, or the power of poetic imagery. Although he was a native of Poland, a certain unfamiliarity in his Yiddish idiom, spoken in a Polish-Russian accent, was detectable. Nevertheless, his speeches were listened to most attentively. In those years he was the unquestionable leading Jewish political personality in Poland. He grew up in Płock, where as a youth he founded a Jewish library. After completing his law studies at the University of Warsaw in 1901, he served for a while as Naḥum Sokolov's secretary, while himself supplying articles to the Hebrew, Yiddish, Polish, and Russian press. During World War I he lived in St. Petersburg, then returned to Poland in 1918 to assume the leadership of the Zionist movement and the editorship of two papers, *Ha-ẓefirah* and *Dos Yiddishe Folk*, which later merged with the widely distributed *Haynt*.

Gruenbaum found himself in a fierce political fray right from the beginning of Poland's statehood. The new state was immediately caught up in the nationalistic enthusiasm of its intelligentsia, the religious fanaticism of its clergy, and the rigidity of its bureaucracy. Heedless of the country's geopolitical position between two major powers, Russia and Germany, and of the Slavic, German,

Yizhak Gruenbaum, most prominent Jewish political leader in the 1920s

and Jewish minorities in its midst, Poles clamored for a Poland exclusively for Poles. To establish mono-ethnic rule, they introduced economic and cultural discrimination against the minorities, including pogroms and other forms of terror. From its birth, the independent Polish state began with abuse of Jews—in the terrible pogroms in Lvov (November 1918), Pinsk (April 1919), Cracow (early 1919), and elsewhere. As early as 1919, a secret order was given to remove high-ranking Jews from the military. Jewish soldiers, who had fought for Poland's freedom, were now deemed untrustworthy and were confined in a camp at Jabłonna (1920). On August 18, 1920, the Poles court martialed and executed Rabbi Ḥaim Shapiro, rabbi of the Płock community, under the vicious accusation that he had secretly signaled to the Bolshevik army, similarly to what the Russians had done to the rabbi of Radom, as I will relate later.

In the face of such hostility, Gruenbaum called for action. "I am a Polish citizen," he declared, "Make use of the creative talents of three million Jewish citizens for the benefit of the state, and for their own benefit!" In his articles in *Haynt* and other papers and in his speeches, he recognized that in political life there were no free lunches, that equal rights would only be wrested by struggle.

By education and background he was a liberal democrat, but he opposed compromises that put the Jewish community in jeopardy of discrimination. Although he was an ardent Zionist, affiliated with the pioneering labor movement in Ereẓ Israel and in Poland, he was also a promoter of the Helsingfors Program[7] which called Jews to stand up for their civic rights wherever Jewish communities existed, and declared that all communities should be harnessed to the national "work of the present."

Gruenbaum's greatest influence became manifest in 1922 when he organized the Jewish public for the elections to the *Sejm*, the lower house of the Polish parliament, by negotiating agreements with the other major minority groups—Germans, Ukrainians, and Belarusians—to run in one bloc. Together the alliance of minorities won one hundred seats, of which forty-six by Jews—thirty-four in the *Sejm* and twelve in the senate. This was the high point of parliamentary gains for Jews and other minorities, for thereafter the Poles, fearing the power of the minorities, increased their pressure. In the years 1925–26, contrary to Gruenbaum's position, a number of more conciliatory Jewish delegates from Galicia negotiated with the government, which sought to obtain loans from Europe and the United States by making a number of concessions to the Jews. But in May 1926, Marshal Jozef Piłsudksi regained power in a *coup d'etat* and Prime Minister Kazimierz Bartel abrogated the deal signed just a year earlier with the Jews.

By the 1928 general elections, the Jewish political parties suffered a big setback: of their 46 representatives, only 22 remained. The fragmented, endlessly bickering Jewish parties failed dismally, together and each one separately. Agudat Israel and the Zionists in Galicia, under the leadership of Leon Reich, allied themselves with the government. An even more difficult period began for the Jews. The second decade of Polish rule was full of abuses. Anti-Semitism became official practice, and throughout the period, especially after Pilsudski's death (1935), the discrimination, disturbances, confiscations, and plans for deportation ("voluntary immigration") did not cease.

I remember the early enthusiasm in the Zionist camp, and its steady growth after World War I: "The beginning of redemption" is how it viewed itself. In 1921, the number of paying members of the Zionist levy reached 770,000 (compared with only 130,000 before the war). In Poland, Gruenbaum was the chief champion of Zionism, national pride, and equal rights. But toward the end of the fourth *aliyah*, I heard his speeches interrupted by cat calls from people returning from Ereẓ Israel in disappointment. The Zionist Federation had duped them, their money was gone, there was no work and no livelihood in

Ereẓ Israel. The hall was in an uproar. The hecklers' reports could not be denied with flowery rhetoric, they could not be dismissed as simple fabricators. The audience sensed that their outburst was genuine, that they spoke of things they had personally experienced. Gruenbaum would try to soften their sorrow and to explain.

The situation in 1928 was indeed difficult in Ereẓ Israel as in Poland. I could not help thinking about the squandered opportunities of the Zionist cause. Had the Jewish people responded to their leaders' appeal in the post-war years energetically, with all their might and soul and resources, the struggle with the British Mandate government and with the Arab national movement would have taken quite a different course. The history of that entire generation would have been very different, and perhaps we would have escaped Hitler's Holocaust. Even in Poland, Gruenbaum saw the struggle as a very difficult one, and already then as one almost lost. Not many years later, in 1933, he took his leave of the Jews of Poland and immigrated to Ereẓ Israel, a disappointed, beaten, despairing leader.[8] The tide of Polish hostility swept away all his achievements.

In January 1927, a year before my tram ride to Aleksander, Aḥad Ha'am had died in Tel Aviv and a large crowd attended the memorial service at our concert hall. Dr. Yirmiyahu Frenkel, a teacher at the Hebrew High School, was one of the eulogists. In those days I was already well acquainted with most of the essays comprising *At the Crossroads* (*Al Parashat Drakhim*), a complete philosophy on how to live as a Jew, both in the privacy of one's home and as a citizen of the world. I was even tutoring these essays to private students. I felt, however, that Aḥad Ha'am's death marked the end of an era of "spiritual" Zionists and that the establishment of the Jewish "spiritual center" that he had advocated was no longer enough. The needs became more pressing. Jewish life and property were in real physical danger, and it was imperative to build the Land of Israel with the greatest energy and with all possible means.

I heard many speakers on that stage and on these subjects. Yaakov Zerubavel, the brilliant Yiddish orator speaking for the labor party Po'aley Zion, would intersperse lively popular anecdotes and jokes in his sharp polemics, much to his public's delight. I was deeply impressed by the leaders of Mizraḥi, an Orthodox Zionist political movement, which developed and spread rapidly in the post-war years. In Lodz, I believe, it rivaled in numbers the General Zionists. Rabbi Yehudah Leib Kowalski, head of the rabbinic court in Wlotslavek, Rabbi Yehudah Leib Zlotnik, head of the rabbinic court of Gombin (later Rabbi Y. H. Avida, who became my friend in Israel), the rabbis Shmuel Brodt and Yiẓḥak Nissenbaum, Amiel and Grobart, were all relatively young leaders and powerful speakers. Mizraḥi's chief spokesman in Poland was Joshua Heschel Farbstein, but I preferred listening to the rabbis and preachers. In their disputes with non-believers on the one hand, and with the anti-Zionist Orthodoxy on the other, they marshaled illustrations from the Torah and arguments from political life in a brilliant string of radiant and joyful words that filled one's heart. I loved the charm of the sermons and the acumen underlying their complex argumentation.

The foremost speaker at our concert hall was without a doubt Vladimir Ze'ev Jabotinsky. In those years he resided in Poland, or visited it frequently, and I heard him speak several times. The walls of the Concert hall were lined with pillars supporting the ceiling, and I recall how Jabotinsky compared the *aliyah*, the Jewish brigades, and the "colonial rule," i.e., the rule by which the British Mandate government awarded land to the Jewish immigrants in Ereẓ Israel, to pillars upholding the Zionist edifice. Without those pillars, he intoned, the entire edifice collapses. The Zionist leadership was not doing enough to buttress these pillars, and it would take the fall of only one pillar—and here he pointed to the colonnade where I was sitting—to bring the roof down over our

Ze'ev Vladimir Jabotinsky in World War I uniform of the British Jewish battalion

heads! I was shaken by his speech. However, already in those days I learned to take issue with his views; but the impression left by his rhetoric—the powerful magic of a great orator—was unforgettable.

His personality and political career in the Zionist movement always generated controversy in the Jewish world. We argued about him a great deal in school. No Jewish leader of that era, I believe, inspired so many followers and foes. In February 1928, the *Ha-ẓefirah* reported on a speech he gave at the Tarbut[9] convention in Warsaw to an audience of Hebrew teachers and Tarbut officials, where he generated great enthusiasm by his attack on Yiddish-language schools and his advocacy of exclusive Hebrew-language instruction in all subjects of the curriculum, in lieu of the bilingualism (Hebrew-Polish) advocated in the schools founded by Dr. Markus Braude, such as my *gymnasia*. Only total immersion in Hebrew, regardless of whether or not the diplomas would be recognized by the Polish government, could save Jewish culture, he argued. "In New York I never heard children speaking Yiddish among themselves," he claimed, and he laid the blame squarely on their parents, who were sending them to non-Jewish schools. Even Yiddish could not hold its own. Yet in the great battle that raged in those days over the future of the Hebrew-language school in Poland, even the Zionist public largely rejected his proposals. Nevertheless, his speeches were enthusiastically acclaimed wherever he appeared. They were, as experts attested, rhetoric at its finest.

The Zionist element in the inter-war period was significant not only for its very existence and for its considerable size, but from another aspect too. Polish Jews were attempting to rejuvenate their diaspora in its dual struggle against assimilation on the one hand and "stagnation"—the fixation with the past—on the other. Tremendous energies were invested to create the possibility of national life in exile, the special life of a people living on foreign soil. The Zionists were the chief contestants in this struggle. In Lodz, the Zionists succeeded in wresting control of the community's leadership from the hands of the assimilationists, members of the elite, whose fathers had established the city's industry.

Also appearing in the concert hall was Noah Prilutzky, the prominent Yiddish philologer and ethnographer and head of the Folkists party, who, in the name of the "breite Yiddishe massen" (the broad Jewish masses), advocated Jewish autonomism in the spirit of historian Simon Dubnow,[10] national autonomy that would allow Jews an independent existence as a minority in Poland. A few great orators of the Bund, the socialist workers' party, also appeared, notably Israel Lichtenstein, a gifted teacher and speaker, who argued against all the other parties and inspired the masses in support of the "Doykeit" ("hereness") policy, as articulated in the Bund's famous slogan, "Wherever we live—that's where our country is!" ("Dorten vo mir leben—dort iz unzer land!"). Both Folkists and the Bund, the latter much stronger than the former, were parties committed to the struggle for Jewish rights, to dignity, to taking one's fate into one's own hands via political action. Even though they opposed the Zionists, it was obvious that they too, as members of the young generation, wished to endow the Polish Jewish polity with a new sense of its uniqueness.

Finally, in parting from the concert hall, I too had the honor of standing on the stage upon which so many luminaries of that generation had spoken. As class valedictorian, I delivered an address of greetings, thanks, and farewell in the presence of a large crowd of parents, teachers, and students at the graduation ceremony of my class in May or June of that year 1928. I spoke in Hebrew. Then one of the three principals of the Hebrew high schools spoke, followed by Dr. Braude, their founder. I remember that a child, the son of Zalman Silberzweig, composer of the Yiddish theater lexicon, presented me with a bouquet of flowers. There was loud applause. My father, ever sparing in his praise of me, said my speech was "not bad," in the spirit of true English understatement.

CHAPTER 5

Lodz Economy and Politics

A glimpse of the city's frenetic energy, commerce, political parties and ideologies, the Jewish press, and the growing poverty in Baluty, the town's proletarian slum and later ghetto.

A PRODUCTIVE CITY, ENERGETIC AND ENERGIZING

Let us return to the tram ride to Aleksander, to the court of the *ẓaddik*. We are still on Zielna Street. On the left beyond the concert hall stands a large building whose ground floor lodged a printing press where my mother's cousin Avraham Mordekhai Rogowy edited and published the weekly *Die Yiddishe Stimme*. Avraham Mordekhai was only ten years my senior and already a publisher, a co-founder of the Beis Yaakov network of girls' schools, an Agudat Israel politician, and later a member of the Lodz city council. Before arriving in our town, he had already participated in Warsaw in editing Agudat Israel's daily *Der Yud*. In Lodz, he edited a collection called *Friling* (1922), as well as a magazine for youngsters with the interesting title *Unsere Treibkraft* (Our Motivating Power), where he encouraged young sons of Ḥasidim to express themselves in writing. He left our town for Warsaw upon his appointment as editor of the chief organ of Jewish Orthodoxy in Poland, *Dos Yiddishe Tageblatt*. Even in those early years when he invited me to his editor's office and asked me to write something for one of his papers, I saw in him a man of great talent, creative himself and promoting creativity in others within the Ultra-Orthodox camp; indeed, he was the personification of all the young fresh forces within the camp of the faithful. He perished in the Holocaust. He had had a chance to escape, but was not prepared to part from his wife and children. His friend Benjamin Mintz came to Ereẓ Israel in 1925 and later became a member of Knesset, representing the Agudat Israel party, adherents of the Rebbe of Ger.[1] These gifted and energetic young men wished to reshape the future of Ḥasidism in Poland. They were very far from the "stagnation" so often attributed to them by their secular opponents.

[Only on one occasion did I get to see the leader of these bright young men.] Their rebbe had frequently visited the Holy Land between the two wars. Upon his return from a visit in 1926, my friend and neighbor, Leibele Cohen, who had been named after Reb Yehuda Arieh (Leibele) Alter, father of the presiding Gerer Rebbe, invited me to accompany him and a large throng of Ḥasidim to the Kaliska Station. There the special train wagon transporting the rebbe and his close associates was halting for an hour or so. A multitude of Ḥasidim, and the two of us young fellows among them, jostled for the chance of giving him a *sholem aleikhem* greeting.

Our tram arrived at the junction of Piotrkowska Street, Lodz's main artery, and turned right toward the Old City and the suburb of Balut. The immediate continuation of Zielna Street, on which we had been traveling so far, was Zielona Street, home in those years of Reb Beẓalel Yair, younger son of the Old Rebbe and uncle of the rebbe toward whom we were making our way.

Most of the town's trade was centered along Piotrkowska Street, which stretches through the whole length of Lodz from south to north, and in the streets that feed into it. The houses were three to five or even six stories high, fronted by businesses, large and small shops, offices, restaurants, and above them apartments. Entering through a building's gateway, one would find in the inner courtyards more houses on all sides: a warren of dwellings, workshops, small manufacturers, and storehouses. One could exit onto a parallel street through gates on the opposite side. Each such yard was no less busy than the street outside.

On weekdays the city was teeming with myriad and varied sounds. In no way did its streets and yards resemble the "Idlers' Town" ("Batalon") or "Fooltown" ("Kessalon") of Mendele the Book Peddler's satiric descriptions. In that part of Piotrkowska Street where we took the tram to Aleksander, at least every second person was a Jew. The road was not wide, and two trams on each side and a cart on the right and the left would easily clog it. However, the sidewalks were adequately wide. There Jews preoccupied with their business or trade hurried about, assembling and dispersing, opening and closing deals. Porters carried merchandise, peddlers called out their wares.

Jews were a key factor in our town's development. According to the census of 1921, 43 percent of Jews worked in industry, as laborers or employers, the remainder in trade and services, transport, and office work. Knowledgeable people claimed that the Jewish population of Lodz was the most active and productive of all Jewish communities in Poland, and "possibly of all diasporas in modern times."[2]

On this street it was possible to hear a great deal of Polish spoken by Jews. Even though the city was still predominantly characterized by Ḥasidism, Jewish learning and traditional piety, the native language began to penetrate. The number of Jews in Lodz who were fluent in Polish reached a few tens of thousands in those days (1928) and possibly even encompassed a third of all Jewish inhabitants, and was steadily rising. Still, in this unparalleled intensiveness of Jewish existence, whether religious-traditional, or Zionist, or Yiddishist, there was no movement toward assimilation. Nonetheless, the atmosphere in Lodz was pragmatic and goal-oriented, and the Polish language served the needs of work and trade.

We passed Café Astoria with its two spacious halls, which served as a meeting place both for business people and for the Jewish intelligentsia. I used to play chess there whenever I had a free moment between one private lesson and another when I tutored in the neighborhood in the afternoons. The jokes about the shrewd Jewish waiters with the quick, insolent retorts that were told in New York (Avrom Reyzen excelled in them) were copied, perhaps, from the Astoria that I experienced in those days. The atmosphere was flippant but not wanton. In the first month of the city's occupation at the end of September 1939, the Nazis killed 12 Jews there.

The streets to the right and left of the tram's course buzzed with the life of Jewish organizations and institutions. In one of them stood the Scala Theater, where Yiddish-speaking troupes performed and where Habima[3] appeared when it came to Lodz. Public assemblies and festivities were also held there. These organizations, theaters, libraries, sports clubs, and banks received no government support. They were founded by Jewish volunteers, often with the assistance of the Joint,[4] as were the hospitals, schools and adult education courses, or the various mutual help organizations, a dense network of organized Jewish initiative. Members of political parties also assembled in these streets.

All the political parties and movements established branches in our city. Political divisions led in multiple directions, and no movement escaped inner fragmentation. The Mizraḥi movement, for example, gave birth to Young Mizraḥi and to the Mizraḥi Worker. The Mizraḥi Worker movement proposed a particular innovation that interested me greatly: a worker who could be both religious and Zionist, observant of the *miẓvot,* but participant in the national movement. The adherents of this movement saw in productive work one of the Torah's commandments: Eat the fruits of your own labor, and you will be blessed in this world and in the next. I heard young speakers of the Torah and Labor (*Torah va-Avodah)* movement, an organization within the Mizraḥi party, who spoke up against the Mizraḥi movement itself, but especially against the socialists on the one hand, and, on the other, against Agudat Israel, the ultra-Orthodox anti-Zionist party that separated religion almost entirely from Jewish nationhood.

I heard speakers who demanded personal self-realization through *aliyah* to Ereẓ Israel and physical labor there. They strove to inculcate self-improvement in the private sphere, but to the commandment "love thy neighbor as thyself," they added the commandment of labor, only through which, so they believed, could one reach the supreme level of love of humanity and realize the ideal of justice enunciated in the Torah. These young people who had emerged from the *shtibels*, agonized over how to forge an ideology that would fuse Zionism with Torah observance. They believed the Talmud's words, "Greater is he who enjoys the fruits of his labor than he who fears heaven." A young thinking Jew in Poland was troubled by a complex web of theoretical and practical problems, in an atmosphere unconducive to theoretical investigation.

In one of the streets parallel to the tram's course, in Zachodnia Street, stood the Great Shtibel of the Aleksander Ḥasidim. This *shtibel* next to the Lithuanian synagogue occupied the top floor of a large building. It was considered the central and most important venue of prayer for the Aleksander adherents, who had dozens of *shtiblachs* throughout the city. This was where the rebbe came when he was in Lodz. Every Sabbath approximately 700 Ḥasidim would pray in the Great Shtibel, among them the best known and most esteemed, the "face" of the Aleksander Ḥasidic community, such as Reb Simḥa Oberbaum, Reb Mordekhai Włoszczower, one of Lodz's rabbinical judges, members of the Makower family, who to this day attend the Aleksander court in Bnei Brak, Reb Yossele Feiner, Itche Meir Woidislawski, and Shabtai England. The Russ family were among the most distinguished. Their father, Reb Moshe Neḥemia Russ, had hosted the rebbe known as *Tif'eret Shmuel*, Reb Shmuel Ẓvi, for nearly five years during World War I. Reb Shabtai Hecht was cantor, *gabbai* and renowned *mohel*, a wonderful, multi-talented personality whom everyone revered.

Among them also was Reb Mendel Woler, who was friendly with my father, who, in this *shtibel*, was called Mordekhai Dovid Woler (instead of Szmulewicz), but I do not know if they were related. In Aleksander my father was known by this nickname because he had spent a few years in Zdunska Wola. A Ḥasid was frequently given the name of the town where he lived when he first joined the community of Ḥasidim, and even if his place of residence later changed, the congregation did not change the name they had given him at the first encounter.

Piotrkowska Street ends at Freedom Square (Wolności), site of City Hall and a large statue commemorating the national hero Kosciuszko. The Nazis destroyed it in November 1939, and hanged a number of Poles and Jews on that site. In my day the square was wide and impressive, one of the more pleasing sites in this industrial and unattractive city. The continuation of the street was called Nowomiejska, an entirely Jewish street, similar to Nalewki in Warsaw. Shops here were small, huddled together and crowded with diverse products and wares. You could hear vendors calling out their beverages and delicacies. They sold soda water, warm bagels, and warm peas. At every corner stood carts loaded with goods. It was more crowded here, but the pace was just as frenzied.

This was the densely populated heart of the city's Jewish district on whose streets I spent a great deal of time in my childhood. One of them, on the left of our tram route, was Ogrodowa Street. In one of the courtyards lived Grandfather Moshe, Father's father, and there, in the house and its courtyards, one in the front and one in the back, resided a large number of Jews, as though it were a small town in itself. At the front of the house, facing Nowomiejska Street, there was a large Jewish tavern with a strictly kosher restaurant. The place was always frequented. Whenever I went to pick up a few bottles of beer at Grandfather's request I did not see Jewish drunkards, and non-Jewish drunkards did not come here. The owner, named Karo, was a lame, red-headed Jew, who would shake his cane at us children. His grandson, with whom I used to play in the courtyard in our childhood, I later met again in the Jewish Theological Seminary in Breslau, and our friendship resumed.

We entered the Old Town. From this spot, the city of Lodz had grown and spread in all directions. There were already some newer high-rise buildings, but the old buildings of 60–70 years earlier were still standing. In these small wooden houses lived some dozens of descendants of the first generation of artisans and tavern keepers. Many Ḥasidim and business people, artisans and the first industrialists, had moved out of this neighborhood to the better neighborhoods, to Piotrkowska Street and its vicinity. They were replaced by Jewish newcomers from all parts of Poland, especially from the environs of Lodz, who arrived in droves and settled in the old neighborhood. With no room for further construction, the crowded conditions worsened.

Had these newly arrived Ḥasidim, *mitnagdim* and *maskilim* gone overseas, they would have separated and created individual communities. In the Old

Funeral of Rabbi Majsel, Lodz, 1912

Synagogue (Altschul), Lodz's Chief Rabbi Eliyahu Ḥaim Meisel (Majsel), popular with the entire community despite his origin in Lithuania, had presided. He treated all with impartiality—the rich, the Ḥasidic rebbes, or the rabbinic scholars. The rabbi himself was a distinguished Torah scholar and many appealed to him for *halakhic* rulings and written responsa. However, by no means did he make do with prayer and fasting. When at the beginning of the century a cholera epidemic broke out, raging especially in this old neighborhood and in the adjacent Bałuty, he saw to the sanitization of houses and the hospitalization of patients. Assembling a team of physicians whom he would send to the hospitals as needed, he himself would visit the sick in their homes, oblivious to the danger of contagion. The mass funeral he received in the streets of Lodz in 1912 testifies to the love he had earned from simple folk and the esteem felt by the educated elites. The city never saw his equal again. After his death, the sects and parties of Lodz, immersed in a drawn-out bitter dispute, failed to unite in electing a successor. Rabbi Eliezer Lajb Treistman (Lejzer Trajstman), elected at the height of the dispute, was accepted by only a small segment of the public, even though the authorities confirmed his appointment. After World War I, in my time, Lodz had judges of rabbinic law, but not a universally accepted Chief Rabbi.

Following the 1924 elections, the composition of the Lodz community leadership was as follows: Agudat Israel—11, Aleksander Ḥasidim and other *ḥaredim* (Ultra-Orthodox)—7, Zionists, chiefly members of Mizraḥi—6, Bund—3, Po'aley Zion Left—2, Po'aley Agudat Israel—1, Folkists—1. Dr. Uri Rosenblat, a leader of the Zionist faction, was elected to chair the Jewish community's committee at the head of an anti-Aguda coalition, and Shlomo Bodzinger, a factory owner and an Aleksander Ḥasid, was chosen to head the community's council. However, the elections did not reflect the composition of the population and its political-organizational aspirations, because community affairs captured little attention among the Jews of Lodz in my day, and only a few tens of thousands voted in these elections. As prescribed by the authorities, the committee dealt only with the administration of synagogues and cemeteries, and with some of the organizations that served religious needs, such as the ritual bath, the *mikveh,* and a little with charity for the poor. These elections, in contrast to elections to national or public institutions like the Polish parliament, did not reflect the political aspirations of the city's Jews. The principal participants in these internal elections were religious Jews and members of parties that wished to wrest the governance out of the hands of the oligarchy and prevent it from falling to the Ultra-Orthodox. The distribution of mandates showed that the Ger Ḥasidim who voted for Agudat Israel on the instruction of their rebbe, gained over their opponents, the Aleksander Ḥasidim: twelve against approximately seven. In subsequent years, the Ger Ḥasidim gained even more power. The Aleksander Rebbe who died in 1923, Reb Shmuel Ẓvi, proved to have been a more formidable opponent to Ger than was his son later on.

THE PRESS

The editorial offices of the Jewish papers were concentrated in the last row of houses on Piotrkowska Street, and in their courtyards, the press machines hummed. Located at number 16 was the Zionist *Lodzer Tageblatt,* the most widely circulating paper, whose founder and first editor was Yeshayahu Uger, one of the town's leading activists during World War I. At various periods it faced competition from other papers, such as the *Lodzer Folksblatt, Neier Folksblatt, Lodzer Extrablatt, Lodzer Folkstimme,* edited by Israel Kahn, and others. Also published were papers on business, finance, and even sports. In 1912 a special magazine for chess came out.

Most of the parties published their own papers, journals, brochures, and leaflets. Other than the daily *Republika* whose Jewish editors preached assimilation, the papers were sympathetic to the Jewish revival movement. I learned a great deal in my youth from reading the *Wiadomości Dzienne* (*News of the Day*), which was published with the support of the city's Zionist Federation and its editors and contributors were mostly drawn from among the teachers of the Hebrew high schools. The paper began appearing in 1926, but because of competition, especially from Zionist papers that came from Warsaw and Cracow, it did not last for more than a year and some months. I recall that in its pages I read for the first time extensive explanations of psychoanalysis, which began appealing at that time to wider audiences. The author of these explanatory articles was my high school teacher for Classics, Dr. Moshe Freilich.

Of lesser credit to Lodz was the absence of book publishers. Yiddish and Hebrew publishing concentrated in Warsaw and Vilnius. Nonetheless, in the first decade after the war several hundred books and pamphlets, especially schoolbooks and poetry books, were printed in our city, as well as some Ḥasidic and rabbinic books.

The Jewish press attempted not only to reflect but also to direct and instruct the many creative forces of Lodz Jews. It featured the activities of organizations and parties and brought to the public's attention appearances of public figures, artists, and writers. Theater performances, such as Habima's, received detailed and enthusiastic critiques. Concerts, exhibitions, assemblies, protest demonstrations—in brief, all the events in which the pulse of the city's life was expressed—received coverage. This awakening of the masses to activism assumed four main expressions. Politically, it meant the formation of parties that campaigned against the Polish government for the amelioration of living conditions and for the Zionist effort to build the Land of Israel. Socially, it found form in a plethora of associations and institutions, charity organizations, etc. Economically, it created loan and mutual help cooperatives, and organized protective action against disenfranchisement from work places. Culturally, it was expressed in associations and clubs for education and the arts, such as Ha-zamir (Hebrew: The Nightingale) and Harfe (Yiddish: The Harp), in elementary and high schools, in Torah schools and *yeshivot*, in works of literature, science and the arts, and in the spiritual life of both traditional and new synagogues, the latter founded by members of the Mizraḥi movement and the Zionists. Most of these organizations disseminated their messages in print.

A young man such as I sensed these turbulent forces concentrated in the city precisely in those last houses on Piotrkowska Street. Here, with stubborn persistence and no small talent, the daily struggle of the Jewish masses for their livelihood, their welfare, and their spiritual image, was waged. True, the papers were full of mutual critique and complaint, censure and recriminations, not always politely phrased, something like a wrestling arena, and it was sad to witness the "Wars of the Jews." Nonetheless, all their differences were subject to the consciousness of the overriding shared Jewish destiny, a commonality in the struggle for its amelioration.

Lodz got, of course, all the large daily newspapers which appeared in Warsaw: nine dailies, and in some years—even ten. The Zionist *Haynt* and the popular, unaffiliated *Moment*, edited by Noah Prilutzky (who was nonetheless the leader of a party, the Folkists) had hundreds of thousands of regular readers. The Hebrew press in Poland also enjoyed a regular readership of some tens of thousands. These papers published a great deal of literature. This was the golden age of Yiddish literature in Poland, the generation following Y. L. Peretz and his colleagues. Most of the authors, major and minor, contributed to the daily papers and their famous club in Tłomackie Street 13 in Warsaw was a center of creative talents of all types and levels.[5]

As the conditions of Polish Jews were not determined solely by their own doings, the papers devoted much space to the Polish government and its leaders, to incidents, events and trends, political and economic analyses, speculations and sensations. Journalists and publicists would strive to enlighten the public that the events affecting its life were not divine decrees but the deeds of human beings, bad intentions and errors, that things could be otherwise, that there was hope for the future. The papers would patently demonstrate that it was the government that determined the destiny of Jews, that its activities affected every home, and not only through the agency of taxation, and that it was necessary to oppose its vicious caprices.

The papers were snapped up as soon as they reached the streets. When great events occurred, bringing earth-shaking news, special editions bannered them in huge letters.

THE STEIGER (SZTEIGER) CASE

For a whole year, we were bombarded with news of the Steiger trial, a case that deeply agitated the entire Jewish community. This is what happened:

On September 15, 1924, when the State President Stanisław Wojciechowski and his entourage reached a square in Lvov in order to officiate at the opening of the Eastern Trade Fair, a sound of an explosion was heard. Immediately, a witness was found, Maria Pasternak, a hysterical old woman with a criminal past who swore by Jesus and all the saints that she had seen with her own eyes how Shlomo (Stanislaw) Steiger, who had stood next to her, had thrown a bomb at the President. Steiger, a student at the Lvov University, denied it but was brought before a summary court martial. Luckily, the judges could not agree on the verdict, and the trial was moved to a civil court of jurors. The petard proved to have been harmless, and its throwers apparently wished only to create the noise of an explosion and to raise panic in order to remind Poland and the entire world that eastern Galicia, formerly part of the Ukraine, did not recognize Polish rule.

A number of revolts had already been quashed there, but the struggle of the Ukrainians for their national rights continued. They considered the Polish government an occupying force, and Ukrainian youths were encouraged to refuse service in the Polish military. In 1921 a secret military organization was founded, which initiated acts of terror against the government, against large Polish landowners, and against groups of Polish peasants who had been transplanted to Poland's eastern areas in order to dilute the local population. The authorities harassed the Ukrainians, confiscated their newspapers, and turned many of their schools into Polish establishments. The Ukrainians were pushed out of local government, the justice system, the police, and the rail service. The Poles treated them as they treated the Jews, and perhaps even worse, due to the magnitude of the threat they saw in the rebels, who aimed at establishing a state of their own, or joining Soviet Russia.

When Marshal Józef Piłsudski paid a formal visit to Lvov on September 25, 1921, a young Ukrainian shot at him three times, missing by a hair's breadth. In this assassination attempt, the governor of Lvov Province who stood next to the Marshal was killed. The Ukrainians declared that they were protesting the annexation of Lvov and eastern Galicia to Poland, that they would react in similar fashion in the future and would not be pacified until the wrong was righted.

And now again an assassination attempt in Lvov. Since the Ukrainians never publicly accepted responsibility for the deed, and since the Polish authorities were embarrassed to admit that there was still a problem with imposing Polish sovereignty in eastern Galicia, they found it convenient to blame Jews. For a long time they concealed the truth, even when it became evident to them that one of the members of a Ukrainian military organization, Teofil Olshanski, had thrown the bomb. He escaped to Germany where he received political asylum, but the propaganda in Poland vociferously insisted that Steiger was the assailant, and that he had not acted alone but with the help of fellow Jews. The entire state apparatus and most of its press ganged up on the peaceful, modest student, and on his people. This period of anxiety lasted over a year. Steiger's renowned defense lawyers unveiled corruption in local and national authorities, acts of stupidity and ignorance and anti-Semitism in the administration, in greats and would-be greats. Finally, in December 1925, the jury court set Steiger free.

BAŁUTY—THE POOR DISTRICT

The tram taking us to Aleksander on that cold winter afternoon was approaching the lodgings of toil and poverty in Bałuty, at that time perhaps the single largest indigent Jewish community in Poland and possibly the most congested in the Jewish world. Through the tram window, I could see the one or two story wooden houses and the tall brick buildings, with their wide wings and courtyards, in which additional dwellings had been constructed. Most of the inhabitants were handworkers, weavers and dyers, day laborers, workers in the neighboring small factories and workshops, porters, and wagon drivers. As a young man I experienced Bałuty's poverty first hand. I had an uncle there, a weaver, who worked at home with his family from morning to night at their handlooms, or on rented looms, and with great difficulty eked out a living. We would visit them and their neighboring friends.

Old houses in the Baluty poor quarter, still standing in the early twentieth century

A number of Yiddish narrators have described Bałuty, notably Israel Rabon.[6] In a 1929 issue of *Ha-sneh,*[7] A. Z. Aescoly (Eshkoli) wrote about the district's thugs and their "rebbe", the "rebbe" of the underworld, the "chief justice" of the congregation of thieves and scoundrels.

A labor intelligentsia also arose here, civic leaders and Yiddish writers and journalists. The leftist parties—Communists, Bund and Po'aley Zion—drew the masses. The names of Froyem Lejzer (Efraim Elazar), Izrael Lichtenstein[8] and Leib Holenderski[9] were revered here, though most of the district still observed the commandments and kept the Sabbath.

What caused the poverty of this district? Why did an underworld of prostitutes, pimps, and thieves arise there, some of whom, when they quit Lodz as accomplished professionals, became infamous among the police authorities of Europe?

This is a lesson in rapid industrialization gone awry, mainly for political reasons. When my grandfather Moshe Szmulewicz from Bełchatów—a mostly Jewish town near Piotrków—arrived in Lodz in the 1860s, because livelihood in Bełchatów was scarce, he could look forward to a range of attractive opportunities. In those days, the Jewish community of Lodz numbered about 40,000, and worked at a number of professions, but mainly in the textile industry, where they played an important role in supplying raw materials to foreign weavers who came from Germany and the Czech areas, and then selling the latter's finished products. Some Jews established ties with markets in Poland, gave and received credit, and distributed the city's wares. Others opened factories which increased in size in the course of time, especially after customs between Russia and Congress Poland were abolished (1850), and the large Russian market opened wide to Lodz textiles. Moreover, Jews leased various revenue-raising branches of the government, the municipality and of the community, such as the marketing of liquor, beer, salt, and matches, the stamping of measures and weights, the tax on bridges and tax on kosher meat. Jews ran the agencies of the national lottery. The entrepreneurial pioneers were soon joined by an army of clerks and supervisors, and, of course, the hired labor in the factories.

Nonetheless, the majority of Jews remained handworkers: tailors, haberdashers, glove makers, metalworkers, tanners, glaziers, shoemakers, butchers, and similar trades required for everyday communal life. The factories too really resembled large workshops, where spinning and weaving was still done by hand. One such factory, belonging to Avraham Prussak, a Kotzk Ḥasid, already employed 132 Jews in 1860. Prussak wanted his factory to cease all labor on the

Sabbath and employ only Jewish workers. In this matter, as it later turned out, he was a rare exception among Jewish industrialists.

In the 1860s, the industrial revolution reached Lodz. Thousands of peasant youths streamed into the city and, under the guidance of German experts, quickly learned the textile business. Jews too flocked into the city from the smaller towns, but it soon became obvious that they would be unable to become absorbed in large industry, for three main reasons. First, they had not been trained to work the machines and the German textile experts refused to teach them. Second, the automated factory did not suspend work on the Sabbath. Third, the Christian workers did not want to work with Jews. Despite these three serious obstacles, the Jewish population continued to increase, reaching 98,000 by 1897. Eight percent were large industrialists and rich merchants, a significant and rapid achievement, but sixty percent were hired laborers in small factories and workshops, where handwork was still the rule, and many were outworkers, working at home on leased looms, or on looms they managed to purchase by the sweat of their brow.

It is easy to see how poverty spread: A mechanized factory worker earned 600–900 zloty per year, skilled workers and expert instructors as much as

A Jewish hand-weaver at his loom in the Baluty neighborhood, 1920–30

2,000 zloty, whereas a tailor earned only 400 zloty per year. At the beginning of the twentieth century there were 61 factories owned by non-Jews and 36 owned by Jews. In addition, there were many smaller Jewish-held textile workshops, so that together Jews made up about one-half of all the production in a branch that constituted 92 percent of the town's industry. Ostensibly this was a tremendous economic force and could have served as a respectable source of livelihood for our people, however the non-Jewish factories denied entry to Jews, the Jewish-owned factories employed few Jews, and most of the Jewish workshops were small and poorly mechanized.

Statistics from 1901 are illuminating, or rather, depressing: they point to the source of Bałuty's poverty, and that of the Old Town and other neighborhoods. In that year, the industrialized factories owned by non-Jews employed 31,000 workers, of which only 61 were Jews. The Jewish-owned industrialized factories employed 11,000 non-Jewish workers, and only 1,184 Jews. In the un-mechanized factories held by non-Jews only two Jews were employed compared to 688 non-Jews, and in such factories under Jewish ownership there were only 779 Jews and 1,900 non-Jews. Clearly the industrial revolution did not devolve its blessings on the Jews of Lodz. It has been calculated that from the days of Julius Caesar until the industrial revolution, through all those generations, no laborer, anywhere in the world, ever succeeded in earning more bread for an hour of labor. Only the industrial revolution achieved an increase in bread and other necessities in exchange for labor.

This Jewish labor force counted many young boys and girls who had never attended any kind of school, and more than 1,000 women. A renter of looms or a piecework contractor working from home with his wife, sometimes with their children, often 12 to 16 hours a day, earned 3–4 rubles per week, about half the wages of a worker in industry. He was usually also the first victim of a crisis in the markets, an easy prey to catastrophe. In 1904, there were 2,000 unemployed weavers.

Most instructive are the statistics from 1897, from my father's childhood. Among Jews, 40 percent worked as artisans and in industry, 30 percent—in trade and loans, 19.3 percent were hired employees, servants and salespeople, 3.8 percent retirees-pensioners, 2.2 percent white-collar professionals and clerks, 2.2 percent transport, prostitutes 0.1 percent (20 women). In the course of time, migration into the city increased, birthrates rose, and medical developments helped sustain the life of newborns so that poverty increased still more. Young people were generally untrained for any other occupation than that of their fathers. The city's industrialists Poznanski, Bielschowsky, Jaroki, Eitingon,

Yeraḥmiel Lifshitz and others built great mansions. Handsome homes of the well-to-do (upper, middle and lower middle-class, as defined by sociologists) arose in streets inhabited mostly or partly by Jews. On the other hand, the dilapidated homes of the lower classes became increasingly overcrowded. In my father's day, Lodz became one of the largest industrial and trade cities in the Russian empire, and its products spread even far beyond it, but the economic gap within the population kept on widening.

THE CITY'S PAUPERIZATION

The Jews of Lodz were especially hard hit during periods of economic slowdown. As ill luck would have it, every few years the European and Russian markets were rocked by crisis, and worse of all was World War I, during which the Germans plundered Jewish factories and homes. The entire city was hard hit, and tens of thousands of citizens left, many returning to the small towns from which they had come.

It took industry a few years to recover from the war. In my day, there were about 30,000 Jewish laborers in the city's workshops and factories, mostly in textile. In 1921, inflation began to soar. The policies chosen to counteract the raging inflation were stymied by drastic errors and intentional discrimination, for which Jews were forced to pay a heavy price because it was from them, from the country's traders, that most of the taxes were extracted. Their tax assessments were grossly inflated. The treasury compounded its rapacity: When Jews could not pay income and sales taxes, their property and possessions were seized.

In those days, I saw horrifying scenes of dispossession and confiscation proceedings and heard the laments and protests of shop owners and small traders on our streets. Economic dispossession was an overt and insolent policy. Particularly shocking were the scenes of property and work tools confiscations. Trade houses were permanently or temporarily shut down and many were threatened with closure. In panic, they scurried to obtain loans to pay their taxes. There were, of course, also tax evasions and fraud. The middle class became poorer, and among the lower classes poverty spread even more. As mentioned earlier, this situation, severely aggravated during the Grabski premiership (1923–1925), prompted many Jews to leave Poland for Ereẓ Israel (the fourth *aliyah*).

For Poles too, of course, the situation was precarious. Masses of Polish workers emigrated in that decade to France and Germany. In 1926, 20 percent of all industrial workers in Poland, one in five, were unemployed. The standard of living declined dramatically. Still, the Jewish worker suffered more than did the non-Jew. The country's 150,000 Jewish employees worked mostly in small factories and workshops, as noted above, at lower wages than those of the non-Jewish workers in the large factories. More than half of the Jewish artisans, and there were about half a million of them in the first decade after the war, could not afford hired help. Where a Jew was in partnership with a non-Jew, his taxes were ten times higher, even though he had no additional income outside the joint business with the non-Jewish partner.

I remember clearly two strikes. In the year that I left Poland, in October 1928 to be precise, a long and bitter strike erupted in a number of factories where Jewish workers also took part. The demand was for a 25 percent wage increase. In the end, the workers settled for the promise of a mere 5 percent increase. Another strike that year broke out in Eitingon's factory: The Polish employees refused to work because a Jewish mechanic was hired. I read about this strike in *Ha-olam* when I was already enrolled for studies in Breslau, and I

Lodz, 1933. In the Baluty neighborhood marketplace, a street merchant with geese for sale hung around his neck

saw in it not only testimony to the struggles of Jews in the present—in the days of Piłsudksi, who was reputed to be "favorable" to the Jews—but an ominous sign for the future.

Bałuty, then, suffered from compounded problems: the poverty of the Polish state, the economic dispossession of its second-class citizens, the Jews, the particular occupational structure of the Jewish workforce, the residents' technological backwardness, the horrific congestion, and the inadequate sanitary and housing conditions. World War I with its attendant destruction, hunger and lawlessness, and the periodic national economic crises, continued to pauperize the neighborhood. When I left Poland, statistics showed that 80 percent of its Jews belonged to the underclass, 15 percent were middle class, and the rest well to do and wealthy. The most productive of all Jewish communities in Poland saw scant reward for its labor, and the Jews of Bałuty were among the most disadvantaged and afflicted.

COMMUNITY LEADERS AND THE REINCARNATION OF RELIGIOUS ENERGY

No wonder that Bałuty was the seedbed of the labor movements. At first they fought among themselves in the *shtiblach* for the souls of workers, artisans, and apprentices, and then they established parties with public stages, crowd assemblies, organizational cells, pamphlets, and newspapers. During the first Russian revolution and the subsequent rioting in Bałuty, heroes of Bund, the Zionist Socialists (S. S.) and Po'aley Zion acquired fame. They demonstrated, protested, and defended their brethren against the rioters, among whom were Russian policemen. Father told me about the exploits of these heroes, and what he left out was supplied by our neighbor C. A. Tobiasz, a former *yeshiva* student, who in those days (1905–06) had been a young worker who began to induct his friends from the Ḥasidic *shtibel* into the Po'aley Zion party, and was one of its early founders in our city. In their defiance and self-defense in those heroic days and in the struggles during World War I and subsequently, it was clear that despite the collapse of faith in the sanctity of the Torah as conceived by tradition, faith itself had not waned. True, in the eyes of these young people, human history on earth was no longer a divine drama with the Jewish people its chief protagonist, next to the Creator Himself. For the problems of the world, of God, and of social and economic conditions, they no longer sought answers in the Holy Scriptures or the *Shulḥan Arukh*. Quite purposefully, they rebelled and protested against the faithful and their leaders, the rabbis and the Ḥasidic rebbes, whom they viewed as innocently deluded, if not hypocritically deluding others. However, in the paths taken by each of these parties, each with its individual *programa*, these young people, imbued with great dedication, longed to bring salvation to the individual and to the community.

The old Jewish religious energy was now channeling itself into new directions. I sensed this palpably, for it was as recently as just one generation earlier that their fathers had been enthusiastic Ḥasidim, and they themselves were at first content to follow their fathers' footsteps. Now the members of these new and rebellious parties set before their adherents new commandments and demands, which they were to fulfill "with all their souls and all their might," underpinned, however, by a new rationale. The conception of the redeeming enterprise that removes evil and injustice from the world took on a secular garb, which in the eyes of traditional believers was an abomination, a desecration of God's name, the "law of the Gentiles." It is impossible today not to regard the endeavors of these modern activists as another expression of the "light of Judaism," perhaps stemming from the selfsame motives and impulses which previously supported the structure of traditional faith in the Torah, the commandments, and the customs. The bitter disagreements among the new parties were very reminiscent of the strife between *Ḥasidim* and *mitnagdim*, and the disputes among the various Ḥasidic sects themselves. Beliefs and experiences were transformed from the traditional mold to be reincarnated in secular varieties and, perhaps one may say, in new varieties of religion animated by great enthusiasm and creative energy.

Bałuty too had its "rebbes," and I do not mean that "rebbe" of the crime underworld so ably described by A. Z. Aescoli, even though he too performed an important public-spiritual mission, and it is regrettable that no rabbis from among the establishment responded to the challenge of improving the lives of these embittered and hardened poor. I am referring to leaders like "Froyem Lejzer" (Efraim Elazar), in whom the working masses saw noble qualities, a fearless fighter (he scored a number of achievements, and finally a square in Bałuty was named for him), a man irreverent toward heaven and its religious deputies, who wished to do the right thing by his people. I am not certain that the rebbe*s* of Aleksander paid attention to him and leaders like him. No doubt in their eyes they were heretics, defamers of God's name and "troublers of Israel."

The extent of neglect was everywhere to be seen. The sphere of "life" and the sphere of "religion" had really drifted far apart during the city's era of dynamic growth. Rabbi Meisel, as related earlier, had worked among the poor in their time of need, especially during the acute distress of the cholera epidemic, and they had reciprocated with affection and respect. But by the end of the nineteenth century, the leadership had already lost the last remnants of control over their Lodz community.

The loss of control was general, and was due mainly to two factors. The first were the living and work conditions that weakened deference to authority, and increased skepticism and criticism. The "de-authorization" corroded the established social order, the age-old accepted hierarchy, by undermining the faith that the affairs of this world were indeed governed in a permanent order stemming from divine providence or from the state's power, on whose justice and grace one could rely. The crisis in confidence tarnished the leadership's halo of authority and even undermined the foundations of the family. The urbanization of the *shtetl* dwellers who flocked to Lodz increased tensions within the family and subverted parental authority, as in every country of immigration. The individual saw himself alienated, isolated and dependent on unfamiliar powers with which he was untrained to cope. As so often happens, an unfamiliar environment tends to promote lawlessness and makes imperative new forms of organization.

Add to this the population increase. The old forms of life had been structured for small communities, not for large urban centers, just as the narrow streets of an old town are unsuited for modern traffic. In a *shtetl* that counted at most a few thousand souls everyone knew their neighbors. The community leaders, the rabbis and *gabbaim* could oversee each person's conduct. This socialization process made the community's external authority an internal individual necessity, a movement of the heart, to observe the commandments and the customs without afterthought, such that members of a community kept an eye on each other, ensuring that each walked the straight path. For generations, these frameworks and modes of conduct had stamped a uniformity on all members of the community, but with demographic growth, and especially with migration to the big city, these ancient norms were no longer adequate, although one should say to their credit that they certainly held out well for many generations.

The rabbinic culture, strengthened by the Ḥasidic movement, had vested enormous resources of thought, organization, and historical experience into buttressing the Jewish community. This culture founded and secured a religious-political organization which few in the world could rival in terms of strength, cohesion, and the ability to withstand enemies from without and skeptics or heretics from within. However, the structure of the community with all its formerly efficacious institutions could no longer properly contain and sustain the Jews, who had so increased in number in the modern era. To give just one example: the traditional private *ḥeder* could handle only a small number of pupils who studied in the teacher's house, and even the later public Talmud Torah primary school had become too small for the increased numbers. I could see that the courts of Aleksander and the other great rebbes had become rearguards, last holdouts of desperate resolution trying to maintain the rabbinic-Ḥasidic culture, as if the world around them had not changed.

THE GHETTO

The tram was about to reach its destination. It was by now very crowded. Most of the passengers were Ḥasidim, engaged in lively conversation. From afar, I could see that Reb Beẓalel Yair was dozing off in the midst of this moving tumult. In 1928 he was already an old man, perhaps over seventy, who looked more like eighty. Upon seeing him, Father wondered about him and his family. Usually, due to his frailty, he did not venture out of the house.

We passed by the unpaved narrow streets of Bałuty, where the ghetto would later rise in early May 1940. Approximately 200,000 Jews (the Nazis listed 163,776) from Lodz and some of its surrounding towns were confined here in a prison of hard labor and a reality of extermination deportations. Jews from Germany, Austria, and Czechoslovakia were also sent to this ghetto. For all of them, this was the last station before the extermination camps, mainly Auschwitz. In 1944, after the final deportations to Auschwitz, only 887 Jews remained in the ghetto.

Recently, detailed documents about the history of the ghetto have been published in *The Chronicle of the Lodz Ghetto, 1941–1944*. This chronicle is shattering in the matter-of-factness with which a team of educated ghetto inmates reported on daily life, from the price of potatoes on the black market to the deportation of children to extermination camps and shootings along the barbed wire fence—precise systematic reports replete with details, written from a wide perspective. The abridged English edition appeared not long ago in the Yale University Press.[10] The first two volumes were published in the 1960s in Polish, but the authorities then prohibited the appearance of the subsequent three volumes.

Father, Mother and all our other family members, some from Zdunska Wola, were immediately thrown into the congestion, filth, and typhoid epidemic which raged here fiercely in the first few months, and into a daily expectation of death. Indeed, Father died of typhoid fever about two weeks after moving to the ghetto. Mother held out until August 1944, that is, until the liquidation of the ghetto, perhaps thanks to her connections with Mordekhai Ḥaim Rumkowski,

"King of the Ghetto," with whom she used to work before the war on the board of the Helenowek Orphanage. The Jewish population of Lodz held out longer than any other Jewish community in Poland, apparently because it had tremendous production capabilities which were useful to the occupiers. Nearly four and a half years it maintained itself, closed off and isolated, until the final extermination. Of this huge, once so vibrant Jewish community, only a few hundred survived, broken in body and soul. The Lodz ghetto had no chance at all to revolt. It had no arms and no contacts with the outside world. It was impossible to connect with the city's Polish citizenry. Its labor leaders, who had close associates in Bałuty's political parties, were already deported early in the war.[11]

Let us now return to the trip to Aleksander, some eleven years before the Nazi takeover.

CHAPTER 6

Sanctity and Sin

Sketches of the life and personality of two Ḥasidim, reflections on the education of girls, on prostitution, and on the ultimate failure of the Ḥasidic leadership to cope effectively with the desertion of its sons and daughters.

It was possible to get to Aleksander by carriage or coach. That is how one traveled formerly, and in my day, some wealthy adherents still did so. At the corner of the square one could still see covered horse-drawn wagons from the previous century. Each had two facing benches where six passengers could sit on either side. Taking this vehicle, one would reach the rebbe's court after two or more hours of a jerky ride. In my day the main transportation to Aleksander from this transit point was the blue tramline. Young bachelors and recently married men would walk on foot a few stops in order to economize, for even the relatively cheap tram ticket was too expensive for them.

In the square around the tram stop a large crowd waited, most of whom, but not all, were Ḥasidim. Father knew many of them, and nodded to them in greeting.

AN EXEMPLARY ḤASID

Here I would like to describe two Ḥasidim who were waiting with us at the tram stop. I knew them both well.

Reb Avraham Moshe was a tall Jew, 60 plus years old, with a high forehead, thick and threatening brows, but with kind, smiling eyes. The entire handsome cut of his face was encircled with a white beard and side locks. He was thin, and his long thin fingers gestured expressively. His nickname in the rebbe's court and among the Ḥasidim was "Strykower," although his name was Goldman. After his marriage to a woman from Strykow, he had been supported there for a few years by his father-in-law, hence the name.

My father had asked him to teach me Talmud and *tosafot* once a week and we had already studied together a few times, about an hour and a half before the afternoon prayers at the Wiślicki prayer house. There I learned to appreciate the qualities of an exemplary Aleksander Ḥasid who had absorbed the Vurka and Biale Ḥasidic traditions in his youth and had frequented the Old Rebbe of Aleksander, the current dynasty's founder. He had learned a great deal of Torah and Ḥasidism during his sojourn at Strykow, a town of 4,000 inhabitants, half of whom were Jewish. It had been the former residence of Reb Efraim Fishel Strykower (1743–1822), a disciple of the *maggid* of Mezeritch[1] and of Reb Elimelech of Lizhensk.[2] This Strykow Rebbe was known as a saintly man and a disseminator of love for one's fellow, *ahavat Israel*. His issue and that of his disciples numbered several rebbes, among them Reb Dov Berish (Beresz), the Rebbe of Biale. I loved to hear stories of Reb Efraim Fishel Strykower's greatness—a fabled figure in Polish Ḥasidism. My maternal grandfather, after whom I was named, had the same name, and his family name was Strykowski. Reb Mendel, son of the Rebbe of Biale, was a friend of my grandfather and uncles and associated with them when he resided in Zdunska Wola, my mother's hometown, as indicated earlier, and where I spent my infancy when my father was supported by his mother-in-law.

Reb Avraham Moshe did not talk much, and it was not from him that I heard about the vicissitudes of his life. The Ḥasidim used to tell a miraculous tale. While he still lived in Strykow, already burdened with the care of a wife and five children, two sons and three daughters, his small textile shop caught fire. He got up and travelled to the *Yismaḥ Yisroel*, cried in his presence and begged him to pray on his behalf for his livelihood. The rebbe replied, "Your lottery ticket will win, your salvation is near." When the Ḥasidim heard the rebbe's words, they immediately congratulated Reb Avraham Moshe with *mazel tov* and pointed at him as the new *gvir*, the town's "rich man." In those days, and already in the days of Reb Yeḥiel, the Old Rebbe, the *gabbaim* in the Aleksander court would sell Czarist Russian government lottery tickets. The Aleksander court served as a sort of agency for this lottery. Reb Avraham Moshe bought a ticket, and his number won 25,000 rubles, which was an enormous sum in those days. He left Strykow, settled in Lodz and traded in textiles. He used to pray in the Great Shtibel on 56 Zachodnia Street, where he spent many hours of the day studying Torah. He gave liberally to the poor. For his three daughters he set aside generous dowries.

In the meantime Lodz underwent the first catastrophes of the war—the economic collapse and the German plunder, troubles that hastened his wife's demise. After World War I his eldest son Yeḥiel immigrated to New York where his uncle lived, and shortly thereafter, before the gates of immigration closed, brought his younger brother over. The rebbe, Reb Shmuel Ẓvi, disapproved of migration to America. In America, he knew, "hell's fire" burned. The capitalist ethos of entrepreneurs in quest of novelties in a society that was becoming increasingly hedonistic and materialistic was breaking down the values of rabbinic-Ḥasidic culture. This the rebbe and his Ḥasidim in Lodz felt instinctively, needing no sociological analyses. How could a young man, even one from a good family, preserve his Ḥasidic faith in a world abandoned to all manner of desires and instincts? The *midrash* expounds a phrase from the story of young Joseph seeking his brothers—"They have moved on from here"—as: "They have moved on (away) from the good qualities of the place." Still, when the young man came with his father for the last time to take his leave of Aleksander, the rebbe gave him his blessing, that he may succeed and prosper with God's help and be of succor to his father, for he was being sent for the purpose of bringing a livelihood and should return to the home of his ancestors quickly.

Indeed Yeḥiel did well in America. With pride, Reb Avraham Moshe showed me a letter he had received from his eldest, in whom the rebbe's blessing was being fulfilled and he was going from strength to strength, thanks to his uncle's help. In flowery rabbinic language, Yeḥiel informed his father that the two brothers had entered into partnership, that they and their wives and children lived in two lovely adjacent apartments, and that they would soon be sending their boys to *ḥeder*. The sons would send their father money for his living, as he was by now impoverished, especially after the severe inflation of 1922–24. The Ḥasidim related that once, when Yeḥiel stopped sending money, the rebbe appeared in his dream and ordered him to honor his father. Reb Avraham Moshe's youngest daughter, an able seamstress, worked in their apartment at the sewing machine. They moved not far from us to a first-floor apartment consisting of one spacious room, divided by a partition, and a small kitchen. This daughter had attended a Polish high school for a few years, spoke in a gentle, feminine voice, and at only thirty years old was already considered an old maid.

Reb Avraham Moshe was a great scholar, in the Biale tradition, which sought to curb the enthusiasm and abandonment of the Vurka Ḥasidim. The latter, so it was related, would enjoy big spreads: on *rosh ḥodesh*, upon completing a Talmud tractate, on *miẓvah* meals for every occasion, besides Sabbath and holy days feasts, joyously regaling themselves in company to fulfill the saying "The desire of a man is His kindness," namely, that desire in man, when it serves matters of holiness, is a blessing from the Lord.

Reb Avraham Moshe, however, tended to deny himself the pleasures of this world and sanctified himself in what he felt he was permitted. Although he was impoverished, he would, as indicated, give generously, openly or discreetly, whether from any remnant of his earlier fortune or from the dollars he received from his sons. Modest and humble in all his ways, he worshipped the Lord in restrained, sober ardor. He was proficient in the *Mishnah* and the *poskim*. I heard that he had been offered a position as a rabbi but had declined. I recall that in those days I was already losing the sweet taste of a page of Talmud and my only satisfaction lay in the achievement of the difficult study, as in a sports contest. I did not admit this to myself, but I was attracted to cracking specific problems, to Maimonides' *Mishneh Torah*, to consulting the works of the great *poskim* and then returning to examine the Talmudic give-and-take in their light. Reb Avraham Moshe did not approve of this circuitous pursuit, yet nonetheless he went over some responses of the *Noda Biyehudah*[3] (Part One) with me, which we found in the Wiślicki prayer house.

He loved to tell me about the Aleksander rebbes. He venerated the author of *Yismaḥ Yisroel*, but for some reason was particularly attached to the Young Rebbe from Vurka, Reb Mendel[4] who would "hold Tish" in such profound silence that one could hear the wings of a fly in the room. And yet, the *Tish* was full of questions and answers, and the communicative power of the rebbe's silence reached every single Ḥasid, each according to his level. The greatest cry, the rebbe used to say, is the one kept locked in one's heart.

Many a cry did Reb Avraham Moshe bury in his heart. What should a living man complain of when he is granted to worship the Lord and study His Torah? The Lord impoverishes and enriches, lowers and raises, and everything He does is for the good. When I once tried to express my doubts about the way this world was run, he responded with a profusion of quotes from our ancient Sages, from saintly men, past and present, ending with what is essential in Judaism as he had received it from his forefathers namely, "You shall be blameless before the Lord your God." Since the Lord, Blessed be He, oversees everything, and indeed is in everything, one may say that in its essence, the whole world is the Lord, Blessed be He; therefore one should conduct oneself in all worldly and human matters as one conducts oneself in the worship of God. Reb Avraham Moshe had a complete and innocent faith, without sophistry. In his every simple articulation and daily deed there was a kind of profound intentionality, by no means simple, an intimation at other dimensions, at lofty horizons.

Although we lived at the same time and in the same place, it was clear that Reb Avraham Moshe belonged to another generation, in the sense explained earlier, i.e., that the boundaries of a generation are the boundaries of the distresses that preoccupy it. His world picture had crystallized into forms of thought and faith around quandaries and reactions different from mine. I was asking questions that he did not know, or that he chose to distance from himself. On the other hand, I felt that despite the distance, I could not help share the experiences and crises of the previous generation and the responses it gave to its quandaries. I loved to hear him quote the Old Rebbe's explanation of the verse from the Psalms, "Let everything that has breath praise the Lord"—for every single breath, for every moment of living, we should praise the Lord.

A few years after I left Lodz, so I was told, someone knocked on our door at night. Reb Avraham Moshe's neighbor called my father to come quickly: Reb Avraham Moshe had fainted from pain. My father was known in the neighborhood as an "expert" at healing the sick, a sort of paramedic or medical consultant, and if a sudden emergency arose before a doctor could arrive, one would call him for first aid. Reb Avraham Moshe died of a stroke while he was studying the *Zohar*[5] at night. His soul departed in sanctity, in a "kiss of death," and he was spared the atrocities of the ghetto and suffocation by gas. His younger daughter married a widowed rabbi or rabbinic judge from Strykow, where she was born. I met one of his sons some time ago in a religious kibbutz in Israel.

SORROW OF RAISING DAUGHTERS

In the square, waiting for the Aleksander blue line tram, there were a few dozen Ḥasidim and about a dozen of the town's residents returning home from their affairs in Lodz, carrying a motley assortment of packages, baskets, knapsacks, bags, and sacks. Although I was rather embarrassed to see there a neighbor, Reb Ḥaim "the lame," I nodded a greeting, and he, recognizing me beneath my new Ḥasidic outfit, smiled with a mischievous wink, as though promising to keep my secret. He too was going to the *hillulah*.

People said that he was not lame from birth, but that the medic associated with the court of Aleksander maimed him deliberately, to disqualify him for service in the Russian army. In the days of the rebbe known as *Yismaḥ Yisroel*, young men called to present themselves before the medical boards of the Russian military would gather at Aleksander during Sukkot and the rebbe appointed a number of Ḥasidim who were "in the know" to act as a sort of examining committee. They would order this one to lose weight, another to have his teeth pulled (this was Father's lot), and a third some other impairment. The four-year service in the Russian army was intolerable to a pious young Jew who observed the commandments and studied Torah. Ḥaim had this limp inflicted upon him, after which he hobbled on his left foot, and was known on our street as Ḥaim the Lame.

He moved into a house adjacent to ours only three years prior to our outing to the *hillulah.* I would see him on the street, a man of about fifty plus, short, broad shouldered and firm of build, striding-limping slowly as he carried his *tallit* and *tefillin* bag under his arm. Sometimes he would carry in and out of his home various packages, apparently containing cloth. We spoke to him only in the *sukkah* on the Feast of Tabernacles. In the building where he lived and in which he was the only Jewish tenant there was no *sukkah.* Its owner, a non-Jew, was a butcher who kept his meat shop in the front. Reb Ḥaim was a man of few words, a brooder. He was a widower with three daughters, all buxom girls.

His worry was his second daughter, Hanna, if I remember correctly, who was a prostitute, according to the consensus on our street. In those days, prostitutes were still easily recognizable by their dress, even though women's fashion in the 1920s already shortened the hemlines, by their heavy make-up, high heels, deep neckline, provocative gait, and other signs. It was difficult to mistake this young woman of about 22 when she sallied out of her house with a friend, equally gussied up, along our street, apparently headed for neighborhoods distant from the home of her pious father.

One should keep in mind that in those days modesty in the conduct of boys and girls was still taken for granted. One of the greatest revolutions in my generation was the dissolution of the norms of traditional modesty, also among Jews. All of a sudden, it was as though the relationship to the body, to sex life, to the authority of public conventions, to the duty to honor father and mother, were all changed, and that change came as a shock. Prostitution in Lodz increased significantly after World War I. Dozens, perhaps hundreds, of prostitutes walked the streets and loitered around house entrances. Most, though not all, were registered with the police. Poverty was not the only motive. Hanna, the daughter of Ḥaim the Lame, certainly suffered poverty and want, perhaps even hunger, although his eldest daughter worked, as I recall, in a factory and Reb Ḥaim himself lugged those packets of cloth in and out, and I don't imagine he worked for nothing. Apparently Hanna wanted to work, like her sister, but to earn more. As she saw herself mistress of her own charms, she offered them for sale. Perhaps she lacked love and sought it in lovemaking. Perhaps she was expressing her independence by protesting against the traditions of her father and the conventions of family life. I assume that Reb Ḥaim saw this and that his heart grieved, but who knows, maybe he did not wish to see. Father once told me of a similar case of a God-fearing father, whose daughter had become immodest, though not yet sunk to streetwalking. He expounded on Scripture: "When the man saw that he could not throw Jacob, he struck him in the hollow of his thigh"—likewise, when the Evil Inclination, Esau, the Angel of Uncleanness, sees that "he cannot throw" a God-fearing Jew, he touches "the hollow of his thigh," that is, he goes after the issue of his thigh, his children. Therefore, right after this tale of our patriarch Jacob, we hear: "Dinah, the daughter of whom Leah had borne to Jacob, went out . . ."—and a very nasty business ensued.

I do not know why Hanna did not leave her father's house. Perhaps, in her own way, she was attached to him. Perhaps this was just a beginning, her early career. On the first day of Sukkot a year before my departure, she came to our tenement's *sukkah* to lay the table for her father's meal at one end of the table in the place reserved for Reb Ḥaim. The landlord, Ichi Meir Schlosser, got all heated up, swearing and cursing, "Get out of this holy place, you slut!" Reb Ḥaim paled for a moment, then broke out in loud vituperations against the landlord: It was because he, Schlosser, was a Ḥasid of Ger that he was humiliating her, a kosher Jewish girl, daughter of honorable Ḥasidim of Aleksander, poor orphan that she was. He would allow no one to insult her! "And furthermore, here's your own son, Benjamin, the fool, the idiot, bothering her, and she would have none of him!" The *sukkah* was full. After the initial stupefaction, people tried to calm things down and make peace. The following day, it was Reb Ḥaim's eldest daughter who brought him his meal. It was, after all, obligatory to make the blessings and eat in the *sukkah*. However, this disgraceful and agitating spectacle was the talk of our street that day, and for a long time thereafter. A year later, he participated in the expense of putting up a *sukkah* in his own yard, a more elaborate booth, constructed as a sign of protest and independence by a widowed wagoner, a simple and friendly man who, too, was burdened with daughters, albeit younger ones.

FATHERS AND SONS

I did not see that Hanna mended her ways. After I left Lodz I heard nothing more of Reb Ḥaim and his daughters. I know that these good-looking, fleshy girls led me to many sinful thoughts. A propos the breakdown of sexual taboos: Many non-Jews on our street were equally unhappy when two Polish prostitutes, one older and plumpish, the other younger and thin, rented the grocery directly opposite our apartment building for their trade. They covered the door and windows with curtains, and men entered and exited. I was a teenager, and I could say in the language of the Book of Proverbs: "I glanced out of the window of my house, I looked down through the lattice ... suddenly a woman came to meet" me. And she seduces: "Let us drown ourselves in pleasure." However, the Polish neighbors harassed them, and after some months, they departed.

The difficulty of raising sons and daughters became more acute in the decade after World War I. Western Europe culture, together with the "laws of the Gentiles," broke through traditional modes of life and undermined the three pillars of tradition on which the House of Israel rested. These were:

(a) Religion with its institutions—the Torah and its scholars and teachers, the decisors and interpreters of the Law, and the *halakhically* loyal community leaders.
(b) Family—honoring father and mother according to the Torah's injunctions, "Ye shall fear every man his mother and his father". The Midrash explains: What is fear? He will not sit in his parent's usual place, will not speak in his stead, and will not contradict him. This was the foundation for Maimonides' Laws of the Rebellious Ones (*Hilkhot mamrim*). Authority was also strengthened through the lineage of families, and of course, a family's wealth would enhance the power it could wield over its offspring.
(c) Government and fear of authorities—even though according to the *halakha*, it is only the general law of the land that is to be accepted as binding, not laws that are applied to Jews only, a Jew is obligated to "pray for the welfare of the government, since, but for fear of it, men would swallow each other alive." Even more so were the internal Jewish governing bodies to be respected, at least nominally, however, in reality, disputes and dissensions abounded.

The change after World War I was most evident, I believe, in our dynamic, ambitious, industrial city which lacked a tradition of Torah study and leadership, unlike Cracow, Lublin, and Vilna. Young people were abandoning the *shtiblach*. Many like me were straying from the fold, leaving, returning, and leaving again. They saw their parents as prisoners of the past who interpreted the present in the light of the past and its language, the language of biblical stories, rabbinic tales and the omnipresent divine providence. These young people felt that there was no point in sitting in inaction waiting for the Messiah; rather, that the acts of wonder had to be replaced by the wonder of acts, useful acts, which would bring liberation closer. The Jewish street was proposing activist messianic solutions. Sons and fathers drifted apart.

Faced with emptying *shtiblach,* Aleksander leaders tried to respond. They felt that the modern schools were leading Jewish children "astray," and forbade their followers to send their sons to such schools (daughters were exempted from this ruling). Shortly before his death, the *Yismaḥ Yisroel* circulated a "holy epistle" against the attempt in Cracow to found a modern Zionist school, the curriculum of which included *Mishnah* and *Gemarah.* Thus wrote the *ẓaddik*: "To the honored great and famous rabbis who sit in judgment in the holy congregation of Cracow, may their Rock keep them and grant them life, against a certain doctor who wished to found a *gymnasium* where Talmud too will be taught, to cast a net for ensnaring innocent souls." In this admonitory epistle, the *ẓaddik* complains of the "loss of the generation's soul," of "those who are wise in their own eyes, who sway with the breeze of the day, all of them against the Holy Torah." With such wise men, the rebbe does not wish to argue, because they would not heed him. He addresses himself "only to those who are wandering in their thoughts and debating which way to go, those who say, 'it is good for Torah study to be coupled with *derekh ereẓ*.'" His polemics are aimed at the modernizers, the founders of educational institutions in the spirit of the Mizraḥi movement, or of the new Tarbut schools, or of the Hebrew high schools founded by Dr. Braude, and even the heads of the Reformed Ḥeder[6] movement, telling them that their schools were nothing but "a cover to mask the blight." These educators were using the instruments of holiness in order to strip the Torah of her fine embroideries and adorn her slave-maid, who would repudiate her mistress and eventually usurp her position. True Torah scholars, the rebbe argues, were those who watch over the House of Israel, who apprehend the evil that is about to descend and stand up and warn that "the impure should not, God forbid, mix with the holy." For God's work, the *ẓaddik* explains, is to rectify the original sin, by which "the evil became mixed with the good, and we are under obligation to sift out and separate the evil from the good." He calls on them to lift the veil of blindness and not to walk "in the crookedly deflected path of those who walk backward instead of forward." Finally he implores the readers of his epistle to raise their sons to Torah study and piety in the ways of our ancestors and not in the new way, the counterfeit, the destroyer, Heaven forbid, of the Torah.[7]

My father too read this epistle at the end of the *Yismaḥ Yisroel.* Many times, I imagine, he must have pondered its warning. In that same book, in the rebbe's sermon for Simḥat Torah, he also read "that the chief form of worship is to anchor in the heart a simple and complete faith, like that of a simpleton."[8] It is possible that in his youth my father could accept the rebbe's words in simple and complete faith, "like a simpleton," but since then many changes had rocked his world. Good and evil were very much mixed together, and it was often difficult to discern who were those walking forward and who backward. When his sons grew, and the world changed after the terrible war, he decided, with a heavy heart, upon the advice of his sisters who had already finished high school, to disobey his rebbe's instruction. I imagine that in all his subsequent life he was plagued by a sense of guilt. Without actually making a conscious decision one way or the other, he tried to walk between the raindrops and to raise me to Torah study and observance, but also to *derekh ereẓ*. At any rate, he feared lest his son become alienated from him.

Reb Shmuel Ẓvi, who was the first rebbe I knew in my childhood when he resided in Lodz during the war, saw the quandary of his flock and tried to respond according to his lights. He opened a *yeshiva* in Aleksander, Beis Yisroel, named after his brother. His son, Reb Yiẓḥak Menaḥem, the rebbe to whom Father and I were travelling, tried to establish *yeshivot* all over Poland. In 1927, I believe, a *yeshiva* was founded in Lodz, where a few hundred boys and young men studied. Perhaps this effort stemmed the epidemic of desertions. The tragic rift, however, did not cease, and with it the struggle over the ways to mend it. This war between parents and children tore apart many Ḥasidic families.

Among the crowd of Ḥasidim waiting for the tram that would bring them to the rebbe's court, no doubt many wished to pour out their sorrow of raising sons and daughters in the *ẓaddik*'s ear, and receive his counsel and blessing. My father too, on a previous occasion, had asked the rebbe to bless me. He had told the rebbe that I was continuing my study of holy subjects, but that I was also studying in the secular Hebrew high school. The rebbe had sighed and had blessed Father that he may derive *nakhes*, satisfaction, from his son.

The movement of *aliyah* to the Land of Israel, another salvage route from the wreckage, was weak among the Aleksander faithful. It began in the days of Reb Shmuel Ẓvi, at the beginning of the fourth *aliyah*, and continued in a trickle. The rebbe ordered the purchase of a plot of land in Bnei Brak, on the eastern periphery of Tel Aviv. In 1928, the first *shtibel* of Aleksander Ḥasidim, Beis Yisroel, was founded in Jerusalem, and later a *yeshiva* named Yismaḥ Yisroel was built. I do not recall that this made any impression in Lodz. Only in 1933 did a member of the Aleksander Rebbe's family come to Israel: This was the afore mentioned Reb Moshe Yehuda, son-in-law of Reb Beẓalel Yair, thereby saving a branch, an all too small remnant, of this illustrious family.

CHAPTER 7

A Town and its Ẓaddik

Composition and economy of the *shtetl* Aleksander. Ḥasidim assemble at the rebbe's "court." A somber memorial service at the cemetery. Demons and souls, spiritual traffic between heaven and earth.

THE "EARTHLY ALEKSANDER"

This was not my first visit to Aleksander. I had sat in the rebbe's great *beit midrash* a number of times and had also danced with the Ḥasidim in the large square in front of it, young and old joined in a large circle of swaying happiness and fraternity, circle within circle. I had also occasionally rambled through the town's streets. When I began forming my own opinions and started looking about me with open eyes and the critical thinking tools acquired through my high school studies and my readings, I pondered quite a bit about the nature of Aleksander. I considered it the path of knowledge and faith, a symbol, "the heavenly Aleksander," but I also looked at it with the sober realism of a Lodz native who had already learned about the power of economic forces, class struggle, demographics, ethnic relations, and other topics that were not considered of great importance in our world. Half inside, half outside, I saw Aleksander in double vision.

The visible Aleksander was similar to so many other *shtetls* where Jews and non-Jews lived side by side, both groups recently arrived, driven by the dynamics propelling the vigorous capitalism that built Lodz and its surrounding towns. According to the statistics of 1921, its population numbered about 8,000, mostly Germans, 3,000 Jews, and a smaller minority of Poles.[1] In municipal elections during the 1920s, the authorities interfered to the detriment of the Jews, thereby skewing the demographic reality: Eleven Germans, six Jews, and five Poles were elected to the council [the Jews who constituted over 37 percent of the population, received only 27 percent of the seats.]

True, the Germans merited primacy. The town had been founded by German weavers fleeing their homeland in the first half of the nineteenth century due to hunger, drought, and oppression. Similarly to the "Swabians" (as they were called by the Poles) who had settled in Lodz, they too lived on weaving and excelled as specialists with a tradition of high artisanry. Most of the streets in Aleksander looked like a German town of those days: wood or brick houses, small and clean, with red tiled roofs, and fronted by cultivated gardens, vegetable beds, and flowers.

Work was hard, the days long. The handloom would bang ceaselessly, its thrusts shaking the houses. Eventually a number of weavers introduced steam-powered machines, established factories, and prospered. The "Swabians" built a large Lutheran church in the town's main square.

In the streets inhabited by Jews the houses, mostly of wood, were less well-kept and usually lacked gardens. I saw windows stuffed with rags, or covered with metal sheets. However, there were a few large red or black brick, or stone, houses. A number of wealthy Jewish industrialists wished to honor the rebbe, the author of *Yismaḥ Yisroel*, and paid for the construction of a handsome synagogue, inaugurated in 1909. At that time, the rebbe was also the rabbi of the town, and he encouraged them to build. In my day, the town's rabbi was R. Yiẓḥak Meir Singer, a Jew of small stature and nimble movement, abounding in Torah wisdom and everyday talk who was often seen in the rebbe's court. He was a son-in-law of the Rebbe Shmuel Ẓvi, and brother-in-law of Reb Yiẓḥak Menaḥem, the last Rebbe of Aleksander. After World War II, Singer's sons published in New York a facsimile edition of *Yismaḥ Yisroel*, which still exists today.

The town's Jews were artisans, tailors, hatters, furriers, bakers, butchers, day laborers. Servicing the rebbe's court and catering to the needs of Ḥasidim arriving from afar (guest lodgings, eating-houses, rented beds) supported a few families, but in the summer months, when the rebbe and his entourage left for a recreation or spa resort, these families would look for other sources of income.

However, a large number, perhaps the majority, made a living in the hose industry. According to the statistics of 1921, there were in Aleksander 196 Jewishly-owned hosiery workshops and factories which provided work for their owners and their family members, as well as to some 220 Jewish workers and 180 non-Jews.

Thus, while the "heavenly Aleksander" was a center of Ḥasidism, the "earthly Aleksander" was a center for the manufacture of socks and stockings. The Jewish workshops were generally un-mechanized, and their owners, and certainly their workers, eked out a poor living. As in Lodz, the problem here

Yiẓḥak Menaḥem Dancyiger (1880–1943), fourth ADMOR of Aleksander (1923–1943) walking with his sons and student in the spa of Marienbad, 1937

too was that the larger factories, even when owned by Jews, did not employ Jews, mainly because of opposition by non-Jewish workers. Due to the competition with Lodz and the towns within its precinct, like Zgierz and Pabianice, the textile industry in Aleksander declined and only the specialized hosiery manufacture survived successfully. This profession too underwent crises and long periods of unemployment.

Even though the town's heart was the rebbe's court, not all its Jewish inhabitants were Aleksander Ḥasidim. Politically and culturally, the town was very different from what it had been in the days of my grandfather, and even from those of my father's youth.

After the German army expelled the Russians from Poland and the formation of political and social parties and unions was permitted, it became clear that the Jewish population of Aleksander was not of one mind and will. In the 1924 elections to the community's board, the Mizraḥi movement won two seats, Agudat Israel (i.e., the Ger Ḥasidim and their supporters) one seat, and the Aleksander Ḥasidim, in their very own home base, only one seat. The Zionists, the Po'aley Zion and the Bund did not bother competing for seats on a board whose powers had been reduced by the new rulings of the Polish government to matters of cult and charity. I believe that of all the Jews of Aleksander, only some 200 families, maybe 800 to 900 people, perhaps even fewer, were devotees of the Dancyger dynasty, which had become a magnet for thousands of Ḥasidim throughout Congress Poland. As though indeed "a *ẓaddik* is honored everywhere except in his own hometown." Aleksander devotees, unlike those of Ger, did not favor political involvement and the rebbe did not encourage them to organize in modern public activities. As mentioned earlier, Rebbe Shmuel Ẓvi established a large *yeshiva* in his court, subsequently enlarged and strengthened by his son, the dynasty's last rebbe in Poland, whom we were about to see. This was Yiẓḥak Menaḥem Dancyger, who, following his death in Treblinka, was named *Akedat Yiẓḥak* (The Binding of Isaac), the title given to the posthumous collection of his sayings.

During World War I and subsequently, a number of secular cultural institutions made their appearance: libraries, theater clubs, sports associations, a culture center ("*kulturhois*," established by the Po'aley Zion party in 1922), where the Ha-zamir choir members met. In 1918, the Mizraḥi movement established a school, and a few years later a girls' school, Beis Yaakov, was founded. Most boys attended a *ḥeder*, but it already had to compete with the state elementary school, which did not operate on the Sabbath. Aleksander also had a Zionist group of the *He-ḥaluẓ* movement, which prepared young people for immigration to Ereẓ Israel.

The "earthly Aleksander," then, in its hard labor and indigence, and in the political and social remedies that the diverse parties offered for the spiritual ills of the day, revealed the position of the rebbe's court in the overall struggle. Clearly, in my day the court was no longer central.

ḤASIDIM ASSEMBLE. BEGINNINGS OF THE ALEKSANDER DYNASTY

We arrived by tram to the stop near the *ẓaddik*'s court and walked together in the snow. We saw a number of groups, a few tens of Ḥasidim, who came on this day of *hillulah* to the cemetery and the *beit midrash*. Geographically, the rebbe's court was nothing more than a wide piazza bordered by several buildings, most notably the *beit midrash*. This was an old house, built of strong wood that had been repeatedly repaired in a number of places, especially following a (relatively minor) fire in the days of the *Yismaḥ Yisroel*, when a Torah scroll also caught fire. Not far from the *beit midrash* stood a number of brick and stone houses, two and three stories high which served as the residences of the rebbe, his brother, sons and sons-in-law, and other relatives and close associates who were, you might say, the court "bureaucracy." Nearby there were a few houses for lodging visiting Ḥasidim. Their rooms were small and accommodation was tight and crowded. Nonetheless, I saw Ḥasidim get up in the morning fresh and alert to run "fleet as a gazelle" to divine service with the *ẓaddik* in the great *beit midrash.*

On the wide piazza stretching out in front of the *beit midrash,* Ḥasidim would assemble when the weather was mild to sanctify the new moon and to dance in circles. The piazza was bustling all hours of the day and evening. From there one accessed the surrounding houses. The *beit midrash,* which served also as the prayer hall for the rebbe and the Ḥasidim, was furnished with long tables along the walls and bookshelves laden with books: the Talmud and *poskim,* Kabbalah and Ḥasidic works. The singsong of the Talmudic hum never ceased day and night. Who can count the thousands of pages studied there in concentration, in enthusiasm, in sanctity! Or the number of tears shed in whispered prayer and in wall-piercing sobs, a streaming lament of men hungry for salvation, crying from the anguish of their hearts.

To assuage their troubles the tables in the *beit midrash,* as in the *shtiblach* of Aleksander Ḥasidim everywhere, offered the "bitter drop" (liquor). As soon as we entered, we saw a group of Ḥasidim standing near a table, greeting one another, talking together loudly. One of them opened a bottle of brandy and poured some glasses. Honey cake was distributed among the group, some sitting, others standing about. The beadle brought some herring. Glasses were raised *leḥayim,* to life. This was the drinking order: First, they would take the glass and make the blessing, sip a little, stretch out their hand and shake, not strongly, the hands of all the other drinkers, and toast a "*leḥayim* Reb so-and-so," adding good wishes for health or livelihood, depending on the need. After the blessings-wishes, each would down his glass. They did not clink glasses in the non-Jewish custom. Often they would pour a second glass, and a third. Their opponents called them the "Aleksander drunkards." They would drink brandy, wine and beer. At the rebbe's table during a meal, when a number of tables were joined, only wine was served. Between one sip and the next, the conversation flowed: words of Torah, everyday talk, Ḥasidic stories, personal matters.

The history of the *beit midrash* was bound up in the history of Aleksander Ḥasidism. Prior to the establishment of the Dancyger dynasty, the forefathers of local Ḥasidim would journey from Aleksander to Kotzk, then to Vurka and Biale, until a disciple of Reb Menaḥem Mendel of Kotzk settled in Aleksander. This was Reb Heynekh of Aleksander[2] who was considered a great miracle worker. When he died, Ḥasidim would travel to Biale, and when the latter's rebbe, Reb Dov Baer (Berish), died in 1876, the Ḥasidim bought the *beit midrash* in Aleksander from the heirs of Reb Heynekh. They invited the son of Reb Shraga Feivel Dancyger, the *ẓaddik* Reb Yeḥiel, to Aleksander and chose him to be their rebbe. The dynasty began with him. Reb Heynekh was mentioned only rarely by the Aleksander Ḥasidim of my day. However, I have found a two-part Yiddish book about him by an author named Yiẓḥak Heynekh Sonenberg who wrote tales of Reb Heynekh's sanctity and many miracles in "A Very Beautiful Wondrous Story about Reb Heynekh from Aleksander."[3] In brief, the rebbe Reb Yeḥiel to whose grave we were heading, was the founder of the Aleksander dynasty, but the courtyard and the *beit midrash* were already permeated in sanctity in the days of Reb Heynekh.

AT THE CEMETERY

The air in Aleksander was far less polluted than in Lodz with its smoke and soot, smoggy air, and stinking gutters. The factories here were not located in the middle of town and there were few of them. Just a few steps through Aleksander and already you were in the fields, in a wood, or a patch of grass by the lake where the rebbe and his Ḥasidim would cast their sins during the *Tashlikh* ceremony on the afternoon of the first day of Rosh Hashana. Now it was frozen and I could see its ice glittering in the distance.

A few hundred Ḥasidim were already gathered at the cemetery, and it was difficult to get near the *ohel*.[4] From a distance, I could see the rebbe, his brothers, and their entourage. The Rebbe of Aleksander, Reb Yiẓḥak Menaḥem Mendel, whose name the Ḥasidim did not usually pronounce, though of course they could never for a moment forget it, was on this day of *hillulah*, the fourteenth day of the month of Shevat, 1928, about 53 years old. To me, he looked older—bent in posture, with his long beard already largely turned white. He was wearing a brown fur coat and a fur hat of the same color. Next to him walked his two brothers, Reb Yakov Simḥa Bunim, who was considered very smart and energetic, and Reb Avraham Ḥaim. Both traded in some goods in Lodz. I believe that they also involved the rebbe in their affairs, because the Aleksander court did not depend solely on donations from Ḥasidim. The funds funneled from the business were spent on charity and on maintenance of the *yeshiva*, which the rebbe had expanded and to which he had added an adjacent dormitory for young men. This, however, was not simply the traditional Jewish arrangement whereby the worldlier, business-oriented siblings supported their more learned or more pious brother who devoted himself exclusively to Torah study. For the rebbe's two brothers were also Torah scholars, esteemed for their deep learning and many virtues. One could say that their business really was Torah and piety. They too were an adornment to the Aleksander court. They were cordial and accessible to the Ḥasidim who sought their counsel. The only one missing was their brother Reb Shraga Feivel, whom the Russians had hanged in Radom at the beginning of World War I.

During the war Russian military authorities harassed the Jews in the border towns under their command with expulsions and confiscations under all manner of pretexts and false charges, chiefly for spying for the Germans and betraying Russia. When the Russians succeeded in re-taking the town of Radom from the Germans, Jews were accused, based on slanderous claims or on testimony from non-Jewish informants, of abetting the enemy.

Reb Shraga Feivel, a Torah scholar and a man of sharp wit and noble virtues, was one of the community's outstanding leaders, esteemed and beloved not only by Aleksander Ḥasidim. He had married a Radom girl, and had spent some years there, as was customary, "at the table" of his father-in-law. He was the second son of the rebbe Reb Shmuel Ẓvi, who would visit Radom from time to time to rejoice with his son and his relatives, and to inspire the community with his presence. There were about 20,000 Jews in Radom at the time.

On September 3, 1914, the Russians executed three innocent Jews in Radom's town square. Wrapped in a *tallit* and crowned with *tefillin*, Reb Shraga Feivel was the first to "sanctify the Name." Along with him they hanged his brother-in-law, Ẓvi Mordekhai and Jacob Eizman, a relative of Reb Shraga Feivel's wife. His death was mourned for many years in Radom, and deep sorrow descended on the court of Aleksander. The Ḥasidim recounted that the rebbe cursed the Czar in unwonted fury that he would not complete his days in peace, and that his children would be killed before him. And so it was, an eye for an eye. Yeḥiel Lerer's[5] book *Beit Aba* contains a poem about the three martyrs.

I am sure that I was not the only one at the cemetery to recall the deceased, who had sanctified God's name at Radom's town square. For the day of a *hillulah* is, by its very nature from the Ḥasidic perspective, a day for return to the origins of the *ẓaddikim*, the Righteous Ones. It was a day for self-examination and for putting one's spiritual house in order, for reaffirming one's loyalty to the first founder, his sons, and their sons. The day of the *hillulah* is meant to strengthen the social bond, to revivify affection, awe, and elation. The Ḥasidim come to partake of the spiritual radiance emanating from their leaders, from those deceased and from those living.

There I saw the sons and grandsons of the rebbe and his brothers. One could easily distinguish them from all the other young Ḥasidic men and boys. I confess, albeit with shame, that these boys of the rebbe's household irked me for the impertinence they exhibited toward the Ḥasidim, even the learned and the old ones, and certainly toward one such as I. It was clear that that which was forbidden to boys and young men like me was permitted to them. One had to indulge misbehavior by this "holy seed," the son or grandson of the rebbe himself, or of his brothers, as though it were a trifling matter. Pinchi, Pinchas Shraga, the rebbe's son, was only eight at the time. He died in Aleksander in his adolescence. Should I reproach him for his naughtiness? Clearly, in matters of behavior one was not strict with the boys. On the other hand they were burdened with a heavy yoke of Torah study, piety, and prayer to prepare them for leadership of a Ḥasidic sect in the future. No wonder that from time to time they loosened their yokes and horsed around a bit.

At the cemetery, of course, there was no play. Psalms were already being recited: "Man is like to vanity: his days are as a shadow that passeth away" … "But God will redeem my soul from the power of the grave for he shall receive me. Selah." All were deep in mourning. Standing in or near the *ohel* were Reb Beẓalel Yair, his son Reb Avraham Yidl, son-in-law Reb Moshe Yehuda, as well as his brother-in-law Reb Eliezer Lipszyc, who was a rabbinic judge in Lodz. There I also saw Reb Yiẓḥak Meir Singer, rabbi of the town of Aleksander, and a number of other rabbis and old Ḥasidim whom I did not know.

Not far from me stood Reb Mordekhai David Maroko, head of the rabbinical court of the congregation of Burzenin, and his father, Reb Yidl of Złoczew. I was happy to see them both. The dense crowd prevented me from approaching them immediately. Reb Yidl was my grandmother's brother, a kind and wise granduncle whom I liked and respected enormously. He was a much-esteemed veteran Ḥasid who exuded the joy of being and shone a great light on his interlocutors. I drew close to him and learned to appreciate his fine qualities during one summer vacation I spent at Złoczew with my mother and younger brother. When I would meet him at Aleksander, he would keep an eye on me, making sure that I did not withdraw from the circle of dancers. He liked warm Jewish togetherness and was worried that I might be drifting away. His words and deeds were all prompted by a kind, generous heart. His son, Reb Mordekhai David, the rabbi of Burzenin, was endowed with a superb memory and could easily quote by heart, verbatim, from the vast rabbinic literature. When I was fifteen and sixteen I studied Talmud in his home two summers in a row. From Burzenin I would return home to Lodz and the secular high school full of piety and would recite the daily prayers with full conviction. I would imitate the gestures of this rabbi and his style of prayer.

There I observed the routines of the inhabitants of a tiny Jewish *shtetl*[6], noting their daily dealings and the respect that they bore their rabbi. Earning a living was tough, and their rabbi too lived in scarcity. He merited a rabbinic position in a much larger community, but people in those days joked that in Poland there were more rabbis than *shtetls*. He recorded his "innovations" in Torah matters in an elongated, thick copybook like that of a bookkeeper, and I saw that he had already filled several such notebooks with his beautiful handwriting. I recall that he occupied himself with tractates from the order of *Toharot* (Purifications) and *Kodashim* (Holy Things), a rather uncommon concern in Poland. From his tiny Polish town he took flight to the priests and their offerings, the Levites and their psalmody, to the service of the Holy Temple in Jerusalem when it stood in its glory. To elucidate the minutiae governing the proper conduct of the Temple service, he invested infinite *pilpul* on what was or wasn't, or should have been, according to the Talmudic Sages and generations of *poskim*.

Only after the conclusion of the ritual part of the ceremony: *El maleh raḥamim*,[7] *Hazur tamim po'alo*,[8] recital of psalms, *Mishnah* segments, especially Chapter Seven in the Tractate *Mikva'ot*,[9] and *Kaddish deRabbanan*,[10] could I approach Uncle Yidl and his son, the rabbi of Burzenin, and stand with them near the tombstones in the *ohel*.

Uncle Yidl reminded us of the testament of the Old Rebbe wherein he bade his sons to pray for the rectification (*tikkun*) of his soul in order to "mitigate the judgment" set upon him in the next world, and, on the day of his *hillulah*, to study all day, from morning to night. My father added: "They should also afflict themselves with deprivations." But Uncle doubted whether one still did so. The rabbi, Reb Mordekhai David, commented that in the rectification of the soul, the Old Rebbe had referred to profound mysteries, and the main thing in the rectification, so he had commanded his sons, was "weeping, from the bottom of one's heart and soul." Indeed the cemetery resounded with the weeping of Reb Bezalel Yair, his pleasant voice bathed in tears as he recited the psalms, together with the many sorrowful sighs and sobs of the brothers and the Ḥasidim.

Later in life, I read the Old Rebbe's testament as it appeared in *Tif'eret Yisrael*[11]. One cannot but be impressed by the greatness of this soul, by his humility. He requested that no *ohel* be erected for him, and that he not be called a saint or a *zaddik*, not in his lifetime and even less so on his tombstone. The tombstone was severely plain. All it said was "Here lies our Teacher and Rabbi, Reb Yeḥiel, son of the honored Teacher and Rabbi, Reb Shraga Feivel." Indeed, until the year 1910, so Uncle Yidl told us, there was no *ohel* at all. However, when the *Yismaḥ Yisroel* died and his testament did not explicitly *prohibit* an *ohel*, the Aleksander Ḥasidim set up a court of three rabbis who decreed a compromise: to build a wall around the plot where the rabbis were buried and where family members would be buried in the future, but without a roof. This was done. The tombstones of the Old Rebbe's two sons stood one next to the other, these too simply inscribed: "Here lies our Teacher and Rabbi, Reb Yeraḥmiel Israel son of our honored Teacher and Rabbi, Reb Yeḥiel." The inscription on the stone of Reb Shmuel Ẓvi Hirsch was similar.

The memorial service lasted above an hour, and even though we were standing in the freezing snow, it was a stirring and thought-provoking occasion. Many thoughts about the rebbes of Aleksander and their Ḥasidim of three generations went through my mind as we stood there near the graves. Here stood Uncle Yidl, his son, my father and I, generations of diminishing Ḥasidic piety, you might say, especially in the leap between the second and third generation.

The *ohel* ("tent") structure sheltering the graves of the rebbes of Aleksander and their families with the tombstones of Reb Yehiel (the "Old Rebbe") and his three sons on the exterior wall

THE GREATNESS OF REB YEḤIEL: TEARS AND JOY

The Old Rebbe was known for the power of his prayer. His Ḥasidim called him the "pillar of worship," or the "pillar of prayer," and his son the *Yismaḥ Yisroel* said of him that no one really knew his father except the angels and seraphs who were born of the *yiḥudim*[12] made in his prayers. I suppose that among those present at the cemetery on that day there were quite a few Ḥasidim who believed wholeheartedly, even though they did not speak of it, that the *ẓaddik*'s spirit returning on the day of his *hillulah* to his burial place was surely accompanied by those angels and seraphs created by the power of his prayer.

Reb Yeḥiel's prayer, as I said, was all supplication, in a heart-rending, tear-drenched voice, emanating from a broken and humble spirit, ever cognizant of God's boundless supremacy and the lowliness of man. Yet with all the submission and self-deprecation, the rebbe wished his prayer to reach the ears of the Holy One, Blessed be He, who listens to the prayers of His people Israel. Seemingly, it is difficult for man to attain a level of sanctity that would make the Holy One, who both "fills all worlds and encompasses all worlds," listen to the prayers of a mere mortal. The rebbe's opinion was that a human being is of two constituent aspects, the aspect of nothingness, as King David said in his Psalm: "But I am a worm, and no man; a reproach of men, and despised of the people", but also, only "a little lower than the angels." Man, as it were, elevates the whole structure of the world and God himself. That is how the author of *Yismaḥ Yisroel* interpreted his father's faith: "I will extol thee, O Lord; for thou hast lifted me up," because despite the Old Rebbe's belief that he was "the worst of the worst," he had confidence that his prayer and his good deeds added, as it were, power to the Creator.

The Old Rebbe's prayer expressed the paradox of knowing one's own limited value, as in "I am but dust and ashes," and at the same time faith in one's utmost importance, as in "for my sake was the world created." This paradox he had learned from Reb Simḥa Bunim of Pshyscha, who used to expound on "Know from whence you came." Whence (*me'ayin*)? From the nothingness (*ayin*) of the Most High: Your soul is quarried from beneath the Throne of Honor, but it also comes from a "putrid drop" of a creature born of woman.

A similar paradox appears in the juxtaposition of the characteristic Aleksander lachrymose grief with the outpouring of joy. How can sorrow and joy dwell together? I have read much deliberation on this in the writings of the Aleksander rebbes. From these, and from the sayings of Ḥasidim with whom I spoke, I learned that all the rebbes had commanded the banishment of sorrow, which derives from the Evil Inclination, whereas the tear-drenched prayer was "therapeutic" (needless to say, they did not use this term, but I believe this is what they meant). The tearful prayer not only crushed and broke hearts, but also healed and mended. It pulled a man back to his roots, that is, to his inward communing with the Holy One. In this inwardness he finds joy, his own personal joy, and that of all his people.

I was not "at home" at the rebbe's court, yet every time I visited there, whether on the Sabbath of Ḥanuka, on the Days of Awe, or for a *hillulah*, I saw Ḥasidim dancing and rejoicing. On Simḥat Torah, of course, hundreds of Ḥasidim would surround the rebbe as he danced with the Torah. At Aleksander I felt, maybe for the first time, that sadness and joy were really not far apart, that there truly are tears of joy, a weeping that relieves one from anguish and elevates the soul. There is also a dancing sorrow which turns into an impassioned, ecstatic joy to the point of shedding one's corporeality.

THE OLD REBBE'S INNOVATION—TORAH STUDY WITH *DVEIKUT*[13]

It has been said about Ḥasidism that it was the triumph of "sentimental" over "cerebral" Judaism, i.e., the rebellion of the ignorant poor, the *am ha'areẓ*, against the Torah-scholarly elite. In the days of which I speak, however, Ḥasidim devoted much more time to the study of a page of Talmud than to the life of "sentiment," or to contemplative or emotional *dveikut*, or to the study of ethics. It seems to me that at the beginning of the Ḥasidic movement's growth, and perhaps until the second half of the nineteenth century, they still drew a distinction between *dveikut* and the soul's preparation for it, and the study of Torah. In the meantime, however, the study of Torah spread in Poland and its status rose. The Old Rebbe sought a new way of forging the two tendencies. He wished to study the Torah, but out of a mystic *dveikut*, or, as his son the author of *Yismaḥ Yisroel*, wrote (*Parashat Vayeẓe*) in the name of his father: "Words sweet like a honeycomb embedded in the syllables and the letters of the Torah" gladden the reader's heart and open his eyes. In other words, the very letters and syllables of a Torah text become focal points for crystallizing the learner's contemplative and emotional concentration. One needs to keep connecting the external forms of the letters to the supernal spiritual exemplars from which they originate in order to cleave to the "infinite light" inherent in the letters.

This was a sensational novelty, though I am not certain that it indeed originated with the Old Rebbe. He may have received from his forefathers the idea of not separating between Torah study and *dveikut*, and instead, of making the study of the Talmud or the *midrash* and even of the legalistic *poskim* an opportunity for contemplation of and cleaving unto the Holy One. Perhaps this teaching was his protest against the path taken by the Young Rebbe of Vurka who had taught *dveikut* through the power of silence.

I believe that my granduncle Yidl and Reb Avraham Moshe and others among the chief Ḥasidim knew what the rebbe's real view was, and how one attains joy through *dveikut* during Torah study. In my youth, I saw that the study of Torah among Ḥasidim had spread widely, exactly in the regular, "cognitive" form of their opponents, and unlike that of the kabbalists, who sought in study a way to achieve spiritual adhesion unto the Holy One. Either way, all believed wholeheartedly that the Torah was a "Tree of Life to those who take hold of it," and that those who study it gain joy and confidence in the Lord. The Old Rebbe's path, however, was not accessible to all.

Even though the Old Rebbe fasted every Monday and Thursday and denied himself all worldly pleasure, he spoke in praise of eating and drinking, in sanctity and purity, saying that these too increase joy. By assuaging worries they chase away the Evil Inclination. Through food and drink we can draw closer the divine sparks which had dispersed far from the source of holiness. This is what our Talmudic Sages meant when they said, "a mouthful … draws near those who are distant," that is, the sparks that have dispersed in the distance coalesce again when one drinks a *Leḥayim*, over which one says a blessing. All the more so is this the case during a *miẓvah* meal, and needless to say, at the rebbe's table, or in his proximity.

BETWEEN THE LIVING AND THE DEAD

The dead, even though departed from this world, were still not far from us who mourned them. In those days, they would still visit us in our dreams, appear in reincarnated form, and as *dybbuks*, returning to the place of their burial on their memorial day. Between heaven and earth there was not a vast empty expanse, but a host of beings rising and descending, a constant back and forth, a live connection in a hidden and overt spiritual traffic. This in-between territory was peopled with descending angels and seraphs, and similarly, with their adversaries, devils and malefactors. In the opposite direction, souls arose, heading for their original home beneath the Throne of Honor, to await their judgment. Above both the living and the dead there was, after all, the Judge of Truth, who snuffs out and breathes life, and to whom every creature gave thanks. The world was one, and its Master one.

Faith in the providence of God, the Master of all souls and of heaven and earth and all their creatures, assuaged the fear of death and delivered a person from the terrors of non-being, destruction of the world, and the futility of good deeds and their merit. A Jew believed that the Holy One who created all creatures in justice knows the number of them all, dispatches them justly, and will in due course restore their souls to their cadavers.

For those standing around the graves of the Aleksander *ẓaddikim* on that day of *hillulah*, the fear of death was, as it were, removed. No, nothingness does not nullify the soul. The soul does not vanish with the death of the body. The Ḥasidim believed that the unison of their hearts with their rebbe continued, even though he had died more than thirty years earlier. In the grave's soil, under the snow, and between the grave's stones, the Ḥasidim left little notes on which they wrote their secret requests. All the graves of rebbes in that cemetery were full of these scraps of paper. Some had been scattered by the wind. That day, the Old Rebbe returned to his Ḥasidim and members of his household. This is how his second son, the author of *Tif'eret Shmuel*, described his father at another *hillulah* held in his memory: "He was pure, and pure he is eternally, as it is written: 'The fear of the Lord is clean, enduring forever', and surely, he is with us."

Since Reb Yeḥiel died at the close of a Sabbath, at the time for the meal in honor of David the Messiah King, a propitious moment for the traditional triple petition for sons, good health, and a decent livelihood, the Ḥasidim hoped that the Holy One would bestow these blessings, and all good things, both spiritual and material, upon those who attended the *hillulah*. They also said that since the Old Rebbe had declared everyone else greater than he was in wisdom and virtues, he induced in heaven a great *zekhut*, great merit, over his entire generation, as no one up there challenged his opinion. We had no doubt that on the day of remembrance of the *ẓaddik*'s death the light of his holiness appeared and enhanced his merit ever more potently, to protect us all.

Even the Ḥasidim in my small group there, who did not accept popular beliefs literally, had no doubt that the day of the *hillulah* bestowed a bounty of holiness. Perhaps they followed the reasoning laid out in one of the later books of the Aleksander Ḥasidut, *Emunat Moshe*, namely that the holiness of the *ẓaddik* in his lifetime made an impression "up there," and after his departure from this world the impression remained. On the day of the *hillulah* "all those unifications (*yiḥudim*) and the devotion that he practiced in his lifetime reawaken, and are re-endowed with their living breath. These lights bring grace to people, and this is the meaning of 'The righteous are greater after their death, more so than during their lifetimes', that is, in the hour of death, their rank rises and they become a very great light."

Students of magic, myth, and religions have taught us that even when faiths erode it is extremely difficult to extirpate from the human heart the belief in the continuity of life in one form or another. Belief in the soul's afterlife, which attempts to overcome our terror of the negation of being, is rooted deeply in the human psyche. On the day of the *hillulah,* as we stood in front of the *ẓaddik*'s gravestone, we contemplated this faith.

CHAPTER 8

Portrait of a Ḥasidic Rebbe (Admor)[1]

Authority in traditional Jewish communities and the emergence of "charismatic" Ḥasidic leadership. How did the rebbe deal with capitalist exploitation? Was the rebbe a miracle-worker? What did a rebbe know about medicine and healing? Wherein lay his power?

THE WISDOM OF *YISMAḤ YISROEL*

I wish to evoke here the memory of an archetypal community leader that became prevalent among the Jewish people only with the spread of Ḥasidism. The *ẓaddikim*, the great rebbes, especially the founders of dynasties, were considered by the multitudes of their adherents as possessors of extraordinary powers, as men raised above all others whom the holy spirit had endowed with qualities of redeemers. These were leaders of the "charismatic" type (in Max Weber's terminology[2]). This archetype had already appeared previously in the mystic culture, especially in the Messianic movements, but in Ḥasidism (mysticism's later offshoot) this model gained prominence and spread widely.

For many generations, the authority to exercise leadership in Jewish communities was achieved in two ways. The first was in the realm of the holy. The Master of the Universe, who had singled out His people through His Torah, had invested authority in students of the Torah and teachers of its laws, and in all those who strengthened and upheld it. The second way was through political and economic power. The ruling sovereign, for whose welfare a Jew was commanded to pray, bestowed the authority from which power devolved unto ministers, court officials and congregation leaders. In general, there was friction between community leaders chosen for their prestige, wealth, and connections to the ruler, and the rabbis and scholars. The two types of "elites" vied for power.

With the spread of the Ḥasidic movement there appeared the "charismatic" leader whose authority, unlike that of the Torah scholar and *halakhic* teacher, emanated from on high. He had the right to lead by virtue of the holiness, as it were, of his personality. The *ẓaddik* who has a direct connection to the uppermost spheres does not need the endorsement of "traditional" authority nor that of a "legal-rational" authority, according to Max Weber's distinctions. His leadership is above these. He ordains and the Holy One fulfills his petition (according to numerous sayings of the Sages).

Clearly, this type of leadership which rests neither on law-based authority nor on selection from among a number of candidates, but is entirely dependent on the community's faith in the holiness of "a man over the congregation, which may go out before them" is by its very nature the archetype of a revolutionary, rebellious leadership. The Baal Shem Tov (the Besht, for short) and his early disciples in the eighteenth century had rebelled against the order then prevailing in Jewish communal governance. Since then, a few generations had passed and the "charismatic revolution" had solidified into routines; the novelty of the Ḥasidic movement had worn off. *Ẓaddikim* multiplied, especially through inheritance, whereby the sons, who usually did not match the stature of their fathers, inherited the leadership as though "charisma," that gift of grace from on high, was a birthright.

The Old Rebbe, Reb Yeḥiel, was venerated by multitudes as a holy man, and even though he forbade the Ḥasidim to call him a *ẓaddik*, a Ḥasid, or even rebbe, he was their *ẓaddik* and rebbe. He was considered the rebbe of the "lowly ones," simple Jews, the humble of this earth, and perhaps it was in his image that Sholem Asch modeled the *ẓaddik* in his story *Der T'hilim Yid.*[3]

His son, Reb Yisrael Yeraḥmiel Yiẓḥak Dancyger (1853-January 1910), saw himself as the "interpreter, *shofar* (proclaimer), and oral transmitter of the holy words" of his father. Yet he was a very different spiritual personality from Reb Yeḥiel. For while he considered it as one of his important roles to transmit and elucidate his father's sayings, and prayed that he would be granted to serve as his father's assistant even in the Garden of Eden, as though he had no desire to innovate anything of his own, all his words and acts gave proof of a strong streak of originality. He knew that he himself was a sort of living spring, or one whose mouth emitted "sparks of fire." Indeed, on the first Sabbath that he "held Tish" after his father's death, he opened his "Torah" with a statement that he was only a transmitter of an idea he had heard from his father ("*es is nor anibergezogener*"). Yet, he also hinted that there was in him a *zoger*, an independent speaker, a sort of *maggid*, who was not merely repeating the ideas of others.

In fact, he taught that every man had a personal *maggid* that was his alone, the power of which he must learn to awaken inside himself.

No wonder that his Ḥasidim and adherents venerated his spiritual originality. Even though the rebbe was, as mentioned earlier, odd in his external appearance—he lacked any sign of a beard or moustache and had a long, prominent nose, very dark skin, and rather peculiar facial features, his Ḥasidim accepted him with love and respect. The rival Ger Ḥasidim would joke at his expense with a pun on the verse "Only where the children of Israel were, was there no hail," they would pronounce *barad*, the Hebrew for hail, as *bard*, beard in Yiddish. However, with intellectual and leadership capacities that surpassed those of his father and of many other rebbes, he was clearly endowed with that "magnetic force that connects all hearts together."[4] Wherein lay his power?

Our cousin, Reb Mordekhai David Maroko, the rabbinic judge in the Burzenin community mentioned earlier, testified to the rebbe's phenomenal memory. He had memorized the entire Babylonian and Jerusalem Talmuds by virtue of a "photographic" memory, that is, he could see before him lines and pages, and recalled by heart things he had not seen in thirty years. He had an eye for faces, which he committed to memory, and subsequently never erred. He was also gifted with a superlative auditory memory. He knew the contents of the Ḥasid's petitionary note, the *kvittel*, in advance, with no need to open it and would give answers before the questions were asked. Hundreds of people came to him every day, and he listened as they poured out their woes. With all his heart and soul, the rebbe devoted himself to the leadership of his flock. No wonder that this flock kept increasing over the years.

How did he act upon them? What was his method of leadership? When I put together what I heard about him in my youth and what I read later, the image that emerges is of a sensitive man, wise of heart, who used psychoanalytic tools long before this method gained wide recognition. He acted not as a doctor observing from the outside, with the objectivity of a researcher, but as a participant in the other's emotions and quick to intervene. In a prayer printed at the head of the chapter on Leviticus in his book *Yismaḥ Yisroel*, he prayed: "May You remember all the childless ones and grant them perpetual seed, a good and kosher seed." Childless though he was, he saw himself as fertile and procreating through the power of his influence, thereby giving life to many disciples and Ḥasidim who felt his spiritual bounty and thought of him with love.

They stood in long queues, anticipating a moment of conversation with him. For many hours the rebbe sat or stood conversing with his visitors.

Occasionally, he complained that he had no time either to pray or to study. "Almost all my life I have been their servant, attending to their welfare in every possible way," he once remarked about his burden[5]. He saw himself as a "hewer of trees," i.e., a simple man, one who worked with "the world" at least twelve hours a day (the quota for laborers in his day).

His "technique," if we may use this term, because he never thought of the guidance of his Ḥasidim in an instrumental way, was first to listen attentively to every slight shift in their voices as they confided in him. He listened with empathy, would pale, moan, shed tears, get angry. In this dialogue, the Ḥasid could patently see that the rebbe felt for him, that his troubles affected him. The conversation was usually intimate, couched in everyday words or clothed in holy language—about conjugal matters, social strains or theological dilemmas. He would warn the young men regarding the laws of family purity, menstruating women, beds laid out alongside each other, about ablutions in the *mikveh*. He knew how to give practical advice, when to direct to a doctor, to suggest a useful address, and even to offer certain medications himself.

The Ḥasidim related that when he looked at their faces "from bottom up and from top down," their hearts would melt; each man knew that the rebbe was penetrating his soul's innermost recesses. Sometimes he would scold a Ḥasid and uncover the man's deepest secrets, which he was trying to hide from the rebbe and even from himself. They would marvel that he knew everything, and believed that he drew his knowledge from the power of the holy spirit. But the rebbe admitted, "Know this: It is you yourselves who tell me everything." At times, he would call to mind the words of the Baal Shem Tov that every transgression that a man commits at night, in darkness, he is compelled to blurt out, in the hearing of others by day. His listeners, however, have no ears to grasp his words, and he too is not aware that his mouth has just given evidence against himself.

The rebbe would draw to himself Jews whom he knew were transgressors: "They come to me, these *sheyne Yidn*,[6] and I know that hell is gaping at them. But what can I do? If I reprimand them for everything, what will I be left with?" Sometimes he would shame people in public, scold and show anger, but during the admonition, he would say: "I know that I will have no part in the World to Come. I have lost my share long ago, from the day that I assumed the rebbe's chair." Nonetheless, those who were chastised felt that they merited the censure and that the rebbe, in his own way, loved them. Indeed, the rebbe would say that if holding this chair caused him to lose his love for his people, then it was a real sin to continue occupying it.

People who came to him downcast and miserable, laden with worries and broken of heart, afflicted by internal discord and at odds with the world, would leave his presence exhilarated and joyous, appeased, full of hope, trusting in him, in God, and in themselves. Besides his quick grasp and penetrating insights, he also gave of his own money from the salary he received as rabbi of the town Aleksander. Like his father the *ẓaddik*, he never accepted *pidyonot* money, and whatever donations he was given he distributed as charity, and prompted others to help the needy.

A ẒADDIK IN A CAPITALISTIC WORLD

The fifteen years (1894–1909) of his tenure as the Aleksander rebbe were the years of economic growth in Lodz and its neighboring towns. The rapid industrialization that enriched many facilitated corruption and iniquity. The newly rich—the industrialists, the brokers, the traders, the commercial credit lenders, a large crowd of climbers who achieved success in a short time—had been uprooted from their former orderly lives in the *shtetls* from which they had migrated to Lodz and now found themselves in an unruly, disharmonious environment of acute capitalist competition. There were many among this layer of *nouveaux riches* who walked over the bodies of workers and servants, exploited, defrauded, oppressed, declared bankruptcy, obtained damages from their insurance companies for real or fake fires, defaulted, and brought ruin upon those who had entrusted them with their money, their daughters' dowries, and savings of widows and orphans. No doubt there were also among these newly rich Jews some decent men, but in general, their activity in the factories contradicted their pious professions in the synagogues or the *beit midrash*. It is before these *sheyne Yidn* that the rebbe laid out the specter of a gaping hell.

Authors, albeit only a few, described the blights and blemishes that the extraordinarily rapid industrial boom had brought to Lodz. Most successful were I. J. Singer[7] in his novel *The Brothers Ashkenazi*, and W. S. Reymont[8] in his two-volume *Land of Promise*. The latter was not without an anti-Semitic tinge. The party of the anti-Semitic Endaks, headed by Roman Dmowski,[9] had commissioned the author to describe Lodz Jews as using their financial power to gain control of the town's industry, to supersede the Germans and oppress the Poles, especially the farmers, who were streaming in multitudes into the factories.

People came to consult the Rebbe of Aleksander in every weighty affair, be it money, layoff from work, trade, and production disputes. The sounds and quandaries of the changing times all reached the rebbe's court. Of course he was also consulted on matrimonial matches, for there was no *shidduch* for which the rebbe's consent was not sought.

How to mend the "world of chaos" into which the generation had fallen? Commenting on the verse, "He causeth them to wander in the wilderness, where there is no way," the rebbe said that according to Kabbalah, the world of "no way" (*tohu*) refers to dots that do not connect one to the other. Similarly, he who separates himself from the body of Israel, who imagines "I am, and none else beside me," walks where there is no way, in the wilderness. "This is not the way!" the rebbe told his Ḥasidim.

How to be a pious Jew, in private and in public, and not be tempted to sin in the modern world of *tohu,* of brutal, coarse, capitalism, the practices of which were so rapidly spreading in Lodz, as in other industrial towns, such as Bialystok, and had even made inroads in the settlements in the rebbe's vicinity? How can one mend the damage caused by hard, cold rationalization and rigid bureaucratization, which prizes the machine over the worker? How to connect the lost souls, as dots that have lost contact one with the other, in one body of *klal Yisrael* (All of Israel), which observes the commandment to love one's fellow?

The rebbe had no political-social program. In his day, no one in Aleksander dealt in politics. The Old Rebbe his father had objected to public assemblies and to wrangling over positions of power and benefits. Certainly there were fights between and within *shtiblachs,* and large and bitter disputes over rabbinic posts in Aleksander and the *shtetls* in its orbit, of which the most famous was the rancorous dispute in Zdunska Wola, as I describe in Chapter 14. There was no thought in Aleksander in those days, not until the end of World War I, about political organization and systematic, directed action. Nor did it occur to the rebbe to make any social program to improve living conditions, to minimize exploitation and abuse, to create charitable institutions, to find jobs for the unemployed, to feed the hungry, and to take care of the helpless elderly.

The standard of living rose in his days, but although wealth increased, poverty did not diminish. In fact, there developed a new urban underclass of the unemployed, of all those jettisoned from the speeding capitalist train in its frantic course. Former life in the *shtetl* had been far from idyllic, and the rebbe surely did not indulge in nostalgia, unlike certain Romantic writers who sang the (unmerited) praises of the small town's routines of daily life. In his childhood he had seen poverty and want. The jokers used to say about certain rabbis that if they had not been in the habit of fasting every Monday and Thursday, they would have died of hunger. However, the traditional *shtetl* life style did alleviate some of the hardships, and inculcated certain modes of decency. In contrast, the big city was tempting and stimulating, raising expectations and testing one's mettle. To some men it gave much, in keeping with the measure of their ambitions, and even more than they dreamed of, but for the majority big city life was harsh indeed.

The rebbe responded to these new distresses with Torah and prayer and the old charitable institutions, by bringing people together, by exerting himself on their behalf, and by arranging loans which Ḥasidim, by his order, were obligated to extend to each other (usually modest amounts). Money was expensive. Interest was high, the pursuit of money frenetic. The rebbe wished to mend the conduct of the individual, to make him behave justly and kindly, but it never occurred to him to interfere in the way Divine Providence ran the world. Is there not a "Master to the City?" He provides for all His creatures, be they rams or lice. What should a Ḥasid do? Help as far as he can, but mainly, accept God's will. The rebbe taught humility, piety, submission. Even though he would not afflict himself with abstinence as his father had done, he made do with little, eating and drinking sparingly, and thought that this is how a Jew should live. God is nearest to the broken-hearted.

In private audiences with his Ḥasidim and with many who were not his Ḥasidim, and in his brief exchanges with those who came for "sholem nemen" (for a greeting), there were rich and poor, mighty and lowly, all equal in his eyes. None received preference. Uncle Yidl told me that he had heard with his own ears how the rebbe once asked the *gabbai*: "What is so-and-so doing at the head of the *Tish*, among rabbis and Torah scholars?" The visitor was a well-known rich man from Lodz who had been very helpful in getting young Ḥasidic men exempted from service in the Russian army. Nonetheless, the rebbe did not permit him to sit at the head of the table in the company of rabbis and Torah scholars.

He would stand near the door of his room adjoining the *beit midrash*, and the Ḥasidim would pass before him, reminding him ("mazkir zein") aloud of their name and that of their mother, and touching his soft hand in greeting. He touched, but did not squeeze, the many hands. He knew their names, and that of their mothers, and had no need of reminders. With his sharp tongue he would sting the rich, often with humorous anecdotes, but neither did he spare the poor. Since he knew the weaknesses of each of them, he prayed for mercy for them all. He was a *ẓaddik*, a rebbe of a Ḥasidic following, not a social worker, nor a political or social thinker.

NO REWARD IN THIS WORLD

Our group walked slowly through the snow on that cold winter day, which was already beginning to darken. The Ḥasidim around us were greeting each other with a nod or conversing in whispers. The rebbe and his entourage had already left the cemetery and they were in a hurry to catch up with him. As we bade *shalom* to acquaintances, Uncle Yidl, who loved retelling stories about the old rebbes, especially witticisms, playful Torah extrapolations and jokes, recalled some of the sayings of the *Yismaḥ Yisroel.*

Once the rebbe had asked an *avrekh*: "Where have you been all day?" The young man replied, "What a question! In the *shtibel,* of course." "I didn't ask about your body, I asked about your heart."

On another occasion, the *Yismaḥ Yisroel* became tired, his spirit weak with all the troubles he was hearing from those who came to him with their petitionary notes. He sighed. What can one do? The Holy Torah commanded us: "One who swallows the *maẓẓah* without chewing, has fulfilled the obligation of eating *maẓẓah*. However, one who swallows the *maror* (bitter herb) without chewing does not fulfill the obligation of eating *maror*. The bitter herbs must be thoroughly chewed, only thus can one fulfil the commandment and gain salvation. A Jew must believe that even the harshest and bitterest commandments stem from the Holy One's mercy and grace. In this way one can sweeten the commandments at their root, as Scripture says, 'The judgments of the Lord are true and righteous altogether,' namely, that at the root of judgment is justice, and the internal core of the commandments is mercy and grace."

Uncle Yidl told me the story of an old man who came to the *Yismaḥ Yisroel* and told him that with God's help he had succeeded in extirpating all lust from himself—lust for a woman, for food and drink, for clothes, and for all forms of envy. The rebbe replied: "Good for you, but I see there still remains a lust for honor and a zeal for your honor, which has grown as a result of these triumphs of yours over the Evil Inclination. Surely, you must know what our Sages said, 'Envy, lust and honor-seeking drive a man from this world.'"

I did not suspect that our Uncle Yidl might have been that old man. However, in the days of the *Yismaḥ Yisroel,* that is, twenty and more years earlier, he had sat at the *Tish,* close to the rebbe. He had been one of the leading figures in the congregation of Złoczew, where he had settled, and was frequently called to assist in complicated arbitration cases. Can one ever fathom the measure of honor for which a man lusts?

Father said little in the conversation, preferring to hear what older Ḥasidim than he had to say. His cousin, the rabbi of Burzenin, who was ten or more years his senior, recalled the story of the sterile Ḥasid who came to the childless rebbe and begged him to pray for him. The rebbe replied, "I have 600 more sterile men like you, myself among them, and if I include all of them in my *Shmone Esre*[10] prayer, the heavens will burst out laughing." This old story, which my uncle and his son, the rabbi, knew well, would still bring a smile to their lips. I did not understand the joke. What exactly did the rebbe mean? After all, he prayed on behalf of thousands of Jews for the Holy One to send them a decent living. Why was there no laughter in heaven over that? Apparently, the rebbe was joking, or maybe it was his way of refusing the Ḥasid's request. Perhaps he thought that a Jew who cannot perform even the first *miẓvah*[11] in the Torah is ridiculous, both in his own eyes and in the eyes of the angels and seraphim in heaven.

Our cousin, the rabbi of Burzenin, would also relate tales of wonder or some witty turn of phrase. He would speak sparingly, and his stories about the rebbes were "the little that held the much," sometimes mere allusions. On this occasion he spoke more explicitly. Once, when it came time to take his leave of the rebbe, a poor Ḥasid who had invested all his money in a fruit orchard he had leased, lamented that a storm had brought down all the fruit before it could ripen and that soon, if the wind did not abate, he would lose everything he possessed. The rebbe bade him to stand with him for a while. Wouldn't you know, soon a Ḥasid came up to the rebbe, lamenting that his mill was idle because there was no strong wind to move its sails. The rebbe turned to the fruit grower: "Now, God willing, both of you will be contented—the wind will go to the mill and leave the orchard in peace."

I had difficulty deciding whether this was said jokingly, or whether it was a tale of a miracle. Surely, the rebbe meant to say that Divine Providence would give to the one without injury to the other, and that all would benefit.[12] However, according to all the stories about him and the teachings he wrote in his own name, it is evident that he knew very well how imperfect the world was and that human relations were far from harmonious. His teaching was strictly traditional: One must not expect reward in this world, the destinies promised us in the Torah are not meant as payment for having fulfilled commandments. The essence of the blessing that God gives to Jews—"Behold, I set before you this day a blessing … if ye obey," is that they will be able to obey His commandments and perform them in well-being and without distress.

MIRACLES AND THE SPHERE OF WONDER

If even piety, including that of quick-witted Ḥasidim who had learned the secrets of manufacture in a city rife with duplicitous wiles, did not guarantee worldly success, what could? The many thousands who flocked to the rebbe—not only Hasidim, but also a large crowd of "Litvaks" from near and distant Russian provinces who had settled in Lodz and its environs, all came in quest of something special. This something was called luck, or *si'ata dishemaya* (heaven's help)—that which separates the rich man from the pauper, and the man blessed with *shlom bayit* (domestic peace) and *naḥat* (gratification from his children) from he who does not gain these and suffers in secret, or in full view of others.

Many believed that the rebbe was a *ba'al mofet*, a miracle worker. His benediction is efficacious in heaven, his prayer is heard there, his counsel brings success. Israel Kalmanowicz Poznański, Markus Silberstein, Tuvia Bialer, Shlomo Bodzinger, Yankev Wojdysławski, Khayim Yankev Wiślicki, and many other of Lodz's wealthy industrialists and merchants, and needless to say Asher Cohen (Oskar Kohn), the king of industry in my day, all sought benedictions from *ẓaddikim* and the benefit of their miracles. This is what multitudes of Jews believed. I stress: Multitudes, and not only poor, simple people, believed in the *ẓaddik*'s power to perform miracles. They patently "saw" that thanks to his benediction, prayer, or counsel, people rose to greatness, that a cornucopia of wealth and well-being came showering upon them from above: good sons, good matches, relief from government oppression, in brief, material and spiritual well-being.

True, the more learned among his Ḥasidim, those who knew the literary corpus of Ḥasidism, felt ill at ease with stories of their rebbe's miracles, and all the more so those of other rebbes. A well-known pun went, "Signs and marvels in the land of Ḥam,"[13] meaning that signs and marvels were for simple people, who needed them because of their low intelligence (*cham* in Polish is a boor, an ignoramus). The rebbe's very being, his singular personality, his prayer that sundered heaven, his piety, were in and of themselves "marvels." I do not recall that my father, uncles, or cousins ever told me tales of miracles performed by *ẓaddikim*. But Father did relate, quoting old Ḥasidim, the following anecdote. The *Yismaḥ Yisroel* always knew exactly who had taken proper leave of him at parting and who had not. It once occurred that he did not wish to greet a certain merchant; both the man and the Ḥasidim who stood with him wondered why. The rebbe smiled and said, "Because over two years have passed and he has not yet taken his leave of me." This impressed Father.

I was a boy when I read about the miracles worked by the early and later *ẓaddikim* in the Hebrew and Yiddish books that were then widely circulating in Lodz,[14] and I could not get enough of all this wonder. Father did not try to restrict my reading, because there were not many other books in those days for boys of ten to thirteen. Later, I read that the disciples of the Besht related that he would get angry when people talked of the miracles he had performed rather than of his path in the worship and fear of God.

In my day, many jokes already circulated about the *ẓaddikim* and their miracles. They were heaped ridicule by the press, in the theater, in street corner chats, and in conversations of the educated. This world of wonders, miracles, marvels, and portents began crumbling progressively under the blows of critique levelled at it by the newly educated *maskilim*. The exponents of the new scientific culture now proposed a reasoned causality to explain conduct and deeds.

In the *shtibel*, however, I once heard the contrary argument: that it was good to tell miracle stories of the *ẓaddikim* precisely at this time, when heresy was on the rise, and that this faith contributed to piety. I also heard someone quote these clever words: "Anyone who believes in all the stories praising the Besht is a simpleton who'll believe anything, but anyone who denies these stories, why, he is a heretic (*epikores*)."

For indeed, even in the practical world of hard-nosed, business-minded Lodz, one could still thrill at the experience of wonder which intimated that things were not to be accepted at face value. No, the world does not pursue its course with no hope of change, without possibility of reversal of its entire order. The experience of wonder, usually a kind of spiritual jolt, surprises the wonderer about the matter before him and about himself. How did I not see this previously? "And I knew it not," Jacob is jolted into exclaiming upon waking from his dream of the ladder that reaches heaven and realizing that "the Lord is in this place." Wonder reveals something new. It intrudes unexpectedly, ripping or tearing open a wound in consciousness and in the continuity of time. Some languages perhaps reflect this connection: wonder-wound, in English, Wunder-Wunde, in German.[15]

For the Aleksander Ḥasidim the *ẓaddik*'s whole being, which moved people to marvel, his wondrous deeds, his wisdom and inspiration, were certainly intimations of dimensions of being and of power of a world order that was not prosaic, calculating and basely utilitarian. Like followers of all the other *ẓaddikim* of Poland in those generations, indeed like believers of all creeds, Aleksander Ḥasidim saw in wonderment and wonders, in those "signs" given by the rebbe, a revelation of the truth of their faith. Wonderment elevated them to thankfulness, joy, and exaltation. Throughout the existence of Ḥasidism in Poland, the believers flocked to the *ẓaddik*'s court in order to inhale the spirit that he brought down from on high. I, too, on this day of *hillulah*, sensed the batting of the wings of that spirit.

WONDERS AND DOUBTS

I felt deeply the difference between Lodz, the town and all it stood for, and the court of Aleksander and its aura of holiness. Young people such as I were reading the books of the *haskalah* movement, the stories of Pereẓ Smolenskin,[16] the satires of Yiẓḥak Erter[17] and the poems of the leading *haskalah* poet Y. L. Gordon (YaLaG).[18] I already saw men who just a short time before had been strict Torah observers and had now become, after just a short period of study, rebellious sons, all inflamed and eager to ignite others, propagandists of slogans about religion as the opium of the masses and their pastors as idlers who mislead the people and exploit their facile credulity.

My *gymnasia* teachers Jonah Braverman and Dr. Nathan Eck taught me the views of the Hebrew Enlightenment authors, mainly that adherence to the old ways was the source of all our age-old troubles, that their strictures contradicted the human spirit, especially its intelligence—"source of everything useful, a stronghold in time of destruction,"[19] and its scientific and practical achievements. However, I did not accept this simplistic *maskil* ideology. The evidence of my eyes denied it. Pious Jews who believed in the rebbe would rise to their day's work every morning, industrious and able, full of life and love of life. They were not sick souls alienated from real life, as their critics supposed. On no account would they have uttered the words that Y. L. Gordon put in their mouths: "I will not plough, I will not thresh, for I am scion of 'a kingdom of priests, and a holy nation.'"[20]

I knew from youth, from what I saw among my own family members, that human life moves between the "gates of purity" and the "gates of impurity," but the main thing for me was that sanctity and purity indeed existed in this world and that they were not "opium" for deluding people with hallucinatory nonsense. Their power may not be great, their measure modest, but without them, how is man superior to the beast?

The wondrous *ẓaddik* and no small number of Ḥasidim that I have known in my life, like my Uncle Yidl and Reb Avraham Moshe, arouse wonder and reveal the sphere of wonder in this world to eyes that wish to see. However, many young Jews like me in Poland in those years had to concede that the rabbinic culture had neglected philosophy and the sciences and had closed itself too hermetically, putting up fences within fences, fearing that the slightest relaxation of rules would cause all fences to collapse.

And this doubt too: Was the sphere of wonder inherent in sanctity and purity particular only to Jews? The foreign literature we were reading and studying in high school revealed a long line of world geniuses, "miracle masters" they too, by virtue of their works and the inspiration they gave to people.

In my childhood, as mentioned, we had no children's books, but we felt no need for them. In the *ḥeder* we read the Pentateuch stories, stories that entertained and stirred the imagination, great dramas that thrilled our hearts. Are there children's stories in world literature that can rival the story of Joseph and his brothers? When we grew up we read the *Book of Jossipon*[21] and the legends of the Sages in the Talmud and the *midrash*. The terrifying stories of the Brothers Grimm that I read later did not cause me greater horror and pain than did the tales of the torture endured by the Ten Martyrs.[22] I was seven when I learned in the *ḥeder*, in Tractate *Berakhot*, about Rabbi Akiba, whose flesh the Romans had flayed with combs of iron—a spectacle hard to match in its harrowing cruelty. And how our young hearts were wrenched when we learned in Tractate *Gittin* about the destruction of the Temple and the fall of Betar![23] Then followed the many stories in praise of the *ẓaddikim* and their miracle making.

In the court of Aleksander, the heroes of these stories seemed to me like the patriarchs or like members of the family whom the rebbe*s* of Aleksander appeared to resemble, though not entirely. Rather, they resembled their predecessors, the earlier *ẓaddikim*, in that they too continued to draw down the plenitude of grace and wonders from above unto God's people "assembled below."

ẒADDIKIM AND THE POWER OF HEALING

We returned from the cemetery to the piazza in front of the *beit midrash*, washed our hands and prayed the *minḥah* afternoon prayer. The rebbe and his entourage, and many Ḥasidim, had already prayed before leaving for the cemetery. The *beit midrash* began filling with a huge crowd. Many others already went to get in line in front of the rebbe's room and the queue was lengthening. Father and I decided to get in line too. The rebbe had retired to his room for a short rest. Perhaps he was fasting, as his grandfather the Old Rebbe had commanded his son, and now, at sundown, he may have taken a bite to eat. The rebbe in those years, as I mentioned, was the fourth *Admor* of Aleksander, Reb Yiẓḥak

Menaḥem Mendel Dancyger (1875–1943). He led his congregation after the death of his father, Reb Shmuel Ẓvi Hirsch (aka *Tif'eret Shmuel*) in 1924. On the eve of 15 Shevat, 1928, when I stood in line in front of the door to his room, he was 53 years old, in the fifth year of his tenure as *Admor*. He was renowned for being a prodigy, proficient in Talmud and the *poskim* and in the *Book of Zohar*. He too was much admired for his excellent memory and could recall entire pages, as needed. His eyes had weakened, and in that year when I stood before him for the last time, people said he was almost blind. Nonetheless, he led his congregation with great ability and sensitivity, and, some said, even surpassed his predecessors, both in drawing an even greater number of Ḥasidim (approximately 25 *shtiblachs* were added, or were strengthened, in his time), and in adding a boarding facility for a few hundred young men to the *yeshiva*, Beis Yisroel, founded by his father. This was a significant economic-public achievement in those days of impoverishment. He was sweet tempered, "having patience with each and every one of them according to their awareness." He knew perfectly well that the opinions of those who came to his court varied, and that it was necessary to direct them patiently. I do not know if he felt he possessed the powers of his uncle, author of *Yismaḥ Yisroel*, of whom they said, in the language of that same *midrash* which argues about the nature of the good leader, that he could "go against the spirit of each and every one." The present rebbe was not the combative type, but he accomplished a great deal in his quiet and confident style.

Young and old stood there waiting their turn for a moment with him. Many came with medical problems, ailments of body and soul. The rebbe*s* of Aleksander were renowned for their competence as advisers in medical matters. Even though medical science was already widespread, much more so than in the days of his predecessors, people still came to consult with the rebbe.

I often heard in my childhood and youth that one consults with the rebbe about ailments, even in life-threatening situations, indeed especially when the danger is greatest, for it is then that the need of his benediction and prayer is greatest. Mother told me that when I was four years old, Father woke up in the night with excruciating pain in his abdomen. He rose quietly so as not to wake her, and made himself a cup of tea. Having drunk two cups of hot tea and not feeling any better, on the contrary (given that an inflamed appendix does not stand heat), a doctor was summoned. He examined the patient and concluded that Father must be operated on within twenty-four hours. *Operazia*, surgery, was considered in those days a mortal danger, a scary prospect. A messenger was sent to Aleksander, to the *Admor* Shmuel Ẓvi Hirsch. He decreed not to operate, to postpone, to wait. Indeed, the pain passed, Father recovered, and the appendix troubled him no more. How did the rebbe know, and what did he know?

An Orthodox Jew knows that one must consult doctors, that more than prayer is required when life is in peril. True, the Sages of the Great Assembly[24] had included the prayer "Heal us" among the Eighteen Benedictions, and the Talmudic Sages believed that a righteous man's petition on behalf of a sick person was efficacious. But the Sages had also decreed that one should consult doctors and one of them, Shmuel,[25] called by his peers "doctor of rabbis," boasted: "I know how to cure anything." Jews learned in the Talmud: "[It is written], 'He shall cause him to be thoroughly healed.' From this we learn that permission has been given to the physician to heal." Maimonides listed healing the sick among the 613 commandments. R. Ḥaim Yosef David Azulai (the ḤIDA) in his commentary on *Shulḥan Arukh*, the last, most authoritative code book for the observant Jew, determined, "Today, one should not rely on a miracle, and the patient is obligated to call a doctor."[26]

Can there be any doubt that the rebbe knew all these references-caveats, and many more? How could he take the liberty, how did he have the temerity, and whence had he the knowledge to treat patients?

Having examined various testimonies, I infer that our rebbe, like most *admorim*, adopted a number of basic rules, nuanced by some secondary rules, to guide his approach. The first major rule was the psychosomatic connection, namely, that the soul, in all its facets, affects the body. For the rebbe, an articulation of this rule would have been Proverbs 18:14: "The spirit of a man will sustain his infirmity," "that is, in all matters of disease, God forbid, whether of the body or of the soul, the most important thing is to hearten the mind, which is the head ... a clear mind and brain to hearten ourselves."[27] In "heartening the mind," the rebbe meant not only that which is taught in modern psychology and psychoanalysis. In all likelihood he meant peace of mind which the believer attains by acknowledgement of God's omnipotence and by confidence in Him.

The secondary rules that supported this primary one were rules of suggestive therapy by the power of faith, such as reciting chapters of Psalms according to the stipulated order, or reciting selected chapters. However, not all rebbes took this literally. A well-known anecdote relates how the Rebbe of Kotzk received a Ḥasid who was suffering from intestinal pain and had come to ask him to recite a few chapters of Psalms for his recovery. The rebbe responded, "What on earth are you thinking—that King David composed his Psalms in order to cure your stomach!" Our *admorim*, like all the *ẓaddikim*, did prescribe the recitation of Psalms, so and so many chapters, in this or the other sequence, and with deep concentration. In case of failure, the patient or his relatives could blame themselves for not having concentrated seriously. The rebbe believed that the cure depended on the faith of the patient and his family and on the Healer of all flesh, the Healer of the sick among His people Israel.

The array of healing methods mentioned in the Talmud, the *midrashim* and the medieval literature, was available to everyone. A Jew who studied Torah, and certainly a rabbi, knew the basic anatomy of beasts and fowl from the laws of ritual slaughter, basic gynecology from the laws pertaining to menstruation, and something about sexual problems and diseases from the laws of ritual uncleanness, defects, and sores. Relatively speaking, he would have known quite a bit about health and disease. True, the decisors of Jewish law in the Middle Ages had already warned not to rely on the medical prescriptions of the Talmud, in order not to put the Talmudic Sages in an embarrassing light—this was the official reason given, but maybe, simply, because "the medicines in the Talmud are not good in our times." Likewise, the RaSHaL[28] wrote that there exists a ban (*ḥerem*), ordained by the early ones, not to rely on the Talmud's medicine, because if it fails, it puts the Sages in a bad light.[29] I have no doubt that the rebbes of Aleksander knew all these warnings. If they nonetheless counseled in accordance with the Talmud they certainly turned these matters over in their minds and checked them in the light of all the information available to them from other sources. From the Talmudic Sages they could learn, most importantly, rules of hygiene, such as "A person should not drink from a cup and give it to his friend, because of mortal danger," laws regarding the washing of hands, ablutions in the *mikveh*, and various warnings regarding hygiene.

Modern experts have already noted that although the Sages were quite knowledgeable about animal and poultry diseases, they did not research them with the aim of healing humans or beasts, as the modern mindset might expect. Nonetheless, they knew quite a bit about human diseases too. Medieval scholars and physicians followed the Sages' footsteps and added their contributions, some of which the rebbe certainly had in his hands, such as the *Book of Toviya*[30] by the eighteenth century physician of that name. My father too used to pore over these "recent" medical books.

Since the days of the Besht, a number of *ẓaddikim* adopted a "natural" approach, using herbs, plants and minerals, various potions and concoctions known to popular medicine, as practiced by healers and "masters of the name" in the villages. Their diagnostic methods, popular therapies, including methods of telepathy or telekinesis, have, of course, been rejected by modern medicine.

We tend to think that modern medicine brings good results, but the rebbe and his Hasidim could make a similar claim for their methods. Some of these methods have reappeared in our days, in guises of "alternative medicine."

The rebbe heard hundreds of stories about illnesses, some quite detailed descriptions, with the names of physicians and the medications prescribed, and he himself visited and consulted with doctors. The author of *Yismaḥ Yisroel* even traveled to Berlin for eye surgery, and the *Admor* we were visiting must have also consulted eye doctors. The *admorim* knew very well to whom to direct patients. There were doctors in Lodz and in Warsaw whom they trusted, and there were others, even renowned ones, in whom they had no confidence. In general, surgery was unacceptable, as we have heard.

An additional therapy the rebbe recommended was giving charity. As we know, charity, like repentance and prayer, "annul[s] the severity of the Decree." The *Mishnah* says, "The following are the things for which a man enjoys the fruits in this world while the principal remains for him in the world to come." To the four basic ethical precepts spelled out there, others were added over the centuries, and appear in the Prayer Book. They include, in this order: visiting the sick, providing a dowry for an indigent girl, and accompanying the dead to their grave. Aleksander rebbe*s* would point out to their sick petitioners the order in which these precepts were listed, prodding them and their families to contribute to the dowry of a poor bride, in order to be spared a funeral.

Finally, there was magic healing with charms and amulets. I remember two amulets. One bore the verse: "Lead me, O Lord, in thy righteousness." The other contained the prayer *Ana BeKho'aḥ* (Please, by the great power of thy right hand), and especially the phrase *Kra' Satan*—an acronym formed from the first letters of the words in this poem's second line, a manipulation that means "destroy (literally: rip up) Satan." However, more learned, deep-thinking, no less pious Ḥasidim argued that there was room for doubt regarding charms and amulets. They were fodder for the jokers, and, instead of strengthening faith, they may, God forbid, destroy it.

In my youth, when skepticism regarding amulets and protective charms had already spread, there were well-known popular songs that made fun of them and of the rebbe's miracles. I believe the *ẓaddikim* too became more cautious in prescribing these. Instead, they recommended recitation of psalms, learning *mishnayot,* praying with concentrated intention and giving charity.

CHAPTER 9

Farewell to Aleksander

Finally admitted into the rebbe's presence, the author realizes he cannot speak candidly. More memorable than the rebbe's words is one unforgettable gesture. Lessons learned about the nature of religious faith.

ḤASIDIM THRONG TO THE GREAT *BEIT MIDRASH*

Outside it was getting dark and the *beit midrash* filled with light. Numerous electric chandeliers illuminated the bookcases, the raised platform, the Holy Ark, the tables and benches, and the large throng of Ḥasidim that had assembled in Aleksander on this day of *hillulah*. Ḥasidim sat and studied or browsed through a book. Some walked here and there, although it was difficult to make one's way in the dense crowd. Some went out, washed hands, returned. Others sat and chatted. The door of the *beit midrash* was in constant motion. They came and went and came back again. More Ḥasidim arrived.

I saw good-looking Jews, *sheyne Yidn* in the best sense of the term, faces that expressed mental alertness, spirituality. The Jews who came here were accustomed to perusing books; all knew Torah, in greater or lesser measure. They delighted in telling and listening to "words of Torah," sayings of Talmudic Sages, tales of *ẓaddikim*.

Each individual Ḥasid stood within a sphere of relationships at the center of which was the rebbe. From him, from the rebbe, filaments of grace extended to the Ḥasid. Standing in front of the rebbe's door, each Ḥasid's interest was keenly focused on this field of relationships: A Ḥasid has just "received shalom," or is about to "receive shalom," is entering now, or will enter shortly, has heard from the rebbe and feels intoxicated by his aura, or will hear soon. All expected to receive the exhilarating, redemptive inspiration which emanated from the rebbe's person.

I said *sheyne Yidn*. True, there were among them faces furrowed by sorrow and care, prematurely aged, but this yearning for the elevation of the soul, this thirst for the living God, endowed their faces with a touch of grace and benevolence. Most of them wore the *kapota* customary among Polish Jews, and underneath that the *tallit katan*[1] over the wide shirt, with pants tucked into boots or into long black knee-high stockings (the rebbe wore white stockings, even on weekdays). Lodz textiles and tailors supplied the whole country with quality wares, but here you could still see tattered and patched *kapotot*. Most of the *shtreiml*s were tall and full, bushy, and shiny, but some were crinkled, flattened, looking as though plucked from front and back. The *maskilim* made fun of them—wearing clothes of Polish nobility from the Baroque era, thinking they thereby preserved Jewish tradition! The Ḥasidim, however, paid no attention to ridicule coming from the modern Jewish educated class, and even less to that of non-Jews. In their view, the Jewish people were spared destruction only because they had not changed their ways. This is how it was in Egypt and in all subsequent diasporas. It had been their forefathers' tradition, hence they would not budge from it. Of course, anyone who refused to yield to the "ways of the Gentiles" and continued instead to wear Jewish clothes exposed himself to humiliation and persecution. People threw stones at him and set their dogs on his tail. It took courage to be different, but that was just the point: to differ from the *goyim* and their impurity.

Was this deliberate aloofness the cause of anti-Semitism or its result? Who can say? It was in Germany, where Jews believed in the possibility of "symbiosis" with the denizens, spoke their language, and adopted their manners, that it became permissible, even obligatory, to exterminate them.

Most Jews in the generation before the establishment of the Polish state viewed the Pole as synonymous with physical labor, drunkenness, prostitution, theft, and murder. Passing by their churches, a Jew would spit and whisper, "Thou shalt utterly detest it, and thou shalt utterly abhor it; for it is a cursed thing." These *goyim* were held to be idol worshippers. Altogether in those days, the prestige of the Poles was very low not only among Jews, but also among others who had settled in their midst—the Russians and the Germans. Only after the reestablishment of Poland's sovereignty did we come to see that they too were human beings, but also that it was they who now had the power to harm and destroy us.

Who knows if doubt sometimes crept into the Ḥasidim's mind? The Bible had said of us, "Thou shalt be blessed above all people," and yet we were mud at their feet in this world. Will it never end? Should we not rise and do something to change our condition? Many young people in Lodz and its environs began preparing themselves for *aliyah* to Ereẓ Israel. Aleksander Ḥasidim, unlike those of Agudat Israel, often allied themselves in the elections with the Mizraḥi movement, that is, with the religious Zionists. Was this not a sign of awakening, a desire to struggle against fate in new ways?

Here, in front of the rebbe's door, there were also some Jews wearing short jackets, "Deitch" (western) style. They were "Litvaks" coming from afar, immigrants from Russia and Lithuania, who spoke Yiddish with a strange, almost incomprehensible accent. However, they too were the rebbe's adherents, although most Litvaks were not Ḥasidim. They had their synagogue and a large *beit midrash* in the courtyard next to the Great Synagogue of Aleksander on 56 Zachodnia Street in Lodz.

Most of the Litvaks who settled in largely Ḥasidic Poland continued to be either *mitnagdim*, or adherents of the *mussar* movement.[2] The latter affiliation infused them with a certain melancholy: Every stage attained in the process of ethical improvement appeared to be only one more step on the endless path to a still higher grade of perfection, in the austere battle with evil, the eternal enemy. Perhaps in order to find relief from these torments of conscience and to rejoice, like Ḥasidim, in the service of God, some of these Litvaks accepted the Polish Ḥasidic variety of piety. At any rate, the Rebbe of Aleksander welcomed them, as his father and uncle had done before him, and his Ḥasidim were used to them. In the rebbe's court, all were equal, although Ḥasidim in traditional garb were "more equal."

IN THE REBBE'S PRESENCE

Before the *gabbai* collected our *kvitlach,* where we had written our names and the names of our mothers, and in one sentence, the essence of our requests, I stood a few minutes in front of the open door to the rebbe's room. I saw there a sight that I have never forgotten in all these many years. The rebbe sat at his modest table on which *kvitlach*s and money bills were piled up. Next to him stood a Jew, wiping his tears. I could not hear his voice. A man in trouble, obviously, living in penury perhaps, or struck by sudden calamity. Wide-eyed, I watched as the rebbe swept from the table a handful of bills and thrust them into the Ḥasid's hands. As mentioned, the rebbe, although not totally blind, could barely see; he surely could not see how much he was giving.

I had little time to contemplate this scene. We were summoned into the rebbe's presence. In my note, I had written something about "fear of heaven," i.e., that I needed to be strengthened in piety. The rebbe asked whether I was still studying with the rabbi of Burzenin. I answered that I was now studying with Reb Avraham Moshe (Goldman). "A Jew of gold," the rebbe replied. "Learn

Yiẓḥak Menaḥem Dancyger (1880–1943), fourth and last rebbe of Aleksander, only 63 at his death in Treblinka

Torah. As you know, 'everything is in the hands of heaven except the fear of heaven.' A man must work at it." I did not tell the rebbe that I was about to quit Poland for Breslau, to enroll in Judaic studies at its famed Jewish Theological Seminary, concurrently with secular studies at the university, all in preparation for *aliyah* to Ereẓ Israel (according to my plan, which was already pretty firm in my mind by then). I was afraid he would not understand, maybe he would get angry. I did not want to make it difficult for my father. I did not lie or deny. I just did not speak the whole truth. I did not open my heart to him, and I was a little ashamed of it.

By "fear of heaven," I meant that spiritual equilibrium which I had reached in that last year of my life in Poland, a kind of compromise between the demands of secular life and the obligations of sanctity. The main thing was to cling to "I am the Lord thy God," regardless of the many diverse forms He might assume.[3] However, I considered the Jewish Theological Seminary in Breslau preferable to the *beit midrash* in Aleksander, and even to the new *yeshivot* that had been established in Warsaw: Taḥkhmoni, established by the Mizraḥi movement, and the Metivta (*yeshiva*) for the sons of Ger Ḥasidim, where cousin Avraham Mordekhai Maroko, Uncle Yidl's grandson, was studying. (The *yeshiva* of Lublin first opened in the summer of 1930). I had concluded that only study abroad could equip me with the requisite tools for teaching and research in Ereẓ Israel, and this I could not tell the rebbe outright. My avoidance of candor stemmed, apparently, from the same desire to maintain the equilibrium.

The rebbe blessed me with success, and we left stepping out slowly, with our backs to the door, our faces toward the rebbe sitting at his table. I left in agitation, and perhaps that which agitated me most in that meeting was the spectacle preceding it: the rebbe giving *ẓedakah* with a sweep of the hand, paying no heed to the amount.

The conversation with the rebbe, rather than setting my mind at ease, greatly disturbed me. Why was it not possible to speak more honestly with a great spiritual leader? After all, there were many among his adherents who saw no future for their children in this country. In Poland, national awakening in the form of Zionism and everything it meant in terms of secular, activist thought was not merely an intellectual current that sought, as it were, to rival Ḥasidism. Rather, it was a genuine endeavor to answer the great life question that so troubled the new generation, all those young people who knew themselves to be discriminated against and unwanted, targeted with insults in the Polish schools and universities, in government offices and in the street. They felt entirely in exile and lacked tools with which to confront its distresses, except by setting themselves apart. The author of *Yismaḥ Yisroel* had warned, "Lest they budge one iota from the ways of Torah, and alter any custom whatsoever of the customs of our forefathers, may they rest in peace." This warning, originally published in his "Holy Epistle" (*Igeret Kodesh*) to his adherents, was reprinted in 1926 in the Passover *Haggadah*, in the edition issued by the two brothers of the rabbi with whom I had just spoken. This *Haggadah* was very popular among Aleksander Ḥasidim, and I too have frequently perused it, together with the two Holy Epistles that were added to it. In an epistle from 1917, I read: "It is now a matter of some years that the cloud of the accursed *haskalah* has spread upon the face of the earth, and many books of incitement and seduction have appeared, uttered in smooth tongue and with defiled lips, and, for our multiple sins, have led many in Israel astray." These were the arguments repeated by all the *ẓaddikim* of the age, including Poland's "three greats": the Rebbes of Belz, Ger, and Aleksander.

Twenty years later they were still speaking the same language and had changed none of their arguments prior to the Holocaust. Were they the ones who could save the new generation? My thoughts were fuzzy, not clear. I saw before me much Jewish suffering, impoverishment, also bloody riots, pogroms, confiscations, and banishments. Occupations practiced by Jews, artisanry and trade, had suffered from the surplus of people engaged in them, especially in the big cities. Artisans lacked adequate professional training, petty traders lacked sufficient capital, and the mechanization of industry finished off many of the home laborers. All were easy prey to expropriation. And the unemployed? About 28 percent in that year. Father was one of them, having been laid off from his job at the Silberstein factory in 1927 and having found no permanent work thereafter. I became responsible for helping with the family upkeep by private tutoring. What would our fate have been without this "accursed *haskalah*" and everything it gave me for understanding the world around me? "After the sons become sated with the bitter fruits of their defiled study, they will betray their fathers, and shut their ears to their weeping and distress," the rebbe had warned in that "Holy Epistle." I, and many like me, were an unfailing mainstay to our parents, as far as our ability allowed.

Nevertheless, I did not say to myself, "What succor can this one offer?" I sensed in him, and in all of Ḥasidism, a tremendous spiritual power, a fecund and fecundating force, within its limits. This power needed to be adapted to the general atmosphere then regnant in the Jewish street, which was full of yearnings for a thorough mending of Jewish life, both in Poland and in Ereẓ Israel, by confronting reality neither with pie-in-the-sky hallucinations nor with misleading and overshadowing myths.

Leaving the rebbe's room I felt acutely the inherent tension between continuity of a cultural tradition, which had ennobled a Jew's spiritual world with so many great virtues, and responsiveness to inevitable change. In order not to lose the former, to preserve its core and chief idea in the face of harsh and rapid permutations, the foreign, modern environment impelled us to break through the walls of tradition and let in the winds of change.

Later in life my thoughts and feelings in the rebbe's room, still quite nebulous on that occasion, became a principal subject of my theoretical studies.[4] Many years passed until the things I had felt in my youth became intelligible to me through scholarly research, eventually culminating in a philosophy of historical perspectivism. This approach sees in the wide expanses of Jewish history and in its depths, a ceaseless contention between forces of continuity and of rupture. The continuity is one of seven evolving, though distinct cultures, which are forever invading each other's territory, subverting, reinterpreting or reinventing their predecessors, in their endless battle over the right path to salvation, each according to its own ontology.

THE *TISH*, THE MEAL AND THE "REBBE'S WISDOM"

The rebbe emerged from his room for the evening prayer. The audience in the *beit midrash* had thickened and packed the hall. I do not remember who led the prayers, but the melody was the Aleksander *niggun*, melodious and tending to tearfulness. Even in the evening prayer of an ordinary weekday there was enthusiasm and *dveikut*, for on this day of *hillulah*, many believed that the Old Rebbe's soul returned also to the *beit midrash*, thus energizing the prayer with an intensity of holiness.

After the prayer, the rebbe returned to his room and in the *beit midrash*, Ḥasidim began moving tables and benches. They laid out the *Tish* for the festive meal. By the time the rebbe re-entered to take his seat, which was not at the head of the table, some thirty of the most important Ḥasidim were already seated. These were rabbis and Torah scholars, among them my uncle Yidl and his son, the rabbi of Burzenin, as well as Reb Avraham Moshe, and a few others whom I knew. However, I did not know most of them (some sixty or seventy altogether). Behind them, a huge crowd huddled and shoved, everyone trying to squeeze through and wrest a place as close as possible to the table or on one of the benches around it.

Naturally I wished to see and hear what the rebbe had to say, but I was held back by fear that I might tear my borrowed *kapota* in the crush. Nonetheless, I got on a bench, squashed in the crowd, hanging on, and fairly close to the center of the table.

The meal at the *Tish* is a symbolic, or if you will, a magical expression of the renewal of the Ḥasidic believer's vitality, by virtue of the ingestion of material and spiritual food. This is the secret of eating the "leftovers" (*shirayim*) from the rebbe's plate. The leftovers themselves, of course, were of no importance. One ate a morsel ("as much as an olive") of meat or rice, fish or *ḥallah*, a spoonful of soup, or a sip of wine. The important thing was the eating together with the rebbe, partaking of his holiness. That is what the Ḥasidim who ate and drank with the rebbe around the *Tish* felt, and so did the large crowd behind them, those who lucked out, or not, to receive something from the table, and participate at least symbolically in the meal. My father and I were not so fortunate, although Reb Yidl apparently thought of us and made gestures as though he wished to pass us a piece of *ḥallah*. The Ḥasidim around the table ate. The rebbe partook of the food only sparingly. The *gabbai* announced donations of wine for the *Tish*: "The Ḥasid so-and-so contributes three bottles of wine," or four, or five. He announced the names of all the rich men and of many other Ḥasidim. The number of bottles consumed was never as high as the number declared at the *Tish*. It was a form of fundraising, or a way of honoring a donor's name, or simply mentioning a name in the rebbe's hearing. To my amazement, I heard: "Mordekhai Woler donates three bottles of wine." I was sure that Father had no money for such a large donation. The *gabbai*, apparently, meant well by him.

The rebbe's "Torah" was quite lengthy. I could not catch it all. The rebbe spoke in a low voice and rapidly. Several times in my youth I had an opportunity to hear *admorim* "saying Torah" at the *Tish*, and I always saw that they spoke in a whisper, and as though in a hurry. For a number of years I used to visit the rebbe of Pabianice who lived at that time in Lodz, a tall Jew with a white beard, a dignified face, very much the rebbe image although with only a small following. Adherents from out of town, only a few dozen, showed up only on Ḥanuka and Holy Days. I could stand close to him, as there was no congestion there at the Sabbath meal, and saw that he too did not raise his voice above a whisper. I heard this style with the Rebbe of Ger years later in Jerusalem. If it were not for the young people, wearing torn *kapotot* especially reserved for the jostle to get near the rebbe, I would have had no idea what he was talking about on that Sabbath of the first of Elul in the year 1978, at his court, in the holy community of Jerusalem.

Based on what I could grasp, and on what Father and a few other Ḥasidim added, I can more or less reconstruct the Aleksander Rebbe's "Torah" on this occasion of his grandfather's *hillulah*. He began with words of praise for the Old Rebbe. Then he mentioned the fifteenth day of Shevat and the commandment to eat on this day from the fruits of the Land of Israel, and indeed there were several oranges and carobs on the table.

The main thrust of his talk, in homiletic style, was approximately this: Commenting on the verse "*ami ata*" (Thou art My people), the Talmudic Sages said, "read it as *immi ata*" (Thou art with Me). The Holy One has left Israel a part, a role, in mending the world, that is, the mending is divided, as it were, between the Holy One and Israel. The rebbe quoted the verse, "But I am poor and sorrowful: let thy salvation, O God, set me up on high," and expounded, "I know the poorness of my condition, that I have nothing, that everything comes from the power of the Holy One, from the treasure of His unconditional gift and that only Your salvation, O God, will set me up on high, when I help God, and God, as it were, is redeemed in Israel's redemption. This is the meaning of what we read in the Rosh Hashana liturgy 'Salvation is His crown,' the salvation of Israel is His crown, and it is on this account that I beg you to set me on high."

I liked what the rebbe said about good and evil. I was already very sensitive then to the problem of "the righteous suffer and the wicked thrive," arising from capitalist and other forms of exploitation, and found it hard to believe that there really was reward for performing *miẓvot*. The Psalmist declares, "I have been young, and now am old, yet have I not seen the righteous forsaken, nor his seed begging bread." But I *had* seen a righteous man forsaken and his seed seeking bread, and I began to doubt whether the Lord really was omnipotent and providential to all His creatures. I felt that one must rouse oneself and help God, as it were. And here, the *rebbe* had declared a certain religious activism, a need to help God, very much in the spirit of my thinking.

The rebbe then recalled again the memory of the Old Rebbe, his grandfather, who had been so humble in the knowledge of his small worth, but had known that only thanks to God's grace our people have not perished and would not perish despite our sins. The Old Rebbe had been afraid of no man, had had no fear at all. Only by virtue of such confidence, which is the foundation of faith, can a man mitigate God's judgments in times of trouble and draw down life from above, in the sense of "the just shall live by his faith," and "The Lord is my portion, saith my soul." This is the ascendancy of the light of the soul, which endures forever. In these words, however, I again felt the rebbe's propensity to passiveness, the acceptance of fate in submission and humility.

In his last words, I felt the rebbe was directing himself especially to me. He quoted from Ḥasidic literature, in the name of the Besht. The Sages, commenting on the words of Jacob "How dreadful is this place! This is none other but the house of God," extrapolated a warning: "Woe to him who has no courtyard yet makes a gate for same!" That is, woe to him who has no house (i.e., no piety), but has made a gate (Torah learning) to the house. Our Patriarch Jacob studied Torah fourteen years in the *beit midrash* of Shem and Ever, but only now, after having awoken from the dream of the ladder that reaches heaven, is he ready to accept fear of heaven and piety, which is the house, God's house. Learning Torah up to this point had only been the gate to heaven.

I felt that the rebbe's insistence on the primacy of piety over Torah study sought to strengthen my resolve, but I was not sure whether he and I meant the same thing by the concept of piety. I had much to think about.

The rebbe ended with words of comfort: Even though Israel is in exile, "He hath set me in dark places, as they that be dead of old," "yet for all that … I will not cast them away, neither will I abhor them, to destroy them utterly, and to break my covenant with them"—God forbid. The rebbe's "Torah" imparted faith and consolation. Like me, everyone felt that the rebbe had spoken directly to him, reaching into his heart. Feeling strengthened, they again toasted *Leḥayim* and proceeded to recite the blessing after the meal. When the rebbe left the *beit midrash* to take a brief rest before beginning to receive more Ḥasidim and saying goodbye to those who came to take their leave of him, a murmur rippled through the great *beit midrash*, swelling into loud tumult. They discussed the rebbe's "Torah" and exchanged views about allusions they found in it. A group of Ḥasidim danced and sang, others began to take leave of each other, though with little relish. It was getting late, time to hurry to the tram and get home. Tomorrow was an ordinary weekday, but it would be easier to bear having basked in the aura of Aleksander.

As I leave here the world of the Rabbinic-Ḥasidic culture, and turn my attention to the National-Israeli[5] culture (the Hebrew high school, the new Hebrew poetry), I would like to summarize the lessons I learned from the Ḥasidic world.

FOUR THEOLOGICAL LESSONS

Everything that I saw and heard in Aleksander, in that year and earlier, contributed to the crystallization of my systematic thinking about religious faith in general, and Jewish faith in particular. I learned the following:

a) Faith is essentially transcendental, if we may use philosophical terminology, and all the concepts, opinions, and deeds regarding faith depart from the boundaries of the natural-empirical. They contain an addition, an enhancement, which lies beyond the reach of our rational consciousness and our overt will, far above any realistic reasoning. One must differentiate between knowledge of objects in this world through scientific investigation and philosophic conceptualization, and the understanding of that distinct enhancement which is rooted in wondering and in wonder, beyond the visible and its comprehensible symbols. There exists an "extra soul," there is always more and more of the beautiful and the virtuous in the treasures of meaning, which nurture music and poetry, philosophical thought, and silence. No being, act, or event exists in and of itself, as is; rather, it becomes burnished by the "holy sparks" inherent in it, and which represent absolute meaning.

b) Just as the world is not self-evident, neither is man, even less so a Jew. Jews are comrades, from near and from far, in their roots, partners from the time of Abraham, Isaac, and Jacob. If you do not act properly and even more than just properly, toward other persons, especially toward someone near you, toward a fellow Jew and a Ḥasid, your conscience pricks you, you feel a moral and emotional failure, Satan's work, resulting from your neglect. On the verse "Love thy neighbor as thyself, I am the Lord," the *Yismaḥ Yisroel* commented that "'I am the Lord,' is as though the Holy One were saying: let Me in too" ("*lozt mich oich aran*"). This is the emphasis on spiritual enhancement and ascension.

c) Matters of religious faith touch a person's heart; his affinity to them is profound, absolute. This is also what I later learned at the University of Frankfurt on the Main from my teacher Paul Tillich, who explained that God is "that which concerns us absolutely," that is, He is one in which you have an absolute interest, an "ultimate concern,"[6] not a partial interest. In religious faith, the "I" clamors for a superior power, for an encounter with words of teaching, which call you, grabbing you by the roots of your hair—"My soul thirsteth for God, for the living God." On the other hand, conscience calls and awakens, as though it were seeking me, "Where art thou?" and I cannot hide from it. It is as though everything is directed at me, and there is nowhere to flee.

d) All opinions and acts in religion relate to overall intentionality, or in Ḥasidic language, to that which "surrounds all worlds, and transcends all worlds." Without faith in an overall intention, in cosmic and all-human meaning, which encompasses all things, there is no true faith. The main question of every believer is how the overall intention fits the significations of everyday life, that is, how it reveals itself in effect and how to see this meaning in the contingent and occasional. A Jew must seek this intention in order to confirm the significations of the daily deeds and events throughout his life. This implies that there are, of course, varying degrees of faith, and that questions and doubts arise. The energy of faith in the supreme and overall intention is not uniform at all times and under all circumstances. We should say, however, that faith for its part always gives an answer, directs one to the answer, to resolution of doubts, and does not permit the negative possibility to become total reality. God is never absent from the world, but one must open one's heart to see Him. Sometimes He hides His face in a hazy cloud of precepts, rituals and their minutiae, and of foolish delusions.

In later life, I studied and researched these and similar ideas, inalienable assets in Aleksander, in Judaism, and in religious faith generally.

True, from a social-spiritual standpoint, Ḥasidism sought to preserve the old Polish version of education and way of life, and it saddened young people like me to see it growing increasingly conservative and fanatic—a conservative-clerical party, withdrawn within itself, and losing its sons. In the 1930s, when only one party ruled Poland in a government hostile to the minorities, and especially to Jews, there was hardly any Jewish representation left in the parliament, except for Agudat Israel, that is, the Ḥasidic party. We need hardly say that Ḥasidic politics seriously warped the Ḥasidic spirit.

Even though the political and social orientation of Ḥasidism in Poland had become objectionable to many young people who left its fold, surely it was still possible to deepen the study of its origins and derive insights which had not dimmed in the transformations and quandaries of the last generation.

CHAPTER 10

A Hebrew High School in its Heyday

A new model of teacher-educator, a new type of student. Discrimination against Jewish schools by Polish authorities. The brilliant career and sad end of Dr. Mordechai (Markus) Ze'ev Braude, founder of the Hebrew high school network.

ZIONIST ENVIRONMENT AND JEWISH ACTIVISM

On the cold dark morning following the *hillulah* at Aleksander, after my early prayers at the Wiślicki prayer hall and a hasty breakfast, I ran to school, the Second Boys' Hebrew Gymnasia (in Polish it was called the *Jewish Gymnasia*), founded by Dr. Mordekhai Markus Braude. Mounds of snow had piled up on the sidewalks and a thick white blanket of snow covered some of the streets and the fields which one could make out in the distance. The school was only a seven-to-ten minutes' nimble "hoofing" from our house, but I would always arrive at the last minute, just before the closing of the schoolyard gate.

The two Hebrew high schools for boys stood on either side of Gistracka Street. The first to be established was at #7, under Dr. Avraham Perlman (who succeeded in reaching Israel in time and continued working here as an educational supervisor). Diagonally opposite, at #16, stood the second Hebrew high school, headed by Shaul Rieger (1893–1966), where I was enrolled. These two schools numbered no more than one thousand male students.

The girls, as I mentioned earlier, had a high school on another street, where they too obtained a thorough Jewish and general education (26 weekly hours of general subjects, 11 hours of Hebrew subjects: literature, history, Bible, Mishnah). Its first principal upon its founding in 1921 was Dr. Bromberg-Bitkowski, an important Zionist writer-poet in Polish and German, possessing a dignified countenance and much charm. I remember reading his translation of the Song of Songs into Polish. He was succeeded by Dr. Michael Brandstetter, son of the Hebrew writer of humorous tales about the Ḥasidim of Galician towns, which were published a generation earlier in Pereẓ Smolenskin's journal *Ha-shaḥar*. This Hebrew writer of the *haskalah*, Mordekhai David Brandstetter, was still alive (he died at the end of 1928), and from time to time some of his witticisms were recalled. His son was a serious principal: strict, but kind. He assembled a superb team of teachers, of whom Dr. Shmaryahu Ellenberg and Ḥaim Ormian later became educators in Israel.

Tardiness, of course, was forbidden. Sometimes the principal stood at the gate in person, and latecomers got their due from him directly. Sometimes they were even denied entry. Although still a young man, who was, like some of our teachers, a product of the Ha-shomer Ha-ẓa'ir youth movement in Galicia, Rieger imposed discipline and easily imparted authority. At first he was appointed as a young deputy principal (to Michael Brandstetter, before the latter transferred to the girls' high school), and then as principal and able captain at the helm. Order in the school was exemplary, and not too oppressive, largely due to his power of persuasion and to voluntary consent. In my last school year Rieger was also our teacher for European History and for Contemporary Poland and particularly excelled in familiarizing students with historic source materials, which gave us a vivid picture of the realities they described.

Indeed Shaul Rieger and the teaching staff were a new type of teacher-educator. They had pursued academic education—acquiring expertise both in a specific field of learning and in modern pedagogy, knew modern Hebrew, and were enthusiastic Zionists (generally affiliated with the Zionist-socialist Hit'aḥdut[1] movement). Most of them were in their late twenties or mid-thirties, and the principal was around thirty-five. Most had been counselors in youth movements and had an open, direct approach, free of mannerisms, yet respectful and supportive of the student. Some were scholarly researchers who shared their scientific pursuits with their students and at the very least gave them a sense that what they were teaching was not a regurgitation of book-based material, but something new, discoveries emanating from their own independent investigations. Others were creators in literature and the arts. They were prepared to innovate, to dare, to try out new ideas. They themselves wished to test their strength. Although each of them carried his or her bundle of personal and family problems, and even if didactically their methods were not always the most effective, in a wider pedagogical sense their impact was powerful. They awoke in us a thirst for knowledge, for becoming innovators rather than receptacles of accepted truths. All of them radiated a powerful attraction upon thousands of students who swarmed to the Hebrew high schools of Lodz.

In their university studies, mainly in Vienna, our teachers, mostly from Galicia, came under the influence of the new creative mindset in education which preached not only the importance of knowledge, but mainly the development of a student's intellectual independence: the ability to think through and deal with difficult situations. To be sure, our teachers still believed that one needed to know a lot and did not reject even the old method of rote learning, but more than anything they wished to develop a student's abilities and ethical conduct. A great effort was required of them to weld together the wealth of general education with the treasures of Hebraic-Jewish learning so that these would not line up one next to the other in separate, hermetic compartments, but would nourish each other creatively in both thought and deed.

The revolution that took place within this generation of educators was particularly evident in the way they related to traditional beliefs, to the old Jewish way of life, to nature, to the state, to the essence of exile, and the return to Zion. They really wished to mold a new Jewish person in their own image and even better. Although they did not elaborate on their arguments against the traditional Jew, it was clear to us, based on what they said in class, in our school fests and ceremonies, whenever the opportunity arose for a "revolutionary" sermon, that they detested exile life, the *galut*. They detested everything it implied—submission to a fate that condemned us to acceptance of the yoke of alien rule with its abasement, its baleful decrees and dispositions, its indifference to our desires or opinions. In other words, they wanted to inculcate Jewish pride in the spirit of the great teachers of Zionism. They wanted to empower their students with a Jewish education that would serve them effectively, both in struggling against their environment and in adapting to its altering situation, but the main goal was achieving dignity without subservience or self-denigration.

The school exemplified the rebellion against the ways of life of "old Poland," that is, against *shtetl* life, whether as satirized by Mendele or as idealized by Sholem Asch. We read Asch's stories *A Shtetl* (1904) and *Reb Shloyme Nogid* (1913), and while his *shtetl* was already quite different from Mendele's "Beggarsville and "Idlers' Town," we knew it too was portraying an image far removed from what our eyes saw.

As to Ḥasidism, to our teachers it did not appear as a movement of renewal, though they admitted it had been such in its heyday. With its expectation of the Messiah and the Kingdom of Heaven, of miracles and the goodwill of *goyim*, its response had been one of accommodation and submission. In particular they viewed the Ger Ḥasidim, who allied themselves with the authorities against the national camp, as a reactionary, retrogressive camp.

Even bright journalists like my cousin Abraham Mordekhai Rogowy and his associates, who were activists by their very nature, appeared to my teachers as upholders of outdated customs, too willing to appease the government. No doubt, the dark wonder of our existence in the diaspora was a great enigma for our educators as they struggled to decipher it with us, but on no account did they believe that divine providence, if such existed, liberated man from responsibility, as though "The Lord shall fight for you, and ye shall hold your peace." On the contrary, one was obliged to raise the banner of action, to rise up, to change. This was a dramatic new worldview.

At all our school functions—the start and the end of the academic year, at the award of matriculation certificates, at Ḥanuka celebrations and Lag ba-omer excursions—our teachers, and occasionally Dr. Braude, the school's visionary founder, articulated their educational philosophy. The premise was that notwithstanding the respect genuinely felt for the past, especially for its great heroes, fighters and creators, it was now urgent to examine *all* of its treasures in order to select those most suitable for our generation. In other words, one should not hesitate to relegate to oblivion the dream fabric of traditional Messianism. Instead, one should strengthen the striving for salvation in a "mended" world and within a renascent Jewish people in the Land of Israel. Even though the words were grandiloquent and flowery, they were clear and unequivocal to us. Perhaps in this lay their charm, for they pointed to the future and interpreted the past and the present.

Our school truly aimed to be the crucible for forging the young Jewish generation. One might assume that it is more likely for the external conditions and internal mores of a community to fashion the character of its education system than for education to change the mores and conditions of a community. Here, however, within the walls of the Hebrew high school, an attempt was made to change the world. The school prepared us to confront the dangers lying in wait for Zionist education in the diaspora: the specters of the past (the Rabbinic-Ḥasidic tradition), assimilation (including its socialist and Communist expressions, which were gathering momentum before our eyes), and the Polish nationalistic fanaticism. Implicitly and explicitly, we were taught that it was our responsibility to confront these challenges, and to do so without any sense of inferiority.

JEWISH EDUCATION AND THE POLISH AUTHORITIES

According to statistics, in the years before World War II there were more than half a million Jewish children in Poland, of whom only 40 percent received their education in a *ḥeder* or in a Jewish school. Only 15 percent of all Jewish children in the country studied in schools that promoted Zionist Hebrew education. In my day, in my neighborhood and its vicinity, there were at least three other boys' high schools under Jewish ownership, but these offered no Jewish studies at all.

High school studies in those days cost a lot of money. On the one hand the government imposed mandatory education, but free tuition was allocated only at the elementary level. High schools would award a number of scholarships to talented poor students with funds raised through the efforts of their patrons, usually at festive school functions. However, the rule was that whoever could not pay was kicked out. Even in our school, sometimes an entire third of the class was sent home for a day, or for a number of hours, creating an awkward situation if a test had been scheduled for that day.

Since I belonged to the Union of Jewish Student Youth (called Yardenia, which later changed its name to Herẓlia, and finally to Zionist Youth), I heard from my male and female friends there about the schools in which they were enrolled. The schools were usually named after their principals or founders. The Starkiewicz School on Sienkiewicz Street, which enrolled a number of assimilated Jewish youths, was renowned for its high standards. Its principal, Leon Starkiewicz, was a well-known science teacher and educator who treated his students with great respect, teaching through explanation and persuasion, almost never resorting to punishments. Some of the leading Lodz intelligentsia emerged from this school, among them Julian Tuwim, later recognized as a great Lodz and Polish poet. Some institutions, for example, the municipal vocational schools, attempted important pedagogical experiments, such as self-management and independent organization of assignments by the students themselves. Boys and girls studied together there—a great innovation. My friends in Yardenia also spoke highly of the Copernicus State Gymnasium. However, an unpleasantness occurred there in the year I am speaking of when it was discovered that three teachers had accepted bribes from students scheduled to be tested for matriculation.

A number of my friends attended the Orzeszkowa Girls High School, a progressive institution for daughters of wealthy families from the city's industrial and trade circles. They would talk about a wonderful teacher, Stefania Skwarczynska (1902–1988), whose classes in Polish literature were for them a great illumination, full of mystery, as though their teacher was a "witch." It was difficult to extract from them wherein exactly lay the power of this teacher, and this mystery intrigued me. But they also talked about a scandal that had occurred in their school—a Communist cell had been uncovered. Later I read in the newspaper that 14-year-old Hanna Spiro and her friends were accused of having "spread Communism within the ranks of the military!" The attractions of the Polish Lit class apparently did not save them from the "foreign fire," and maybe, on the contrary, it increased their disaffection with contemporary Poland.

For a similar reason—a Communist cell among the students—our school too lost its privileges in 1932. As I later heard, the police caught some of our students attending a meeting of young people involved in organizing a Communist Party cell in Lodz. The police seized a brochure containing names of Communist student cells in other schools and a government supervisor wrote an indictment against the school for promoting unpatriotic education. Only with great effort did Shaul Rieger succeed in convincing the authorities to restore the school's privileges and confidence in its staff. However, truth be told, already in my time four years earlier, there were a number of boys in our school who had Communist sympathies, and, who knows, maybe they too organized a Communist cell. I remember the gossip about fellow student Hanoch Bzoza (1907–1964)—that he was caught up in Communism. Indeed, he later became one of the leaders of the Communist Party in Ereẓ Israel, but then left the party and founded a sort of nationalist Hebrew-Zionist-Communist organization.

Every school had its distinct student uniform, or at least student caps, so that one saw in the city streets a wide range of colors: green, blue, white and red, with stars and stripes and various emblems. Jewish boys and girls were to be found in most of the city's high schools, even in the German Gymnasium at the corner of Zamenhof and Kościuszko streets, in a large handsome building, with its sports field and gym halls. I had a number of friends who spoke to me in German and whose Polish was marked by a distinct German accent. The *Hitlerjugend* and a number of Nazi leaders of the German occupation later emerged from this school. Most of the Germans in our town, the *Volksdeutsche,* joined the Nazis. Even their Social Democrats, who published a daily newspaper in my day, were swept up in the torrent, or else they were silenced and ostracized. This is a sad story unto itself—the exploits of the German citizens, scions of the founders of the city's industry, who later donned SS uniforms and took part in the government of "Litzmannstadt," i.e., Lodz, and the entire province of the Warta River.

As I ran every morning (except on Saturdays and festival days) to the Boys Second Hebrew High School, I had no time to take note of my fellow laggards running to the other schools around us. I could just make out the caps of the Braun Gymnasium, the Wiśniewski Gymnasium, and the students of the Commerce School. These three schools were located up the street, as you approached Staszic Garden, on the way to the municipal tram parking lot. Lodz

University was later established there. One of its principal buildings, which I visited in 1982, was formerly the Commerce School.

In accordance with the treaty signed at Versailles between the victorious powers and the representatives of the Polish government in June 1919, the new state undertook to establish and maintain at its expense schools for the minorities living within its borders, in their own languages. The Polish government also agreed to permit the establishment of special minority schools, such as middle and high schools, at government expense. It expressly committed itself to allocate to minority schools "an appropriate portion of the enjoyment and use of the sums to be allocated by the state, cities and other organizations to educational institutions."

However, the government not only dragged its feet in fulfilling these commitments to Jews, but trampled upon them with a haughty nationalistic boot. It did not allocate regular, permanent funding even to Jewish elementary schools—the only national minority thus deprived of state support. Rather, its education policy was to establish its own network of elementary schools, which refrained from instruction on the Sabbath in Jewish neighborhoods and *shtetls*. This was the only concession made to the Jews, and usually the only Jewish feature of those schools. This Sabbath-keeping school was in fact a Polish institution in every respect, and its eager-to-assimilate teachers, mostly women, were unfamiliar with Jewish culture, ashamed of speaking Yiddish, and strict about forbidding its use by the children. The chief goal of these schools was to produce Polish patriots, alienated from the destiny of their own people and lacking any knowledge of its culture.

It may seem baffling, and yet it is entirely true: The same Polish authorities who discriminated against Jews more than against all other citizens, hoping in fact for their *evakuatzia* elsewhere, at the same time set out aggressively to impose Polish culture upon Jewish students. The aim was to cause their identity to crumble from within, to make them a non-people that would rapidly acculturate within the Polish population.

Immediately after World War I, a number of Jewish educational networks were established throughout Poland, each affiliated with a religious or political party which fought its battles with the authorities, raised funds, and assisted as best it could in the many problems faced by Jewish schools. All these institutions, regardless of their strands and substrands, were dependent on their support organizations. A certain contribution came from the Joint, especially in the early post-war years and very little from the government or from the limited resources of municipalities. It was up to the impoverished Jewish communities, and mainly the parents, to shoulder the heavy burden of maintaining the schools. Given the overall economic conditions of Jews in Poland, it is no wonder that school budgets were tight and never adequately secure.

No less difficult was the legal status of Jewish schools, especially those whose language of instruction was Yiddish or Hebrew. These were denied the accreditation accorded to recognized public schools and were subjected to frequent harassment. Under the guise of humane progressiveness, the authorities would pester Jewish schools with all kinds of new ordinances. Local and provincial supervisors, whom we would see periodically on the school premises, would declare the building unsuitable, or the hygiene deficient, or that the students' health required a spacious sports field. In the name of pedagogy and psychology—not to overburden the students—they would demand a reduction in the number of hours in Hebrew. Only in 1926, after long, wearying negotiations, did they formally agree to approve the Hebrew curriculum, which had already been in effect for a number of years.

The Hebrew high school's major struggle was over its accreditation as an institution authorized to award the state matriculation certificate, which enabled its graduates to enter university. The state divided the Jewish high schools into four categories: (a) A high school with full accreditation—its students took the matriculation exam in their own school, the examiners were their teachers, and the examining committee was chaired by the school's principal. I believe that our school attained this status only after my departure from Poland. In my day it belonged to the second type. (b) Students were examined in their own school, the members of the examining committee were their teachers, but with the addition of a government supervisor-controller, and the committee chair was an external government official. (c) In some high schools, students were tested by external supervisors exclusively. (d) Lowest in the ranking were the schools deprived of accreditation, whose graduates were considered external examinees, that is, they had to take the matriculation exams in a Polish high school to which they were assigned.

The authorities knew that the teaching standard at the Hebrew High School was superior. Every year, the results of the matriculation exams testified to the great efforts and achievements of teachers and students alike. Nonetheless, fear of hostile governmental interference was always present.

The accreditation issue was, of course, a fateful matter—the *tachlis* question for us and for our parents who wished to set us on a career path. It was also existential for our school, which had to contend not only with the outside world, i.e., with the authorities, but also to compete with other Jewish educational networks. It had to vindicate the moderate, middle-of-the-road course it had chosen—teaching Jewish subjects in Hebrew and general subjects in Polish. Absent state accreditation, many parents would send their sons and daughters to Polish schools, to an education of Jewish alienation.

Not everyone attached so much importance to accreditation, or, if you will, to opportunistic arguments, to *tachlis*. Quite a few parents and students enthusiastically supported the idea of education exclusively in Hebrew. In the city of Baranowicze, parents and students went on strike when their all-Hebrew high school was turned into a bilingual school. Much was written at the time about this incident in the Hebrew press in Poland; the Yiddish press too gave it some attention. The student youth, they announced, favors full Hebrew education, even at the price of not obtaining accreditation. In 1929, the Hebrew journal *Sneh* commented on the Baranowicze strike: "The young people want something different from their parents—a purpose for the future yet to come, not a purpose for the present." The Baranowicze bilingual school did not succeed in taking hold and had to return its concession to the government. In Lodz two attempts for the long-term maintenance of an exclusively Hebrew language high school also failed. In Poland it was, as indicated, the bilingual high school which spread most widely.

Many of my friends wanted to study at university in preparation for a profession. In theory there was no *numerus clausus*, that is, no official quota that limited the admission of Jews to university, but the institutions of higher learning were "autonomous" and had the right to decide whom to admit. Our history teacher, Dr. Friedman, found that in the academic year 1921–22 there were 35,000 students enrolled in Polish universities, of which 8,228 were Jews, some 24 percent. Fifteen years later in the academic year 1936–37 there were only 5,700 Jews out of a student population of 48,000, that is, less than 12 percent. The universities limited Jewish admissions, especially in medicine, law and engineering, to a bare minimum. In 1923–24, 30 percent of all medical students were Jews, but in 1937–38 only 9 percent. Jews could more easily pursue liberal arts subjects, but here there was a large excess of talent and very few prospective teaching positions. At the universities, Jewish students would find themselves periodically under attack from their Polish fellows, yet most of the professors did not protest against this mistreatment. Jewish students were even assigned separate benches in university lecture halls. Many refused to sit on them, preferring to stand throughout the lectures. However, all this was after I left Poland. In my day, hopes still bloomed, and voluntary Polonization was progressing rapidly.

POWER OF THE POLISH LANGUAGE

Our school was very punctilious about teaching the Polish language and its literature. The governmental supervisors decreed this, but it was also the desire of many parents who began preening themselves on their Polish, and especially that of their children. In my day, use of Polish spread widely among many middle class Jewish families that were sending their children to high schools.

Even though the traditional Jewish life style, whether totally *ḥaredi* or more secular, was still maintained by a large majority of Jewish families—*kashrut,* a little prayer, candles on the Sabbath, festival days, and an intermarriage rate of no more than 1.5 percent in 1927 (compared to 21 percent in Germany, 12 percent in Holland)—linguistic assimilation became widespread. Both the successful scalers of the social ladder and the classless class of those who lacked any kind of permanent status and material base—brokers, clerks, *luftmentshen*—increasingly began to feel ashamed of speaking Yiddish. My classmates' mothers began showing off their fluency, speaking a vulgar, non-standard lingo, and yet—it was Polish. My friends' names changed during their high school years: Shlomo became Stashek or Stanislaw, Moshe—Mietek or Mieczysław, Joshua and Yeshayahu—Jerzy. The dominance of Polish was most common among the girls. Our friend in the youth movement was ashamed when her father called her in front of us by her Yiddish name, Libbe; we knew her as Ludka or Ludvika, and on no account would she utter a word in Yiddish.

From its very beginning, the Polish state emphatically rejected the Russian and German languages. In my earlier years, my mother took me to Yiddish or German theater performances. Later, however, I joined my friends in attending Polish theater. Needless to say, when the Habima Hebrew theater came to Lodz, it swept all of us to its first five plays.

Many Jewish homes already subscribed to Polish language newspapers (whose editors and publishers were Jews), wherein they could also read literature, original and translated. There was a visible effort to think in the terminology being disseminated in newspapers and popular books.

During the relatively brief period of my school days, I saw the great transformation—Polonization, and with gusto. True, the Jewish past still lingered, like a hump, on the back of every alienated Jew, to hinder his absorption into the Polish polity. Polish society was fairly closed, but many Jews began seeing themselves as straddling the two national cultures.

Before World War I, the Jews in the territories of the Russian and Austrian empires had acted as intermediaries between the ruler and the local populace in matters of culture and economy. In this lay their unique role. After the war, however, the newly created states discovered that they possessed powerful forces of acculturation. Nations whose literate-intellectual culture had been far poorer than that of the Jews, like the Ukrainians and Belarusians in the Soviet state, and the Poles, Lithuanians, Latvians, Romanians and Serbs in their states, began, with the vigorous support of their governments, raising themselves up on the rungs of the culture ladder, and assimilating their minorities. In schools and universities, newspapers, literature and art, a new national culture came into being in which Jews participated willingly, or under compulsion. Whereas

The Reform Synagogue in Lodz

previously the educated Jewish public, having acquired one or two languages (German or Russian), had formed a sort of ethnic entity that overarched the countries of Europe, the new pressures of assimilation no longer left any room for this national Jewish distinctiveness. In every new nation-state Jews were now obliged to adjust to the new order of things—regime, language, culture, and economics. With the disappearance of the large empires of Russia and Austria-Hungary, lost was the former vista of spaciousness, of wide horizons; every Jewish community concentrated henceforward on its own needs, measuring Jewish welfare in the light of its own particular needs.

Left alone on guard over the nation's overall welfare in its newly established states of dispersion stood the Zionist movement and several transnational Jewish organizations. Jewish national sentiments also grew, thanks to the national movements, and especially thanks to the Jewish high schools, like ours. Generally, however, the entire structure of Jewish reality weakened progressively.

DR. MORDECHAI (MARKUS) ZE'EV BRAUDE, FOUNDER OF THE HEBREW HIGH SCHOOL

Our high school was founded by the Association for the Establishment of Hebrew High Schools in Poland under the initiative and leadership of Dr. Braude (pronunciation of the name was German, even though the name originated in the Galician town of Brody, or in Hungary). This enterprising public figure deserves to be more fully recognized[2] for his work and great achievements in the field of Jewish education and politics in Poland, especially for his overall Zionist orientation.

Dr. Braude (1869–1949) came to us from Galicia, scion of a distinguished rabbinic family. His great-grandfather was R. Jacob Meshulam Orenstein, *Av Bet Din* (presiding judge in a rabbinical court) in Lvov, author of a book of responsa titled *Yeshu'ot Ya'akov*, upon whom the *maskil* Yiẓḥak Erter (1792–1851) poured his ridicule in one of his well-known satirical parodies. Mordekhai Ze'ev Braude parted ways with his strictly traditional ancestors, although he did not distance himself from them and from their vocation. He too was ordained a rabbi, albeit in the liberal Orthodox Berlin Rabbinical Seminary, and completed his studies in philosophy at the University of Freiburg. He was thus a *Doktor Rabbiner*, a "progressive rabbi," the new type of rabbi-educator, preacher, and public spokesperson who began to make his appearance before World War I in East European Jewish communities, first in the Polish provinces under Austrian and

Dr. Markus Braude, 1926, charcoal drawing by Marek Szwarc (Schwartz)

Prussian rule, later also in Congress Poland. Braude had been a Zionist from youth—he was a delegate in the first Zionist congress in Basel in 1897, later in all subsequent Zionist congresses, and wherever he resided he took part in Zionist activity. At first, in 1900, he served as a rabbi-preacher in the synagogue of the "Progressives" in Stanislawow, Galicia, where he coordinated Zionist activities for the provinces of Galicia and Bukovina. Thanks to his efforts and lobbying, Zionist representatives entered the Austrian parliament in 1907—an achievement that surprised and excited the Jewish public.

As a young rabbi and educator—lively, bold, endowed with a creative imagination, he arrived in Lodz in 1909 to take the position of spiritual leader of the Progressive (Reform) congregation in the sumptuous new synagogue, completed just two decades before his arrival. He quickly acquired a prominent position, even though he did not hesitate to challenge both the Orthodox, who could not accept a rabbi of this new type, and the upper-class community of acculturated Jews. Many of the latter, Jewish industrialists and traders, especially their educated young, swarmed to hear his style of prayer and sermon in a setting that was a great novelty in our town: a setting of beauty, decorum, excellent cantors, order and quiet, and instructive, pleasing words. Braude at first preached in German, and later switched to Polish. He was a bright, combative, energetic, and persuasive speaker, delivering well-constructed addresses, at times tending to florid oratory. His approach to the Jewish world was preservation of tradition, adaptation to the environment, and achievement of success through one's own honest endeavors—in the spirit of "historical Judaism" as propounded at the Breslau Jewish Theological Seminary (similar to Conservative Judaism in the United States). On Saturdays and other occasions, I heard his fascinating speeches on matters of the day in which he was well versed, and which he would combine—quite artistically—with the explication of the weekly Torah portion and Talmudic exegesis. He was not in the habit of writing down his sermons. I believe that after his death not even a single sermon was found among his papers, only fragmentary memoirs, incomplete chapters, which he barely managed to jot down at the end of his life.

Aḥad Ha'am, in his article "National Education"—which he first presented as a lecture in Russian in 1902, and then wrote in Hebrew in 1907—outlined his ideas for the desirable profile of a Jewish school. Among other things, he expressed this belief: "The burning question, the one that bores into the very depths of our national life, will not be resolvable except by the people as a whole, and the people will resolve it in the near future, more or less in accordance with our views. This cannot be doubted because the people's instinct for the will to live will demand this solution." Dr. Braude, although an enthusiastic Herzlean, was a fervent reader of Aḥad Ha'am and accepted his views on the development of the Judaic spirit (Herzl had nothing to offer in this sphere). He certainly saw himself as a sort of emissary of that "instinct of the national will to live," which mandated action, most importantly through education of the young, on the road to a Jewish state. He indeed was just such a man of action, not merely a talker. In 1912, he founded a Jewish bilingual school in Lodz. This was a great novelty.

Jewish Zionist modernizing education at that time was still embodied mainly in the Reformed Ḥeder movement (begun in the 1890s), and this already showed considerable progress, but its programs and needs had many opponents. The Orthodox, as had been their custom for generations, sent their children to the traditional rabbinic *ḥeder* and *yeshiva*, where the old instructional methods prevailed. Only after World War I was a network of Orthodox schools founded—Ḥorev for boys, Beis Yaakov for girls—where a number of modest innovations were introduced. Braude's enterprise in Lodz was preceded by Hebrew kindergartens, such as the one founded by the poet Yiẓḥak

Katzenelson, as well as an elementary school for the lower classes. During the war, the Bund (anti-Zionist Marxists) and the Po'aley Ẓion (pro-Zionist Marxists) movements founded a number of Yiddish-language schools.

Modern Jewish education in Poland grew and spread only after World War I.[3] In the country's eastern provinces, whose borders were not yet recognized, a number of newly founded Hebrew language elementary and even high schools managed to function reasonably well. For diverse reasons—political and cultural—pertaining to the local populations in those regions, it was from there that the full Hebrew-curriculum education system spread all over Poland, through the Tarbut Association, which had been established in Russia immediately after the revolution of Spring 1917, and had moved to Poland in 1922. This association, truly a magnificent educational enterprise, realized through the tremendous efforts of parents, teachers, and principals, established a network of kindergartens and elementary schools in every *shtetl*, and numerous high schools and teachers' training seminaries. Tarbut institutions trained for Zionism: The Jewish people and the Land of Israel were at the heart of the curriculum and all educational activities. I have seen it claimed that about 60 percent of graduates of Tarbut elementary schools made *aliyah* to Israel.

Indeed, these schools fulfilled the dream of the bold champions of full Jewish education and culture in the diaspora. In his day, Ze'ev Jabotinsky stood at the head of these leaders. As mentioned in Chapter 3, he argued that what imprints itself on a child's soul is not specific national values, but rather the *language* in which the child acquires the images and concepts of its world. His sharp slogan: "In national education, language is the core, and content is the shell," gained attentive ears.

This, however, was not the view of Aḥad Ha'am and his adherents, such as Dr. Braude. They took into account, more realistically, both pedagogical concerns and pragmatic factors, or, if you wish—opportunistic arguments. I already mentioned that the government shortchanged schools whose language of instruction was that of one of the minorities and that their graduates could enter universities only with great difficulties, first taking external examinations, and then too, only a select handful gained admission. For this reason, the purpose of Dr. Braude's schools (in 1921 the Girls' Hebrew High School was founded, and a second high school for boys) was, in the words of the school's internal charter, "to give the students a general secondary education according to the government's curriculum for state high schools, as well as a Hebrew education and knowledge of Judaism, suitable to high school level."

After World War I, Braude's enterprise grew at an astounding rate. In 1928, there were already some thirty bilingual high schools, most founded by Braude, numbering more than 6,000 students. Additional high schools with similar Zionist leanings were founded, especially in the former Russian-held territories of Poland. The association founded by Braude also established elementary and vocational schools. He succeeded in surrounding himself with education promoters-functionaries, parents' committees, and, above all, with outstanding teachers and principals. His prestige and influence further increased when he was elected to the Polish Senate—a Jewish Senator, one of the very few from among the multitudes of Jews in Poland. I believe that for some years he was the only Jewish Senator from Lodz.[4] With good reason, it was said of him, "Torah and greatness in one place, *saifa vesafra*" ("sword and book", i.e., action and learning), and similar flowery epithets, which, in this case, really did apply to the man and his actions.

On occasion, we students would catch a glimpse of him as he jumped briskly out of the carriage that brought him to the street of the high schools, where Dr. Arie Tartakower, the nimble young secretary of the Association for the Foundation of Hebrew High Schools, was already expecting him. The principals of the two boys' schools would be standing at attention next to him, ready to accompany him on his round. As he was rather heavy, with a potbelly preceding him, we boys would giggle at the sight of his descent from the carriage. He was only in his late fifties at the time. Notwithstanding his corpulence, he would step with great agility, quick and full of life. In walking, the burden of his years and responsibilities seemed to fall away from him and he would joke and relate anecdotes of his student days. From him we learned the student anthem *Gaudeamus igitur*, which he would sing to us with the gusto of youth, or nostalgia for it. Truth be told, we also made a little fun of his Hebrew, which he spoke in a strange mix of Ashkenazi and Sephardi accents.

His class visits always commanded attention. His questions were surprising in their acuity, and there was always something to learn from him. Our class already knew his little weakness: He was delighted when, in the Hebrew Literature lesson, mention was made of that great-grandfather, R. Jacob Orenstein, who had been the scourge of the "Enlightened," the *maskilim*, and upon whom Yiẓḥak Erter the *maskil* had wished to take his revenge. He spoke of the *maskilim* with no rancor, but also without great appreciation. We had already heard his sermon-speeches a number of times when he addressed the school at the opening of the academic year or at school celebrations, always reasonable, level-headed, always with something new to say. In the elegant Reform

Synagogue on Spacerowa Street (which the Nazis later burned down), as in our school, we could patently see his efforts to raise the status of Poland's Jews in general, and the condition of Jewish education in particular. From time to time, we also read one of his speeches in the Polish Senate. Indeed, we knew that we were not without a leader.

I need hardly say that in my eyes Dr. Braude was a superlative model of a modern rabbi, knowledgeable in Torah and engaged in worldly affairs. I confess that during my first years of high school, after I had just left the *ḥeder* and its total Ḥasidic influence, biblical and Talmudic texts were alien to me in their original languages, and still more so in Polish translation from the pulpit of the Reform Synagogue. I was used to hearing them only in Yiddish. Is it possible to feel close to the spirit of a text in a foreign language, which happens also to be the language of the street? In fact, the question was whether the ancient texts were amenable to modern translation, or transposition, to revivification and fructification in new forms of thought and expression. After all, even the modern Hebrew which we spoke had already considerably changed Rabbinic conceptions. I therefore realized that it was indeed possible to transfer from the past to the present, to pour from an old vessel into a new one, without diminishing the uniqueness of either, even if something of their full primal essence is lost. Moreover, only by its rebirth in the present does the tradition of the past regain life—and the "perennial fund," the *keren kayemet,* yields its ever-new fruit.

I got close to Dr. Braude while still a student in Lodz. My teachers tweaked his ear regarding me, especially because of my knowledge in Jewish subjects; altogether, my status in the class drew his attention. When I decided to further my studies in the Jewish Theological Seminary in Breslau, that is, to follow his example, he drew me even closer. In 1928, his initiative led to the opening in Warsaw of the Institute for Jewish Studies, aimed at training rabbis and especially high school teachers and public functionaries in the spirit of the new age, with Hebrew as the chief language of instruction. However, Dr. Braude did not try to persuade me to enroll in that Institute. He knew I had decided to study in Germany.

I visited him in his home a number of times, where we would sit in his large library discussing various matters. I also visited him when I returned to Lodz during my student years in Germany. In November 1929, he joined us in Breslau for the celebration of the 75th anniversary of the founding of the Jewish Theological Seminary. In Lodz, prior to the outbreak of World War II, he still had the pleasure of inaugurating the new elegant, multi-storied building, where the two boys' high schools were to be lodged together.

With great difficulty he managed to escape from Poland a few weeks after the Nazi occupation, with his wife Natalia (Martin Buber's sister, she too a teacher in the high school). In 1940, at the age of 70, a man of great accomplishments and—as a witness to the early stage of the destruction—of much sorrow, he arrived in Ereẓ Israel. I would occasionally meet him on Mt. Carmel in Haifa. He lived another ten years, and not idly. He was busy with the Rescue Committee of the Jewish Agency and with educational matters, but it was obvious that he was in deep melancholy. The ship, whose captain he had been, was a wreck. In retrospect, one can say that it had been merely a flimsy raft, loaded with Jews bobbing on treacherous waters. Its only security lay in agreements promising to safeguard minority rights and in whatever organizational power a minority could muster. What was the strength of reams of paper and of minority endurance in a period of violent nationalism? Dr. Braude and his colleagues fought courageously and wisely. He produced many students, and multitudes of Jews in Poland uttered his name in affection and admiration, but most of them perished.

I do not know why—maybe due to a sense of failure, maybe because he himself had been a preacher-eulogist for many years—but in his will he forbade all eulogies for a period of three years. Not a word of eulogy! At the end of the three years, Mrs. Braude asked me to say a few words over his grave in the cemetery near the Haifa beach. These words were printed in 1953 in *Hed ha-Ḥinukh*, the organ of educators in Israel—reflections on a fraction of the deeds of a man of true Jewish nobility, whose acts were so interwoven in the lives of his students and admirers.

His consolation in his last years was the *Judenstaat*, Herzl's State of the Jews, for whose establishment he had campaigned since Herzl's day. He lived to see the great moments of its creation, its early years of taking root, and the ingathering of many immigrants. His grief was that most of Poland's Jews whose representative he had been did not reach safety in the state that was designed to deliver them from the woe of exile.

CHAPTER 11
My Teachers

A day in school: Hebrew literature takes on existential problems, Physics teaches methodology and philosophy, Jewish history is taught by first-rate scholars, Polish literature raises mixed feelings, Civics shows up the gulf between political promise and reality, and nothing is livelier than Latin.

FIRST PERIOD: HEBREW LITERATURE—DR. NATHAN ECK

I knew it was better to get to school early, better to prepare for the lessons at home, better to go over them again in the few remaining minutes before the bell rang, but for some reason I was never able to arrive early nor prepare my homework with requisite attention. At that time I was preoccupied with many matters that appeared to me to be most important, and doing homework was not one of them.

Fortunately, my teachers treated me with indulgence and gave me good grades in most subjects, even very good. They were not strict with me regarding trifles, even if they did not view them as trifling. In most subjects—even if I say so myself—I was the best student in the class, and an exemplary student in the entire school. I read a great deal, easily understood the principles as well as the fine points, discoursed with the authors we studied and with myself, and in the humanities I was certainly "above and beyond," as they say today, even without preparation. Thus, I was not worried about arriving at the last minute.

About thirty students sat in the senior high school class preparing for their matriculation exams. Most of my classmates came from affluent homes of industrialists and merchants—"modern" parents. A minority of us had Ḥasidic parents, strictly observant, and decidedly poor.

I would arrive running and sweaty just before the gate was locked and the bell rang as I entered the classroom. The room was heated and noisy with conversation. I had no time to join in, for Dr. Nathan Eck, short and energetic, strode into the room, a copy of Volume Four of *At the Crossroads* under his arm. We were about to complete our study of the essays of Aḥad Ha'am. Although

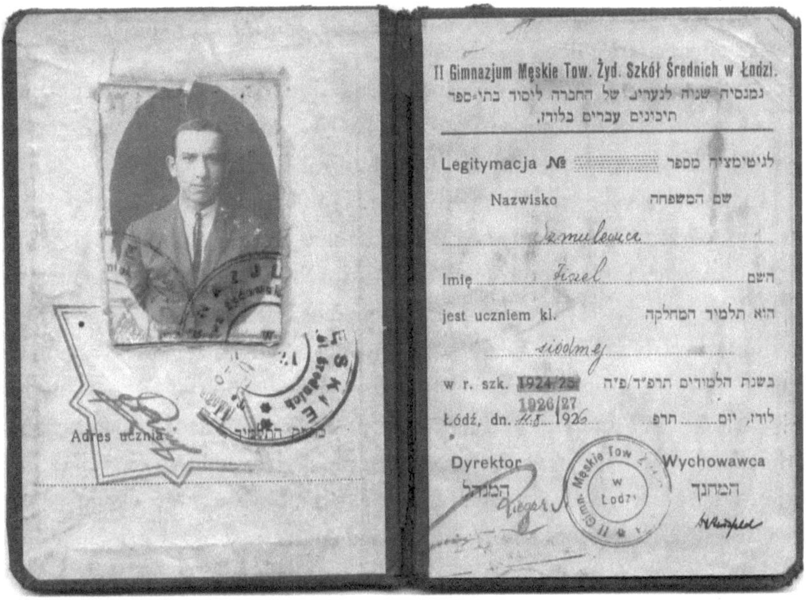

A student in the Hebrew gymnasia, aged 18

reading his essays was not easy for many of us, he always held our interest. Aḥad Ha'am—so we learned—was very instrumental in awakening Jewish national activism. We marveled at his integrity, at the logic of his arguments and the lucidity of his language, and at his courage in confrontations with Herzl and the "political" Zionists. In his essay, "Slavery within Freedom," we felt vindicated reading that most Jews in the West, despite having attained civic rights, remained in spiritual slavery, uncertain of their power and always apprehensive "like slaves who have entered the palace of their masters" lest the latter kick them out. Hence their self-abnegation and groveling before the Gentiles. I liked his characterization of the "People of the Book" as a slave to the book, a people whose soul had departed from its body and ensconced itself completely into the written words, as opposed to a "Literary People." His call for a "resurrection of hearts" echoed in our own hearts. The essay "Moses" had aroused our admiration when we studied it with Mr. Jonah Braverman. We also heard of the Benei Moshe society established by Aḥad Ha'am—a select sect of Ḥovevei Zion[1] who were to look to Moses as their model. But now, in the senior class, our teacher Dr. Eck brought us an essay by Shmuel Tchernowitz,[2] published, if I recall correctly, in the anthology *Sifrut* (edited by F. Lachower) that painted a more critical picture, both of Aḥad Ha'am's concept of the prophet Moses, and of the

Benei Moshe society and the relations among its members who were supposed to be an elite group, guided in all their activities by the national purpose and by a vision of absolute justice. Eck also succeeded in sowing doubt in our minds regarding several of Aḥad Ha'am's other ideas—primarily in respect to his view of Ereẓ Israel as a spiritual center, spiritual only.

In the same lesson we dealt with Aḥad Ha'am's essay "Negation of the Diaspora." We already knew that Aḥad Ha'am denied the possibility of our continued existence in the diaspora once the bastion of religion was destroyed. We could no longer escape the impact of foreign cultures that sweep away, swallow up, and assimilate our national identity. The end to our existence as a nation was nearing. This situation—the essayist writes—gave rise to the camp of "nationalists," headed by Simon Dubnow, who proposed a solution for Jewish existence in the diaspora: Jewish autonomy in our countries of residence. We did not read Dubnow's writings, as at that time very little of his work, written in Russian, had been published in either Hebrew or Polish.[3] We learned of his principal thesis from the essay by Aḥad Ha'am, and I cannot say that it pleased us.

Speaking for many of us, Aḥad Ha'am advocated "negation of the diaspora" in the sense of negation of the subjugation imposed by the exile and all

Aḥad Ha'am ("One of the People," pen name of Asher Ginzberg, 1856–1927)

that it entailed in both matter and spirit—a lamb among wolves, in danger of destruction or assimilation. Negation of the diaspora, Aḥad Ha'am teaches, is the denial of any possibility of our future national existence in the diaspora. However, Aḥad Ha'am was also unhappy with the Zionist claim that we would be able to continue our national existence only in Ereẓ Israel, namely that whoever wants to assimilate among the Gentiles, so be it, but those who cannot or do not want to assimilate, will go to the "Jewish State." This is an extremist theory, the author claims, and the Jewish people will not "buy" it. Just as the Jewish people have not heeded the promoters of assimilation who wish to hasten the end, it has also not embraced "political" Zionism. "The will for national survival" counsels the people that although the diaspora is bitter, in order to live we need to, and we can, live in the diaspora. End of the diaspora is a hope only for the End of Days. The question is how to build a new bastion that will replace the collapsed religion. Aḥad Ha'am's reply: a spiritual center in Ereẓ Israel. Dubnow replied: national autonomy in the diaspora, in which we will safeguard our rights, and which will allow our people normal conditions of development, even if only as a minority among the nations. Autonomy will permit education based on Judaism. Aḥad Ha'am rebuts Dubnow's arguments: The nations will not recognize the historical right of a foreign people to live its own national life in countries, which, from its very first arrival among them, were never considered to be its national home, not even in its own view.

The entire essay was most pertinent. Already then opinions divided on the four solutions presented: (a) assimilation; (b) "Herzlean" ("political") Zionism; (c) "autonomy" in the countries of residence as advocated by Dubnow and the proletarian party (the "Folkists") and others; and (d) Aḥad Ha'am's thesis of a spiritual center in Ereẓ Israel. At that time, after the failure of the fourth *aliyah,* he held views close to those of Chaim Weizmann as well as to those of a great part of the workers' movement in Ereẓ Israel, albeit with a different emphasis. We were nearing new elections to the Sejm and the Senate, the parties had already mobilized their masses, and debates flew high. The debate heated up in the classroom as well. Moshe Schoenfeld[4] viewed favorably the idea of autonomy, if only it were possible to obtain and maintain it in Poland. A powerful debater in command of an excellent Hebrew style, Moshe studied Talmud every day with his scholarly father, a graduate of a Lithuanian yeshiva. I too sometimes had the privilege of taking part in these studies. He was seconded by Aharon Savitzky (later Saviv, educator, author and researcher, employed by the Israel Ministry of

Education): Our lives in the diaspora must be ameliorated and our foundation broadened to the greatest extent possible; we should fight for minority rights and simultaneously seek the complete solution beyond the confines of the diaspora.

Shmuel Pacanowski (later Gavish, a leader of the Kibbutz Movement and the Mapai Labor Party), at the time a counselor in the Gordonia youth movement being organized in those years in Lodz, differed. He leaned more to the views of Aḥad Ha'am, except that instead of spirituality he sought to find in the renewed Ereẓ Israel people tilling their own land, working in crafts and industry and building a new order of society in the spirit of the *kvuẓah* (an earlier, smaller version of the kibbutz). He was joined by Ozer Obzhensky[5] (in time Ḥuldai—a founder of Kvuẓat Ḥulda). Morgenstern, whom we called the "youngster" (he really was the youngest of the group, an adolescent whose talents matured precociously and who later became a doctor in the large Poznansky Jewish Hospital and perished in the Holocaust) was in favor of extensive, political, Herzlean and Revisionist Zionism.

The very alert orchestrator of this debate was our teacher, Eck (in time Ekron, a Holocaust researcher in Israel), who arrived in Lodz from Vienna in 1924, replacing Shlomo Szpan,[6] who had left for Ereẓ Israel. He too was from Galicia. Unlike our other teachers, he was educated in law and political science. I believe that in Vienna he also attended the famed Hebrew Pedagogical Institute of Rabbi Zvi Pereẓ Chajes, and I know that he was the Rabbi's secretary. Eck was well versed in subjects relating to the Jewish people and the new Hebrew literature, particularly its academic aspects. He was folksy, informal, and lacking affectation. His speech was spiced with popular sayings, proverbs, and juicy Yiddish words. He was sharp and energetic, an excellent journalist in Hebrew, Yiddish, and Polish. His essays were always direct and accurate and his arguments well-ordered, with surprising innovative angles. His Hebrew style was businesslike, an easy Hebrew, not detached from the sources, but seemingly just flitting above them.

Before me is his book, *Wandering on the Roads of Death,*[7] describing his three escapes from the Nazis, and I quote a passage from the opening chapter as an example of his style. After informing the reader that these words were written shortly after the occurrence of the events, he continues: "This fact adds to their documentary importance, for human memory is usually not a 'lined cistern' (i.e., hermetically sealed), but rather a broken vessel that loses a great deal in the course of time! And whatever it doesn't lose, it 'processes', changes and interprets—not consciously, but in accordance with the spirit of the changing times." A clear and elegant statement, pertinent to my own memoir as well.

In the classroom he was cordial, avoided excessive fervor, did not rebuke the students, but neither did he excite them much. He imparted a sort of sobriety, or composure. On the other hand, we saw him as a man burdened by his occupation, diluting his strength with essays on diverse and sundry matters, and troubled by no small degree of anxiety. The discipline in his class was not exemplary. His speech consisted of volley after volley of clear, rapid sentences, which would suddenly cease, followed by a sort of embarrassed mumbling, which he then managed to overcome by firing off a new volley. It was apparent that he swallowed and repressed a great deal before succeeding in establishing this composed image of himself. When angry with the class, he would sit on the podium, take out a sheet of paper and fill it rapidly with his writing.

His affinity to poetry was "proprietary." He was interested in its content, in the public, human, and national "message" it contained. When we read with him the poems of Bialik and Tchernichovsky, or of Zalman Shneur and Ya'akov Cahan (previously a teacher in the First Boys' Hebrew Gymnasia), he did not dwell on their aesthetic values. In those days I was devoted to poetry, and succeeded in having some poems published in magazines for children and youth, and even the editor of the weekly *Ha-olam*, Moshe Kleinman, accepted my poems for publication (published at the end of that school year). Eck did not relate to my poems, and perhaps I did not show them to him, fearful of a frosty reception. Once he warned us against *meliẓa*, flowery language: He who pitches his words higher and higher is called a *meliẓ* (advocate, supporter), while he who bends them downward is called a *leẓ* (buffoon), and it would be best to avoid both, and write a Hebrew sentence that is both simple and correct. I recall that once during a test on Aḥad Ha'am I explained the words of the great thinker in one of his essays without including any comments of my own, which displeased me because I so wanted to add a personal touch. Eck gave me a grade of "Very Good." That was the point: not to add, nor to detract, but to understand the text thoroughly.

It was a pleasure to listen to his explanations on matters close to his heart, on subjects that he expounded because he wished to, not forced upon him by the syllabus. He did not like the *haskalah* literature. Mendele, in his opinion, was not the portrayer of the Jewish people. He depicts defects, base acts of degradation and humiliation. Bialik was too much the poet of the diaspora; he shone as a great artist only in his nature poems. Eck viewed Hebrew literature as a system of works forming a secular Hebrew culture, which in time would nurture the soul, just as formerly the sacred culture had done, without disconnecting it from the lofty and the noble in our long history of spiritual creativity. Its mission is to bring the present generations closer to the spiritual fountainheads that had been plugged up by a unilateral rabbinic culture, by a religiosity imprisoning the past in a perpetual present, a religiosity stuck in the past only. Literature needs to renew for us the full and broad world of sights and sounds and human pleasures. We have been intimidated by the "shadows of life," of which Feierberg[8] had spoken, and need now to come out into the broad daylight of life.

It seemed to me then that not even an iota of poetry clung to Dr. Eck. However, I did learn to appreciate him for his purity of expression, so simple and to the point, which resisted any ornate embellishment or lyrical expression of emotion. He was confident of his assertions, needing no assistance from flowery language, and intolerant of murkiness. Rather, he cut and ruled one way or another, saw every argument set before him clearly and sharply, and yet was able to embrace a great variety of opinions. His homey generosity whispered in his ear that arguments that differed from his own also had the right to exist. In the books and essays he published in Israel after the Holocaust I saw that he had softened a great deal. I realized that he also knew how to tell a story such as in *Wandering on the Roads of Death,* wherein he related his riveting experiences in tangible details and scenes. Having twice escaped certain death, he was deported by the Nazis with his wife and daughter to a detention compound in Vittel, a town in eastern France, thanks to a forged Paraguayan passport which earned him a brief reprieve from deportation to a death camp. At Vittel he was incarcerated for several months together with Yiẓḥak Katzenelson. When deported from there to Auschwitz, he managed to jump off the train and survived. In Paris, he published the newspaper of the Labor Movement and upon arrival in Israel, began to work at Yad Vashem, where he wrote his comprehensive book on the Holocaust.[9] He passed away at a ripe old age on 22 February, 1982 in Tel-Aviv.

The bell rang and Eck only had time to say that it was difficult to see today how a permanent spiritual center for nationhood was possible, when most of the Jewish people were not living in their own land. However, he did concede to Aḥad Ha'am that if one did not believe in miracles, it was hard to see how to get rid of the diaspora. The Hebrew literature lesson ended on this skeptical note, unsatisfactorily for the hungry soul. The solutions were not convincing and those that were did not elate the spirit or relieve its thirst. A great benefit of Eck's lessons was that he would inform us of what was happening in Hebrew literature with news of contemporary authors and books.

PHYSICS AND SCIENTIFIC FAITH—DR. EMANUEL ANISFELD

Only a few minutes remained for me to glance at the physics textbook and at the copybook of my neighbor, Stashek Platau (Shlomo Platau, later an engineer at the Tel Aviv Municipality), who from early youth began to focus on math and physics. We were studying solids, fluids, and gases—regrettably without a lab, although in truth thermodynamics is largely based on abstract thinking. Still, my classmates and I, who grew up in an atmosphere of verbal and abstract education, felt the absence of observation of nature or of lab experiments.

I had barely managed to copy a few formulas, when Dr. Emanuel Anisfeld entered in calm, measured steps. He had recently joined us from Cracow, where he had completed his studies in math and physics. His dissertation, however, was on the philosophy of the exact sciences—on the theory of scientific hypotheses, actually—a philosophical inquiry into the limits of our trust in science, which, ever since Galileo, seeks to master nature through its mathematization.

Anisfeld had no problems with discipline in his lessons. He had perfect mastery of both the material and the students. Whereas Eck would often enter class without having prepared for the lesson, Anisfeld always had notes to guide him as he progressed, step by step, until he reached his precisely calculated end point. Indeed, we advanced at a rapid pace.

Although the syllabus was concentrated and challenging, Anisfeld was able to inject into it a sort of entertaining elegance. The subject matter was most informative, perhaps thanks to Einstein's relativity theory that Anisfeld introduced to our class. There are no absolutes, everything is relative, time and place, top and bottom. The physicist-scientist who examines the materials of the world is not only their observer, he also affects them. Anisfeld thus made physics more human and personalized for us.

The transformation of materials was discussed: Solids become volatile, liquids vaporize, gases turn into liquid—a vast movement of abundant energy that assumes and changes form. The laws of thermodynamics which we learned in that lesson were fascinating, and even offered moral instruction. The first of them formulated the principle of energy conservation. In every isolated system, that is—when heat does not escape or enter—the overall energy will remain constant. Every system that transforms heat energy into the kinetic energy of a moving mechanism is a heat engine. However, one cannot change heat into work, that is, into energy, without establishing a difference between the heat absorbed by the system and the heat emitted by it. As energy is transferred or transformed, more of it is lost, and the more disordered events are, the greater the degeneration of the system. This is the second law of thermodynamics. The contingency in nature causes the rupture of order, or of the system—and that is entropy.

Anisfeld took out a pack of cards. We had not heard that he played cards, so realized that he meant them for making a point. One can see there is only one way to determine perfect order in cards when you begin with the ace of clubs and continue according to the same principle until you reach the last card, with each card in its exact assigned order in the pack. On the other hand, there are endless ways of arranging the cards randomly. There is one path to the truth, the teacher added, and many paths to falsehood.

The second law of thermodynamics was scary. Order degenerates when no energy is introduced into a system, i.e., a system returns to chaos when energy diminishes. On the other hand, work injects energy, introduces order, conserves it and increases it. A system is easy to destroy, that is, it is easy to diminish order and difficult to establish order. That, if you like, was the moral lesson derived from the physical processes, according to Dr. Anisfeld.

Since Anisfeld was also class "educator,"[10] we would meet with him in the afternoon for informal conversation. We would quickly wrap up routine class business to listen to him talk about reality in a constant process of becoming, in ever-changing creative processes. Science establishes boundaries in order to establish the order and permanence of lawful unity. Since life is a fount of ceaseless creation, conceptual orders are neither absolute nor permanent. In brief, instead of ostensibly absolute and permanent laws bestowed from heaven above, what we should recognize is the human person who believes that true knowledge is within the bounds of possibility; by virtue of this belief, man may establish rules, which should be acknowledged to be nothing more than hypotheses. The key element is human creativity. No faith can guarantee that it has found absolute truth; faith is, in effect, no more than an exploration and a quest. Its enemies are skepticism and nihilism.

The teacher's words got through to us, more or less, and surprised us. Although he brought us close to his subject and even to methods of philosophical thinking that went beyond his subject matter, he himself remained distant. Thin lipped, always concentrated and serious, engaged in a dialectic with the world concerning the nature of human cognition, he exuded a chilly aura. It was rumored that during World War I he had been in Russian captivity and had spent a number of years in the frozen plains of Siberia where he must have witnessed many horrors. It seemed that a recalcitrant, solid bitterness had settled deep within him, which he could not dissolve, even in the relaxed atmosphere of our school. He, who so intelligently explained the power of faith, was by nature doubting and suspicious, as though he himself had been targeted by those very enemies of scientific faith of whom he spoke.

To my surprise, about a year after my graduation, Dr. Anisfeld showed me his just published (in Cracow) dissertation, written of course in Polish. Its title was approximately this: *Introduction to the Philosophical Grounding of a Believer*, a strange title for the work of a physicist and mathematician who occupied himself with the methodology of the exact sciences. It was, in fact, a brochure of only about seventy pages, but chock full of information and ideas. The author hardly mentioned names of other thinkers and scientists, and I do not recall that he cited other philosophers, that is, he did not direct the reader to known sources of orientation. Rather, he presented arguments originating from his own thought, crystallized and condensed, if not downright compressed, on which he wished to endow validity by virtue of his own assertions without reliance on external sources.

I did not understand everything, and when I reread the work I grasped only the general direction of his thoughts. Anisfeld asked me to try to translate his book into Hebrew. Someone else would correct the manuscript, if needed. I was surprised at the request and wish for his essay to appear in the Hebrew language, which, at that time, was very poor in systematic philosophical writings. Philosophy instruction had not yet begun at the newly established Hebrew University in Jerusalem. It was only at that period that Hugo Bergmann's[11] first philosophy book in Hebrew (on Kant, 1927) appeared. Even after a year of philosophy study at the University of Breslau I was not prepared for such a task. I remember sitting down to translate six-seven pages of Anisfeld's work. I found it very difficult and returned the brochure to him, dissatisfied with my work. I was also pressed for time, since I was about to wind up my stay in Lodz and return to Breslau. However, I was touched by his faith in the value of Hebrew literature and in the plausibility that Hebrew readers would be in need of philosophical inquiry and would find interest in his composition.

I have already mentioned the essence of his inquiry. As far as I recall, and based on what I later read in a critical article by Benzion Rappaport[12] in the Hebrew monthly journal *Ha-Sneh* (1929), Anisfeld courageously, even aggressively, explained that all scientific knowledge is a process of birth and renewal, both in its fundamentals and in its laws, and not only in its particulars. Thus, no science is complete and certain, as its assumptions might change from truths to falsehoods in the light of new discoveries. Science builds itself as it develops. Moreover, what we call truths or ideas are not a reality independent of the observing individual. In Rappaport's critique I found this sharply formulated citation from Anisfeld's book: "We must learn to give up on the absoluteness of knowledge, as we have learned to give up on knowledge of the absolute."

It was clear to me already then that Anisfeld was protesting against mechanistic-positivistic philosophy, and that he accepted Henri Bergson's theory on the creative formation of all things through the energy of life. Rappaport, who in those years wrote about philosophy in Hebrew and was, apparently, a friend of Anisfeld in Cracow, praised the book for dealing forthrightly with important problems, and for containing innovations, even if the conclusions it reached were already known in contemporary philosophy. "There is great interest in the quandaries of a thinking person who struggles with problems independently." This is what we sensed in class: "the quandaries of a thinking person." However, it puzzled me that even though he spoke a great deal about openness to argument, about coming into being and renewal, about the power of the creative personality, which opens itself to the world, he was an introverted man. Often his lips parted as though he were about to say something, but for some reason he would clam up. In school, there was whisper of a disappointed love affair or maybe he lacked colleagues for discussion. Surely he must always have longed for situations of genuine openness, but for some reason it was difficult for him to gain such moments and this tormented him.

Eventually, I found out that his main thesis, namely, that science proposes hypotheses, and is a matter of faith, which must be reconfirmed each time anew, was close to Karl Popper's thesis that theory is not the discovery of a fixed and eternal truth about reality, but a hypothesis ("faith" in Anisfeld's language) that is valid only temporarily when it responds to the hitherto known facts, until a new hypothesis explains it better. There is no eternal proof, theories are disproven and rejected. Moreover, that which cannot be disproven belongs to the realm of political ideology, or to poetry. Even though Popper's first book *The Logic of Scientific Discovery* appeared (in German) only in 1934, the two authors were clearly of one generation, both animated by the same critical fervor. They both agreed about the destructiveness of dogmatism on the one hand and of doubt and nihilism on the other.

In Dr. Eck's aforementioned book *Wandering on the Roads of Death,*[13] I found a description of a meeting between our two teachers during the

Holocaust. In the town of Częstochowa, where Anisfeld had become director of a Hebrew gymnasia similar to ours:

> We had not seen each other for a number of years. Now, as we met, we were happy to be together. We spoke of various topics close to our hearts—until we got to the subject of Ereẓ Israel. 'For some years, I have had the intention of making *aliyah*,' Dr. Anisfeld told me, 'but I delayed all this time because I did not want to arrive there empty-handed; I will go there immediately after the war. I will wait no longer.' I did not wish to ask with what might his hands be fuller after the war than they had been before it but he read my thoughts with no words exchanged. He went to his closet, rummaged about for a moment, finally brought out a large package wrapped up in yellow paper, and said: 'This is what I plan to travel to Ereẓ Israel with.' He began to untie the package slowly, as was his habit. Indeed, I was curious to see what treasure it contained. It turned out that he was holding in his hand a thick manuscript, a composition of his philosophy. That was the contribution that he planned to bring to Ereẓ Israel.

His dream never materialized. Dr. Anisfeld was shot by the Nazis in Częstochowa.

Again, the school bell rang. While some of my classmates truly excelled in the thermodynamics lesson, I was not among them. My afternoon hours in those years were taken up with private tutoring and other occupations, and I did not invest energy in lessons that required more intense preparation. Even though I was attracted to the ideal objects of mathematics, to abstract thought unfettered by reality, and to postulates of unity and lawfulness in physics, especially to the moral instruction derived from the laws of thermodynamics, these ceased to be the subjects that I tutored. For this reason, I also had no time to acquire them for myself properly. Nonetheless, I did well in the baccalaureate exam, although much less so than in the humanities subjects.

There was a short break. For a number of years I was head of my class committee, and in my final year I was elected as head of the student council for the entire school. Student social life was lively and varied, and many of the council's activities were carried out by a subcommittee: lectures and balls, mutual aid, class newspapers, and drama performances. One needed to consult, give instructions, execute tasks, speak to students from other classes, confer with teachers and the principal. Generally, I was very busy during the breaks. I was also about to hand over my role in the council to a student from a lower class.

JEWISH HISTORY—DR. PHILIP (FILIP) FRIEDMAN

I had two teachers for Jewish history in high school, and both were researchers who became famous thanks to their important writings. The first was Jacob Naftali Simḥoni (1884–1926), one of the greatest scholars of his generation. He came to Lodz by invitation of Dr. Braude during World War I. While in our city, he wrote comprehensive articles on Solomon Ibn Gabirol, which were published in installments in the quarterly *Ha-tekufah*. Here he also translated the writings of Josephus Flavius from Greek into Hebrew, composed a three-volume Hebrew textbook on the history of the Jewish people, and wrote several important articles, which spread his fame.

I see him before me, standing in front of the class with his hands clasped behind him and his back turned to the heated brick stove, lecturing to us about the Hasmonean era, without raising his voice, with no special intonation, in pure fluent Hebrew, not flowery, but neither very easy. He lectured without notes. His phenomenal memory was legendary. We were young, and he was not a very fascinating teacher, not for kids our age at any rate. A number of times I heard him lecture about the Second Temple period at People's Hall on Saturday afternoon and the great throng that attended, even in winter (and there was no heating there) drank in his words with profound emotion.

Simḥoni, renowned as a prodigy, an *'iluy*, and a great expert in all areas of the "Science of Judaism," was invited to take part in the editorship of the Jewish encyclopedia *Eshkol* in Berlin. After working there for only one year, he died suddenly in May 1926, only 42 years of age. Mourning descended upon the Hebrew-reading public and on scholars in Judaic studies. All the newspapers and journals in the Jewish world eulogized him in admiration and affection. I will not elaborate on him here, as I have written a comprehensive monograph on his life and work.[14]

Dr. Philip Friedman (1901–1960), the man invited to replace Simḥoni as teacher of Jewish history in our school, came into the class running, tall and agile, and immediately began talking in simple, colloquial Hebrew, quite different from Simḥoni's style. He specialized in modern East European Jewish history, especially in Poland. He had just recently graduated from the University of Vienna and from the Hebrew Pedagogical Institute in that city with a Doctor of Philosophy degree for his thesis on *The Jews of Galicia in their Struggle for Equal Rights* (printed in German in 1929). His teacher had been Salo Baron.[15] Friedman was my teacher for two or three years in the upper classes. We students discovered that within a short period he published numerous articles,

Historian Dr. Philip Friedman

long and short, in four languages: Hebrew, Polish, Yiddish, and German—an unstoppable torrent.

Philip Friedman (we never heard his Hebrew name) belonged to a group of young historians which arose in Poland after World War I, of whom the best known were Emanuel Ringelblum, Raphael Mahler, Bernard Dov Weinryb, and he, Friedman. The distinctive attributes of these new historians, as I see them now, were the following: (a) Emphasis on social and economic history: livelihoods, social stratification, economic competition, structure of the Jewish community and its internal conflicts. (b) Each of them deliberately chose a limited sphere of research in an area of regional and local history: one city, one community or area. In the narrow field to which they confined themselves, they introduced as many details as possible, with the aim of producing a full, accurate picture. (c) These historians gleaned from archives a multiplicity of data, in great accuracy and detail, without making a particular effort, as their predecessors had done, to reach general conclusions and to deduce comprehensively valid principles. Indeed they recoiled from generalizations. Eventually, however, they broke the boundaries which they had set themselves, and which had characterized their work at the beginning, especially Raphael Mahler.[16]

Friedman dealt largely with the minutiae of Jewish life in Galicia, where he was born and raised, and later—of the Jewish community in Lodz. As I saw him, he was a diligent man, a prolific writer, astounding in his output. His class lectures were dry—facts, dates. Like Simḥoni before him, he would read-dictate his notes from his blue notebook, which he later turned into textbooks. In our class he taught what he later published in a brochure titled *History of the Jews in the Modern Era from the French Revolution until the World War* (Lodz, 1934, in Hebrew). I do not have the brochure, and perhaps I never saw it; I know of it only from the bibliography he compiled of his writings.

To our regret, we had no Hebrew books on the history of the Jewish people in the modern era. Reading only the little that was available in Polish, our knowledge in modern Jewish history was feeble. Graetz's *History of the Jews from the Earliest Times to the Present Day*, reached only as far as the *Haskalah*, and dealt little with political and social history. A. S. Kamieniecki (Kamenetzky), the translator of Graetz's opus (after its first translation into Hebrew by Shaul Pinchas Rabbinowicz), lived in our town, but his translation had not yet been published. Dubnow's multi-volume *World History of the Jewish People* appeared in German only in 1925–29. In our work in the youth movements in those days we keenly felt the acute lack of books on modern Jewish history, on the history of Zionism and on the national movement generally.

I remember how he came to us all skin and bones, with a high forehead and large eyes expressive of wisdom and energy—the mien of a famished *matmid*. After two years his face became more rounded as he put on some flesh. Matrimony, together with a steady job and absorbing research pursuits, apparently contributed to his well-being. Viewed from the outside his life seemed to be one of contentment. His spirit, however, knew no rest. He was ceaselessly writing in a number of languages in daily newspapers and in scholarly journals, without too much attention to the aesthetics of his compositions, in any language. In 1935, he published in Polish his comprehensive *History of the Jews in Lodz from the Beginning of the Jewish Settlement until 1863*, a tome of about 400 dense pages. Chapters from this book were published during my high school days in the town's newspapers, in Yiddish, Polish, and German.

Shortly thereafter, in an article I published in *Davar*,[17] I opened in this grand style: "In a period of unbridled anti-Semitic rampaging in Poland and of Jewish economic impoverishment and spiritual collapse, we might perhaps find a measure of gratification and comfort in calling to mind Polish Jewry's era of glory and enterprise in the previous century, based on the only book to appear thus far about the second largest community in Poland, a major industrial center—a work recently published by Dr. Philip Friedman." After presenting the book's contents I commented that it should be of interest to every person who reflects on the development and fate of Polish Jewry. I expressed the hope that in the book's second volume, which was about to appear, the author would also deal with the community's spiritual character (because up to that moment he had dealt only with its economic-social development). I concluded with a comment which must have sounded a bit strange in those days: "One can only regret that this important research work, which has presented interesting historic material from primary sources and has subjected them to a scientific, wide-ranging and deeply knowledgeable examination, was not written in Hebrew … One would like to hope that the sequel of the monograph on Lodz will be presented to the Hebrew-reading public." Indeed, a strange comment for its time. What on earth? How many readers would this book have found had it been written in Hebrew in 1935? On the other hand, in retrospect, maybe it was not so strange after all. How many Polish-reading Jews could it have found after the Holocaust?

The sequel to that book did eventually appear, but it already dealt with the Lodz ghetto, with Rumkowski, the "false Messiah," and with others like him who deluded themselves into thinking that they would save lives by organizing the ghetto to work for the Nazis. Friedman fled to Lvov, hid in that city or its vicinity, and returned to Lodz after the war, there to research ghetto survivors and other witnesses. He proceeded to compose several important studies on the Holocaust period, on *Martyrs and Fighters: The Epic of the Warsaw Ghetto* (1954), on Auschwitz,[18] on the non-Jewish populace and its attitude to Jews in Poland, on hygienic conditions in the ghetto, and more.

Friedman's first study of the Holocaust, one of the first on this topic, was printed in 1946 in Polish and English by the Central Commission for the Investigation of German Crimes in Poland. Based on detailed economic and social findings that he collected and carefully examined, he described the situation of the Jews before the Holocaust and the unfolding of the extermination and its methods. He saw in the extermination of Poland's Jews the result of the Nazi plan to conquer Eastern Europe—requisite for solving the essential problem of German policy, as Hitler conceived it, namely, the need for *Lebensraum* for the expanding German people. To realize this plan, the "Third Reich" was planning also to murder millions of Slavs. However, Friedman did not minimize the unique character of the Holocaust, which he recognized as a unique catastrophe in our history in its scope and its execution: The Final Solution made use of rational scientific methods in order to develop the very same industrial processes and managerial techniques that had propelled European culture to the height of human achievement.

Friedman was also one of the pioneers who devised scientific tools for the study of the Holocaust: methodological instructions, guides, bibliographies. The last collection of Friedman's Holocaust studies appeared in English translation posthumously—*Roads to Extinction: Essays on the Holocaust* (1980). Down to his last days, he labored to discover details and summarize guidelines.

I do not recall what we studied with Friedman in that lesson, the third of the day. I believe we were still stuck in the nineteenth century due to a considerable lag in our studies. Friedman read out of his blue notebook. There was no discussion, no arguing with facts, dates, and statistics. I do not recall conclusions, earthshaking assumptions, or other basics that become stamped on memory. Only our classmate Yeshayahu Frishman (later an educator and school supervisor in Israel) was devoted to Friedman's method.

Recently when I returned to look at his writings, I realized that we judged him too harshly at the time. For besides the abundance of material that he would bring with great diligence and rigor by the sackful from printed sources, and especially from archives, he did in fact wish to uncover basic trends. In the history of Lodz, for example, he unveiled the clash between the liberal-capitalist orientation that championed free competition, and the feudal conservatism of the pre-capitalist era, which joined forces with the nationalistic movements. He also highlighted the differentiation that occurred during the nineteenth century in the social stratification of Lodz Jews, and of Polish Jews in general, as the urbanization process accelerated and economic opportunities broadened, especially after the Russian market opened to industrialists and traders from Congress Poland. From then on, a Jewish financial-industrial plutocracy came into being and with it a multitude of poor artisans and laborers. Friedman did try then to introduce these historic events into a framework of trends and laws that had a certain general validity.

However, as I said, in my youth Friedman's research orientation was not sufficiently clear to me. The truth is that he did not reach a more comprehensive synthesis of the details and the rules, and perhaps never intended to do so, as explained above. In this, he resembled his fellow historians of that generation. The Holocaust interrupted and put an end to his preoccupation with Polish Jewry of the nineteenth century, his chief contribution to historical research. With his great talent, energy and diligence, he turned his attention to the study of the terrible calamity—to understand what had happened and how it happened.

Remarkably, my three teachers described thus far and the three I will describe next, and many others like them in the parallel high schools, shared one salient biographical detail—they all came from Galicia. Intellectually, these young men and women, who settled first in pre-World War I Congress Poland, then in the new independent Polish state, came as a sort of spiritual-intellectual storm, which opened new horizons for Polish Jewry. They played a significant role in its educational institutions, newspaper editorial boards, public organizations, and in private employment. Polish Jewish historiography in the interwar period produced basic research works that presaged brilliant development. Young Galicia-born historians were imbued with a vision of renaissance. They had witnessed the destruction wrought upon Jewry by World War I, and they were troubled about the future. For this reason, each one, according to his lights, labored over buttressing its foundations—until the Nazis razed the whole house down to the very ground.[19]

THE ANCIENT CLASSICAL WORLD—DR. MOSHE FREILICH (MOJŻESZ FREJLICH)

The big recess after the third lesson brought me some respite. One could carry on calmly with the student council affairs, eat, and read the class paper, which hung on the wall, mostly in Hebrew, partly in Polish. However, we had to get out of the class to let in some fresh winter air through the windows.

After 25 minutes of this breather, the bell rang again and into the class strode Dr. Moshe Freilich, our teacher for Latin language and literature. He checked to see that we were all standing erect at our desks, not slouching, until he seated himself at the podium. He took his time (one's bearing is important!). He was a handsome, charming man, punctilious about his dress, polished and spotless, his black hair neatly combed, his facial features well chiseled. To all appearances, a picture of classical harmony.

He would enter the class as an actor on a stage, expecting applause. The histrionic aspect also characterized his lessons. We benefited from his talent and advice as stage director in the school festivities we organized and in plays that we put on. In all our school events, his word was decisive. It was he who discovered the theatrical talent of my classmate Israel Schumacher, who later became a famous comedian with his colleague Shimon Dzigan.

Freilich indeed exhibited many different faces, as I saw in class during the academic year and at the school's summer camps, which he directed. In each role, he played his part well, but from time to time there were hitches. He had days of discontent and irritation; at such times, the entire mantle of calm classical dignity, with its ornaments and frills, just slid off him. In these stormy hours he would fill the house with his scolding—unless he was enacting Jupiter hurling his thunder?

He too, like all our teachers, was still young—in his early thirties, but he had experienced the horrors of war in the Austrian army and, according to his account, had excelled in the campaigns against Italy and was proud of his officer rank. He, like Anisfeld, carried within him the horrific sights he had witnessed in the war, but his delicate charm and gentle poetic-dramatic spirit overcame, it seems, the hardness and bitterness. He loved beauty and would often talk to the class about works of art and poetry, its forms and meter, about the great artists, and on whatever interested him most at that moment. These special "bonuses" of information, stories and descriptions in all areas of humanistic studies that dropped into our lap from time to time, charmed and delighted us. During my last years in school his hobby was psychoanalysis and the interpretation of dreams, a subject on which he published several articles in the daily press and which he would frequently mention in class. One could not relate to Freilich with indifference: You either loved or hated him. I felt much attached to him. Although, at times, even I was intimidated and repelled by his outbursts.

Immoderatus, one who breaks the bounds—he would teach us—was most reprehensible in the eyes of all authors of the classical world. However, he himself was without bounds, alarmingly sensitive and vulnerable, an irritable, cantankerous man with a stinging tongue, born, it seemed, under the sign of Mars. Eventually, I got used to his moods and was not afraid of his sharp tongue. I knew that before long he would calm down, and, although he would not apologize, his sunshine would return.

Freilich was a well-rounded scholar. One day, he invited the high school students to a lecture about the prophet Amos and the beginnings of literary prophecy. To our surprise, we who were used to hearing from him only Polish and Latin, now heard him lecture in correct, beautiful Hebrew. Except for the teachers who taught their subjects in Hebrew, Freilich was the most knowledgeable and fluent in this language—an added advantage in his lessons.

Our school deemed it important to reinforce our Hebraic education via the general, secular curriculum we were studying in Polish. The lessons covering our national heritage should not stand alone, as though cut off from any affinity to the languages and cultures of other nations. Thus from time to time our teachers proposed topics such as Jewish themes or Jewish characters in Polish literature; comparison of descriptions of nature in Polish literature and in Hebrew literature; affinities in form or substance between the two literatures, etc. The problem was that there was no teacher of Polish literature who also knew Hebrew literature, or had an interest in it.[20] Not so with our classics teacher.

Freilich liked to present combinations and confrontations, comparisons and contrasts, and his lively lessons threw light on both worlds, the Jewish and the Roman. We could clearly see how close they were to each other, and how distant. Freilich encouraged us to translate into Hebrew the rhetoric of Cicero and the poetry of Ovid, Horace and Virgil. Naturally it was easier to translate the prose of the historians Sallust and Tacitus. Freilich himself would enlarge upon the spiritual affinity between the Stoics and the Sages of the Mishnah in *Ethics of the Fathers*. He always surprised us with his broad knowledge without ever compromising his particular analysis of the uniqueness of each culture.

The Polish supervisors who frequented our school did not view this trend favorably. I remember how I once nearly "collided" head-on with one of them, a classical philologist who sat in on our class while we read and explained "Scipio's dream" at the end of Cicero's *Republic*. For some reason, I felt impelled to get up and make a comment. I said that our Sages, who lived more or less around the time of Cicero, never reached the point of negating the world and the importance of this life on earth. Even after two and a half years of debate between the adherents of Hillel and the adherents of Shammai on the value of life, they finally agreed: "It would have been preferable had man not been created than to have been created. However, now that he has been created, he should examine his actions that he has performed and seek to correct them." I explained my position in Polish, basing myself on Aḥad Ha'am's famous essay "Flesh and Spirit": The kind of cancellation of the world as Scipio here declares ("that which is called life is really death"[21]) is reminiscent of Christianity. The supervisor did not approve of my comment, of my entire approach, and remarked that one should not introduce here "Talmudic *pilpul*." I responded that there was no more *pilpul* here than in Cicero's text. For almost immediately after Scipio the Elder says that man's exploits and glory in this world are not important ("Of what worth is that human glory?"[22]), he declares that if his grandson, Scipio the Younger (the dreamer of this conversation), should arise to perform a great deed for his people's welfare, for example, destroy Carthage, he would immediately be granted an abode among the stars of heaven and everlasting life. I pointed out this contradiction, with all due respect, of course. I absolutely did not want to trip up Freilich, who was to a certain extent the dispenser of my bread, or at least, the butter on my bread, thanks to the private tutoring jobs in Latin that he helped me obtain.

In this particular lesson, we were studying the fifteenth book of the *Annals of the Excesses of the Augustan Gods* by Tacitus. We had already read a number of chapters ("books") in this great historical composition. I was thrilled with the dramatic description of the exploits and events—the fine craftsmanship of a great artist. Tacitus always placed the agency of a personality at the center of each episode, and proceeded to describe with creative zest its character and motives, both manifest factors and secret desires: lust for honor, for money, or for a woman. His description of the cunning and cruelty of Tiberius Caesar made us shudder. "An exemplary tyrant!" It was in his image that we envisaged other despots of antiquity—both foreigners and Jews, like Herod—and modern ones.

Now we were in the last chapter of the life of Nero. We read how he sentenced friends and foes alike to death, or exiled them and confiscated their property. A conspiracy against him was being hatched, or so he imagined. Paragraph 60: Seneca, his teacher and advisor, sits down to supper with his wife and two of his friends. The tribune enters and brings him an enquiry regarding his involvement in the conspiracy; namely, Nero wishes to know whether he knew of the plot or of the conspirators. Seneca replied what he replied (that he did not). Dissatisfied with his answer, Nero asks the tribune, upon the latter's return to the palace, whether he had detected in Seneca any signs of fear. Nero orders his teacher to die—"the last necessity." When the emperor's verdict is brought to Seneca, who is still at table with his wife and friends, the philosopher says that he would bequeath to them the most precious legacy in his possession—"the example of his life" (*imaginem vitae suae*)—so that his life and the good wisdom they had learned would be their reward for loyal friendship. Seeing them in tears, he added, "Where are the precepts of philosophy, and where the words of wisdom, which for years have taught us to meet the calamities of life with firmness and a well prepared spirit?"[23] (*Ubi precepta sapientiae, ubi tot per annos meditata ratio adversum imminentia?*)

According to Tacitus, Seneca's suicide under Nero's order was very cruel. In fact, he died four types of deaths: by the sword—he slit his veins, and when death tarried, he drank a cup of poison. He then entered a hot bath—death by boiling water—and still death did not come. Finally, he suffocated in the vapors. Long beforehand, when he was still at the zenith of his wealth and power, he had ordered in his will that his body be cremated without a funeral ceremony (Book XV, 64).

Freilich read with emphasis, recited aloud and acted out, even where Tacitus offered no dialogue. As I said, he was an entertaining teacher—Purim and Yom Kippur, jest and gravity, rolled into one, and a philosopher when he so fancied. For me, he incarnated an Italian humanist (he knew Italian and would often talk about his trip to Rome, to museums and exhibitions), surely with all the well-known weaknesses of the humanists, as I later described them in my books on the Renaissance culture in Europe.[24]

In this lesson on Seneca, or perhaps it was in another, he explained that the philosopher was not blameless. Seneca composed Nero's wicked speeches, replete with lies, guile, and plots to entrap his master's enemies. Nero was thus the first Roman emperor to employ a ghostwriter. All the emperors who preceded him, even Claudius, who was not very bright, spoke independently, and delivered their own speeches. Seneca had also received many benefits from the emperor, mostly property confiscated from persons deported or executed by imperial order. One may assume that he knew about Nero's intention to murder his own mother Agrippina, and did not hinder him, and apparently also heard about the plotters against Nero, and perhaps even was in their confidence.

Freilich would widen the scope. He read to us several of Seneca's letters, from which we learned that even though Seneca was born in Cordoba, in his pragmatic bent he was every inch a Roman. Remote from all metaphysics, even from the Stoic school to which he was closest, he had no inclination for any philosophy that dealt in abstract notions, such as logics or epistemology. He was a practical thinker, with neither heights nor depths. He wished in his thinking to resolve difficulties of everyday life and to guide people to the realization that their real possession was their own intelligence, with which they should make do. In this way, Seneca came to articulate some famous ideas: He who acts according to wisdom acquires happiness, the substance of which is "unalloyed freedom from care, and … unshaken confidence."[25] Seneca asserted that only one thing is required of man: to live according to his true nature.

In Tacitus, however, we read how little the Romans—both the people and their ministers and emperors—lived in accordance with the nature of true intelligence, making Seneca's precept sound like a downright joke. Another thing Seneca taught: Intelligence is a great equalizer. Differences in status among people do not stem from nature. Seneca, so we learned from our teacher, was one of the first in the pagan world who spoke so emphatically about the equality of all human beings, reminiscent of the prophet's "Have we not all one father?": "All men, if traced back to their original source, spring from the gods. You are a

Roman knight, and your persistent work promoted you to this class ... Socrates was no aristocrat ... Philosophy did not find Plato already a nobleman; it made him one."[26] Moreover, our teacher continued, the words "knight" and "slave" are nothing but appellations, born from acts of iniquity and the pursuit of glory.

The words of Seneca could have served as a turning point in the history of slavery, but, if I am not mistaken, they failed to alter the customs of the ancient world. A few classmates raised the question as to what Seneca had learned from our Sages or what the Sages had learned from him. Freilich could not answer this question conclusively. I believe that until today there is more doubt than certainty in this area of comparison.

The ringing of the bell ended the interesting lesson on the *Annals.*

POLISH ROMANTIC LITERATURE—MRS. PENINA STRAUCH BAR-YEHUDAH

Miss Gleicher, later Mrs. Strauch, and, when she reached Israel, Mrs. Bar-Yehuda, knew neither Yiddish nor Hebrew. She had studied in Cracow and trained in Berlin. From her youth, she had been a friend of the woman who later became Mrs. Rieger, our principal's wife, a physics and math teacher in our school who apparently drew her friend to Lodz. Mrs. Strauch was a few years older than were all our other teachers; in 1928 she was already 40-plus and her colleagues treated her with respect, and not only because of her age. In a class of grown, lively boys, this teacher, small of stature, simply and neatly dressed, whose every word and act expressed high intelligence, just captivated our hearts. She specialized in both Polish and German literature.

In the fifth lesson of the day, we reviewed and prepared for the upcoming oral and written baccalaureate exams in Polish literature. Romantic literature, and especially the works of Poland's three great bards[27] was particularly attractive to young Jews, perhaps because Poland's political failure, coupled with the greatness of its artists and their vision of independence, echoed our anguish over our exile and our yearning for Israel's redemption in its land. The Polish poets sang a messianic, religious song of life, one that heartened and spurred the Poles to fight their oppressors. The Romantic poetry of the bards was a sort of spiritual homeland for Poles, a "portable fatherland"[28] (although, in contrast to us their homeland was palpable under their feet), and it is in no small measure thanks to this poetry that they won their freedom. For us this poetry brought great tidings—a vision that was powerful enough to redeem a nation from exile and subjugation, "if you will it, it is no dream,"[29] so to speak. Piłsudski ordered the bodies of the "bards" in exile to be exhumed and brought back to Poland.

Poet Adam Mickiewicz – Poland's great "Bard"

Exam material surely included the epic *Pan Tadeusz* by Adam Mickiewicz, a distinctly national tale, albeit about the *szlachta* (the nobility) in its period of decline, focused on small landowners, their exploits and chicanery. The poem describes Poland as reality and as vision—as it was at the end of the eighteenth century and under Napoleon, and as it never was. It expresses the mood of an exiled poet—in the sense of Halevi's "My heart in the East/ But the rest of me far in the West"[30]—as he experienced it in France, the center of Polish émigrés, after the failure of the 1831 rebellion against Russia. "I longed to pass by in my flight, bird of feeble wing, to pass by regions of storm and thunder, and to search out only pleasant shade and fair weather—the days of my childhood, and my home gardens."[31]

The book is "Polish" through and through, with its fanaticism, licentiousness, and disruption of public order, and at the same time, it is very human, compassionate, and full of radiant descriptions of sun-touched wheat fields and the moon's enchantment for love and its yearnings. The book abounds in descriptions of persons and landscapes, soothing idyllic scenes and rattling scenes of hunting, battles, disputes and arguments, passions and yearnings for deliverance, heroic deeds and remorse, many rejoicings and great griefs. No wonder that *Pan Tadeusz* was a mandatory subject in every Polish school. Good taste has counselled the current regime[32] to declare this poem "kosher" even for Communism.

We Jewish readers who learned about the *szlachta* of that period were well acquainted with its harsh oppression of Jews. Ber Bolochower[33] recounted in his memoirs how Polish noblemen abused "their" Jews, how the poor wretches were forced to dance before them, singing "Majufes."[34] This is the period of the Council of Four Lands,[35] and the Besht and his associates and disciples are busy with "redemption of captives" from Polish landowners. Only one year before our review of Bolochower's memoir, in 1927, the Jewish Polish historian Majer Balaban published the memoirs of the nobleman Jan Duklan Ochocki from the beginning of 1774, and they speak for themselves:

> 5 January. The lessee of the tavern still owes me 91 gold pieces for the past three months. I was authorized, according to the contract between us, to take severe measures and imprison him, his wife and children, until he pays his debt, but I ordered to seize only the swindler himself and to confine him in the pig sty, whereas his wife and children I allowed for the time being to remain in the tavern. Only his youngest son, Leizer, I took to my court and ordered to have him taught the Lord's Prayer and the catechism, since he is a bright boy. I would like to have him baptized and have already talked this over with the priest who promised to come to court in order to prepare the young soul for baptism. At first, Leizer refused to cross himself and to say "Our Father," but the estate steward succeeded in whipping him into submission. Today he already also ate pork. Brother Boniface has worked hard at breaking the boy's stiff neck.
>
> 27 January. Jews came from Berdichev, paid the 91 golden pieces for the swindler Herschko. In addition, they gave a gift of one sugarloaf and six pounds of bad coffee. I ordered Herschko released. I wanted to retain his son, as he was already destined to enter the Church, but the Jews did not let up and I had to release him too. I hope that he will come back to me: Herschko will surely be unable to meet his payments also at the next due date, and then Leizer will become a Christian.[36]

Mickiewicz speaks of the following generation, and his affection for Jews was well known. His mother and wife were daughters of Frankists. Israel is Poland's "elder brother." The poet once confessed to a Polish nobleman: "I am half a descendant of Lech [i.e., a Pole], and a half Israelite …—and proud of it!"[37]

Pan Tadeusz includes the Jew Yankiel, who is an exemplary Polish patriot and aids the underground forces and the uprising. An excellent musician, he plays Polish ballads at their festivities. "The honest Jew loved his country like a Pole!" the poet testifies—a phrase repeated in my day at every Jewish-Polish official function. Thus, Jacob is not a guileless scholar who sits and studies in the tent of Torah, as Jewish tradition would have it, but a political Jew, endowed also with a great ethical soul who joins the Poles in their struggle for liberty.

Unlike Dr. Eck who taught us Hebrew literature, our teacher for Polish literature was particularly sensitive to the lyrical and philosophical aspects of the works we studied. For this reason, she preferred the second bard Juliusz Słowacki to Mickiewicz. In that lesson, for dessert, she read to us a few lines of Słowacki's poetic drama *Kordian.*[38] I have taken the trouble to find these wonderful, sensational lines. I bring them here in my translation, without rhyme or meter. The poet prophesies the day when his homeland will be liberated:

> And then our country—free! Then a day of brightness!/
> Poland stretches to the sea,/
> After a stormy night she breathes and lives/
> Lives! ... When on the first day of freedom joy kindles,/
> And it bursts from people's hearts to hit the sky,/
> Then they will pass through the long darkness of thralldom,/
> They will sit and with great weeping, they will sob like children,/
> And then will they hear the immense cry of resurrection.
> *A potém kraj nasz wolny! potém jasność dniowa!*
> ...
> *I słychać będzie płacz ogromny zmartwychwstania.*

We listened attentively and savored the beauty of expression, the depth of joy accompanied by weeping, a weeping of spiritual elevation, following the resurrection of the dead homeland. However, we could not help recalling what the Poles had inflicted upon their "elder brother" in the early days of their resurrection. The great weeping did not mellow their hearts to affection, or even to mere toleration. Later in life I thought of this weeping—when we burst out in joy over the UN declaration of 29 November, 1947,[39] and once more, at the declaration of Israel's independence in May, 1948.

Polish literature was not all Romantic. For the baccalaureate, we needed to review also the positivistic, realistic, and neo-Romantic writers, in whom the fervor of grief over exile and hope for redemption had waned. The next lesson would be devoted to Stanisław Wyspiański's *The Wedding*, a poetic drama, which parodied the Polish intelligentsia of the late nineteenth century for its delusional Romantic dreams of return to an idealized "simple and sane" peasant life, from which, as it were, Poland's salvation would spring. Wyspiański appears to continue the tradition of the bards, but unlike his predecessors, he no longer saw in the spirit of man and folk a force that could generate action. Rather, like the positivists, he believed in the necessity of political strategies and economic organization. Piłsudski revered him. The drama's gist: The peasants are indeed a great force, and may, possibly, bring salvation to Poland one day, but not the way they are today—sloppy, ignorant, and irresponsible. A recurring verse in the poem is about a golden horn, which the peasant possessed, a magic horn with which to announce the tidings of redemption, but he lost it.

Again: It was a marvel to me how our small, thin teacher kept control over thirty tall, strong boys and guided them with a sure hand through the great quantity of material, and even succeeded to instill in them love for works that were not studied in class, such as Poland's new poets, our contemporaries. She was a woman of great intelligence and cultivated taste. It is still a pleasure today to chat with my wise and refined neighbor on Mt. Carmel, Mrs. Penina Bar-Yehudah, now 96 years old, whose mind is keen and her opinions ever judicious and engaging. (She passed away two years after this conversation, in 1984).

TRAGEDY OF JEWISH POETS—ON JULIAN TUWIM AND ANTONI SŁONIMSKI

I have mentioned above only the Hebrew and Polish literature curriculum, but besides the compulsory texts, several of my friends read more widely. Some of us drank in every new poem by Bialik or Tchernichovsky. The new, expressionist poetry of the immediate post World War I period also attracted us. We read Uri Ẓvi Greenberg,[40] Avraham Shlonsky,[41] and Yiẓḥak Lamdan's[42] *Massada,* which appeared at that time. We became acquainted with world writers through the Hebrew translations of the Stybel Publishing House.

Some among us were keener on modern Polish literature. At the dawn of Polish independence a spirit of renewal and new hope animated its literature: A new Poland will arise, a new era begins, one of destiny and solidarity. However, by the end of the first decade of Poland's rebirth, winds of disillusionment were already blowing, chic ridicule, even cynicism. Reality belied the dream, and as Julian Tuwim said in one of his well-known *Poems about the State,* "It is a great misery and torture to be a state, prayed for by poets whose pens were dipped in the bitter inkwell of blood and tears."[43]

Portrait of Julian Tuwim (pastel on paper, 1929) by Stanisław Ignacy Witkiewicz (1885–1939), commonly known as Witkacy. Warsaw National Museum

Tuwim was our townsman, and the papers declared that with him "Lodz had ascended with bold stride to the heights of Parnassus." His style in the new spirit of expressionism and futurism broke formulaic molds, mixed different styles, even introducing simple prose into poetry. Tuwim's poetry was urbane, impatient, critical, remonstrating against the city and ridiculing it, purposely anti-aesthetic, openly violating the rules of harmony and symmetry. The hero of poetry is now the man grizzled by a wearying daily routine.

In his first book *The Dancing Socrates* (1919), he fumed at the corruption of the rich who exploit the common people, but also at the corruption of overly industrious scribblers, who exploit the word and contaminate it with vacuous frivolities. One should firmly establish a good social order and concomitantly restore truth to poetic language. In his poems and articles we found a conspicuous ambivalence with regard to Jews. In several poems he treats them sympathetically; in others, he is hostile and cruel. Tuwim wrote a great deal: lyrics, poetic thought, countless witty, biting epigrams, humorous pieces peppered with *bons mots*—thunder and lightning. For a few years he worked on a history of witchcraft in Poland and its literature. With the intelligence of an investigative researcher, coupled with humor and mischievousness, he illuminated the dark world of the demons that had peopled the imagination of Poles since the Middle Ages—and his imagination too.

We argued quite a bit about Tuwim's poem *The Jewboy,* or *Little Jew* (*Żydek*), published in 1925. It dealt with a Jewish boy afflicted with madness who sings in the courtyard and begs for alms. The poet observes him from the first floor and reflects: "How did we come to this? How did we lose ourselves/ In this vast world, strange and hostile to us?.../And we will never find peace or rest/ Singing Jews, lost Jews."[44] Did the poet refer to *poets* "afflicted with madness" in the eyes of their sober bourgeois townsmen, or did he mean the *entire Jewish people* was mad in the eyes of the Gentiles?

During the Nazi occupation, Tuwim escaped from Poland to Brazil, then to the United States. There he composed a poetic manifesto on the Holocaust that opened with the words: "We Polish Jews." When he returned to Poland in 1946, he suffered from depression. He still wrote and translated, especially from Russian literature, but he was in despair at what he saw in the new Poland. He died in anguish in 1953.

His friend was Antoni Słonimski, grandson of Zelig Słonimski, who had been a man of science and the founder and editor of *Ha-ẓefirah*. Antoni's father was a socialist and a physician, who converted to Christianity when he married a Catholic woman. Thus Antoni was already born into that faith. Together with Tuwim, Słonimski founded and published the journal *Skamandar,* where they offered their poetry, prose, satires, and parodies. Together they also composed a series of feuilletons and humorous skits and monologues for Warsaw cabarets.

In 1928 he produced for the Warsaw and Lodz stages a satire[45] about a Jewish bookseller who is eager to assimilate into Polish society, its language, and literature. The man is depicted as flighty, snobbish, a laughable imitator, a caricature of one who wishes to conceal his true nature and disavow his people. However, in reality, the satire turned most of its arrows against the anti-Semites.[46]

Neither Tuwim nor Słonimski ever denied his Jewish origin. The Holocaust elicited from both a poetry of anguish. In London, Słonimski wrote an *Elegy on Small Jewish Towns* (1947) and a number of other poems of lamentation and bereavement. He was killed in a car accident in Warsaw, in 1976.

In my day, both of these poets were at the zenith of their fame and the flowering of their talent. No doubt they introduced qualities that were distinctly

Jewish into Polish literature. Unlike the attention given to the great Jewish authors of Germany, very little has been written about the tragedy of Jewish writers in Poland—about the cleft that split their souls, about their wounded love for Poland, and of the tragedy of their people, whose talented sons spread their wings like eagles, as Bialik had admonished,[47] to soar on mountaintops, far away from the literature of their own people.

Their works are still considered enduring assets of Polish literature, even under the Communist regime.

LAST LESSON OF THE DAY: "CONTEMPORARY POLAND"–CIVICS WITH SHAUL RIEGER

The sixth and final lesson that day (twice a week our studies extended to a seventh hour) was in Polish civics: the state's components, its constitution and institutions. Our principal Shaul Rieger skillfully stimulated our interest in things that were ostensibly legalistic and abstract. Rieger had not obtained a doctorate in history, but he had completed an M.A. course. The Ph.Ds in Rieger's family

Bust of Saul Rieger, 1930s–1940s, by Max (Mordechai) Farbmann (1889–1950)

were his brother Eliezer, a supervisor and eventually a professor of education at the Hebrew University in Jerusalem, and Shaul's wife, Elisheva. He had pursued his studies during World War I, with inevitable interruptions. Since he had also trained at the Vienna Commerce Academy, his practical background contributed greatly to his success as a school principal in Lodz and in Israel, and eventually, as the director of the Levinsky Teachers Training College in Tel Aviv.

He was a man of action, a Zionist leader from youth, and as the head of a band of teachers who were also researchers and creative artists, an influential educator. He loved reading, especially history, and engaged in some original inquiries himself, which he often brought to class.

In a brochure published (stenciled) by my schoolmate, Dr. Moshe Prywes, titled *Shaul Rieger, the Man and the Educator* (1980), I find this faithful description: "Among the teachers, Shaul stood out—of tall stature, thin, a very serious face, piercing gaze and deep voice—and the students instantly felt that there was something special in this man ..." Further in that brochure, most pertinent to my point here:

> Shaul Rieger succeeded in welding together a wonderful and perfect amalgam of civic loyalty and decency toward the Polish state with overt, proud Zionism. In the ... balanced atmosphere that prevailed in the institution, there was never any doubt regarding double loyalty, or any other aspect of civic status. There was a clear sense of full belonging and participation in the life of the state as citizens informed of their rights and of the obligations incumbent upon the general population, and at the same time harboring a desire to leave one day and to settle in the old homeland reviving in Ereẓ Israel. And when that day arrives, they will be released from the present civic ties, and will take upon themselves the life and obligations of that homeland in whose re-building they will begin to partake actively.

To me it is clear that the words of my friend Prywes about a "wonderful and perfect" welding are too smooth, too harmonizing. Observing the laws—absolutely, civic probity—certainly. One paid one's taxes, served in the army. After I graduated, pre-military training was introduced in our school, all part of the service of Poland. But was the atmosphere really "balanced?" Did we really feel in our school an educational orientation toward "full belonging and participation in the life of the state as informed citizens?" Or perhaps it was only one orientation, whereas its correlative was that at the "same time [we were] harboring a desire to leave one day and to settle in the old homeland" etc. For really, how could such a "balanced education" succeed, when the political reality in Poland was so inimical to it? Was Poland a homeland for us, or a *galut*? And what about all the young people who wanted to destroy its capitalist-nationalistic system?

The lesson was flawlessly organized: the teacher's lecture, questions and answers, discussion and argument. We could feel the young principal's strong and intelligent guiding hand. It might seem as though we were grinding through dry things: the foundations of the state, the Polish constitution, is premises and directives, the three branches of government, the nature of democracy and parliamentary procedural bodies—all according to the Polish contemporary model. However, it was impossible not to digress to the real-life situations that troubled us in this Poland.

The constitution of the new Poland, modeled after the post-war French constitution, was very advanced, redounding to the glory of its legislators and citizens, judging by the high-minded text, which we were obliged to learn. The evidence of our eyes, however, gave lie to that constitution, and made it a *konstituzie*, as Scholem Aleichem joked: "*konnst du—tust du*," that is, manage as best you can. The constitution preaches loftily, but everything depends on your own ability to get by.

In this lesson we learned that the Polish state was one of the poorest in Europe. Many of its provinces, having served as battlegrounds for the advancing or retreating fronts, had been ravaged in World War I. When the state was founded, it had no means with which to rebuild the country and establish an economy commensurate with the size of its population. Polish industry had been heavily dependent on its markets in Russia. When these markets were lost in the Communist revolution, several years elapsed before new ones could be found. Eastern Europe did not tend to embrace liberal theories of free trade, and even in the West, governments were now increasingly turning toward "autarky" and abandoning these theories. The two super-powers Russia and Germany, Poland's neighbors, deliberately restricted its steps. Russia wished to develop its own industry, and Germany, previously a buyer of Poland's agricultural produce, was now intensifying its own agriculture production to avoid the need to import. The Polish army swallowed up a sizable chunk of the state's revenues, about half of its budget.

About 80 percent of the population were peasants, but large landowners held almost half of the land. Most of the peasants had little land or were landless hired laborers. Their education was very limited and they still cultivated the land in age-old methods. In my day the wheat yield in Poland was about half of that in neighboring Germany, and even less compared to Holland and Denmark. The same was true for other crops—rye, oatmeal, and barley. Only when it came to potatoes, the population's main staple, was the situation a little better. The technology of the coal and salt mines was also antiquated, and their outputs relatively low. A serious impediment to the country's development was the inflation that raged in the first five years of Poland's independence and reduced the standard of living still further. Had the government implemented its much-touted plans for agrarian reform and a supportive economic policy for industrial production and export, and had it developed modern transport systems, the country would have changed dramatically. Industry was begging for investments and credit. (After World War II, the government took this action, but by then other obstacles arose—more on this in the last two chapters.)

Nonetheless, slowly, very gradually, the state began recovering. It gained markets, export increased considerably, especially in 1927, and there was an impression of economic recovery. Politically, however, the state faced serious difficulties, including endless party wrangling, so that in the years 1918–1928 the government changed about a dozen times. Piłsudki's coup d'état (1926) interrupted this turmoil, but did not alter the impact of government intervention in every aspect of its citizens' life.

World War I brought to the surface and amplified a number of underlying trends in the development of European nations, the influence of which became decisive for the fate of Jews in Poland. Principally it raised the prestige of the state and the power and value of its apparatus. The necessity of making maximal use of a population's total resources for war motivated the emergence of centralizing regimes, usually sanctioned by compliant parliaments. I hardly need to say that in Poland the government had little faith in its citizens' ability to work for the common good. Security, culture, health, education, and economic affairs all became dependent upon the power of the state, and the latter began to affect every aspect of a citizen's life. On top of that, Poland had a national problem—its attitude toward minorities.

Indeed, the constitution was liberal, and with Piłsudki's rise to power, in my last years in high school, the government began accommodating Jewish demands. Anti-Semitic incitement became muted, boycotts of Jewish businesses ended, the pressure of taxation abated. Jewish high schools such as ours obtained formal rights in 1926, as described earlier. A few dozen Jews were appointed to government positions. There was hope that it would indeed be possible to live in Poland. Concomitantly, the *aliyah* to Ereẓ Israel, as indicated earlier, stopped due to the economic crisis there.

We were very interested in Rieger's detailed explanations of the parliamentary procedures governing the Sejm and the Senate, the elections system, the make-up of the parties and their platforms, the formation of governments, their rise and fall. We could indulge hopes for Poland's economy—a large land, blessed with natural resources and an industrious population—albeit clouded by the shadow of anti-Semitic nationalism. The Polish nationalists saw their country in a different light: Poland was a poor country, which could not—and should not—support a population of "foreigners" who were consuming the little wealth it possessed. We were scared by slogans about "superfluous populations," among whom a large Jewish minority of which one million should emigrate. At first, they would justify discrimination against Jews with reasons taken from the age-old repertoire of Romantic myth: The Jews were exploiting the denizen nation, or they were inimical to its government, or they had joined the country's enemies, betrayed their homeland, and offended all that the nation held sacred. Or they would argue that the Jews' sources of livelihood were needed for Poles. This soldering of anti-Semitism and the economy became the distinctive hallmark of Polish prejudice. In my day, this argument was just beginning to take hold, later it became current and official: Because of the economic crisis, unemployment, and the closure of immigration to the United States and other Western countries, the Jews were "superfluous" and should be evacuated.

In that lesson we heard a short presentation by Aharon Savitzky about the research of Dr. Arie Tartakower, who brilliantly analyzed in three languages (Yiddish, Polish, and Hebrew[48]) Poland's economic situation and the possibilities for its improvement, mainly reform of its taxation system and of its export and import, which, if undertaken, would ensure honorable livelihoods to millions of Poles. As for the Jews, not only were they not superfluous, they would be very much needed. More than a third of them worked in industry and artisanry and a third in trade, areas in which they constituted a large percentage of the workforce. For example, they were about half of all the artisans in the country. In contrast, the percentage of Poles in industry and artisanry (7.7 percent) and in trade (6.3 percent) was very small, compared to Germany or the Western countries.

The occupational problem in the Jewish population was the segment of people without a profession, and those—mostly women—who could not obtain remunerative work and formed a classless class of several hundred thousand living on air, *luftmentshn*. One must widen the vocational education network, Tartakower suggested, to introduce Jews to public and government service, and to add to the ranks of the employed the many young people who wished to work in factories. Only bigoted nationalism stood in their way. The suggested measures would have changed the shape of the state for the benefit of all its citizens.

I do not know if this was the kind of lesson on "Contemporary Poland" that the authorities had in mind, but we learned a lot; it contained both general theory and things that touched our personal destiny—governance, politics, and economics. Rieger insisted on precise articulation, logical argumentation, fairness in disputations among ourselves and between us and the Polish authorities and parties. However, decency was, apparently, not enough. At the end of five years, he packed his things and emigrated with his family to Ereẓ Israel.

The bell rang and ended the school day.

EXTRACURRICULAR; THE ACTOR ISRAEL SCHUMACHER (1908–61)

I have limited myself to the proceedings in only one classroom during only one day, whereas our school had twelve classes, and for some levels, there were two or three parallel classes. Moreover, besides these six lessons we studied a number of other academic subjects, such as Bible and *aggadah*, world history, German or French literature (one could choose), mathematics in its various branches, biology, and botany. We also had non-academic subjects: gym, drawing, and music. Each high school had a choir and an orchestra, and we and our fellow high schools participated in large parades on the city streets, whether on festive days and outings, or for demonstrations and protests—forming a large crowd of close to 2,000 pupils with three orchestras, banners and anthems, and crowds lining the streets to cheer us on.

There was also diverse extracurricular activity within the school itself: clubs and labs, arts and crafts (for some months we had bookbinding), parties, balls, lectures, debates. The students in our high school began publishing a bilingual (Hebrew-Polish) monthly called *Ḥayenu* (*Our Life*). I still managed to participate in its first issue with a Hebrew article on the desirable profile of a teacher in a Hebrew high school, and with a story in Polish in the style of Słowacki's *Anhelli*,[49] for which I won the editor's prize. In most classrooms, various stenciled leaflets or class-produced newspapers were pinned on the walls.

So far in these descriptions of our lessons I have omitted matters that might be extraneous, or maybe not. Jokes and banter, outbursts of hilarity at someone's expense, or giggles of relief and satisfaction, arguments and disputes, rebukes and reconciliations, overt and covert contests of will, awkward silences, searches for the saving answer that failed to come, anxieties and expectations, defeats and triumphs, annoying and sometimes embarrassing mistakes, acts of weakness and vindictiveness and acts of generosity and courage, both by teachers and by students. In brief, a normal day in class.

[My fellow student Israel Schumacher (Szumacher), mentioned earlier, was a great source of animation in our classroom].[50]

Schumacher and I were "neighbors" in the alphabetical order of names in the class register. He came from a poor family and was with us in the last four years of high school. Tuition in our school was high and even after all the discounts it was not easy for children of the poor to stay in school, but his talents stood him in good stead. He was a humanist—Hebrew and Polish literature were his favorite subjects. From the moment he joined our class, we loved to hear him recite aloud the poems of Bialik and Tchernichovsky, and the poems and dramas of the "bards" Mickiewicz, Słowacki, and Krasiński. When we read plays in class, he was the chief actor. As a matter of course he got the lead parts, although he had some rivals. More than one talent filled our ranks.

During the recesses, the teacher's platform often turned into a stage for would-be orators and impromptu dramatizations. We would act out folk gatherings, festive functions (*akademiehs*), and various mock meetings, and would let forth fiery speeches and wisecracks. In those breaks our class was visited by all the "celebs"—popular speakers and leaders of the Sejm and the Senate, Zionists, Revisionists, Bundists, and members of Agudat Israel: Jabotinsky and Naḥum Sokolov, Yiẓḥak Gruenbaum, Noaḥ Prilutzky, Dr. Yiẓḥak (Ignacy) Schiper, Dr. Braude, Dr. Joshua Thon and Leon Reich, Yaakov Zerubavel, and the rabbis Brodt, Zlotnik and Yiẓḥak-Meir Levin. Any classmate who had attended a rally in town felt the urge to enact it for us.

Schumacher knew how to imitate all the leading personalities, but in those days he was especially drawn to the speakers exhibiting the greatest national or social pathos. He would brush aside the curls from his forehead, alter his facial expression to mimic that of the orator, and there, in front of us, stood Jabotinsky, or one of the head Bundists, or a laborer from the Folkist party.

The greatest dramatic experience for our class was the appearance of Habima in Lodz in 1926, especially in *The Dybbuk*. For a long time after the show we continued to hum its tunes and dance its dances. Schumacher was Sender, or the Rabbi, or the Messenger. These informal performances ended abruptly when the teacher walked in.

There were also formal performances during the big festivities celebrated by all the Hebrew high schools together, or small ones with the parallel class in the Girls' Hebrew High School. Dr. Freilich, whose favored genre was dramatized folk songs, was our stage director. Thus we mounted, in Hebrew translation, dramatizations of *Oyfn Pripetchik* (*On the Hearth, a Fire Burns*),[51] *May Ko Mashma Lon der Regen?* (*What's the Meaning of the Rainstorm?*),[52] *Der Balagule* (*The Wagon Driver*),[53] and various small folk scenes.

From time to time, usually at Ḥanuka, we had an opportunity to put on a more ambitious "classical" play, but mostly we made do with light entertainment. Israel Schumacher was the leader in all this activity. He would wear a long *kapota* and transform into a teacher in the *ḥeder*, or put on a wagon driver's boots and hold a whip in his hand, always with lively, natural gestures. He would sing, dance, and stride the stage as if he owned it. Freilich was the prompter, but when his words failed to reach Schumacher, the latter did not bat an eye—on the spot, he would improvise, and even though Freilich would reprimand him, we, his laughing audience, were the beneficiaries.

Happy days arrived when our school went out to summer camp. In a village in the Carpathian Mountains, many of us would spend about ten weeks of vacation in reading, sports, and theater arts. From time to time, we would organize a public performance: a memorial evening in honor of Herzl, or an evening of dramatized folk songs, which many of the Jewish vacationers would flock to see.

We were sure that it would be worth their while. I played a role behind the scenes, usually translating songs or composing small scenes into which we incorporated folk songs. In town, our teachers were strict with us about translating everything into Hebrew, as befits a Hebrew high school, but in the summer resort the leash was loosened, to the enjoyment of the outside audience. So it was that Schumacher began to appear in Yiddish. A sound instinct must have induced our teacher to allow the actors to talk Yiddish in their Polish-Lodz accent, unlike the practice of the Yiddish theaters in Poland which adopted the Lithuanian accent of the authoritative Vilna Troupe in Warsaw.

In these summer camps Schumacher revealed himself as a master of popular Yiddish humor. Just as he excelled in the rhetoric of national and social pathos, so did he shine in mimicking popular gestures, grotesque expressions, plebeian diction. His voice was pleasing, though not strong, melodious and engaging.

The more serious, intellectually inclined among us saw mere fun, and even an inappropriate levity in his popular appearances, suitable perhaps for vacation time, but not for the career of a young man studying at the Hebrew high school. Others, on the contrary, appreciated Schumacher precisely for this.

All his stage appearances displayed the gifts of a born actor, but I confess we never believed that he would in fact choose this art. We viewed his acting as the frolic of youth, and, as I said, he had in class, and certainly in the school, a number of rivals. His joining the Ararat Theater, founded at that time in Lodz by the Yiddish poet Moshe Broderzon, came as a surprise to us. The truth is we also felt slightly hurt. You want to be an actor? Make *aliyah* to Ereẓ Israel and join Habima! The Hebrew high school, as we have seen, did not really approve of the Polish state and of Jewish life in its midst. The school was prepared to abide by the state's official norms and its obligatory demands for patriotism. With the "Jewish street," it was prepared to make peace in a sentimental way, as a sort of concession, as in play-acting, but not more, at any rate not in any way that would take this type of acting seriously. Schumacher's choice, therefore, was a sort of rebellion against the spirit of the school.

Few of us went to see him perform. It is difficult for me to explain properly why so many showed this reluctance. Perhaps they could not see acting as a respectable profession. Those who saw him, enjoyed him, but it was not a complete enjoyment. Some thought that neither his repertoire nor his stage colleagues were commensurate with his dramatic-tragic spirit and talent.

I did not see him after I left for Germany, where he did not appear. I heard about his great success and during the war was anxious about him. When he arrived in Israel, we would meet occasionally backstage after the show or in the intermission.[54]

MODERN JEWISH EDUCATION—LEGACY AND REMNANTS

The Hebrew high schools established by Dr. Braude were modern institutions. One may ask whether they were created out of the "Jewish existential ethos" or were "imported vines," or perhaps they even "chopped down the shoots of saplings," as the Talmud describes the destructive work of a heretic in one's midst. I have no doubt that this modern education was a genuinely felt necessity, even if external factors prompted its creation and shaped the specific forms it took. The school was a product of the socioeconomic and spiritual changes that had taken place in our world, and further expedited them. The Hebrew schools confronted the "Jewish problem" of our era and gave it a response which steered clear of religious and ideological zealotry on the one hand, and relativism and nihilism on the other. As exemplified in its assumptions and efforts, Hebrew education in Poland tried to transform Jewish society and adapt to its real needs of security and dignity, livelihood and faith.

The response, I find, was not entirely unequivocal, namely, education geared solely at *aliyah* to Ereẓ Israel. On the one hand, it quickly became clear that those of our teachers, principals and students who made *aliyah* had no difficulty in being absorbed into a Jewish-Hebraic atmosphere and participating in all areas of endeavor, as though they had been pre-trained for it. On the other hand, at least in Poland's first decade of independence, and especially in the early years of Piłsudki's rule, after his coup d'état, the impression was that one could "get by" in Poland. This vacillation between the two possibilities is precisely the nature of *galut* and the way it is experienced.

***

During my teaching career I taught high school-level courses in a number of institutions. I was also principal of a high school and of a teachers' training college, and I knew many teachers in Israel and abroad. However, it seems to me that it would be hard to find anywhere a teaching staff of such excellence and motivation as I had in Lodz. I believe that the story presented here of the spiritual work of teachers and students on a typical school day can teach us something not only about those days, but also about good teaching and educating in every age. Whereas the multifaceted Jewish education system in interwar Poland has received quite a bit of research and descriptive attention as a whole (its structure and development, its founders and public functionaries), too little attention has been given to the teachers, who were the chief agents of the system's extraordinary achievements.

In a reunion of graduates, teachers and principals of the Lodz Hebrew high schools held in Tel Aviv in 1960, I discovered that of my class, one-third had survived the Holocaust—a far higher percentage than the average number of Poland-born Holocaust survivors overall. We convened on the tenth anniversary of Dr. Braude's death, upon the completion of the memorial book *Zikhron Mordechai Ze'ev Braude*, published that year by the Zionist Library. The book included Dr. Braude's autobiographical memoirs up to the year 1901, i.e., until his arrival in Lodz, and comprehensive articles by Michael Assaf, Arie Tartakower and Menaḥem Gelerter, describing Braude's activity also in later life. The book served as a tribute to one of the great educators of Polish Jewry, and we who remained and came together for a few hours in this moving reunion, were privileged to have been witnesses to his endeavors, and to their purpose.

At that meeting it was obvious that we were a distinct social segment of Israel's professional intelligentsia and leadership. Among us were writers and journalists, high school teachers and professors, doctors and lawyers, political figures of all parties, army officers, industrialists, and bank managers. Those who in their youth had been counselors in youth movements had here become public leaders. Our school did not send us into the world empty-handed. In addition to giving us a fine general and Jewish education, it equipped us with tools for acquiring new knowledge. It implanted in our hearts a loyalty to the Jewish people and a love of the country. Many of our friends and teachers, too many, were absent from that reunion. We remembered them as they had been in their youth, in the bloom of life.

CHAPTER 12

With the Poet Yiẓḥak Katzenelson

Revival of the Hebrew language and inception of modern Hebrew poetry and prose signal the advent of the Jewish national movement. In this context, the author places the luminous-tragic work of the poet Yiẓḥak Katzenelson and surveys his pre-Holocaust poetry of youth, love, and the joy of life.

CELEBRATING THE TWENTY-FIFTH ANNIVERSARY OF KATZENELSON'S POETRY

The posters in Hebrew and Yiddish in the streets of Lodz at the beginning of May 1928 announced an important event: a function (*akademieh* in Yiddish) in honor of the poet Yiẓḥak Katzenelson (1886–1944), marking twenty-five years of his published poetry. I had no doubt—I *had* to be there. The tickets were cheap, and a full program was promised: choirs, a dance company, instrumental music, and several speakers. Besides our townsmen, a number of speakers from out of town were scheduled: Joseph Heftman from Warsaw, the editor of the revived *Ha-ẓefirah,* and later of *Ha-yom,* and the well-known poet and critic, Yaakov Fichman from Ereẓ Israel who was spending that year in Poland's capital.

Several young culture activists from the Jewish community center Beit Ha'am circle, with whom I used to discuss literary matters, urged me to come. True, Katzenelson had recently shown too much inclination for the Yiddishists and was neglecting Hebrew, and Yiddish, as everyone knew, was a sign of despair, of docile acquiescence with the *galut,* but, basically, he was after all one of ours, a Hebrew and Zionist poet, and was to be honored accordingly. The teacher-poet Yeḥiel Rosenzweig also reminded me that I should attend the *akademieh* and that it was only proper that many fellow students do so.

Bur really, what need was there to urge me? I had known Katzenelson's poetry from my early years. When I began preparing for the entrance exam to the Second Boys Hebrew High School, right after I quit the *ḥeder* at the age of twelve, I had to sit and study not only math and Polish—before this time, it will be recalled, I could not even read the Latin alphabet—but also modern Hebrew. I could not utter or write a single Hebrew sentence without grammatical errors. Differentiating genders, declensions, verb types, not to mention getting a grip on the rules of syntax—none of this was taught in the *ḥeder*. As it happened, my Hebrew instructor in the evening classes I took, the teacher Yeḥiel Citrinowski of the Ẓe'irei Ẓion group, was using a new textbook titled *For Adults: A Book of Study and Reading for Seminar and Evening Students*, composed by Yiẓḥak Katzenelson and Yiẓḥak Berkman, Warsaw, 1921. There I found poems by Bialik, Tchernichovsky and Yiẓḥak Katzenelson, stories by Y. L. Peretz and Sholem Aleichem, all arranged, abbreviated, explained and presented with grammar and syntax exercises. I easily swallowed the book's poems and stories in a few hours, but learning the use of the language and responding correctly to the teacher's questions was not so easy. Eventually I read most of Katzenelson's children's books, as well as his other books and pamphlets—poems, dramas, comedies, and biblical plays.

I became acquainted with Yiẓḥak Katzenelson in the winter of 1925 or 1926, when I was seventeen or eighteen years old and he, at only forty, was already a famous poet, the founder and director of a private Hebrew *gymnasia*, author of plays in two languages and a distinguished personality with a large following of warm and admiring readers. His poems that were set to music were on the lips of many: in Yiddish—*The Sun Sets in Flames* (*Di Zun Fargeyt in Flamen*, 1909), and in Hebrew—*Sad Wind (Ruaḥ aẓuv, ruaḥ agum)*, *Rejoice Galileans (Gillu ha-galilim)*, *Beautiful are the Nights in Canaan (Yafim ha-Leylot bi-Khena'an)*, *The Reapers' Song* from the play *The Prophet* (*Nafol nafla el tokh ha-sadeh shirat koẓrim ha-adirah*), and many other folk and children's poems. His lyrical prose about his visit to Lithuania and on his brief military service in the Russian army had also gained popularity. His poems seemed to sing of their own accord, effortlessly capturing a world of bright radiance, a zest for life, young desire scented with perfumed flirtation, although in a style that observed Jewish "decorum," far from any exhibitionist promiscuity. Even the sadness in his songs was sweet and delightful.

On that winter day when I first met the poet face to face, I already had in my hand a number of poems, or, better said, verses, with which I was not very satisfied as to content, but thought them an achievement in form: sonorities and rhymes, meter and imagery, in keeping with my pragmatic poetics in those days. In no small measure I was following Katzenelson's poetics and totally disregarding those of Bialik; for example, my poem had to be symmetric and harmonious, pleasant and delightful, easily penetrating the heart—so I thought. However, my poems are not the point here.

I did not suspect that before I would get to speak to the poet a Bible and Hebrew language quiz was in store for me. Upon entering the Katzenelsons' apartment and being ushered into the drawing room, I learned that the poet was not at home. However, his father and the latter's friend, Meir Foner, who were sitting there sipping tea, apparently bored, immediately set out to size me up. Now they had something to do. They began quizzing me on difficult words in the Bible.

It was impossible not to be impressed by the dignity of the poet's father, Reb Jacob Benjamin—tall, a beautifully styled beard, meticulously dressed, a handsome *kippah* covering a full head of hair. Born in Belarus, not far from Mendele Mokher Sefarim's native town, he too had composed poems and epigrams in his youth and had even published a book of poems. He had also debated the famed *haskalah* poet Y. L. Gordon. I did not have occasion to read Reb Jacob Benjamin's works. Later in life, I read his son's admiring words: "Clear of eye and high of forehead—a king in uncrowned glory" (*My Father, Avi*, 1937). The son paid tribute even to his father's poetry. To me it was immediately obvious that this father, a God-fearing Jew, although in the modern version of the Reformed Ḥeder, one immersed in Torah but also in world literature, and a poet, or one with poetic aspirations, was both a challenge and a warning. With this kind of father in the house, it would not be easy to criticize traditional Judaism; on the other hand, neither was there here total identification. The son belonged to a much more liberated generation, both in his conduct and his literary work. I sensed in the atmosphere of the Katzenelson home a sort of covert tussle over the existence of an artist, and even more, anxiety for its future, an anxiety over talents that shine brightly and wither without warning.

In contrast to the father, Meir Foner made a neglected, slovenly impression. I saw him later several times in the municipal Staszic Garden, sitting in the company of other old Jews, arguing among themselves about this and that, or playing chess. He seemed older than Katzenelson's father and more demanding. No doubt both were Torah scholars, and it was not easy to emerge unscathed from their scrutiny. We sat around the big table, they quizzing and I trying to respond. I tried to divert the questions from the realm of the Bible to that of our Talmudic Sages, in which I was better versed. I quoted homiletic interpretations and even dared mention, in this home of Litvak *mitnagdim*, some Ḥasidic books. Of the latter, of course, they did not approve.

Mr. Foner took a pamphlet out of his pocket and requested I look at it. It was his Hebrew drama *The Death of King Herod*. Later, I found out that he had composed a number of other plays, including *The House of Eli* and *Judah son of Yeḥizkiyahu, the Galilean,* about the rebellion of the Zealots and the destruction of the second Temple. That month I bought two plays from him. Meir Foner (1854–1936) was one of the holdovers from the *maskilim* circle who came to our town in their youth, like Yiẓḥak Katzenelson's father, from Russia's Pale of Settlement and continued to pursue here the styles they had adopted there. Their tragedy, I believe, requires special attention—the tragedy of those who stand or fall by the wayside of Hebrew literature after their wellspring has been drained and their talent is no longer able to develop under new circumstances. Yiẓḥak Katzenelson himself, in the plays in which he featured scenes of local color, described vacuous, prattling types (albeit young, not old people), who presumed to be writers, artists or actors.

Yiẓḥak Katzenelson had still not arrived. He was expected to return soon. We spoke mostly in Yiddish, and a little in *ivris*—Hebrew with an Ashkenazi accent. I was squirming and beginning to get angry at this teasing and finally asked them outright to stop the interrogation. There was silence. The door opened from time to time. I was told that the house was open to visitors and that many aspirants like me came to receive Yiẓḥak Katzenelson's encouragement and blessing, even though the poet himself was not an editor of any journal.

When Yiẓḥak Katzenelson entered after a short while and sat down across from me, I saw that he was no longer a youth. His curls, in contrast to the photo in his book *Dimdumim*, had suffered from the sooty air of Lodz and had begun to expose a baldpate—a hallmark of many Lodzers. Some years later, he lamented in one of his poems: "The hand of time has touched my head, the hand of time/ Has decimated it/ Has removed its jewel and exposed it." Likewise, in a more whimsical and prosaic rhyme: "No longer does the cauldron stir/beneath my scalp's receding hair." He looked at me with kind eyes, perused my poems, commented expertly here and there, made deft corrections with a light hand, and suggested a change in word order. Finally, he asked me if I knew that my relative, Elimelekh Szmulewicz, also wrote in Hebrew.

Elimelekh was my father's cousin, the son of grandfather's brother Yaakov, an industrialist who had moved with his family to Ereẓ Israel during the second *aliyah* a few years before World War I, but had returned to Poland

and founded in Lodz a factory that supported him amply. Elimelekh had learned Hebrew in the high school he had attended in Jaffa, but wrote only a little Hebrew, and this too was mainly, I believe, due to the influence of Yiẓḥak Katzenelson. He composed mainly prose poems in Yiddish in the spirit of symbolic lyricism (*à la* Maeterlinck or Tagore?). He was a regular household guest of Yiẓḥak Katzenelson and his closest friend, so I was told, until he moved to Paris. I believe that he perished in the Holocaust. I recall that we used to visit the home of Uncle Yaakov from time to time, but I remember Elimelekh only vaguely, and for some reason his works did not reach me. However, it was thanks to him—so I now discovered—that I had immediate *protekẓia* (favoritism) with Katzenelson. It did not help me much, however, because after I published several poems and prose items, chiefly in *Ha-kokhav* (*The Star*), a monthly for young people, founded and edited by Aron Luboszycki, and later in *Ha-olam* and in the children's paper edited by Yeraḥmiel Weingarten, I realized that my glory would not come from poetry. When I was about to leave Poland I began to take greater enjoyment in expressing myself in essays and research. Nonetheless, I continued to visit Katzenelson from time to time, and I appreciated his words—within limits, because by the twenty-fifth anniversary of his poetry, I already began to feel that my regard for his work was diminishing.

In the following pages, I will try to recall my impressions of Yiẓḥak Katzenelson's works as I knew and understood them in those days, before the function in his honor and shortly thereafter, when I took my leave of the poet and of Lodz.

The festive hall was full, indeed bursting at the seams. Over one thousand celebrants had congregated, pressed into a relatively small auditorium. The event lasted some three hours. The Ha-zamir choir, of which Yiẓḥak Katzenelson had been a founder, sang. Several of Lodz's outstanding artist-performers were there to honor the poet. The speeches patently demonstrated how much the Jewish public, in all its diverse camps, appreciated him. Most of the addresses were in Yiddish. There, for the first time, I heard Yaakov Fichman, the well-known Hebrew poet and literary critic. He was the same age as Katzenelson and had begun writing in the last years of the "Fertile Decade."[1] His first book, titled *Stems* (*Giv'olim,* 1911), contained elegiac poems of soft end-of-summer sadness, sunsets, and autumn winds whispering through the plains of his native Bessarabia. If I am not mistaken, that evening Fichman wished to refute in his speech-essay the commonly held view that Katzenelson's poetry was one of light-headedness, of reckless and mischievous frolics of youth. True,

The young Yizhak Katzenelson with a proud head of curls in an advertising postcard with a brief bio and a quote

Katzenelson had begun with paeans to the good life of this world, poems that had not even a whiff of the shadow of *galut*. But his poetry also dealt plaintively with the fleetingness of youth and contained much of the austerity of one who had peered into the abyss. The critic was perhaps thinking here, for example, as was I, of Katzenelson's elegiac 1926 poem *My Celebration is Over* (*Avar ḥaggi*): "The age of youth will never return." A vexatious autumn rain begins to drip; the days of celebration are over. "My nightingale (*zamir*) is in a cage/ Together with me he beguiles in song (*zemirot*)." What kind of song can one sing in a cage?

Yiẓḥak Katzenelson responded in Yiddish, thanked the well-wishers, the performers and the audience and explained that he was principally a teacher and educator. His mood was not very upbeat; every poem cost him torment: "We poets, we bang our heads against the wall." To conclude he read a poem in Yiddish *Etti's zun* (*Etti's Sun*) over which I mulled for a long time when I read it in our daily newspaper. What did the poet wish to express and why, of all occasions, did he choose to recite it at this celebration? For many years, the clipping of this poem lay among my papers. I thought that one day its meaning would become clear to me. When I heard it, and even more when I read it, it seemed to me elusive and stinging, an embarrassed expression, surely a result of wrenching quandaries. I believe I had grasped the reason for the embarrassment which the poet felt at this semi-jubilee festivity.

IGNORED BY THE CRITICS

I do not know if the essay which Fichman delivered at that celebration was ever published. Even then I wondered why serious critics, Katzenelson's contemporaries, wrote no comprehensive critical evaluations of his work. They applauded him, patting his back in short reviews, and, especially when a new book appeared, praised the delightful, playful spirit of his poems and stories, but did not bother to explain their quality. Even less did they bother to analyze his plays, neither the comedies nor the biblical dramas, nor the innovations he brought to children's songs. That large coterie of Hebrew writers, who so often wrote about each other, left behind little more than scant, vague notes about a prolific poet and playwright who enjoyed immense popularity. True, he only managed to collect his writings—three volumes of poetry—just shortly before the outbreak of World War II, and these did not reach us in Ereẓ Israel at the time.

Had it not been for his poetry during the Holocaust about the "murdered people," which Beit Loḥamei Ha-geta'ot (The Ghetto Fighters' House—Itzhak Katzenelson Holocaust and Jewish Resistance Heritage Museum) took upon itself to publish, together with his earlier works, in handsome editions with introductions and notes, this author would likely have been completely forgotten.[2] The question as to why this would be so, which perplexed me in those days as well as later on, requires an answer.

One may argue that the new Hebrew literature which burst forth in full force after World War I caused its preceding creators to be forgotten. In the mouths and pens of the new writers in Ereẓ Israel, the Hebrew language became crisper and suppler, richer and more complex. The problems occupying them acquired profundity through the grief and despair and valiant effort of building the country under harsh conditions. A poet like Yiẓḥak Katzenelson, despite his command of a supple and rich language (reminiscent of Shlonsky in its playfulness and surprising twists), appeared somehow paltry, lacking, and "bourgeois," or, if you like, as a young dreamer, one who does not have his finger on the pulse of his own age.

One may also say that Katzenelson expended his energy on two literatures, Yiddish and Hebrew, but writing in two languages did not detract from the reputations of Yakov Steinberg or Uri Ẓvi Greenberg, and others. One might further say that the artistic styles to which he clung—G. Hauptmann's, later Maeterlinck's, symbolic naturalism, and the erotic lyricism and psychologizing of Schnitzler and their likes—were rejected. New styles took center stage.

Another factor that may have worked against Katzenelson was that all the major Hebrew writers in the diaspora of Eastern Europe had made *aliyah*. Among the stragglers were Yaakov Cahan and Gershon Shofman. Zalman Shneur lived in Paris, later in New York, and eventually in Israel, but as of 1933, he was publishing his poetry in Ereẓ Israel. Katzenelson visited Ereẓ Israel twice (in 1924 and 1934), always intended to make *aliyah*, but did not manage it in time. He wrote to Bialik that he would not leave Ereẓ Israel to his fellow writers there alone, "for I will come." However, in the 1930s his high school obtained the much sought-after and hard-won government accreditation, which headed his stationery: "Yiẓḥak Katzenelson's Humanist *Gymnasia* for Boys, Lodz (with Government Accreditation)."

Also of little help was the Ashkenazi pronunciation to which he adhered in his Hebrew poetry to the very end. "Pronunciation is not a trivial matter," he explained in the 1938 introduction to his collected poetry, "it is a critical matter of the soul. I will not lie to myself, I will not exchange it for another."[3]

Finally, in the last dozen years he hardly participated in the main journals of Hebrew literature, and especially not in those that appeared in Ereẓ Israel.

All these explanations, and possibly others, contain grains of truth. Perhaps more persuasive is the poet's own explanation, partly self-justification, partly self-critique, in that introduction. Most of his poems were "a sort of flight and quest for refuge" from all the horrors he had witnessed in real life and in his dreams. "It has now been decades that I am fleeing, that I block my ears from the evil spirits … I have sung about the trees and the stones and things of no consequence," only not about anything capable of depressing his spirit. The truth is, he never sang of inconsequential things. His poems were always interesting, but perhaps he really did not dare come to grips with the terrors of Jewish life in those generations. Perhaps for this reason he rarely participated in the journals that appeared in Ereẓ Israel.

POETRY OF SPLENDOR AND LOVE

When I stood that spring day of 1928 in front of the poster announcing the semi-jubilee celebration, I was surprised that he had already been writing for so long. I remembered that his books had begun to appear only at the end of the century's first decade, and later. But when I went to check this out I saw that his first poem, as it appeared in the collection *Twilight* (*Dimdumim*, 1910), had been written in 1903—indeed twenty-five years earlier. The poet had then been sixteen or seventeen years old, a promising young virtuoso. The title of the poem, *Radiance* (*Zohar*), immediately evoked in the Hebrew reader's mind the poems of Bialik.

In those years, Bialik was publishing his widely acclaimed nature poetry. These poems, the critics wrote, launched a revolution in Hebrew literature. Joseph Klausner wrote: "Poems rich with observation and copious imagery—*Radiance* (*Zohar*), *The Pool* (*Ha-brekha*), *Morning Breeze* (*Ẓafririm*), *At Sunrise* (*Im shamesh*), *From the Winter Songs* (*Mi-shirei ha-Ḥoref*), and more—regenerated the young Hebrew literature and infused it with a new realism and melded astonishing realistic concretization with creative, rich imagination." Other critics wrote in a similar vein.

If comparison may be permitted for the sake of clarifying the young man's path, in Yiẓḥak Katzenelson's poem about light there is little description yet much rhetoric of light. For example, "And the whole thirsty universe drinks from the great splendor and savors it … A mighty mountain bathes in light, also a grain of sand/ Everything … and I too tore the bolt off my heart / And absorbed the light." In a number of its expressions, *Radiance* is directly reminiscent of the Romantic poetry in Bialik's kingdom of splendor. The difference is in the price paid for acquiring the light.

Bialik started out as a poet from a point of utter despair with himself and with everything that he had attained in his youth: out of "complete defeat," he wrote, "unneeded by humankind and God," "shredded in ten shreds." Yiẓḥak Katzenelson started out with light and fluent verses as a life-loving youth unburdened by spiritual quandaries, at one with himself and his world.

True, at the end of *Radiance*, Katzenelson seems to hint that the light did not come to him easily: "And you [readers] drink and drain the warm light/ With the marrow and the blood." Here he introduced another Bialikean motif, from the poem *I Didn't Win Light in a Windfall* (*Lo zakhiti ba'or min ha-hefker*)—the poet's light is the quintessence of his soul and has cost him dearly. The poem also has a linguistic innovation, which shows that the young poet, who knew the Bible well, quarried it for old-new possibilities.

After World War I, Katzenelson wrote a critique on Bialik. Of the latter's radiance poems he wrote: "When a man reads Bialik's *Zohar*, he shelters his eyebrows with his hand from the light—bright, hot, painful in its brilliance." But in his youth, in his own *Zohar*, he declared with strange egocentrism, "from the mountain summit/ To all the meek and bitter: /... Brothers ... I abandon my heart/ And you, drink and drain the warm light, with its marrow and its blood" as though the light did not shine upon the whole earth and all its dwellers, but was given only to the young poet, and he, in his great generosity, is donating his marrow and blood, sharing his light. The light has been substituted for poetry, and the poet must give it to the many, albeit in pain, and not as a liberally distributed gift.

Notwithstanding his admiration for Bialik's poetry of radiance, forest, and pool, he felt these did not constitute Bialik's real world, the world in which he truly lived. No, the essence of Bialik's poetry resided in the poems where he laments the evanescence of youth, the love that never came, the ruined sanctuary. Bialik is "the priest of the sanctuary that has been destroyed," a man who awoke one day to find that his youth was gone and its hopes never materialized. The beloved woman walks away from him, and a dark terror descends upon him. Time has disillusioned him. The poet sees a collapse of faith, a "collapse of being."

In this reading, I sense that Katzenelson has imparted to Bialik some of his own mood as it was in the nineteen twenties when I knew him. Moreover, and this is another motif that was increasingly heard in Katzenelson's writings, Bialik is the Jew who treads on soil that is not his, as though he "fell to earth from one of the distant planets, and the earth is a stranger to him," and for this reason he yearns for "distant isles ... as to a homeland." Thus, boldly, Katzenelson brought Bialik nearer to his own image, as he himself was in those days, after *The Prophet* and after *Tarshish*—still at the height of his powers, but already pondering time's passage and loss, and showing embarrassment at the ceremony in honor of the twenty-fifth anniversary of his poetry.

In my youth, as I noted before, I viewed Katzenelson as an artist of light and pleasant poetry, for although he also wrote about the everyday life of *galut*, and even about the pogroms in the *shtetl*, the main thing was the poetry of love and desire with its attendant sweet-sad disappointments. In the poem *Love* (*Ahava*), a young man drowns himself in the river because his beloved has rejected him. He leaves his knapsack on the riverbank and disappears into the water. The following day his beloved finds the knapsack containing the letters she had written him. Now she is already sending love letters to a new sweetheart. Katzenelson's loves are featherweight, both in their delights and in their regrets. There are many young maidens in his poetry, and for Katzenelson the love for a woman is not as "strong as death."

However, in a poem from 1928, *The Ḥasid's Daughter's Song about [her Father's] Dance* (*Shir ha-maḥol le-vat Ḥasidim*), there is some kinship between the fire—the "scorching flame"—kindling the daughter and the love of God enflaming her father, the Ḥasid of Kotzk. This poem manifests the poet's sympathy for Poland's Ḥasidic world, but the flame of Kotzk, which rises to heaven, does not correlate well with the flesh and blood fire of the Ḥasid's daughter, and if the poem stops short of being a downright profanation of the holy, neither does it hallow the profane.

In a 1926 poem, *To the Mountain* (*Hera*), a youth has departed on a long journey, "His song still rejoices, dives and rises," he goes up mountains and down into valleys. "There is height upon height, abyss upon abyss," and he walks on: Where, in what direction, and with what hope—this the poem does not say. What is important is that this youth is still walking, that the road is "far, far, far" and there is the exuberance of walking in "joyful song."

Katzenelson was never an ideologue. Even though he was close to the labor movement in Ereẓ Israel and in Poland and to the He-ḥaluẓ movement, and his friends were his cousins Yiẓḥak Tabenkin and Berl Katznelson [sic], both labor leaders later in Ereẓ Israel, he did not espouse, at least not in his poetic work, any particular national or social theory. His patron from youth was David Frishman,[4] "a man of good taste and mind," who dealt with general themes in the spirit of West European aestheticism. The problems of the Jewish people and the great transformations agitating that generation are notable in Katzenelson's early work by their absence. He is not concerned with the relations between Judaism and humanity, traditional faith and secularization, between *galut* and redemption, individual and community. The banners have been removed from the high masts, the sublime and the momentous are avoided. The new Jew, who lives outside the strictures of traditional faith, takes on a new stature in this human poetry of exuberance and love of beauty and pleasure. The poem *Ruaḥ aẓuv, ruaḥ agum* was frequently sung in those years.

It tells of a young lover who conjures the wind to carry his sighs to the small white house where his beloved lives and he regrets that the emissary, the wind, does not return. The girl does not receive his sighs of love. The Hebrew reader would remember Bialik's sighs and the wind that carries them. Despite the sad wind in Katzenelson's poem, there is the *joie de vivre* of a young man who will find another girl, or even many.

TALES OF YOUTH

The autobiographical prose poem *Within the Borders of Lithuania* (*Bi-Gevulot Lita*, 1909), which the poet had titled *poema*, did not disappoint me when I reread it again this year. I had remembered its essentials: impressions of youthful falling in love, devoid of carnal lust, yearnings for a kiss and an embrace, an innocent and fresh work, redolent of dewdrops and fragrance. This is not the Lithuania of the great *yeshivot* to which the young, clever, sensitive, and fun-loving youth travels, but a Lithuania of modest Jewish girls, daughters of the family he had left in his childhood. One can see here their faces and their eyes, and there is even talk of their chest (not of breasts). Moved by agitation and imagination the young visitor fondly rhapsodizes about the lovely Jewish girls: "In spotless white dresses the black-curled ones stand out," when they come out for a Sabbath afternoon stroll, not, heaven forbid, beyond the permissible Sabbath boundary. Their ribbons and kerchiefs are tied around their necks so as not to carry them on the Sabbath. In this story the sun is imagined as a man, and the moon as its beloved maiden. The whole world sings a song of love. This is a Lithuania of strolls to the bridge and to the town, a poor Lithuania, but innocent and full of grace.

The story about a meeting with the family members whose daughters are like graceful gazelles, and meetings with other girls, breaks off from time to time, as in the journeys of Heinrich Heine,[5] with poems and rhymes. For every love, however, a disappointment lies in wait. One poem tells about the blacksmith who has made a carriage for the landowner and the latter came and seduced the smith's beautiful wife. The blacksmith seeks to kill his client, the wife's lover. The story contains allusions to pure angels, demons, and demonesses. There is a *nudnik,* a cripple, and a penniless frustrated artist, but the disharmony, the taunting and the ridicule all dissipate in the atmosphere of charm and pleasantness. The story ends as it began, with the young man obtaining what he had sought, "All that evening I stood with my mouth open and into it a small rosy hand tossed the cherries, one by one, one by one."

Even the second prose *poema, Exile* (*Galut*), which deals, ostensibly, with a painful subject, conscription into the Russian army—a terrifying prospect for young men and their parents—is mostly an idyll. The young man carries in his arms a charming girl, "the small and light Rachel," over a swamp. The description of the conscripts, Jews and non-Jews alike, and their consignment to barracks, with all the attendant feelings of estrangement and dread, is bathed in an atmosphere of faith that everything will end well.

Katzenelson did not bother writing any more stories or narrative poems and, except for two later attempts, did not return to narrative prose. Even though they were, as Y. H. Brenner said, "charming sketches," it was clear that they lacked narrative power. No distinct picture emerges—neither of a town nor of its people. Even the girls, those lovely gazelles, only float in the air of lyric sentimentality, without any substance. They are mere objects for falling in love. Frishman, his mentor, had preached harmonious style, beauty and keenness, but not close observation and the precision of whatever is being observed. In a number of his plays, Katzenelson adopted the naturalist style that was by then pervasive in world and Hebrew literature, but he was not really attracted to prose that examined society's defects. Both the norms of Hebrew literature at that time and the qualities of his own talent swayed him in the direction of poetry and plays.

HEBREW LITERATURE IN KATZENELSON'S YOUTH

When Yiẓḥak Katzenelson published his first poems, the new Hebrew literature stood at its zenith. Its great creators—Mendele, Aḥad Ha'am, Frishman, Bialik and Tchernichovsky, had reached the high point of their flowering. Elsewhere,[6] I have described the years 1897–1907 as the most fertile decade in the history of the Jewish people in the modern era, rich in outcomes, both in vision and in deeds. During this decade most of the contemporary parties and institutions of the national movement and of the Jewish socialist movement were established, and most of the leaders—theoreticians and practitioners—who shaped recent generations emerged. Many forces, some that had been repressed for many years, burst out into the open. It seems to me that everything that developed within the Jewish people in the first half of the twentieth century was already encapsulated in this fertile decade and gradually moved from potential to actualization.

Hebrew literature was the inseparable companion of the great changes that were taking place within the Jewish people. In that last generation, before its disappearance from the stage of our history as the nation's main body, the Jewry of Russia and Poland had brought forth a series of outstanding Hebrew creators who sent out deep roots into the sphere of the personal in order to repair the domain of the public and national. Their artistic and public achievements awoke a craving for individual and national pride. Close upon the generation of Bialik and Tchernichovsky, actually just shortly thereafter, an eloquent array of poets and prose writers ascended our literary stage: Zalman Shneur, Yaakov Cahan, S. Ben-Zion, Yaakov Steinberg, Yaakov Fichman, Y. D. Berkowitz, Y. H. Brenner, G. Shofman, U. N. Gnessin, Yaakov Rabinowitz, S. Y. Agnon, A. Barash, David Shimonovitz and others who expressed, each according to his inclination and talent, a yearning for beauty, courage, self-respect, and freedom. On their lips was the song of human suffering, the terror of non-being and the yearning for redemption and consolation. They described what they saw in Jewish *shtetls* and big cities—desires of the heart, everyday events and bold, undreamt of exploits.

As a generality, one may affirm: Hebrew literature heralded and largely paved the way for the new era in which the Jewish people began bringing its spiritual ideals "down to earth." It revealed the generation's tremendous cravings for life's tangible earthy ground and an equally great capacity to conquer the visible world artistically. Incidentally, in addition to the discovery of the visible, covert wellsprings were also revealed, the "concealed within the revealed," as Berdichevsky (Berdyczewski) had demanded, the mystery of the world. In poetry and prose, the nation's inner soul was being revealed, warts and all. The dark nooks and crannies of the spirit, which even the taunting *haskalah* literature had not succeeded in uncovering—a host of personal distresses and the woes of *galut*—were now exposed. A number of writers heaped upon the nation a thick layer of shadows upon shadows, focusing on nothing but flaws, and almost entirely missing all the light and goodness that inhered in the Judaism of old, when it was still at peace with itself. At the same time, Hebrew literature also sang a paean to the nation's dormant forces that, once aroused, would work wonders. Erect and proud, it struggled with both the past and the present, and prophesied for the nation a new birth—even though it was gnawed by doubt whether indeed a nation that for centuries had dwelt in *galut* might be capable of this rebirth.

However, precisely at this moment, on the eve of World War I, when Katzenelson's talent was gathering momentum and he began publishing his first works, this rapid and wondrous flowering of the Hebrew revival literature came to its first conclusion. The palette of colors used in its most recent works had turned dark grey. The lamentation increased—about the disintegration of the nation and of the individual heart, about "clefts," and "shreds," and the feeling that the ground was collapsing beneath one's feet. Bialik fretted, "It is impossible for a people that does not have a full life, but only wilted scraps of life, to have a full poetry and art; it can only have wilted scraps thereof."[7] It was most difficult to build the home of Hebrew literature on foreign soil. "We cannot change our condition in the diaspora," wrote Berdichevsky, "and if the soil collapses under our feet each time anew, surely those who walk upon it must totter."

It was a time of loss of nerve. Faith in the healing power inherent in the renewal of literature died out. Despair among the new Hebrew writers grew, precisely because the reckoning with both traditional and contemporary Judaism became more trenchant and because the new writers no longer contrasted, as the *haskalah* writers had done in their day, a wise *maskil* in command of his country's language and manners with a superstitious Orthodox Jew who knows nothing about the ways of the world. They knew that a healthy, moral life in the present was also eternal life, and at any rate was not worth much less than eternal life. The spirit of "Yavneh and its sages," which had established and made viable the life of Torah study in the diaspora after the destruction of the second Temple has no significance and value without the soil of "Jerusalem," Berdichevsky explained. "The Jewish people have no soil, or even the echo of a soil," he wrote, and because its life, unlike that of the nations who dwell in their own lands, has no real substance, it lacks the power to spin the thread of creativity from generation to generation on a national and territorial scale, in all its acts and for all its needs. Our endeavors, wrote Brenner, are "cobwebs, flapping and dissolving in air."

The despair in literature increased with the dashing of the first hopes for political freedom in Russia after the failed revolution of 1905. The events of this revolution immediately revealed—in full fury—all those destructive phenomena that bring in their wake complete acculturation. Nor did the Zionist movement offer any solid support; it had become a theoretic option, a pretty story, nothing requiring the kind of tangible action that transforms the life of every Jew in his very home and impels him to leave that home. In these difficult days the loudest voices came from those whose strength was fueled by their profound despair, like Berdichevsky and Brenner, the last defenders of the fortress, as it were, heartbroken yet erect. They threw themselves into the battle, consumed by doubts, but in their individual way, full of faith.

The old Hebrew literature, Brenner explained in the year that Katzenelson's *Dimdumim* appeared, had had a homeland which had nurtured it—religion and faith in God. This homeland, though fictitious, airy and unreal, was nonetheless a homeland. "However, the modern, secular Hebrew literature is entirely bereft of a homeland. Until a new generation arises which will pursue natural Jewish work in our small settlement in Ereẓ Israel where they will be sons to their motherland and their literature will be its fruit, our literature will remain dolorous, nurtured only by crisis and yearnings for the impossible, feeding upon this very lacuna, if not to say—upon emptiness."[8]

LOVE AND ART GIVE MEANING TO LIFE

Where in all this was Yiẓḥak Katzenelson?

His poetry blended smoothly into the emotional and literary landscape of young people of his generation who were already feeling the hollowing of communal life under their feet. Facing the great new void, the young Jewish person, the "individual," the "loner," the "detached," or "alienated" (*talush* in Hebrew, a frequently used epithet to describe this figure), began to seek his happiness, the purpose and meaning of life, on his own, or with just a few companions. The individual now in pursuit of his own course no longer presumes to be a sort of Promethean figure who throws off the yoke of conventions in a bold clarion call to "change values" (Berdichevsky). There was no rebel storming of ramparts for the liberation of the individual; the liberation came as though of its own accord with the slackening of the bonds that held collective faith and life together. Katzenelson's work, as indicated, knowingly distanced itself from the Jewish problematics of his age and his individualism too was not ideological.

As a lyricist, Katzenelson articulated his longings and marveled at the power of invention, at the power of the poetic art in his possession. If faith in the living god was lost and the nation's great problems loomed as unsolvable enigmas, it was still possible to relish life, its richness and adventures. His poetry expresses a quest for life's purpose or a quest for its absolute meaning in love and art. How so?

Katzenelson's poetry evinced no mystical affinity to the absolute in life. The basic tune in his poetry was not philosophical; no great wonderment seems to have resounded in the depth of his being to agitate the profound foundations of being itself. It was as though his poetry did not strive to plumb the depth of his own soul in order to find therein the depth of the world and its dark abysses. The cult of life did not lead to an expansion of the personality, stretching neither to heights nor to depths. It seems that when the artist—thirsting for life in its plenitude—opened a porthole to peer into being, its expressions of sorrow, contradictions and fragmentation did not agitate his soul; rather, he wished to divert his mind from them.[9]

In various guises, in many and diverse tones and semi tones, Katzenelson sang the fundamental experience of faith in life, the intensive expression of which is love. In love and in the artistic act, he sought life's meaning. After the poem *Zohar* in his first book *Dimdumim,* Katzenelson composed several additional love poems. The sun sends the world a farewell kiss; the grove and the mountain are a pair of lovers. Love is a cosmic *eros.* With no shelter in the universe and no shared communal beliefs, one seeks the warmth of love.

One may generalize and say that when faith in absolute meaning does not find an answer in rationality and science, and turns to the emotions, to dreams and the unconscious, it crowns the irrationalism of love and artistic creation with kingship. The Romantics of every generation have made love and art the chief focus of a poet's life. In Katzenelson's works too, irrationalism is a sort of supreme wisdom, the wisdom of the heart, superior to and surpassing the wisdom of the mind. Irrationalism is not chaos and transience; rather, it is redemptive, it enchants with the promise of salvation. The acts of artistic creativity and of love are a refuge, balm for the soul lost in the rubble of beliefs and opinions.

"The priests of beauty will redeem the world in song and melody," so thought Yiẓḥak Katzenelson even before Tchernichovsky wrote those words in his famous crown of sonnets.[10] Perhaps under the influence of Y. L. Peretz, or maybe on his own, for he was endowed with a fine musical ear and was a member of a music-loving family, he exalted the melody. In his play *The Prophet* (*Ha-Navi,* 1922), he wrote that melody was "the mother of all, the cornerstone," a kind of substitute for the wisdom of the Book of Proverbs and for the Torah, as described in the Sages' homiletics. In a similar vein, he speaks of melody as an antecedent to the creation of the world and that which made creation possible: "The whole world's space I fill" … "And if there is spirit in man—I am his light/ I say to him: create / I, the melody." The coupling of God with melody created the universe, and this union maintains it in permanence. Melody teems in all of creation; it is the eternal, cosmic ceaseless *eros.* It endows purpose, order, and meaning. Melody says, "Wherever [there is] God's spirit, there am I." Melody without spirit is not melody. This theme of the spirit, which is identified in *The Prophet* with music, is an innovation, and is not present in the poem titled *Melody* (*Mangina*), as printed initially (1916), separately.

In summary, the act of art joins the theme of love. It redeems from the stings of life and, at any rate, overcomes them more easily. It gives courage and hope.

For the generation of the "loners" and the "detached," art became what religion had been for their fathers. For Yiẓḥak Katzenelson's father, writing poems was an entertaining diversion—the essence of his world was intact without it. For Yiẓḥak, it was a temple and an altar. The problem is that the powers of creativity cannot be depended upon to last a lifetime. They are, by their very nature, evanescent. If a poem is not weighty, one might still add weight to the oeuvre as a whole through sheer numbers, by proliferating more poems. However, their quality, and certainly their quantity, cannot silence doubt. Perhaps Yiẓḥak Katzenelson, more than many other poets of his era, was entitled to say, "My poems have dropped into the camp, and now they are familiar to every pretty girl and on the lips of young men." And yet, neither love nor art guarantees permanent salvation; the poet's soul continues to question.

Another thing, also painful. As long as the world, guided by faith in divine providence, remains anchored in its sturdy frame, it accepts sorrow and suffering as part of its order. A community sustained by a clear and stable set of meanings believes that there is justification for its sacrifices. Sorrow and suffering are part of what it expects from life and cause no surprise. A priori, man must accept the bad with the good. However, where the permanent set of meanings breaks down, sensitivity to pain and suffering increases, and sacrifice makes no sense because one no longer knows its why and wherefore. We have seen this in previous generations and much more so, in our era—every voluntary concession engenders commensurate feelings of insult, outrage and unhappiness. Those who used to make do with little, no longer accept their fate. In other words, in the absence of a stable world order governing a united community, conducted according to consensual norms, a person's quest for and expectation of happiness is entirely individual. Both his heightened sensitivity to suffering and his increased expectation of happiness result from the same breakup of his world.

Katzenelson's poetry was born under the sign of the "in between" era, which Bialik described in his poem *To Aḥad Ha'am* (1903). He chose to seek his happiness in love and artistic creativity, to fashion from chaos a new personal order, sustained by melody.

LAST POETRY BEFORE THE HOLOCAUST

Many of the last poems Katzenelson published in 1937 are expressions of sorrow and terror. They end with the poem *I knew* (*Yada'ati*) that heralds the Holocaust and is close in its spirit to the poems he wrote during the Holocaust:

"You, the grandees, you the heroes and the mighty," he calls to the Gentiles, "and we the sheep led to slaughter—woe to us." Similarly, in his introduction to the three volumes of his collected poetry: "We sing and go up in blood and fire and pillars of smoke ... we sing from the depth of the abyss to which we have been cast." Prophetic words.

Before the events of the Holocaust, he had certainly not been a bitter man given to envy or acrimony; but now, with the significant deterioration of the condition of Jews in Poland, his thoughts turned grim. He confesses that in previous years, in flight from our dismal quotidian, he had sometimes allowed his eyes sleep and had seen sweet dreams, but now he had awoken to "panic and sheer terror." He admits that most of his poems, as we heard earlier, were a sort of quest for refuge from the cruelties of oppressive and depressing *galut*.

In those years, after I had quit Lodz, when only a few of his poems reached me, usually via *Davar*'s Friday literary supplement, the change became noticeable. The direction that he had always avoided in his poems and plays now came to the fore, for example, in the poem *Springs* (*Ma'ayanot*, 1933). The poem's idea somewhat resembles that of Bialik in his poem *May my portion be among you* (*Yehi ḥelki imakhem*), but echoes rather a Ḥasidic teaching: we can enjoy each day thanks to the suffering saviors and redeemers who, in their humility, beg nothing for themselves and in their woe, pose no question. By virtue of such passionate paupers, the meek and humble, we draw strength in the ocean of life. "The beauty of this life—whence do we draw it? From those in pain."

Already in the play *The Prophet* (published in 1922, but written earlier), the poet had expressed two ideas in this vein. The main thing is the pure heart. Human beings as they are, lonely and orphaned, will not find each other. Salvation will not come from knowledge and science, with opening the eyes of the blind ("Why should the blind see their misery ... when their defeat is already complete?"), but through a cleansing of the hearts and in mercy. Here a new dimension opened for love—a theme, however, which was highlighted only in his later poetry. Another idea, similar to this, was expressed at the end of the play, and it is the work's essential "message": The prophet Elisha gave back life to the dead son of the Shunammite woman and now he himself is dead. Yet "he who has died for others still has hope for a life; he will rise and save by turns, will live and die again. This is the mission of the prophet and the man of God on earth." The vocation of the prophet is to live and die for others. This is also the way of the poet-artist who has found happiness neither in the love of a woman nor in the act of artistic creation. Salvation for the individual seeking refuge from the terrors of life and meaning for his life and for the world lies in the purity of the aching heart, which aids one's fellows in kindness and mercy. It is not yet clear here whether the sacrifice will be accepted, that is, why the humble and suffering need to strengthen the lives of those who stand at the edge of the abyss of love and death—why they need to extract for others the "beauty of life." For in that same play we also read, "With me the world shall live, and without me it returns to chaos." Do the humble sufferers do this unconsciously, without a thought, or from pure virtuousness?

It seems to me that here I have returned with Yiẓḥak Katzenelson the "Litvak," the *mitnaged* and non-religious poet, to the world of Ḥasidism. He too harbored a "rebbe" within him. At the very least, we can say that he certainly did not share the *maskilim*'s trenchant critique of Jews and Judaism. When he touches upon human lacunae, ridiculous opinions, or stupid and malevolent acts, he never attributes these failings to the Jew *qua* Jew. There is no ludicrous Jew in his works. There is an assimilated actor, a merchant, or an idler belonging to the Jewish people. He never felt contempt for the attributes of the Jew and, even less, of Jewish tradition.

Katzenelson always stressed that the prophets and the great poets, such as Bialik, reprimanded and reproached in order to mend the nation's failings. Moreover, in his poem *With Mendele in Odessa* (*Eẓel Mendele be-Odessa*, 1936) and in the play *Mendele with the Beggars (Mendele im ha-kabbẓanim*, 1936), he wished to separate Mendele too from his weaknesses. In that play, he has Mendele saying to his friends the beggars that they are indeed, as depicted in his writings, miserable, penniless cripples, but that man's distinction is "the spirit of God within him, which nests in him, mourns in him, and breathes even in a wreck, indeed, more so in a wreck. To all appearances, each one of you is nothing but a wreck, a desolate ruin, but a noble soul and a superior spirit peering through rags and tatters is seven times more beautiful." Further on the fictitious Mendele says, "*With* you, Fishke! Not at your head nor at your tail will I drag myself, only with you and within you, inside your torn and ragged band." Was this too a prophecy, Katzenelson's anxious premonition?

CHAPTER 13

The Holocaust Poet

How the poet of sunshine, youth and love became the emblematic "Holocaust poet." Finding words for the unspeakable. A humanist Zionist message of courage and dignity—Yiẓḥak Katzenelson's address to Hebrew teachers in the Warsaw ghetto on Passover eve, 1942.

Yiẓḥak Katzenelson, the poet of children and young people, the poet of love and radiance, of life's joys and griefs, the creator of highly imaginative lyrical and biblical plays, an author who escaped the austere seriousness of traditional Hebrew literature with its preoccupation with the dark wonder of Jewish

The poet in his prime

existence, came to be known as the poet of the Holocaust. The irony of fate and its fury, the cruelty of time and its vicissitudes! Or did an invisible divine hand choose him to turn his song into a dirge?

In September 1939, with the occupation of the city that had been his home since childhood and where he had established with his family an exemplary Hebrew *gymnasia*, Yiẓḥak Katzenelson fled Lodz for Warsaw. After several months of depression and soul searching, he recovered somewhat when his wife and sons joined him and began writing again. Yiẓḥak Zuckerman (Cukierman) and his associates in the *Ḥaluẓ* movement invited him to join them as a teacher in the new Hebrew *gymnasia* they were establishing. The members of the *Ḥaluẓ* "commune" in Warsaw were the first readers of the new works he created in the ghetto: songs, plays, translations of Bible chapters into Yiddish—large and small compositions, altogether about forty works, some of which I discuss below. Most were printed in the underground press. The poet also published several articles about the most important Hebrew writers in the papers of the Dror movement.[1] Considering the conditions for creative work in the ghetto, one can only marvel at this output, both its quantity and its quality. Yiẓḥak Katzenelson wrote in the years of slaughter four times as much as in the preceding ten years. Most of his output was saved from destruction, and this too is a wonder.

His wellsprings, which prior to the outbreak of the war had begun to dry up, suddenly began to gush forth again. He composed works in all the genres that he had mastered, especially in those mixed genres that had characterized his work: descriptive and narrative poetry, or poetic stories, expressed with a vibrant vitality. All playfulness and laughter vanished in this poetry of the destruction. His language, mostly biblical, remained supple and fresh, without flowery embellishments or the weight of ancient grandeur.

All his life he had turned his heart to the light ("The sun is everything!"), and but for the Holocaust he might have said, like R. Joshua ben Korḥa when he was asked for the secret of his longevity, "In all my days I never gazed upon the likeness of a wicked man." Hitler and his associates forced the poet to take a good look at evil men, at the quintessence of evil, and to gather the strength to go on living day by day. He clearly saw that many of the perpetrators of evil acts were, in fact, small people, insignificant in their views and "banal" in their motives—livelihood, privileges, the fulfillment of instinctual needs—but that the system in which they took part was a most terrible evil. For demonizing the world, its likes had not been known before. In his own flesh and with his spirit of great empathy Katzenelson understood the particular novelty of the

Nazi system: It set out to destroy not only the body, but also the spirit—to debase the image of God inherent in a Jew until it is utterly effaced. I believe that Katzenelson also grasped fairly early that the Nazis wanted to kill *all* the Jews—total annihilation—and it is clear to me that he knew this by the spring of 1942 when he led a Passover *seder* with a group of Hebrew teachers in the Warsaw Ghetto, as I will relate shortly.

In his works during this time of catastrophe he aims at comprehending, in his own poetic, humanistic and Jewish way, the fundamentally incomprehensible, an atrocity diametrically opposed to humanism, to Judaism and certainly to poetry. How to allay this horror? How to express the suffering which quintessential evil has planned in every detail and implemented with an overpowering apparatus?

It was precisely a man like Yiẓḥak Katzenelson—blessed with the remembrance of a happy youth, a happy home, success in his educational and literary endeavors, real achievements in things he had envisioned and planned, and with unforeseen gifts of grace from above—precisely an artist of such mental fortitude, in possession of a strong set of beliefs and "integrative" ideas, who was capable of grasping the madness of quintessential evil.

At the beginning of his stay in the Warsaw Ghetto he gave voice to the daily deprivations, a song of hunger and cold: "They are lying bloated-distended, the girdle on their waist/ a whole legion there together its soul exhales/ dying in multitudes …"[2] The poet calls out, "*Kumi ẓe'i*!" ("Arise! Leave from the midst of the turmoil"), but not *from* the turmoil, rather *into* it, not to the vineyards of the Song of Songs, rather "Arise and leave for the street … we shall die like them all." The street is bustling: some walk, some fall, and many are lying on the ground—"our place too is here." And as in some of his narrative lyrics, the poet's memory returns to his former home in Lodz, to the table laid with all good things, to the gatherings of friends, the cups of tea, "the tea that rivals precious wine," and to the ravenous growing boys, "The plate has only just been filled, and already it is empty."

Hunger and cold. "Cold consumes, in the house a pack of wolves rampages / and through the window bears climb and settle in." The poet goes out to the street, and sees many frozen victims. In vain he seeks a bag of coal: "Grains of coal give me, Help!" Evil rages. Already in his early ghetto poems the poet attempts to bring evil down from any mystical spheres to the human measure of people degraded to perform evil and, especially, to the Nazi leadership's lust for power.

Like subsequent writers about the Holocaust, Katzenelson explored a number of explanations, including the (a) political-totalitarian, (b) anti-religious, and (c) nihilistic nature of Nazism. Ostensibly Hitler means to eradicate the Jews alone, but in a dream he discovers that his real destiny is to conquer the whole world, and that the extermination of the Jews was only a pretext to delude the nations into believing that he did not intend to subjugate them. "It was not you [the Jews] I meant when I killed you ... it is the world, that is my goal/ To make the whole world, this foolish world—my slave."[3] The nations willingly accept his plot, because they wish "to see you broken and oppressed, and [there is] no savior."

Moreover, because of love for a crucified Jew, the living Jew is hated. The Nazis have absolved themselves from both this love and this hatred, that is, from the teachings of the Church. They perform the work of malice, guided by a lucid, calculating intention to deceive. They are heretics who hate the Ten Commandments, the conscience of the individual, every value. The filthy venom of Jew hatred, which the Christian Church propagated among the nations, has generated not only atheism, but also total nihilism. For this reason, the Holocaust is a humanity-wide catastrophe. Katzenelson also expressed these views in his last poems and in the *Vittel Diary* (*Pinkas Vittel*): Those who preach Jew hatred and extermination bring upon the world a demonization which counteracts humanity's moral immune system and common sense.

The ghetto heroes who in their desire to live—"to sanctify life"—opposed the occupiers and, even more, those who faced execution heroically were rebels against evil and guardians of human dignity. The Warsaw Ghetto uprising, as we know, lasted more days than the anti-Nazi opposition of the entire Polish army. In the uprising the ghetto remnants fought with no hope of survival, but also Jewish heroes elsewhere, the tortured and executed, preserved Jewish dignity, upheld values, and were magnified in their death through their faithfulness to that which was beautiful and noble in Judaism and in the world. This was how Yiẓḥak Katzenelson described them.

The Song about Shloyme Żelichowski (*Dos Lid Vegn Shloyme Żelichowski*)[4] described the spectacle of a man about to be hanged in the town of Zdunska Wola near Lodz on the eve of the festival of Shavu'ot, 1942, together with nine other Jews. According to the testimony that reached the poet, the young Ḥasid Żelichowski began singing the *Shema* as he stood before the gallows: "Alone, with devotion, a song before death/ and it was as though he was not alone, with him sang all the people of Israel together." Katzenelson hastened to respond to the event with this sublime poem about the Jew "who exalted man's name on earth, who elevated man's dignity."

These heroes are the guardians of the human-divine image. Their only fault in their own eyes was that they had "spoken ill of our portion in this world," their portion in the Holy City Jerusalem "for which we are destined." These heroes had shouldered the burden of the Torah's holiness and the binding precept to love man. Shloyme Żelichowski killed no one in battle, but "the name of man upon earth he magnified, the dignity of man he elevated!"

Similarly, the rabbi of Radzyn in *The Song of the Radzyner* (*Dos lid vegn Radziner*): "He is so young and as strong as a giant / He is so devout and so simply pious!" but not one to accept the traditional answer that the calamity is a punishment for Israel's sins. Tormented by doubts, the young *ẓaddik* reproaches God for being unable to help His people. In great devotion and sacrifice, in order to preserve the dignity of the dead, he brings murdered Jews to burial, and encourages and comforts the living. Suffering is not a punishment for sins and the fulfillment of precepts offers no protection against disaster; nonetheless, it is an obligation incumbent upon a Jew in order to sanctify himself and his life.

In these poems and in his plays Yiẓḥak Katzenelson voiced the silent suffering of the ghettos. A relatively large public drew comfort and strength from his work; an individual no longer felt entirely locked in under the weight of his own suffering in hunger, in isolation, and on the scaffold. In the play *Hannibal*, he says about the Singer: "Both musician and magician! / Our bitter spirit dissipates in the bitterness of your song!"[5]

The solace in the poems and plays was always one: The people that you Germans intend to bury will rise again. Jerusalem will never be destroyed. You crowd of blood-stained criminals, the earth will spit you out in its fury "and you shall be like a vanishing nightmare fading in the wind."[6]

Katzenelson was in the Warsaw Ghetto during the great uprising which erupted on the eve of Passover, April 19, 1943. Miraculously, his friends managed to get him out of the ghetto to a hiding place on the Polish side. After many hardships he managed to get a Honduran passport, authentic or forged, which saved his life temporarily by classifying him as a "foreign national." For such people the Nazis had established a detention camp in Vittel in eastern France, and there he was sent with his surviving elder son Ẓvi. There he met Nathan Eck, as recounted in chapter 11.

In Vittel, for a period of about four months, Katzenelson kept a sort of diary containing reminiscences, meditations, descriptions of events, daily matters, and expectations—the *Vittel Diary*. He composed two plays in Hebrew: *Hannibal*—about the war of the Romans against Semitic-Tyrian Carthage, and

At Army Headquarters (*Ba-mizba'a ha-roshit*)—about a meeting between a Jew from Treblinka and Hitler and his entourage. Toward the end of the Vittel period, the poet composed in Yiddish the long poem: *The Song of the Murdered Jewish People* (*Dos Lid funm Oysgehargetn Yiddishn Folk*), a distillation of the Holocaust events and its entire quintessence.

As this memoir cannot go into a detailed literary analysis of these works, I will only note a few points about contents and style, and say something about the relationship between Katzenelson's Holocaust and pre-Holocaust work—only a fraction of all that deserves to be said about these complex subjects.[7]

LOVE AND ART COME TO HIS AID

Whoever reads Yiẓḥak Katzenelson's Holocaust works, especially *The Song of the Murdered Jewish People*, cannot but be impressed by the great power of these scroll-pages of grief and protest, and ponder at the profound transformation that took place in the poet and his work. If my portrait of him as presented thus far is true, it leads one to wonder why, precisely, from the pen of the poet of love and joy there should burst forth a song of profound, truly unfathomable anguish. In the words of Yiẓḥak Zuckerman, one of the leaders (and survivors) of the Warsaw Ghetto uprising:

> For us, members of this generation, for the people who lived in Poland, there will be no more faithful expression. There may appear a more artistic expression, more musical, more plastic, but it is doubtful whether anyone will rise to the great truth of this poetry in its simplicity, accuracy, fidelity. Precisely this writing, which lacks distance, is what instills a documentary truth in the poet's great testimony, bares his people's tragedy, and raises his song to the heights of monumental poetry.

With these apt words Zuckerman ended his simple, shattering, informative statement which prefaced *The Song of the Murdered Jewish People*.[8]

I shall here try to briefly explain these words of high praise and clarify the nature of the transformation which had already begun before the Holocaust, especially after World War I and its horrors in the face of the pogroms, discrimination and abuse, as Katzenelson described them. For example, in his Yiddish play *Tarshish* (1921): "You can count on a Jew" declares the Russian officer who bursts with his soldiers into the home of a respectable Jew, Reb Shloyme Tarshish, "that three things can be found in his home—an assimilated Ashkenazi, money, and a daughter."[9] The young man, who in his youth had been undaunted by conscription into the Russian army and had even found in the barracks a friendly officer and genial friends, he who had once accepted with equanimity the horrors of *galut* in Russian barracks, or did not even see them—this man vanished from Yiẓḥak Katzenelson's work long before the Holocaust.

Love—the young bachelor's electrifying-bewitching rush of emotion—turned into a steady flame of devotion to his wife, his children, and the entire Jewish people in its woe. In admiration and awe he spoke of the "burning bush" of love that blazes in his heroes' hearts. Such was the Prophet Elisha who gave his own breath, his very essence, to revive the son of the Shunammite woman (*The Prophet*, 1922). Certainly, this bright flame animates the Rebbe of Radzyn, a noble scion of a glorious Ḥasidic dynasty: "It streams into eyes like a beam, / It pierces the hearts of each and all . . . / It streams, it pierces deep within and without / A holy radiance, a nobleness sublime."[10]

Katzenelson, as mentioned, never ridiculed a Jew, never launched humiliating reproaches at the Jewish people as such, and himself suffered from no sense of inferiority for any alleged Jewish "characteristics." How angered he was with the self-hating assimilated, apostate, or semi-apostate Jews! When the wearing of the star-shaped yellow badge was decreed in the early months of the Nazi occupation, he wrote: "Instead of hating the despicable one who has brought upon us this disgrace, many have expressed their shameful hatred for the Star of David." He lamented the sin of "disrespecting ourselves." In particular, he was pained to see the debasement of Jewish honor in which the persecuted and tormented themselves concurred: "At every step I have encountered in this hour of crisis these deficient ones, and have come to despair: Master of the Universe, this is awful, and worse than death!"[11]

With great love he described the town of Włodawa, one of many Jewish *shtetls* similar to the one he had described in his youthful *Within the Borders of Lithuania* (1909) where the Rebbe of Radzyn sought refuge: "Narrow and crowded, and wider than any width"—a town rich in Torah and holiness. Yiẓḥak Katzenelson could identify wholly with people whose "ideology" he did not share. He admired the courage of the Ḥasidic Radzyner rebbe who did not desert his post, did not abandon his flock, and refused to follow an emissary from Warsaw who came to save him. The rebbe accepted only the money offered for his escape, to be used for redeeming bodies from the sealed train wagons and bringing them to Jewish burial. Katzenelson also described Jews in the big cities with warmth: "I have loved simple Jews in Warsaw"[12]—the *Shekinah* is upon them, Jewish grace on their faces. One must not blame Jews.

As for art, how did it prepare him for setting down on paper the songs of suffering? The simplicity and spontaneity characterizing his earlier writings, the joyous directness with which he used to express emotions, images and playful inventions, prepared him for the writing "which lacks distance," as Zuckerman described it. He never lingered long to examine the events, rather he rushed to express them. His position was close to or immersed in the happenings.

Katzenelson's poetry composed during the Holocaust, if not a photographic reflection of the appalling events, is nonetheless a faithful testimony. Shortly after enduring the first shock when his wife and two sons were transported to Treblinka, through an almost unimaginable spiritual effort he overcame his pain to the point of being able to express both the private and the collective lament.

There was not time to mull over events, to let them filter in lengthy maturation. Above all, it was imperative for him to overcome the paralyzing stupor produced by the sight of mass annihilation. The poet believed, based on the information that reached him, that the fate of Jews in Poland was indeed sealed. Miraculously, the poetic spontaneity which had been his natural lot now liberated powers of expression from the muteness of depression, and he came forward to describe the atrocities and to interpret them as he understood them—to approach the horror, to express the inexpressible. At the same time as his understanding of the horrors deepened, so too did his capacity for expression. In a vocabulary easily accessible to the reader—especially when he wrote in Yiddish, the language in which most of the Holocaust poems were written—he strove to voice himself clearly, to be understood without being obvious. This poet was a teacher and an educator in his every fiber. For this reason, even when he described the most nightmarish horrors there was a representative order in which the subordinate was suppressed and the essential highlighted. His system of tensions and balances warrants further separate study. In this writing there are few "code words," few allusions or symbols. The world is historic, not meta-historic.

His ability to describe these agonies precisely, and through this noble exertion to overcome them, brought the poet to the threshold of silence. But this final, holy silence no longer resembled the first paralysis. The structure of his poems, their linguistic forms, the meters, rhymes and stanzas, over which he remained as precise and exacting as in his early work, perhaps more so, served him like a precarious ford across a rapid river. He held on to these and they empowered and sustained him.

THE SCROLL OF LAMENTATIONS OF A MODERN ZIONIST JEW

Katzenelson's Holocaust poetry begs challenging questions: How did the poet address and how did he engage the reader, and on what level? How did he relate to God, that supreme symbol of omnipotence who is assumed to rule the world in justice and mercy? What was Katzenelson's attitude to the uprising, to revenge, to "Let me die with the Philistines," and to the problem of theodicy? Why did he, Yiẓḥak-Isaac, never mention the symbol of Isaac's sacrifice?[13] These and many other questions arise from his work and are integral to it. As for me, I have no doubt that he was a man of deep religious feeling, though not given to ritual orthodoxy, and it is not surprising that he showed empathy for God-fearing Jews like the Rebbe of Radzyn and Shloyme Żelichowski in the hour of the terrifying "hiding of the Face," when God appeared to have abandoned the earth. I assume that he clung even more than before to love and art as barriers and refuge against the calamity.

Clearly, Katzenelson's pre-Holocaust work differed from that written during the Holocaust, thematically and stylistically, even though the latter appears as an unbroken continuity. The differences were not only of degree, but largely also of substance, as one would expect from poetry about "the other planet."[14] In writing Holocaust poetry he had no existing models to which he might relate or refer, other than those obvious models—chapters from the Prophets and the Psalms, some of which he translated to Yiddish in the ghetto. They must have aided him to overcome the strangeness of the topic and gather courage against the depressing muteness. The most salient models for the poet were Psalm 137—"On the waters of Babylon" with its call for revenge in the final verse, the Scroll of Lamentations, and chapters from the Book of Ezekiel.

However, his poetry during the Holocaust lacks the key element of prophetic faith—the idea that Israel has been exiled from its land because of its sins, which have earned God's just retribution, His anger and wrath, but with hope for His mercy. "The Lord is righteous," hence the call for repentance "Let us search and try our ways, and turn again to the Lord." In Katzenelson's poetry, not only is that most solid foundation of biblical literature—the justness of the destruction—absent, there is also no God who is about to appear on the world stage to astound the nations. Nor is there a mythologized Satan who works his evil upon the Jews. Absent too are the consolations we read in the traditional biblical lamentations and the call to repentance. Crushed by the accumulated weight of experiences that lack any human-divine sense, the despair and spiritual anguish arising from Katzenelson's poems is greater than that of traditional litanies. He seeks an explanation. Not everything is irrational contingency; there is logic in this evil insanity, in the senseless malice, in the banal cruelty. "We are doomed!" is the cry of woe that emerges from his poetry. The Jewish fate in exile is sealed, with no recourse. Words of "curse" escape from the poet's lips in the poem that opens with the words *Vey dir* (*Woe to you*), similar to the curse at the end of *The Song of the Murdered Jewish People*: May the evil ones be destroyed by their own hand, without the help of heaven, or earth or seas. The elements should not conspire "to wipe out the wicked from the earth, let them be annihilated by their own hand." (Canto XV, 15)

At a time when even the wildest imagination could not have foreseen the horror, many Jews clung more fervently to the idea of the "sanctification of life"—not to let the oppressors break their will to live, to carry on, to await better days, to escape in every possible way, to fight for survival (as was the slogan of Rav Nissenbaum[15]). Katzenelson too spoke of the duty of every Jew to protect his body, just as the Rebbe of Aleksander had written to the congregation of Mlawa regarding exemption from fasting on Yom Kippur, in the spirit of "I shall not die, but live, and declare the works of the Lord." Existence itself was a triumph, so he apparently thought, as long as there was still a scrap of hope for escape. I believe that after the massive extermination he witnessed in 1942, he no longer held any such hope. However, the poet himself relates, especially in the *Vittel Diary*, that initially the Jewish public in Poland did not break down under the blows, and even recovered somewhat and continued for a while to be active, whether legally or in the underground. Katzenelson especially admired the pioneering movement, the remnant of the various youth movements that resisted and revolted in one way or another, and in this valiant group he included all the diverse camps then active in the "Jewish street."

Besides the poetry of the collective, the lament of the individual over the destruction of his home, over the wife and children taken from him, must also break out from time to time. "I am the man that hath seen affliction by the rod of His wrath"—this biblical man is the symbol of every tormented and oppressed person. If there is a faith in God in Katzenelson's work, it appears, as in Lamentations, in the recognition that "The Lord hath swallowed up all the habitations of Jacob, and hath not pitied." What is missing here is the all-merciful God who forgives and who returns Israel's captivity. The multiple exhortations to "Sing," taken from the Psalms and the Prophets, are meant to rouse the poet to his task. They provide the encouragement he needs in order to immortalize what he has seen, not to forget, regardless of whether any Jews survive or whether their end has really arrived with absolute finality—because the enemy has "swallowed all . . . and not pitied."

GOD AND MAN IN THE HOLOCAUST

The poet is not preoccupied by the speculative problem whether God—the central symbol of the world's permanent order, upon which all human values rest, and the guarantor of the horizon of expectations and duties—exists as an absolute being unto Himself. The poet does not delve into theology. It is clear to him that "the Lord hath forsaken the earth." In the *Song of the Rabbi of Radzyn,* one of Katzenelson's most complete and beautiful works, the rabbi sees God as one who hides His face. If there is pity in Him, His pity is far above the earth. Unable to save, God remains alone in the world—His people have already been burned and consumed. The poet does not hurl reproaches at God, and he certainly does not taunt Him, as did some of the protesters before him and in his own day, for example, Bialik in *City of Slaughter* (*Be'ir ha-harega*), who has God admit: "Your God is destitute like you . . . I've been cleaned out!"[16]

The Rabbi of Radzyn cries over God's grief and participates in His torment. Paradoxical as it may seem, the rabbi pities God. The silent weeping that resonates through the world rises from the forsaken homes of Jews; it is the weeping of the Master of the Universe. The rabbi knows well that in these days of calamity God is not "strong and mighty"; his people "became a prey and derision to the . . . heathen," and He hides His face. Is the young rebbe still a believer?

The literary critic Dov Sadan described Yizḥak Katzenelson's "spiritual transcending" during the Holocaust, when the poet suddenly found himself in the "Valley of Slaughter," not as an individual, but as the nation's spokesman. In speaking of the individual, he means, apparently, the non-affiliated Jew, a modern Jew, perhaps partly religious, partly entirely secular: "From this perspective, we should spell out the decisive difference between the individual and the nation. For the individual it is possible to look upon God as a symbol; for the nation, it is imperative that its God be for it a reality." In Sadan's view, Yizḥak Katzenelson's "spiritual transcending" is expressed in the idea "that the nation's imperative [to believe] became for the poet a possibility for the individual."[17]

I wonder about the validity of this differentiation between possibility and imperative, between individual and nation. It seems to me that God's existence is no more evident to the narrator of the *Song of the Rabbi of Radzyn,* spoken in deep empathy to its protagonist, than to the poet who speaks in his own name in *The Song of the Murdered Jewish People.* True, the rabbi of Radzyn wishes to sanctify the Name, like Rabbi Akiba in his day, "for my Jews, for the Lord," but his faith in a God who loves His people, who rules the world in mercy, is already very much shaken:

> Oh, devout Radzyner, you're no longer devout!
> You still love your Heavenly Father, you do
> In your goodness forgive him, do forgive him,
> He sees the death of his people
> and is as helpless and powerless as you ...

In these words of despair, the non-Orthodox individual and the rabbi are one. The rabbi too deliberates between revenge and sanctification of the Name:

> "He would have pulled a sword from its scabbard/ in hiding here he would pay back the Germans, the wicked ones."

True, the poem is a song of Jewish heroism—this is what the introduction proclaims. The Gentiles' heroism consists of bloodshed and destruction; in contrast, Jewish heroism, especially in the Holocaust, has always been the shedding of their own blood, sacrifice for others, heroism without a sword, with a pure heart and a clear conscience. In this poem, so full of love for the Torah, for Ḥasidism, for Jewish *shtetl* life, it is doubtful that simple faith in God is "imperative" for existence.

Certainly there is still a difference between the God of the Rabbi of Radzyn and that of the play *Hannibal*, for example, where the Bard-Seer brings man's word to God: In vain has He created a world which is a bad, unfortunate business; an entire nation is dying and finds no succor in its day of calamity. Man is God's plaything, "Have your fun with me/, torment me/, Stop! For/ I shall damn you."[18] At the end of the poem about the Rabbi of Radzyn, his wife the rebbetsin begs him not to go to the Gestapo where he has been ordered, and the rabbi replies that he would be happy to die to honor God's name and the dignity of man.

When Yiẓḥak Katzenelson sings about the Rabbi of Radzyn, or about the Ḥasid Shloyme Żelichowski, he surely is not saying, like the Bard-Seer in *Hannibal*, that the world is "a bad, unfortunate business," which God has given to man in order to torment him or to have fun with him. In the *Song about Shloyme Żelichowski* there is an immense love of Torah, the eternal life-giving Torah given on Mt. Sinai on the day celebrated by Jews as the festival of Shavu'ot, and love of Jerusalem: "I remember the city and am troubled." The poet combines here themes from the festival of the giving of the Torah with the *seliḥot* (penitential prayers) of the Yom Kippur *Ne'ilah* liturgy.[19] In the awesome-sublime situation of facing the scaffold, Jews sing their faith in the Torah, "our consolation," which "is given to us again today," and in the rebuilding of Jerusalem.

Was then the difference between the "individual" and the "nation," especially in this time of calamity, really so pronounced? Was there really a great distance between the Hebrew poet living in the world of the new Hebrew literature with its special, selective affinity to the tradition of the past and its treasures, the teacher-educator sitting among the remnants of the ghetto fighters, and the Ḥasidim and *ẓaddikim*, who went to their death honoring God's name and "human dignity"? Was there much of a difference between him and the Ḥasidic Rabbi of Radzyn who performs a *ḥesed shel emet* (true kindness) in bringing the dead to Jewish burial as recounted above? One may say that that which was imperative was precisely the blurring between the "individual" and the "nation," between Israel and Israel's God. This is what the Jew from Treblinka tells Hitler in the play *At Army Headquarters*, which Katzenelson wrote shortly before his death: "And God, if He should know, all of Israel will know. Israel is like its God, Israel wherever it may be, nothing is hidden … that you have fallen, that you will fall, you and your people both." This is the essence of the poet's view on the relationship between God and His people. God is synonymous with His people, and the children of Israel are God-like because many among them are "men of God."

Due to the helplessness of the Jewish individual and of the nation as a whole during the Holocaust, Israel's God, who is no less helpless in offering succor, "requires mercy," as we heard above. "Israel and Israel's God are one"—Katzenelson wrote in the *Vittel Diary*.[20] The people of Israel are a holy congregation. In preceding generations it produced many "men of God" and "in our generation the number of great-souled Jews exceeds that of our prophets who became saints, as it were, in the eyes of the Gentiles (became saints, but their precepts they do not keep)…" In our day, there are many nameless righteous people, *ẓaddikim*, condemned to live in "the midst of the filth of the nations, who have contaminated this godly world." The nations hate us consciously and even more unconsciously because of the divinity that is within us, and because one Jew became their god. So too are the accursed Germans—and the poet damns them with many imprecations—and likewise their helpers, "the slaves of the slaves of these accursed." For this reason, they wish to eradicate the god that is within us, the godly spirit, the spirit of universal justice and the ethics of truth and beauty. "Yes, beauty, because there is nothing more beautiful than justice, truth and honesty."

Katzenelson recognized Germany as the reign of evil infecting many nations with its venom, "a cowardly nation, despicable, immoral, and murderous, which has chosen as its victim a nation of Jobs, whose helplessness is envied by none" (ibid). Similarly, in *The Song of the Murdered Jewish People,* in the imprecations hurled at the German people—they spurred on all their satellite states and all those who stood by, who knew everything and shut their eyes, or pretended to be asleep.

In the *Vittel Diary,* it must be said, he also wrote some very harsh things about those "despicable creatures"—Jews who aided the murderers, especially the Jewish police—"the lethal blow" abetting the German scourge. He held sober, clear-eyed opinions concerning those who stood by in the Valley of Slaughter and those who observed it from the outside.

The most distressing defect in the poet's eyes was self-abasement. "This defiled nation [the Germans] has taught us abasement and self-abasement." As an educator and a Jew, he now made his final adjudication with those who succumbed to the valuations of the Gentiles. Among those who in the past had failed to uphold Jewish honor, he mentions reprovingly the socialist Bund. They had "heaped abominations upon all that was dear to us," on everything holy, on our very souls. Nor did he spare the ultra-Orthodox Agudat Yisrael party: "It too has sinned toward the Jewish spirit, and its feigned concern for religion is merely a mask on its face." These and similar Jews, who had a warped or misplaced self-regard, were among those who have "defied God of the armies of Israel."[21]

THE SONG OF THE MURDERED JEWISH PEOPLE—STRUCTURE AND MAIN THEMES

In the *Song of the Murdered Jewish People,* the poet no longer voices reproaches about objectionable opinions of Jews. Even the Bund and the Communists are now "mine": "Un meyne komunisten hitskep … meyne massen funm Bund" ("and my Communist hotheads … my masses from Bund"), (Canto XV, 14). Though, for some reason, without "my" in the Hebrew translation.

It was with this poem that the poet gained his enduring renown. The work is structured in fifteen cantos, reminiscent of the fifteen Songs of Ascent in the Book of Psalms—ascent to the Temple—only here the ascent is to the scaffold. Each canto of fifteen stanzas opens with the ending of its predecessor. The lines are long and have a rhyme scheme of a-c b-d. Although written with interruptions, the architecture appears to have been planned from the beginning. It is written in Yiddish, in the simple vernacular of the masses, replete with allusions, drawn especially from the Bible, yet readily decipherable. The poet sees himself sharing his sorrow and protest with the ancient prophets who lamented the nation's woe: "Like Saul my king will I hobble, tortured, toward the soothsayer,/... on the path of darkness to Endor will I walk,/ and from the underworld will I raise my prophets all, and charge them ..." (IX, 10).

Canto I. The poem opens with a call urging the poet to rouse himself to deliver the speech-prophecy about "Europe's last Jews." However, no strength is left for song, no tears for weeping. The poet therefore calls upon all the slain and strangled to emerge from the murder camps: "Reveal yourselves to me, all of you, a world audience ... I will see my people, my murdered people, I will behold them with a mute gaze, silently, and then I will sing ...." It is as though millions of Jews are standing around him, listening to his dirge. The immense sadness that envelopes the reader in the first canto increases as the poet relates deeds and events on the axis of time, as though he were unrolling an epic canvas of events, which, in their horror, do not bear interweaving into the canvas.

Canto II. The poet sees before him, amidst the vast agglomeration of murdered eyes, the eyes of his wife and two sons. Poland's Valley of Slaughter does not resemble Ezekiel's valley of dry bones. Of these modern dead, not a single bone remains for future resurrection. The prophets Ezekiel and Jeremiah are of no help to the poet in his anguish.

Canto III begins to roll out the saga of the great slaughter, how people were dragged from their homes in trucks and train wagons to extermination camps.

Canto IV tells of the train wagons sent full and returned empty, only to be loaded again with Jews; the train cars, mute witnesses to the suffering, are the sole attendants in the dead nation's funeral.[22]

Canto VI. The children were the first victims of the calamity, a holy flock of innocents, how they looked after each other! A girl of five feeds her baby brother.

Canto VII reveals that right from the war's beginning, they knew the catastrophe that awaited them without fail: "All of us, ah, all of us, knew. Therefore many wished to escape, but it was too late." There follows a description of flight and despair.

Canto VIII tells of the burning of synagogues, of the desecration of everything held sacred, and of the dignified bearing of the rabbis and the faithful believers.

Canto IX tells of the mute, empty skies. Previously, the poet had so often sung their glory—the sky, the sun, and the moon—like most poets and prophets. Now it is clear that the heavens are desolate and abandoned. In their impoverishment, however, they have won a rich harvest—an entire crucified nation.

This canto ends with: "Rejoice in the Germans, skies above, and may the Germans rejoice in you down here, / and may fire go out from the earth unto you, and may fire descend from you to ignite the face of the earth."

Dr. Nathan Eck confesses in his book *Wandering on the Roads of Death* that during his confinement in Vittel with Yiẓḥak Katzenelson, from time to time the poet would enter his room and read out loud to him and his wife the Song's sections immediately after their writing, but these words made little impression on them.

> All the horrors Katzenelson described, we knew from what we had seen and heard and experienced on our own flesh. It appeared to me that not only was no flesh and blood capable of describing what had happened, or expressing what the dead in their last moments or the handful of survivors felt, but that there was no need of it … Once he came to our room as usual, took out a few pages, and began reading. This was the canto IX 'To the Skies,' which he had just completed. At first, I listened as usual with only half an ear. But those rhymes arrested me immediately, and I was stunned to the depth of my soul. This was the first time in years that a literary work so moved me … The heavens were witnesses to the atrocities and kept silent, whereas he had believed in them and sung their glory all his life … we sat, both of us, my wife and I, and listened in silence, our heads bowed.[23]

Canto X relates how the poet escaped from Lodz. "Oh, if only I had shot him [the German], if only I had killed him at that moment, if only there had been something in my hand"—thoughts similar to those of the Rabbi of Radzyn and to the acts of the Warsaw Ghetto rebels later.

Canto XI is about his wife Hanna, experiences from the Warsaw orphanage, and scenes of the deportation of the children with Korczak and the other teachers marching at their head.

Canto XII. The most terrifying *akzia* on Mila Street. Through this street, more than 100,000 were led to deportation until the city was cleared of Jews. The poet succeeded in escaping with his son. Of the terrible scenes he witnessed on this street.

Canto XIII. The *Ḥaluẓim* shoot at the Germans. About Yiẓḥak Zuckerman and Ẓivia Lubetkin and their fellow ghetto fighters—the last stand. They represent the quintessence of Judaism in the Holocaust. They are the noble bearers of the yoke of heritage.

Canto XIV. The Warsaw Ghetto uprising. Description of scenes of the combatant and burning ghetto: "Over its last Jews the fire flickers and blazes."

Kiddush hashem, sanctification of God's Name—dying without killing anyone—has here made room for "Let me die with the Philistines" in the realization of revenge.

Canto XV. "When all is done." Wherefore have we been exterminated? This canto summarizes the essence of the Holocaust. It tells what has vanished from the world with the extermination of the Jews: "A mother will no longer lull her babe to sleep, no more will Jews die or be born/ and no more will delightful songs be sung … all, all has been wiped out!" The last canto brings the story of the killing into the context of Jewish historical continuity through the ages: "It is a fairy tale, begun in our Bible and down to the present day … A story about Amalek down to one worse than he, down to the German." And his final damning curse—that it be neither the earth, nor the seas, nor the heavens that wipe the wicked from the face of the earth, but that they "be destroyed by their own hand."

Most agonizing in this horrific testimony is the experience of the utter, definitive end of Jews in Europe. In dozens of scenes and images, impassioned utterances, and heart-rending laments, a scene of slaughter is unveiled. The voided world darkens and becomes desolate—an inimical, primeval mass. In this inhuman world, bereft of the breath of affinity to man, the Jew is a stranger.

What remains after us? Only the song, and of this, Hannibal says that it is:

> Our great revenge:
> Song! A song of testimony!
> Its echo will roll on, a thunderous echo
> It is the decisive justness of our cause
> On this earth below
> A song from the end of the world to the end—shrieks
> A reminder of iniquity to the murderous nation
> Until the last generation …
> Until the last, last generation![24]

The song-revenge is not simply the melody which endures forever, as earlier in *The Prophet.* The song teaches a never-to-be-forgotten lesson, or several lessons, that all nations must learn, most especially the Jews. The song will remain suspended in the world's air until a time comes when the sorrow will wane, the insults will abate, and the terrors, like evil, will vanish and perish. It is the outcry of the generation, and a warning for generations to come. The poem opens with the power of song, and ends with it.

The dirge-poem had opened with an agitated conversation with a voice that called the poet to rise and sing about "Europe's last Jews." He refuses: There is no tear in the eye, no strength left to lament. But the muse of his poetry begs him and also promises that in his dirge-poem he will once again see his massacred people "I will eye him mutely ... yes, give me the harp ... and I will play" (I, 15). About this opening, the poet Ezra Sussman wrote in the *Davar* daily newspaper in 1949, upon the publication of the poem's Hebrew translation:

> Such a give and take between the poet and his *Shekhina* [his inspiration, his muse] is unprecedented in the history of ... the great epics. Here sits a poet, like the chief of a tribe, keening over the destroyed nest, and asks the goddess of song only to give him back his incinerated people. The story often sounds like an oral, not a written, narration ... When all forms of life have perished, he remains faithful to the memory of "form" .... For this reason the shrieks in this narration are measured with meter and rhyme. The words weep within a tight prosody and the long line of verse maintains at its center a brief caesura for those weary of the road that lies beneath skies void of God. It is in their face that the rebel hurls his storm, the storm of the cheated nation. Toward them—those empty ones—the mourning bird, which has seen everything, rises. The poet who battles with the heavens, breaches open a path for his people.
>
> 'There is no longer a God within you! Lift up your gates, Heavens, and open them wide, wide,
> Let all my sons enter, all the sons of my slaughtered people, who were tortured to death and died in torment,
> Open the gates for a massive ascent to the Heavens: a whole people crucified, heavy with pain,
> Will enter within ... Oh, each one of them, my perished sons, merits being their God!' (IX, 13)
>
> The poet's mission is to rise together with his people—for life or death—in all their tribulations, and to be their consoler. Not by chance did he choose Yiddish for this last song of the last Jew, because at this moment he needed to talk to them in the language of compassion, in the language of their homes and their outdoors, and of their last moments. But the poem is also the legacy of the generations that came before, and for those still to come.

A MESSAGE OF CONSOLATION

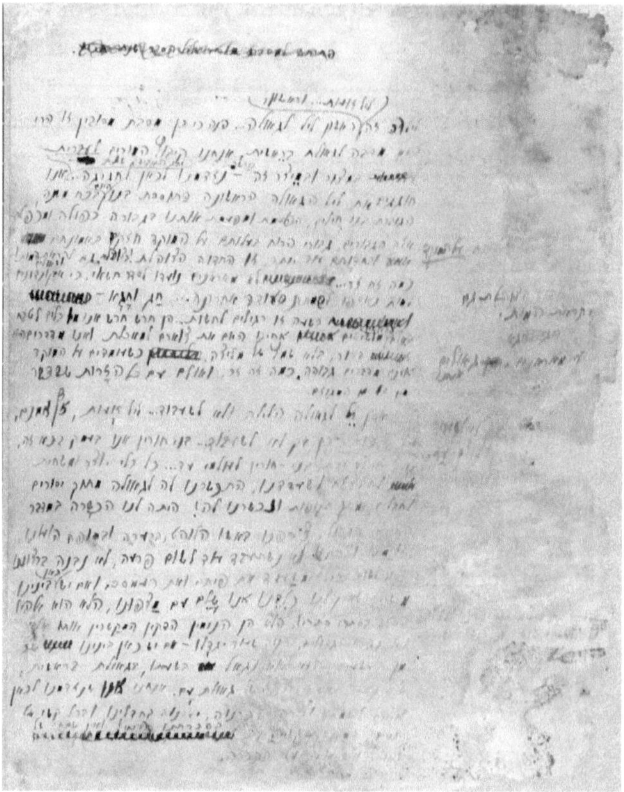

"This night, a night of horrors … and a first, first night of redemption." Katzenelson's address to the Hebrew teachers in the Warsaw Ghetto, Passover, 1942

I conclude this chapter with the message of consolation that the poet delivered—in the ghetto!—an admirable testimony, quintessentially expressive of his mood and thoughts.

On the eve of Passover 1942 (on the second *seder*) in the Warsaw Ghetto, in the heart of Nazi thralldom, Yizḥak Katzenelson addressed the ghetto's Hebrew teachers with a visionary, poetic-philosophical speech, couched in rousing words of invigoration and empowerment.[25] These words merit particular attention because they encapsulate, in allusion and symbol, the essential values and beliefs of a Zionist-humanist Judaism.

"This night, a night of horrors … and a first, first night of redemption … In this siege and strait in Warsaw …, we celebrate the night of our first redemption, which today … fortifies us, pulsates within us, and animates us with redoubled courage." A strange opening line, one that surely surprised his audience, and still today makes us wonder. How, on this *seder* eve, does our first redemption, our exodus from Egypt, animate the hearts of the tormented, suffering-weary and doomed to die, who see no *maẓah* and no wine before them? And with "redoubled courage"?

The poet knew that he was puzzling his listeners. He hastened to assure them: "Strange as it may sound, this is no exaggeration." The doomed "today speak clearly, without a trace of florid speech. When one is bound to the stake, one does not speak ornately." Nonetheless, he testifies to the courage of those who die at the stake, saying that they are "strong in their faith and even more so in their joy, a resounding joy, cheerful even as it faces death." The poet associates the terms "doomed" and "redeemed," and reminds his listeners that theirs was no assembly of "Marranos gathered for a clandestine *seder*." Indeed, the difference is clear—the Marranos saved their lives by accepting the Christian religion, whereas here "the redeemed and the condemned have gathered for the celebration of a last meal." The allusion to Christianity's "Last Supper," which took place on the eve of Passover, is followed by an ironic sad reference to "our Holy Day—and theirs" (*ḥag ve-ḥaga*).

The poet spoke in the present, in this house of bondage at his third Passover in Warsaw (at the fourth Passover, the heroic uprising broke out and the demolition of the ghetto began). The Nazis had already conquered Western Europe, besieged Leningrad, and were at the gates of Moscow. The occupied countries were gradually emptied of Jews. What can one say to a gathering of Hebrew teachers, young and old, who had grown up on Hebrew literature, some upon the Torah, most of whom knew by heart the poems of Bialik and Tchernichovsky, readers of Mendele, Peretz and Brenner, lovers of the Bible and the Sages' homiletics, dreamers of a life in Ereẓ Israel, "to build it and in it, to be built"? They were readers of the Hebrew journals and the annual anthologies—*Ha-tekufah, Knesset* (a single issue,1928), *Moznaim, Gilyonot, Ketuvim*; they had established Hebrew high schools in Poland, and had been educated within the various youth movements. What remnants of hope did they retain in these days? Could one preach to them not to surrender in the daily struggle, to take courage "this very moment, when a murderer's hand knocks on our door"?

It is impossible for an intelligent person, let alone a teacher and educator, not to seek an answer, a reason. Brute facts strike us with force; they are most savage when left with no explanation at all, an affront to the intelligence, more severe even than injuries to the body and the soul. An explanation partially assuages their terror. Was it possible for Katzenelson to present an explanation of a God who rules the world with justice and mercy, who rewards and punishes? Many of the participants that *seder* night must have said in their hearts, and voiced aloud, that there was no God in the land of Poland, that God had forsaken occupied Europe. Their only hope focused on the resisting nations and on the course of the war, a hope that bitterly deceived them.

I am reminded of a vehement phrase, one that cuts right through a believer's flesh, pronounced by Don Isaac Abarbanel in describing the expulsion from Spain and Portugal: "I have seen God do battle face to face with His people." In my book about the life and work of that fifteenth century scholar and statesman, I added, "Whoever has seen this horrific sight could never again find calm, not among the nations, and not in his soul." In his commentary on the Passover *haggadah* (*Sefer Zevaḥ Pessaḥ*), Don Isaac asked the fundamental question, which Yiẓḥak Katzenelson and his fellows in Warsaw, exactly 450 years later, surely pondered. "What have we, people like us today in exile, gained from the fact that our forefathers were delivered from Egypt, and said, 'For it had been better for us to serve the Egyptians, than that we should die in the wilderness' of the nations, amidst annihilations and expulsions, whether by the sword, or by hunger, or in captivity?" The rabbi replied that in that first redemption we gained the dignity of free people and won the privilege of receiving the Torah. Moreover, the festival of freedom is a festival of future promise: "'And also that nation, whom they shall serve, will I judge' … that promise has stood by for them and for us, to our great delivery." This answer is not far removed from that of Yiẓḥak Katzenelson, and yet the difference is great, and is of the essence.

In traditional faith, the justification of God's action (*ẓidduk ha-din*) in our history over the ages was always the same—there is nothing new in these calamities, and we have already been told their meaning: sin and atonement, punishment and suffering, faith in a god who redeems the remnant of Israel. The participants around Yiẓḥak Katzenelson that night did not believe that they had sinned toward God, nor would they accept the accusations launched at them by their ideological opponents, as did many of those whom Yiẓḥak Katzenelson called "apostates" or "those that err and lead others to err out of an obtuseness of feelings and a poverty of spirit, who are being killed here with us." Of the latter, he said, "they have no part and parcel in the ancient House of Israel." However, when Yiẓḥak Katzenelson sang about the devoutness of God-fearing Jews, he never said that they saw acts of evil as a punishment for the sins of Jews. For Katzenelson, God is indeed a "hiding

God," a "conscience," the symbol of sensitivity of all that is good and noble in the world, and "fine filaments" connect us to Him throughout the ages, ever since the days of that "first redemption." He also redeems the individual soul from fears, from brute facts, from the premeditated savagery assaulting us in the anguish of Nazi occupation.

"Indeed, it is a night for redemption, not of enslavement"—this paradox begs the question: What possible redemption can there be in the midst of enslavement and slaughter, in the spring of 1942, in the first months of total destruction, following the Nazi decision to proceed with the "Final Solution"? The poet knows that this is the night of "horrors ... the springtime of lunacy."[26] The springtime of lunacy, and yet also a night of redemption, a time for an awakening of those redeemed. How so?

Redemption is the soul's salvation through consciousness, through self-awareness. "There is no joy of redemption except for those who have awareness." Jews, who possess historic awareness, know that since the days of "the first redemption" and ever after they are "free human beings in the vale of tears" and that no instrument of destruction will succeed in obliterating their spirit: "For eons we were being prepared in suffering and birth pangs for redemption, and we are prepared!" This process has taken place throughout the course of Jewish history in the "great desert of life"—like metal, the people have been refined in their suffering, and purified in their actions and faith. "We have been lifted and we have been cleansed." Jews no longer voluntarily build the cities of Egypt, Pithom and Ramses, for their oppressors. This the poet declares in a time of complete enslavement, when every person's existence depended on work in the Pithom and Ramses of the ghettos of Warsaw, Lodz, Cracow, Lublin, and others.

It was a declaration of independence in the depth of oppression. The Jew is redeemed when he is "at peace with his conscience, that is—with his God, who dwells in his innermost recesses, those fine filaments that connect him to God and his great assets in the hope that these may still increase." Now that we are condemned to die we are brethren in grief and in joy, the joy of redemption of a people whose multitude of sons "stand on the edge of the grave and enjoin the nation to live," in the faith that the "linked chain of eternity is never broken." Eternity is the fruit of the seed that educators-teachers plant in the ears of children. "We come to the nation with our big dreams, dreams of rebirth, as a man comes to a woman."

The teachers who sow and cultivate the holy seed of the future steel the identity of the people even in the forge of poverty and suffering. They add courage and holiness to that awareness of our "first redemption," by virtue of which we became free people forever: "The dreams of rebirth, and the aspirations to create and to liberate the spirit of the nation and of the whole world, emanate from the hearts of those departing to the hearts of those who are coming."

With what, then, could a Hebrew poet console his people crushed under the burden of suffering, sealed within itself, and the entire space of its world filled with the fear of death? He will break through this siege with his words, in poetry and prose, in enlightenment of thought, so that their suffering will not remain an opaque burden of "those led to slaughter in a muteness of mouth and tongue." Remembering Jewish identity negates the terror of death. In giving utterance to their suffering while becoming fully aware of their being, "our brothers extend their necks to the sword, and we speak today clearly." Speech is the Jew's way of soul-searching, in an evocation of the spirit of Zionist-humanist faith in rebirth: "In our remnants, there is consolation. After our death, before which we are standing, looking it in the face without fear."

So ends this noble affirmation. The reader senses that the poet tried here to transform the weight of the dark, mute reality of suffering and non-being into the pain of love for one's people, love for the individual and for the collective, and the ascendance—against the self-forgetting of the "condemned to die"—of free individuals, an ascendance illuminated by the light of awareness, "without fear."

CHAPTER 14

A Small Town in Poland

The author recalls the *shtetl* of his childhood before and after World War I. Some nostalgia, but also ugly rivalry and strife between two Ḥasidic factions. Days of Christian worship and market days. On encountering the Christian interpretation of the Bible.[1]

DREAMS AND FEARS

Several times a year, I travel by plane via Europe, or in a dilapidated, crawling, needlessly whistling train car to Zdunska Wola. I go for a short visit to take at least a quick look at its pleasant visage, to inhale the perfume of its summer mornings—and to partake of its grief. Recently, with the Polish government's attempts to lure tourists via ads about comfortable travel and delights reserved for the foreign visitor, I tend to set out for this town—on my bed, at night—even more frequently.

When I arrive thus, Zdunska Wola is still standing upright in its Jewish presence, exactly as it was, with its Sabbaths and Holy Days, and its days of regular activity, all seamlessly integrated within the Jewish calendar. We still have a place where we were born: a small town, yet a metropolis that contains everything, a whole world. It has not yet been transmuted into the marble frigidity of memories preserved by émigrés and refugees. The town is not yet floating on the roofs of enormous questions and terrors that flutter in alien air. It is still intact, with its houses, squares and large market, in its tangible reality. Trees and shrubs abound, surrounded by green expanses, crop-bearing fields and meadows. No, it has not yet been transformed into a cluster of disconnected dreams, floating in every direction, wherever our fears and expectations have taken us, far from its confines and the rhythm of its calendar.

AN ORDINARY TOWN AND ITS EXTRAORDINARY FEUD

The town of Zdunska Wola, or simply Wola in daily speech, did not sit on abandoned fields, "out alone," as Scholem Aleichem once described a Jewish town in one of his stories. Wola was a link in the chain of Jewish communities from Lodz to Kalisz, and westward on to German Silesia and its capital Breslau. Located about 40 kilometers west of Lodz, you could reach it in a comfortable train ride of an hour and a quarter from the Kalisz Station of Lodz. After Pabianice and Łask, here we are, the third stop—Zdunska Wola. It was one in a variegated fabric of similar Jewish communities, tied by many links to Jewish settlements, old and new, in Congress Poland, but also with ties to communities outside Poland, through the Russian and Lithuanian Jews who gave the town access to the big world. As in other Jewish communities, Zdunska Wola's religious leaders frowned upon emigration. Nevertheless, quite a few did leave Wola in time, escaping the great conflagration and saving others too.

There were about 8,000 Jews in Wola in my childhood, of whom the majority were Ḥasidim. The town did not have the reputation of a Torah study center, although, needless to say, Torah was studied both privately and in groups, and the hum of its study never ceased in Wola's "great" *beit midrash*. However, it did not have an important *yeshiva*, and absent any great local Torah scholars or teachers, it did not attract young men who longed to study. Nor was Wola privileged to be a Ḥasidic center. No rebbe had deigned to settle here, although it was home to some important Ḥasidic followers, people who "sat at the rebbe's table"—were close to a rebbe, could see him personally, figured in his entourage. Neither was there even a small, temporary kernel of Hebrew education. This is not surprising—the communities of Congress Poland played no significant role in the Hebrew Enlightenment movement of the nineteenth century centered in Russia. Ḥasidism attracted sharp minds to its fold in Poland, and whoever wanted a greater intellectual challenge than the Talmud and its subsequent legal literature was encouraged to turn to Maimonides' philosophic *Guide for the Perplexed*. The disciples and the disciples of the disciples of Reb Mendel of Kotsk spread new editions of works by the medieval Jewish philosophers.

Overall, Zdunska Wola was a humble town with mainly laborers, artisans, and small traders, animated by modest ambitions and diligent toil. The town's daily talk centered on looms, weaving, types of threads, on trade trips to Lodz—the chief market for its homemade goods. Indeed, Zdunska Wola was a sort of rural branch of the bustling industrial center, a place where folks still pursued their labors calmly. Wola traders were not rushed and harried, even when they came to Lodz, on whose streets, as everyone knows, one did not walk, one ran, as though pursued and pursuing. This hastiness and jumpiness sometimes turned Jewish entrepreneurship in "Poland's Manchester" to a sort of self-caricature, at least ostensibly. In fact, Lodz's rhythm, intolerant of laxity, was a constructive speed that testified to the strength of Jewish dynamism and creativity.

Young bachelors and those already married but still supported by their in-laws, like my father, a native of Lodz who married a Zdunska Wola girl of the Strykowski-Teich family, studied Torah, whether in the "great" *beit midrash,* or in the Ḥasidic *shtiblach*. But when the day arrived and the "manna from heaven" ended, they too assumed the yoke of work and trade. Some, like my father, returned to the towns of their parents, and some settled in Wola.

Besides ordinary conversation, there was also much religious talk and most secular conversations were peppered with words of Torah as well. Life, however, was not always peaceful. In addition to the perennial feeling of living in exile, the restrictions imposed by governments, the burdens of making a living, and natural calamities, there were aggravations at the hand of one's fellow man, particularly those caused by internal disagreements about communal affairs. Fiercely bitter disputes "for the sake of heaven," i.e., ostensibly purely spiritual and free of all personal motive, dragged on and rankled and brought misery to a good many people. The life of a town is not an idyll, not among Gentiles and not among Jews.

The Wola community divided into two main camps: the adherents of Ger and the followers of Aleksander. The disagreements were about the local rabbi and his election, about the rabbinic judges and the ritual slaughterers, about the number of community office holders, and about all other affairs. One of the nastiest disputes in the first decade of the twentieth century concerned the election of the town rabbi—"better a *goy* for rabbi than an Aleksander Ḥasid!" cried the Ger faction. According to what I was told later and to what I read in the special brochure[2] that described this terrible quarrel, I doubt there was any other Jewish community at that period which experienced such an embittered and long-drawn-out feud. I find it uncomfortable to describe this disgraceful dispute. A number of factors coalesced—spiritual matters entwined with mundane matters of livelihoods—into one dangerous vortex. Ger Ḥasidim and Aleksander Ḥasidim did not marry one another. They would not eat the meat slaughtered by the other. Each made the other's life miserable and denied its members work, loans, and trade. Factory owners dismissed workers and clerks affiliated with the opposing camp, even after Reb Eliezer Lipszyc (Lajzer Liebszyc) was elected rabbi in 1907 and eventually became well liked by a majority of the town's Jews.

It is possible that the Ḥasidic rebbes themselves were not the ones who stoked this fire, but they certainly were not quick to extinguish it. This shameful episode is a poor testimonial to Jewish traditional leadership in the early

Rabbi Lajzer Lipszyc, Zdunska Wola's rabbi from 1907 to 1925. Published in a book in honor of the centenary of Zdunska Wola's establishment, 1925, edited by Ludwik Wicher

twentieth century. Only at the beginning of World War I, when members of the Jewish community were exiled by the German Imperial Army (a temporary exile, indeed an edict of exile more than an exile in effect), did the two camps meet for reconciliation, on the soil of the cemetery. Peace was restored. No doubt like many others I learned a lesson from this feud, one not easily forgotten, about arguments "for the sake of heaven," about the fire that consumes disputants who dress themselves in the guise of holiness.

GERMANS AND POLES—BUSINESS AND TRADE

The town was an "international" community. Of its population of approximately 30,000, about one-third were Jews, one-third Poles, and one-third Germans. The German "Swabians" stamped their imprint on the town, maybe no less significantly than did the Jews. They too worked in the cloth business and owned many houses, yards, fields, and orchards. The Jews lived on the three main streets, many in apartments rented from Germans. Most Jews spoke a Germanized Yiddish, or, at any rate, understood German, and some read German. A number of townsmen even went "abroad," that is to Germany, to trade and return, or not to return. My uncle Beresz Strykowski had lived for some time in Germany, knew German well and was a great admirer of Schiller, Heine, even Goethe and, needless to say, of Lessing and his play *Nathan the Wise*.[3] Often he would pepper his words with quotes from classical German literature. For years he worked for one of the "Swabians" as head artisan and made a decent, if not abundant, living.

The regard for Germany and its culture ended, or at least waned, during World War I, when on September 19, 1914, the Germans conquered the town. I was a small child when I saw German troops march in, and perhaps I witnessed not their first but their second entry. I recall that Jews stood on the pavements and received them with buckets of water on that hot summer day. The Germans of the town, with their sons and daughters lining the streets prepared a very enthusiastic welcome for the soldiers. However, it was already known that in passing through, the invaders had burned the city of Kalisz, most of whose inhabitants were Jews, some of whom had fled to Zdunska Wola spreading fears of these new conquerors. On that occasion, for the first time, I saw a wagon pulled by four horses, Kalisz's public transport vehicle. Since I was being raised in Lodz and was used to its spacious and rapid street trams, my pity redoubled for the poor refugees from Kalisz and their unmechanized wagon. The hope was that once the Germans established their rule, life would return to normalcy, maybe even improve. Everyone hated the Russian regime, this "*Pani* Pig," and certainly had no respect for it. The German Empire was considered the drawing room of European culture. From it, one expected rights, prosperity, and liberty. The conquering general Ludendorff issued a declaration addressed to Poland's Jews replete with sweet promises in the name of his Kaiser.

I do not remember the Poles in the town. I do recall, however, the scene of farmers streaming in from the villages on market day or to church on Sunday and Holy Days. In the *ḥeder,* we learned about the Ephod and ritual clothing of Aaron the Priest with its tinkling golden bells, but in my day bells belonged to the priests of the Gentiles. When the bells began ringing on Sunday morning, a massive stream of villagers would pour through Sieradz Street where we lived. The men came in their long coats and high boots which some carried on their shoulders until they reached the street itself, the heart of town, and the women wore colorful clothes and kerchiefs. From the church they proceeded to the taverns. If the march to the city still appeared organized—a long and quite smart-looking procession of groups upon groups of people—the return to the village was disorderly: a wife helping her drunken husband stagger along, or small groups of families or neighbors wending their way home.

As the villages were only about one hour's walking distance from the town center, or maybe less, the farmers usually did not ride to church but went on foot to spare the beast and the cart on the day of rest. Not so on market or fair days when they loaded their produce on carts. The Sunday processions aroused fears, at least in the heart of a Jewish child—the ominous sound of bells calling the Christian faithful to prayer and the shabby, sorry spectacle of the broken-up groups of villagers, reeking of liquor, straggling home. In contrast, the flow to market was, by definition, a mundane matter, a setting for wheeling and dealing, and thus raised no anxieties. There is nothing like business to bring hearts together.

I came to understand that the respectable is not far from the ludicrous, even an integral part of it. Vexations, humiliations and degradations were closely associated with that which uplifted the spirit. People you respect, people you see focused reverently on an object of sanctity, join the masses in their festivities and end up in taverns, drunk, dragging their heavy feet and participating in demeaning acts. Later, reading Dostoyevsky's descriptions of partying that ended up in total debasement, I knew he was not mistaken. But when I read in the satirical writings of Mendele the Book Peddler, Scholem Aleichem and their imitators descriptions of markets that were unreal—markets that were nothing but tumult and vagaries—I knew that they had gotten it all wrong, or were widely off the mark in their grotesque exaggeration, for on market days I saw the real give-and-take of trade. Usually both sides would do well by it. Both sides were known to cheat sometimes—a Jew might make a mistake to the detriment of a *goy*, and the *goy* likewise might make a mistake to the detriment of a Jew. Everyone knew that in trade and money there is no compassion. However, in general, they traded honestly, and some were scrupulous in avoiding even a whiff of deception, for they were neighbors and needed each other.

The Christians not only had bells, but also drums. A drummer used to pass through the town streets accompanied by a town crier who would announce the news that the authorities wished to communicate to the citizenry. Sometimes the drummer himself acted as the crier, sometimes they were two different functionaries, especially if a very lengthy government ordinance was to be read. We children would run after him a long way, at least as far as his second stop, and would listen once again to his words, which we would not have understood no matter how often he had repeated them. Very few Jews in town understood Polish. However, the local authorities did their duty by the announcement, and indeed its contents quickly became known to everyone. The one who understood ran to tell the others, not sparing them this kindness. The drummer announced the outbreak of World War I, and

Dawny sposób ogłaszania w mieście.

Wola's town crier in a book honoring the centenary of Zdunska Wola's establishment, 1925, edited by Ludwik Wicher

later he, or his colleague, announced the foundation of the Polish state, and subsequently hardly a week passed without drumming. Apparently, there was no newspaper in Zdunska Wola at the time, and, of course, no radio station. The municipality did not provide any public transport. For a fee, one could rent a Jewish-owned carriage. Indeed, there was no other way to get from home to the train station.

FAMILY MEMBERS AND DISCOMFITURE AT NOT KNOWING THE BIBLE

The impact of the Poles on the town increased significantly when they received statehood. They became its rulers and began legislating laws intended to minimize the influence of minorities who, in this town, were not minorities at all, for each group was at least equal in number to the Poles and perhaps even surpassed them in numbers. Under the new government, Jewish youths began learning the Polish language. New Jewish schools, especially those for girls, taught in Polish. No doubt, there was a decline in piety and in Talmudic learning as other interests and needs arose.

The appearance of the town did not change under the new masters. Jews still lived on the three main streets in wooden or stone houses or in the long and not-so-narrow yards. The tallest houses were not above three or four stories. In fact, four-story houses were rare. When additional residents moved to Zdunska Wola, a few new houses were added.

My grandmother, "Black" Rivka (most townspeople had nicknames and members of my mother's family were called "black" because of their very dark hair) owned a house and a yard on Sieradz Street that led to the town of that name. Her husband, my grandfather, died when he was only forty, leaving her with two married sons and four unmarried girls. She worked hard to provide for them and to find them good matches. As mentioned in Chapter 2, Grandfather Fiszel Leib, a Ḥasid of Vurka and Biale, ran in the snow during a particularly hard winter behind a wagon that was to carry him to his rebbe. He came down with acute pneumonia and died within a short time of his return home. He was much praised in the town. What is certain is that he was a friend and associate of the son of the Rebbe of Biale, who later became the Rebbe of Strykow, Reb Menaḥem Mendel, and at the end of his life lived in Zgierz near Lodz.

Both my uncles were Torah scholars. Uncle Beresz seemed to me the noble prototype of the Jewish *maskil* in whom "Torah with the ways of the world," the old life and the new ways, made a true covenant. From him I heard words of Jewish learning and quotes from non-Jewish authors, both of which he prized. His piety was a matter of course with none of the fanaticism born of insecurity. He did everything in measure and with much grace: prayer in its ordained time, work-for-a-living most of the day, edifying conversation, calmly spoken words of wisdom, care and education of the children, responsibility for public affairs. As a founder of the Mizraḥi movement in the town, he was frequently elected to the community's council or to the municipal council. Occasionally, he ceded his position to his elder brother when he too was elected to the same organizations by a different (Agudat Israel) party, as it was not permissible for two brothers to officiate on the same body.

My other uncle, the elder brother "Black" Mordekhai Mendel, an accomplished Talmudic scholar blessed with a sharp mind and a high IQ, and an important community leader, lived in a house on the town's outskirts beyond a small bridge over a stream. It was a very pleasant walk to Uncle's house on summer days, on that long street bordered by meadows and gardens. The house was a duplex. The owner, a German master weaver, caused the house to thunder all day until nightfall with his looms. Uncle had a shop there, a sort of general store which served the farmers in the adjacent villages and his neighbors, primarily Germans. His business knew many vicissitudes. Even though he was busy all day, much preoccupied with the cares of making a living for his wife, son, and seven daughters, he found time to study the Talmud and deal with public affairs. Living in an apartment at the edge of the town—outside its boundaries in fact, posed potential danger but only during the Nazi occupation did disaster reach him there. Though he may not have been saved had he lived in the center of town it appears that the location of his home led to his being one of the first to be killed.[4]

On the road to his house I had occasion, for the first time in my life, to enter into a religious discussion with a member of the Christian faith. In a field, next to an ox-drawn plough, an old man stood and called at me as I passed. It turned out he was a German Lutheran, well versed in our Scriptures and in theirs. He rolled out by heart the famous lines from Isaiah chapter 53.[5] Based on these fourteen cryptic verses, so different in spirit from everything else found in the Holy Scriptures, Christians fashioned their idea of the life of Jesus and the acts of his salvation and repeatedly sought in them confirmation of his history and deeds. I was but a boy, about ten years old. Certainly, I had learned Talmud and *tosafot*, but I did not know the chapters of Isaiah, and I squirmed in my response to the old believer. I realized how difficult it was to hold a religious debate, but I also felt it was needed, and that in order to succeed in it one had to be armed with knowledge, that without knowing what to reply you are likely to end up embarrassed and ridiculous, even if you are in the right. I recall that I was moved by the fact that the Christians revered the "Old Testament," and that we had a foundation for shared opinions. I was ashamed that it was they, and not we, who were well versed in the Bible. True, there is not a single verse in the Bible that is not expounded upon in the Talmud at least seven times, and there are some that appear in the Talmud more than a hundred times, but clearly, sound knowledge of the Bible is not acquired by knowing its verses scattered throughout the Talmud. With what "fundamentalist" fervor my Christian interlocutor adhered to the straightforward meaning of the texts, according to his tradition! In this conversation (followed, later in life, by similar ones), I encountered for the first time one example out of the legion of Christian falsifications of Jewish writings and history, of which the matter of the crucifixion by the Jews was just one detail in the overall subversion, albeit the most terrible and dangerous of all. I felt the hijacking of the Jewish texts, and I was annoyed at the man's goading.

BETWEEN THE TWO WORLD WARS

After World War I, the town did not regain its old equanimity. The wounds did not heal. Things were not as they had been before, though outwardly customs remained unchanged. Some put it down to looseness of mores, godlessness. Others attributed it to innovation, renaissance, the dynamics of development and prosperity. Economically the town recovered after the war. The Jews owned about 70 textile plants that employed altogether about 60 Jewish workers, and many smaller workshops that provided a livelihood for 900 Jews. However, with wages about 20 percent lower than in Lodz, strikes flared up from time to time, especially in the bigger plants (belonging to Moshe Aharon Wiener and Wiśliński-Rozen). The big industrialists in Lodz, for whom Zdunska Wola was a sort of satellite, dictated labor conditions.

Still, the town had what one would call today a better quality of life than the big city. In communal affairs the Agudat Israel party reigned supreme, with seven out of twelve representatives installed in the 1924 elections. In the municipal council its strength was not far inferior—five representatives versus five for all the other parties. However, by this time a few hundred people were already voting for their representatives in the Zionist Congress. To the delight of my Uncle Beresz, half of the votes went to the Mizraḥi movement. The Zionists, the Bund, the right-wing and (the more numerous) left-wing branches of Po'aley Zion founded clubs, choirs, drama groups, evening courses for Hebrew, the natural sciences, history and literature, sports teams and other leisure organizations for young and old, in addition to banks and charity organizations. I attended a number of lectures given by locals or by important guests invited from as far as Warsaw. Yiddish writers and actors recited poems and stories before packed halls. Modern schools were established. While most Jewish children still learned in a *ḥeder*, there was already a Tarbut school, though it did not last long. A Beis Yaakov school for girls was also established. All the parties and organizations of the big city were represented in Wola. The Zionist movement, which competed against Aguda's greater strength, showed considerable vitality—there was an agricultural training farm for members of the local He-Ḥaluẓ branch that assisted young people's emigration to Palestine. My childhood friend Jeremiah Gordon was one of the first to emigrate (he later worked for the Israeli daily newspaper *Davar* and the publisher *Am Oved*).

During the fourth *aliyah* (1924–28), a number of "middle class" people from Wola immigrated to Palestine, bringing with them the good habits of hard working laborers. Unlike "intellectuals" who lived on air, they made a relatively smooth transition to professions suitable to their talents and became productive in the new land.

In this interwar period many young people in Wola were already learning and reading modern Hebrew. I remember that in the summer of 1931, when I visited the town for the last time for the wedding of Uncle Beresz's daughter, I was invited to lecture in Hebrew about the poem *Massada*,[6] and I had attentive listeners. Since I was studying to become a Germanized modern rabbi, half-way toward a *Doktor Rabbiner* degree, the Torah scholars, the rabbinic judge, and the rabbi whom I met in Wola treated me with both familiarity and distance, as if to say: He studies Torah and shows respect for our ways, and yet he is no longer one of us!

Another change was the mutation of the old Ḥasidic fervor into zeal for new secular organizations. Religious fervor when it is poured into secular molds does not cease to seethe or generate disputes. However, there was also a positive legacy: the enduring small-town qualities of modesty, humility, honesty, making do with little, and a certain genuine innocence—very charming and sincere. New winds were blowing with the old—winds of tolerance and forgiveness—good manners were extolled, old virtues were now dressed in new forms, and wherever they appeared, they shone brightly.

Mother Frajda Szmulewicz, nee Strykowska

This grace of the place shone through my mother, who always saw herself as a daughter of Zdunska Wola, and I believe, never felt quite at home in Lodz. She saw life in the big city as cold, hard, and cruel. Since she had been born and raised in a relatively comfortable home before the war, in a Ḥasidic home characterized by generosity and good deeds, she always tried to lend a helping hand. Indeed, by her very nature she could not refuse anyone who requested help, as far as she was able. She simply could not turn anyone away, and many in need appealed to her.

To what social class did my family belong? Max Weber once said that social class is a collection of people whose wives do not consider it beneath them to visit one another and spend time together. Others have suggested three criteria for determining class: assets and their quantity (what you own), income size and its source, and, lastly, the ability to increase assets or income. Useful criteria and definitions. Still, one senses intuitively that the women and their notions of status, or lack of it, offered a more pertinent definition: whose wives were your wife's friends?

Our family did not lend itself to simple definitions. In Lodz, we were a family that could be called "proletarian," with no means of producing earnings, let alone assets. But Mother, who volunteered in the city's philanthropic institutions, associated with the members, both wives and husbands, of the upper-middle or middle-middle class. That is how she came to know Ḥaim Rumkowski, later "King of the Ghetto," as narrated earlier. No doubt there were more sophisticated members than she on the committees on which she served, but I assume that they too felt respect for the generosity of this daughter of Wola who spared herself no trouble to help the needy and did so always with a kind eye and with genuine respect. My wise-hearted mother!

If Zdunska Wola still exists in the history of Poland, severed from the living endeavors of its Jewish citizens, it is a town that has betrayed its true nature, a "deceit of its own heart," in the words of the prophet Jeremiah, a painful betrayal of that which was best and most precious. To me now, it is a hollow specter, terrifying in its non-being, a rebuking reminder of what once was, a monument to absence.

Indeed, that is how I saw Wola when I returned to Poland in the fall of 1982.

CHAPTER 15

Return to Poland

Two parallel impressions of a return trip: the harrowing emptiness of a Jew-cleansed Poland, with memories of all that is lost, and the dramatic developments of the new Poland on the cusp of the Solidarity revolution.

END OF THE STORY AND PROLOGUE TO A JOURNEY

In 1928, the year in focus of this memoir, I left Poland and did not return, except for a few brief family visits, the last of which was in December 1932 just before the terrible year when Hitler seized power, and shortly before my *aliyah* to Ereẓ Israel. I saw then that the situation of Jews in Poland was deteriorating dramatically and later from my new home in Haifa, I followed events in Poland with deepening anxiety. Piłsudski's regime, which at first had brought the Jews some relief, did not withstand the attacks of the anti-Semitic nationalists, the Endaks, who had sworn to make Poland "a national state and not a state of national minorities." Following his death in 1935, during the ensuing unrest and riots in which the police generally refrained from intervening, the government practiced an open, unapologetic nationalistic policy, not dissimilar to that of the Nazis in those years. In September 1934, despite protests by the foreign ministers of France, England, and Italy, Poland reneged—in a public declaration at the League of Nations—on its commitment to honor the rights of its minorities. Its excuse was that the Soviet Union, which had just joined the League of Nations, might interfere in Poland's internal affairs under the pretext of protecting the rights of the minorities.

In the face of an impenetrable wall of hatred, Poland's Jews were isolated. Only here and there did they find allies among the liberal Polish intelligentsia and in the socialist ranks. Consciously or otherwise, the Jews struggled to assert the principle that not only as individuals but also as a collective in exile they were entitled to preserve their distinction, even if their culture was distasteful to their neighbors. And while many tried to get closer to the Poles and assiduously learned their language and culture, they too still wished to be recognized as a minority with national rights.

The history of the Holocaust is known. The fate of Aleksander was the fate of all other Jewish communities. When the Nazis arrived in town in the first month of the war, the killings and arsons began immediately. The central synagogue was burned down, the rebbe's *beit midrash* ravaged, and the houses of the rebbe and family members pillaged. Jews were forced to burn or desecrate Torah scrolls, giving rise to scenes of *kiddush hashem*. The German townspeople, now privileged *Volksdeutsche*, took an active part in the lootings, abuses, and destruction. I heard that some of them and some local Poles did not wish to purchase wooden planks stripped from the *beit midrash*, fearing that these might bring bad luck. They believed in the holiness of the *beit midrash* and its ancient beams.

The Gestapo searched for the rebbe, but he had succeeded in escaping with his family—first to Lodz, then to Otwock, then to Warsaw. On December 27, 1939, on a freezing winter night, all the Jews of Aleksander were driven out under German guard to the town of Głowno, north of Lodz. Several children perished in the snow on that harsh road. After the expulsion, the Nazis ordered the cemetery to be ploughed over in order to transform it into a public garden, so that not a trace should remain. The only thing left standing was the wall of the *ohel* of the Aleksander rebbes and tombstones in the cemetery.

Details of the final years of the last Rebbe of Aleksander, Reb Yiẓḥak Menaḥem Mendel Dancyger, are not sufficiently known. Faithful sources reported that the Ḥasidim had already come to an understanding with Gestapo officials on an enormous bribe, and that the Germans were prepared to let the rebbe leave Poland with his wife and one son. Several Polish *admorim*, albeit very few, succeeded in arranging their escape, or buying it at the price of a huge ransom by their Ḥasidim. The Rebbe of Ger, Reb Avraham Mordekhai Alter, the leading figure among the three "greats" in terms of numbers of adherents (Belz, Ger and Aleksander), managed to reach Ereẓ Israel at the beginning of the Holocaust. He had frequently visited between the two wars and had even spent six months there during his fifth journey in 1936. However, he returned to Poland, probably for the same reason that the Rebbe of Aleksander gave when he refused to leave and save himself: The Jews needed me.

The Aleksander Rebbe's final refusal is not easy to understand, and the matter needs further clarification. In my comprehensive essay, *Kiddush Hashem during the Holocaust* (too lengthy to include here[1]), I speculated about the rebbe's beliefs and reflections during his last journey. Clearly, in this hour of great peril to his people he did not want to flee; he preferred to sanctify God's name. In the Warsaw Ghetto, the rebbe was ostensibly employed in a shoemaking workshop, concealing his real identity under a false name. In one of the *selekzia*s of 1943, he and his family were deported to Treblinka, where they all perished. The *ẓaddik* was not favored with a Jewish burial.

My granduncle Reb Yidl also perished in the Holocaust. His eldest son, the rabbi of Burznin, died previously. His second son, my uncle Yosef Eliezer Maroko, married to my mother's sister, made *aliyah* in 1924. He toiled in a laundry shop in Kiryat Moẓkin, north of Haifa, and died there, aged 70. Uncle Yidl's grandson, Avraham Mordekhai Maroko, whose father had died in Złoczew shortly after his birth, was a graduate of the *Metivta* (*yeshiva*) in Warsaw and an ordained rabbi. This prestigious *yeshiva* accepted only students who were capable of learning Talmud and *tosafot* on their own, memorizing several dozen pages by heart. A student who completed the fifth class and was ordained a rabbi knew almost by heart close to 2,000 pages of Talmud. Although they still clung to the old method of rote memorization, they also introduced a number of secular subjects to their curriculum, two hours per day—Polish, mathematics, and history. Not all rabbis approved of this innovation. The graduates of this *yeshiva* gained fame throughout Poland as young Ḥasidic rabbis with a "new orientation" who tried to stem the tide of secularization.

Whenever Avraham Mordekhai came to Lodz, I felt fortunate that he stayed at our home. On my last visit there he told me about the community of Widawa, near Lodz, where he was serving as rabbi—a small community of 800 Jews, out of a population of 2,000; that is, nearly every third resident was a Jew. He related with pride that in honor of May 3, the Polish national day, he had preached in the town's synagogue in the presence of the entire community and honored non-Jewish townspeople, most notably the *starosta*, the leading official of the province. The latter had praised his words about the importance of equal rights for the Jews of Widawa and about the May 3 constitution. The rabbinic chair in Widawa was really too lowly for his great talents. Not only was he a great Torah scholar and an editor of a journal titled *Degel ha-ẓe'irim* (*Banner of the Young*), in which he wrote in excellent style, he was a man of high ethics, a truly superior individual.

When the Germans entered Widawa in September 1939, they broke into his house and searched it. They found a Torah scroll and ordered him to destroy it, threatening to burn him alive if he refused. My cousin, who was at most four or five years older than I, embraced the Torah scroll and kissed it. The Germans doused him with gasoline and torched him. He and the Torah scroll turned to ashes.

Horrific deeds were perpetrated on members of my family, and I recount here only the fate of those whom I have mentioned in these pages. On the first day of the Germans' entrance to Zdunska Wola, my uncle Mordekhai Mendel Strykowski, Mother's elder brother, was shot to death, along with his son-in-law, near their home at the edge of town. My father died on May 22, 1940, a few weeks after being herded into the Lodz Ghetto, Europe's first ghetto to enclose Jews between walls and barbed wire in "modern times." My mother of blessed memory was deported to Auschwitz in the summer of 1944 with the last remnant of the Jews of Lodz.

In early October 1982, during the week of Sukkot (the festival of Tabernacles), I set out on a journey to the "ancestral grave," *kever avot,* to the Poland of memories and ruins which lay behind the Iron Curtain. After much soul-searching and deliberation, I stepped again on Polish soil. There I wandered alone in the non-being of streets, courtyards, and squares, which had previously hummed with Jews. I found myself once again in Warsaw, Lodz, Aleksander, Zdunska Wola, and Breslau—today's Wroclaw—in the places that I had not seen all these years. In grief, I sought out remnants of the Jewish presence.

What I sought in these destroyed communities and what I found in them and in the Poland of the post-Holocaust era until the 1980s—these impressions are the grim subject of this chapter.

INDECISION AND RESOLUTION

That autumn of 1982 I returned to Poland no longer in those night- or daydreams that had so often come to me during my fifty years of absence nor through the agency of memory, as they had done for many years, especially when writing chapters of this book, but in a real journey, a real encounter with sights and sounds. In a variation on the well-known *midrash* on the verse "And the Lord said, I have surely seen the affliction of my people ... for I know their sorrows," I am now entitled to say: I have surely seen the land of my ancestors—my slaughtered ones, both through memory and in reality.

For many years, I was fearful of approaching the horror of the Holocaust. Beyond all its atrocities as we know them now, there was the fear of the void which the mass extermination left in its wake. I knew: Everything had been obliterated under Poland's sky, and the expunging was still being carried out even now. No memory left and no name; even that which had been erected by way of memorial was nothing but a remote gesture. What was evident was the cancellation of being. All that remained, here and there, was a handful of old, ill and disabled vestiges, some leftists, or some crypto-Jews concealing their origin. In 1970 a study showed that Poland had some 7,000 Jews. Today, I have heard, the number may be closer to 5,000—about 2,000 in Warsaw, a similar number in Wroclaw, and the rest in a few cities like Cracow and Lodz. I was not "seeking my brethren." I knew that they were no more—all our large family, all the House of Israel in Poland. Miraculously, some of us escaped in time. I believe that every Jew who was fortunate enough to save himself from the Holocaust must regard himself as an escapee and a survivor. We must not forget that the murderers also intended to kill us had we been within their reach—particularly the Jewish sons and daughters of Poland.

No, I did not intend to seek the dead. I did not plan to visit Auschwitz, Majdanek, or Treblinka. Rather, it is the dead who visit us, demanding our attention, troubling themselves to come to us in our hours of sleep and wakening. They enter the recesses of our consciousness, its conscious domain and the deep crypts and dark mazes of the unconscious, leaving us no refuge, no escape. It is impossible not to hear the sound of their cries, their entreaties and protests, the stories of the savageries perpetrated upon them and their valiant struggle, in courage and holiness, in their day-to-day deeds in ghetto life and in bold acts transcending their quotidian lives. In a relatively short period, as measured in physical time—and one as long as all our exiles put together—in that fateful parcel of time, the climax of all persecutions and calamities came to be concentrated. This never ceases to shock me.

I knew that I would be journeying to an experience of void and wasteland. As Yiẓḥak Katzenelson described it in Canto XV of his great *Song of the Murdered Jewish People*:

> The sun when it rises in the morning over a town in Poland and Lithuania will no longer find at the hour of *shaḥarit* a radiant Jew at the window, reciting a psalm …
>
> Woe to me, everything is finished … We have all been murdered here on the face of the earth, they have obliterated us all, till nothing remains.

It is hard to say what made me overcome my hesitations. I had no specific purpose in going. Perhaps I felt a reporter's need to return to sights I was describing in these memoirs—Lodz, Zdunska Wola, Aleksander, the Warsaw I had known in the 1920s, and to Breslau, where I had studied for nearly five years before immigrating to Ereẓ Israel.

Once decided, I began to prepare. I read a few books in Polish, vocalizing the words aloud, for I had forgotten their sounds. After finishing two volumes of *The Promised Land* (1899) by Polish Nobel laureate Władislaw Reymont, a story about the development of Lodz at the end of the nineteenth century, I was able to speed up my reading pace. I proceeded with the novellas of Jerzy Andrzejewski, *Holy Week* (1945), where he speaks with sympathy and appreciation of the Warsaw Ghetto uprising as it looked from the Polish side. I could feel the language returning to me. In the garden, our dog, to whom I now spoke in an entirely foreign language, at first showed interest. But his attention quickly waned, leaving me to do my own grappling with exercises in the language embedded in my heart but forgotten by my tongue. It now came back to life—the anamnesis of a sleeping princess.

I had studied and knew what had happened to the Jews of Poland and of the other European lands of exile during the Holocaust, and I had described these events in my books, especially in *History of Our People in the Modern Era, Volume 7*. I had also reflected upon the lessons they could teach us in *The House of Israel and the State of Israel.*[2]

These studies led me to understand how a nation's miseries, whether real or imagined, when coupled with lust for power, can loosen the fetters of murky, hitherto suppressed forces within it. When, under certain political circumstances, the strictures of law and ethics are removed, everything previously held in check bursts out into the public sphere with vicious savagery. In my mind, the "Jewish problem" is not a problem *per se*: It is always linked to and entangled with major extraneous political and social factors. However, one cannot deny that among all the hatreds and jealousies of nations there is one particular ingredient, a distinctive, unique "spice"—Jew-hatred—concocted over millennia, forever conspiring new calamities and preying on Jewish blood. Many have already explained the reasons for this hatred, yet perhaps no explanation will ever be adequate. The incitement against Jews, as I already saw with my own eyes in the 1930s, can become an international force with which to subvert the ethos of nations from within, as Hitler has done. It is a sort of universal, almost omnipotent ploy, like a tried and tested diabolical machine. A foggy mythic lunacy was served up to the nations as an ostensibly rational argument for their self-defense, and implemented with highly sophisticated stratagems and tools, commensurate with the advanced techno-scientific stage of civilization. Whether the murderers used arguments about the supposed spirit of Judaism and the actions of Jews only as a pretext, i.e., as an exaggeration calculated to ensnare nations into their vision of "a new world order," or whether they genuinely felt hatred—substantive, not functional hatred, independent of what Jews did or thought—the results were calamitous.

On the plane to Warsaw, I kept thinking about the nightmare-come-true evoked by Yiẓḥak Katzenelson:

> I dreamt a dream,
> A most terrible one.
> My people are no more, my people
> Are gone.
> I awoke in a scream: Oh! Oh!
> What I dreamed
> Has come, has come.

The poem reads like a nursery rhyme, as though uttered by one who is both a child and an old man.[3]

FIRST IMPRESSIONS

I had always dreamt of a train trip from Vienna to Warsaw and from Warsaw to Lodz, on the line that arrives at the station near where we had lived, called the Warsaw-Vienna Train Station. And indeed, this is exactly how I travelled, though first in a small Austrian plane, half empty, on the Intermediate Days of the Sukkot festival. At noon on October 5, 1982, I arrived in Warsaw after less than an hour's flight. I learned that the Polish state was readying itself for many foreign tourists and had built fancy hotels. I read that in previous years tens of thousands of visitors had arrived from the United States, and many more from other countries, and tourism was growing. People visited relatives, toured the ancient cities, sought out the famous Polish spas, went on outings in the Carpathian Mountains. Many tourists were being sent from Russia. However, my visit took place in the days of martial law imposed on Poland in December 1981 and there was fear of restrictions on movement between towns and inside them, of curfews and other decrees, which do not make for comfortable touring.

A Polish professor from the University of Poznan, a musicologist returning from a conference in Austria with whom I talked on the plane, assured me that there was no curfew and that movement was unrestricted. Music and musicology were quite developed in Poland, he told me. Last month a musicology conference had been held in the town of Bydgoszcz (formerly German Bromberg) by Central and Eastern European countries under UNESCO patronage. Guests and speakers came from "all over the world." They discussed the characteristics of music in those countries and the influence of Byzantium as a center of musical creativity in the Middle Ages, and about the traditions preserved in the churches of Russia and Bulgaria. I learned that Byzantine hymns were absorbed even in the early music of Poland.

The impression was that I was entering a Western, cultured country, hospitable to international meetings, sending its lecturers to conferences abroad, a member of the free world going about its business. After a tasty Viennese lunch on the plane, we agreed to meet at the exit after customs, since the returning professor was of course exiting via a different gate than the tourists.

As there were only a few foreign visitors in Warsaw's rather shabby air terminal, we went through passport control and customs quickly with hardly any checks. The only requirement was to fill out a form: How much foreign currency are you bringing in and how much are you converting immediately upon entry? This form, once stamped by the clerk, was to be presented in every hotel, where the amount charged, as well as any other foreign currency outlay, would be entered. Since foreign currency could only be exchanged at the airport or in a bank, they could thus check at departure how much one spent in Poland, and whether or not foreign currency was used in keeping with the official rate.

My friend the musicologist was already waiting for me at the exit. A cab drove us through Warsaw's beautiful streets and multi-lane heavily trafficked avenues. One could not tell that this large city, a magnificent European metropolis, has been rebuilt from rubble. The driver named the streets through which we passed. I remembered the names, but the streets had greatly changed for the better. Of this, the Poles are proud. With great love and fidelity they have reconstructed historic buildings destroyed in the war, such as the Royal Castle and the Old Town, and have built impressive new edifices, such as the Palace of Culture and Science. The city's population today is over one and a quarter million, the largest in the country.

The driver told us that they were rebuilding the famous large Nożyk Synagogue. For twenty dollars he offered to take me to Lodz, a great bargain, but as I had set my heart on arriving at the Warsaw-Vienna Station near our street, I thanked him and refused. Sticking to one's rituals often beats convenience.

At the large, spacious train station, I parted from the professor, who invited me to visit him in Poznan. On the plane, I had told him that I was a Jew coming to visit *kever avot.* He did not pay much attention to this information and continued until the end of our encounter to talk about music in Warsaw and Poznan.

In the First Class carriage we sat three across fairly comfortably. My neighbor, a middle-aged woman, was returning to Lodz after experiencing the aggravation of running around government offices in Warsaw seeking to obtain an exit permit for Australia. Her husband was trying to get her to join him there. She was not at all sure whether she would obtain the permit or the visa, and she certainly had no idea when she would get it. A lawyer from Lodz who had been in the capital on his affairs had had Jewish colleagues in the past. Today there is not a single Jewish lawyer left in Lodz, or perhaps there is, but he did not know of any. The city, so he told me, had grown tremendously. Today, with its suburbs, it numbered about a million inhabitants, and was the second largest in Poland, just as in the past, and as in the past, it has remained a textile center and still manufactures for foreign markets. After the war many villagers migrated to town, as well as many refugees who came from the border regions. My neighbor in quest of the Australian visa had also come to Lodz from the vicinity of Vilnius, Lithuania. A military man, with whom I chatted in whispers in the wagon's corridor, expressed great admiration for Israel, for its military prowess, but emphasized that in the Polish army, as in all the press, everyone execrated the imperialist Zionists, the Israelis, America's flunkies. Nonetheless,

Lodz central train station, 1930

there were many in the Polish army who admired the Israelis' courage and their great abilities in battle.

I arrived in Lodz exactly where I had wanted, but I hardly recognized the place. The station has been expanded, part of the Station Garden has been torn down, and wide access roads were built. Still, this was the place. From moment to moment it became more familiar. And here is Skladowa Street, our street, a few dozen meters from the station. Across from the street there is now a luxury hotel, the Centrum, which was the one recommended to me by my fellow train passengers. I wished to deposit my things there and rest a bit before beginning my excursions. As it turned out, even though there were few tourists in Poland, the large hotels were quite full. They host conferences, bevies of officials visiting regional offices, and Poles pursuing their affairs. These pay only about a third or a quarter of the official rate exacted from foreign tourists. The hotel was new, more or less equivalent to a five star hotel, and was impeccable: a spacious room with *en suite* bathroom, radio, attractive furniture, and a bowl of fruit on the table. However, here as in other hotels in Poland where I stayed, there was always something missing or out of order. The bedside lamp did not function. If there was a TV set in the room, it did not work. Possibly I did not know how to turn it on, or perhaps the intention was to force me to request help from the attendant, who keeps a watchful eye on the floor and its guests.

"FOR THIS NOW IS WEEPING"

It was already dark when I returned to our street. With no difficulty, I recognized all the houses on the right side; however, on the left, new high-rise buildings had gone up. The section where our house [number 34] stood remained as it had been, only more rundown. A light flickered in the stairwell, and voices of neighbors chatting drifted from the first floor. Someone asked me what I was looking for. My past, I answered. It turned out that one of the neighbors, Leon M., who was standing there talking was a tenant and son of tenants in that building. He had known our family and even remembered me, remembered that we used to play soccer together in the yard, and that he had beaten me at it, even though he was a few years younger than I was. He has remained here, the sole former resident still living in this building. The Jewish tenants had all been exterminated, and the Polish ones had died off, or had moved elsewhere. Leon received me with courtesy, even with affection, as an old friend. We spoke of the past. We sat in his unadorned room, and he told me about the suffering that he and many Poles had experienced during the war: forced into hard labor in Germany and Austria, tortured and killed. He returned from a German factory after the war with a heart condition. His parents had died during the war. I recognized them in the photos he showed me. I had the impression they had been *Volksdeutsche,* but he denied this. Leon had married, they had had no children, and his wife had just died the previous month. He accompanied me to the top floor, to our former apartment. Verses from a Holocaust poem by Uri Ẓvi Greenberg[4] floated in my memory:

> Blessed be the dream that visits us in one of these nights of ours
> And so kindly leads us to the entrance of this childhood of ours!
> ... see, we have opened the door and crossed this threshold of ours:
> Still alive are all our dear ones. Full of charm is a summer's day!
> The *shekhinah*'s radiance pervades our chambers, our clock still chimes its hour.
> Here our father and our mother, not yet slain by these our slayers,
> So joyful moving toward us.
> ...
> For, when wakeful, all this is no more, but in the universe there exists this space of ours,
> And in it, springtime and summer's joy and night's earth go on without us.
> And if we venture there—we shall arrive and find this door of ours—
> We'll stop in dread: a cross is incised upon it, *goyim* live in this our house.
> Using all our vessels, they, these butchers of our family.
> ...
> And the stranger drinks himself sick out of our silver cup of holiness.
> O could we but burn down the house upon its dwellers and our vessels,
> In its ash to wallow, until in rot our flesh dissolve.

I stood and looked around me in silence for a few minutes. What can I say? There were none of our vessels and our *kiddush* cups of holiness. The tenants seemed friendly, decent young people. Our vessels and our *kiddush* cup do exist, elsewhere, and strangers drink from them. I found in the flat almost the same kind of furniture, arranged in the same order, the order dictated by the length of the walls and the placement of the windows. I spoke with the residents of our flat both of whom worked in a textile factory. Her mother looks after their baby.

Leon accompanied me to the hotel. We walked along the part of the route that I described in earlier chapters. The barracks still stand at the end of the street but now serve as an army depot. The sentinel booths still stand, but Narutowicza (or Zielna) Street, which we reached from our street, no longer leads

Skladowa 34, as it looked in 2015

on the right to the tram's night depot, to Lodz's central parking lot and the end of town. From here, new wide streets now branch out. On the site of the former commerce school a university building was constructed after World War II. What I had immediately sensed upon leaving the train station was plainly evident: The town has developed, grown and gained in beauty. Leon told me that there was now far less smoke and soot in the city's air. Factories have moved to the suburbs.

A NEW CITY

In the large Centrum Hotel where I was staying, I had an opportunity to speak to a number of engineers and architects who were attending a national conference dedicated to municipal energy and infrastructure problems. From them

I learned that Lodz had a severe water supply problem, that the city center was deteriorating, and that they were working on improvements. I also learned that the great industrial revolution in post-occupation Poland was produced by just a mere 7,000 or so engineers, architects and technicians who survived the war and who were responsible for the construction and reconstruction of roads, bridges, and buildings and who restored Poland to its beauty, which today shines more brightly than before. Since then, the corps of engineers has grown in number, but once the initial reconstruction impetus ended and the numbers of projects diminished, thousands of engineers and architects—more than half of the association's members—now work in other fields, and many are unemployed, especially the young.

My interlocutors told me that Poland's agricultural production still lagged behind that of other European countries by about twenty-five to thirty years, in particular in use of chemical pesticides and fertilizers. At the conference they decided on a new three-year plan in all areas of construction and development.

The morning following my arrival I toured the town and found that indeed a great deal had improved. The streetcars, still screeching and lurching, rising and sinking, have the same numbers as in the past and travel the old routes, but their terminus is much farther away. New multi-lane roads cross the heart of town, with traffic almost as heavy as in a Western city: buses, private cars, mostly small models (Fiat), trucks, cabs, and trams. The Kalisz train terminal, from which I had intended to travel to Zdunska Wola and to Wroclaw, is no longer at the edge of town as it had been when I left. It was easy to miss it as I focused on the bustling streets and their hazardous, potholed sidewalks. Many houses on the old surrounding streets have been torn down and large buildings erected in their place.

On the way to Balut (Bałuty), the former Jewish slum neighborhood, trees have been planted. From Ogrodowa Street, where my grandfather Moshe used to live, and beyond, a municipal garden stretches out, and beyond it, a new housing complex is under construction. On Ogrodowa Street, the large stone buildings still stand, among them Poznanski's former mansion which is now the regional office of the Communist Party. The whole area has changed beyond recognition—Balut's wood houses and the Old Town have been razed. Where the ghetto once stood, there are now multi-story buildings. Thousands of workers' families live in this old-new neighborhood, bordering wide roads, lawns, and public gardens.

In one public area, I saw what looked like a free marketplace. Leon told me that on Saturdays the square is full of people selling scarce goods, unavailable in government stores, at prices steeply higher than the official rates: spare car parts, men's pants, children's clothes, electric bulbs, flashlights, radio parts, and sundry household items. Also more upscale clothing, such as cannot be found in the stores. Leon said that in a single Saturday the spare car parts vendor could make more than three monthly salaries. The black market is conducted in dollars or German marks. Many people have made their fortune here, buying and selling, accumulating some cash and then moving on to another market.

A young sociologist from Lodz University who accompanied me part of the way, said that equality in Poland was "a joke." A wealthy elite has recently emerged through free market activities, but most of the population is too poor to permit itself even a fraction of its needs in this marketplace. Why are there so many flower-vending stands in the streets? Because previously, when Poles visited friends or family, they used to bring their hosts chocolate, coffee, tobacco, wine, or perfume; today they bring only flowers. Many recall with sadness that until just a few years ago there was an abundance of goods in Poland, and a working family could live without too much worry, albeit modestly, of course, as they received housing and various benefits.

The main arteries in the city center have not changed, but the facades of the old houses look faded and dilapidated. I went in search of places I had known in my youth. Where the prayer halls of the Aleksander Ḥasidim had been, on Wschodnia Street and on Zachodnia Street (the Great Shtibel), there were now offices and apartments. I was told that all the Jews of Lodz were served today by only the top floor of a small house of prayer in an interior courtyard. I went there, to Południową 28, but found no one present at noon. On the veranda I saw a small *sukkah*, barely large enough for making a *kiddush*, but I am sure that a *minyan* of Jews could not stand, let alone sit there.

I visited the sites that I described in earlier chapters. The synagogue of the "enlightened" (the Reform synagogue) where Dr. Braude had officiated as rabbi and preacher had been burned down by the Nazis, and in its place stood a tall building of the university's medical school. Buildings that had housed the editorial boards of the Jewish press were still there, now housing offices and shops. I saw a small printing press, Polish of course, in the place that had once buzzed with activity, spewing out the sheets of the *Lodzer Tageblatt*. The buildings of the Jewish school had not changed, but strangers occupied them now.

Despite my hesitation, I went to the office of the Lodz Jewish community on Zachodnia Street, following the address given to me at the municipal information office. I was told that this office keeps a registry of the names of the thousands of those who were buried in Lodz. In a back building, in the second courtyard, a Polish woman pointed to an office on the first floor. It was closed. While I was looking about me, I saw a man coming up the stairs, also heading to the community office. We struck up a conversation. Usually, he said, two clerks come to the office for only a few hours twice a week. This was indeed the day they were supposed to be here, but, apparently, they had already left. The office houses files on the thousands who died in the ghetto: lists of names, addresses, and dates of death. The man used to be a hairdresser and for many years had run a small barbershop in Balut. Today he receives a pension of 5,000 zloty, on which it is impossible to live. For this reason he makes a little extra money performing all kinds of services, the nature of which he did not disclose. He joined me. We sat on a bench.

I was well acquainted with the neighborhood from my childhood. This is where the synagogue of the *mitnagdim,* known as the Wilker Shul, used to stand, next to the Great Shtibel of the Aleksander Ḥasidim. Nearby was the building containing the *mikveh.* This road used to be a main thoroughfare of Jewish community life. Today everything was strange, alien: empty lots and a few new buildings.

My interlocutor told me that he did not come to this neighborhood often, even though it was not far from Balut. From his youth he had always disliked religious Jews. He knew how religious factory owners mistreated their workers, and, in general, how rich Jews dealt with their poor brothers. Not as brothers, no. Class is stronger than ethnos. From youth he had been a Bundist. Owners of small workshops and factories exploited the labor of Jewish workers, and the moment they had money, they bought machinery and turned to the anti-Semitic Polish labor union N.P.R. for workers to operate them, pushing out the Jewish workers. Even small workshops had to shut down as Jewish workers were unable to compete with the aggressive Polish unions that broke their strikes. This is how his father was dismissed from a Jewish-owned factory and died in penury, after several years of unemployment. For a while, seeing his family's distress, my fellow bench-sitter said he himself lost faith even in the Bund. He then turned to the Communists. In those days, he wanted to transform the order of the state and society from the ground up.

"Do you know," he asked, "that in 1930, in the countrywide elections to the Sejm, 53,700 Lodzers voted for the Communist Party, including many Jews?" He well remembered those elections. There were then more ardent Communists than there are today. The Communist Party won double the number of votes than the Socialist Party and its satellites (the P.P.S. camp). The Bund and the leftists won only 7,000 votes. Among the Jews, the big winner was Agudat Israel with more than 23,000 votes, thanks to which Leib Mincberg, the community head, entered the Sejm in the government's list. Yes, he can recall those days better than what happened yesterday.

Indeed, he churned out facts and figures which were correct, as I later verified. The former Bundist was now a member of Solidarity. He has distant relatives in Israel, but his daughter, son-in-law and two grandchildren live in Lodz, and here he receives his retirement pension. Here he has lived all his life—he is one of the ghetto's handful of survivors—and here he will die. This Lodz Jew, one of the last in his city, still stands sentinel on the agenda of his party, the Bund, as in the beginning: "Doykeit"—only here!

JEWISH CEMETERIES IN POLAND

The Lodz Jewish cemetery was a large area already in my day, surrounded by a wall and fences. Tree-lined alleys led from the main gate to the "tents," those *ohel* structures raised for community founders and dignitaries, and from there paths split in all directions. Lodz's great rabbi, Reb Eliyahu Ḥaim Meisel, who died in 1912, had bought and prepared a burial plot for himself there so that right away trees were planted and necessary small structures added. Herman Konstadt, one of the city's rich manufacturers, built a "modern" (in those days) facility for the ritual washing of the dead. Indeed, this cemetery

Poznanski family mausoleum, Lodz Jewish cemetery

was considered in its day the most beautiful in Poland.[5] Now its area is much larger and is surrounded by low and mid-sized buildings. It is at the junction of some peaceful streets, mostly built after the war (Polish Army Street, Bracki Street).

The main gate was locked but one could squeeze through the gaps in the wall, or enter, as I did, via the back gate, next to the custodian's house. Officially, one can get information and guidance only on Sunday morning at the fixed and limited visiting hours. I came alone, and not during visiting hours. Along an alley of tall trees I saw the tombstones of Herman and Mina Konstadt, the Poznanski family and the Silberstein family, still standing. Many others had been smashed, erased, uprooted, or fallen down, vanishing into the ground without a trace. Not far away, in another plot containing tombstones, some cows were grazing, perhaps the custodian's little herd. I noticed that the headstones from the war and thereafter bore no Hebrew inscriptions. Everything was in Polish—"murdered by the Hitlerites," or "shot by the German murderers." At the entrance there was a big plaque inscribed with the names of Jews from Germany, mostly from Berlin, who met their end in Lodz. The plaque cites the name of the transport and the time of its arrival in Lodz.

Many graves have vanished. My father had little luck in his life, and in his death, no chance at all. Without a guide in these tangled paths and sub paths there was no way of finding the grave of a simple Jew in this "house appointed for all living." When I turned from the central alley, either to the left or to the right, I was immediately lost in a sea of weeds, wild flowers and thick bushes. From time to time my feet hit against stones and bits of burial slabs. Most of the cemetery is neglected, unrestored and poorly cared for. However, I was told that next to the main gate an impressive memorial to the Lodz Ghetto victims has been erected.

I was also told that until the Six Day War, Lodz had a community of Jewish survivors of possibly a few tens of thousands, whose number was diminishing and whose head, Rabbi Ze'ev Moreino, had even been crowned with a title along the lines of "Grand Rabbi of the Polish State." In those days, apparently, there was tighter supervision over the cemetery, but when diplomatic relations between Poland and Israel were severed following that war, neglect of Jewish cemeteries increased. Disruption of relations among the living thus leaves its trace in the damage inflicted upon the dead.

A short time before my trip to Poland, a delegation of the Reform Movement in America had arrived to sign an agreement with the Polish government, whereby it would receive the exclusive publication rights of manuscripts in state archives left by the Jewish greats of the past. In return for this privilege, the Polish government would place under the aegis and supervision of the Reform Movement the remaining Jewish cemeteries, many of which were declared historic sites, or "cultural heritage." According to the agreement, the Reform Movement undertook to oversee the cemeteries, to preserve and restore tombstones and memorials. From the polemics this agreement raised in the U.S. among the three camps—Orthodox, Conservative, and Reform—I learned that there were in Poland about 400 Jewish cemeteries, most of which were neglected and required thoroughgoing restoration and repairs. The Ministry for Religious Affairs and Historic Sites had thus devolved to the Jews all responsibility for the upkeep of cemeteries. I read that of all the remaining cemeteries in Poland, only 22 were in good shape, 129 were wiped out without a trace and the rest are, apparently, in a condition similar to that of the Lodz cemetery. A public committee for the preservation of cemeteries, synagogues and Jewish culture sites was created last year in Warsaw. The official number of such culture sites, so I was told, is 63.

The cemetery in Zdunska Wola, which I visited two days later, is no less neglected than that of Lodz, and perhaps even more so.[6] In this cemetery, communal peace was reestablished after a long, bitter dispute in the early days of World War I. Here I found the tombstone of the town's rabbi, Reb Eliezer Lipszyc of blessed memory, over whom the Ḥasidim of Ger and Aleksander had so bitterly fought ("better a *goy* as rabbi than an Aleksander Ḥasid!"). In this cemetery too, I found the wall broken in more than one place, and mounds of garbage piling up inside. The inscriptions on the stones brought back to mind some of the town's better-known family names. A good number of inscriptions on women's tombstones were in Yiddish. Many stones had sunk or were effaced, broken or uprooted—a depressing neglect. I recalled the opening of Agnon's book *Chronicles of Our Homes*, [*Korot bateinu*, or, as in the Bible, the *Beams of our Houses*]: "Now, after everything the enemies have done to us, turning the whole diaspora into graves—the graves of our ancestors [are] laid waste."

The days of the festival of Sukkot, known as the "time of our rejoicing," are surely not a fitting moment for visiting cemeteries. But then I never imagined that this visit to Poland would fill my heart with joy. The seven days of my visit were like a *shiva* for me. For even on this Festival of Rejoicing, we recite in the liturgy: "For the sake of Your truth—*hosha-na*! … For the sake of Your great mercy—*hosha-na*! … For Your sake, our Redeemer—*hosha-na*!" In these Polish cemeteries I saw the congregations of Israel, over each and every one of which one could say, in the prophet's words, that they were "afflicted and tossed

Tombstone of Rabbi Eliezer Lipszyc at the Zdunska Wola cemetery

with tempest," "killed over You, and thought a sheep for slaughter."[7] My heart cried out with the poet, "For the sake of saints thrust in the fire—*hosha-na*!"[8]

ALEKSANDER EMPTY OF *ẒADDIKIM*, EMPTY OF JEWS

The same tramline that I took on the day of the *hillulah* for the Old Rebbe some 54 years earlier still serves Aleksander, but the landscape has changed. Gone are the fields and woods that stretched between Lodz and Aleksander; all have been gobbled up by large industrial enterprises, such as the one named for Władislaw Reymont, author of *The Promised Land,* a plant for agricultural machinery, if I am not mistaken. Men and women, some burdened with parcels, get on and off the tram near the various plants. No trace of a Jewish face anywhere.

In less than an hour, I reached the town square: in its center, the station, and on its flanks government buildings, two churches (the German Lutheran is now a Catholic church), a car park, and some shops. On this weekday the square was abuzz with people. I could see right away that the town had grown and spread out and improved its appearance.

I asked to speak to some educated people who had known the town formerly. I was directed to Mr. Stefan Rogowski, a pleasant old man, who had been the town's mayor before the war. He was still working in one of the municipal offices and I waited for him until he was free. When he heard my request—a walk down memory lane—he invited me to his office and asked Mr. Olszowski, a former trader and banker, to join us. Olszowski too had known the *ẓaddik*'s court, and he and his father had been in business contact with many of the Ḥasidim.

According to Mr. Rogowski, Aleksander in 1939 had 17,000 inhabitants, of which only 5,000 were Jews, a far smaller proportion than reported in the Jewish sources I had consulted when I wrote Chapter 7 (perhaps the discrepancy is due to inclusion of populations from the vicinity).[9] The two men recalled the names of Aleksander's former wealthy: Goldberg, Kronenberg, Moskowicz, Morgenstern, and Tanzer. Workers who were laid off from the stocking manufacture, so they related, received government unemployment benefits: food packages and money, as well as alternative work in road building or repairs. These statements were news to me, and require corroboration.

Mainly, my two interlocutors spoke of the *ẓaddik*'s house. When the last *ẓaddik*'s father died in 1924, they said, "all Poland" came to Aleksandrow. The streets and the square were black with the multitudes of Jews. The *ẓaddik*'s funeral left an unforgettable impression on the town. Their talk went from one thing to another. The son of the last rebbe presented himself before the conscription board of the Polish army in 1934, together with Mr. Olszowski, but was rejected because he was underweight and had weak eyes. He knew him well. His sister had studied in school with one of the rebbe's daughters (an assertion I must doubt). Moreover, the rebbe would go out on excursions in a sumptuous carriage with one or two horses. Rogowski remembered how the two houses were built behind the *beit midrash*. Furthermore, one of the rebbe's family members was a bank manager, a bank the Poles called the "Rabbinic Bank," and there was an additional Jewish bank in town, the "Cooperative Bank." These institutions, they explained, were a necessity in a major manufacturing town in the days when most buying and selling was transacted via promissory notes. Each transaction deed had to obtain a bank's authorization for the initiator and his guarantors. The trade in deeds was the bank's chief business.

Under Nazi occupation, the Poles could not do much for their Jewish neighbors. They themselves suffered hardships and persecution. The expulsion of the community to Glowno in that harsh winter of 1939 was a terrible calamity. In Aleksandrow, all the inhabitants understood Yiddish, and some spoke it. Mr. Rogowski knew that *tashlikh* on Rosh Hashana had to be performed by a lake that had flowing, rather than standing water. The former mayor has kept an old *ketubah* and a *mezuzah* in his home.

For some reason the two assured me that the rebbe was "very rich," and I had a hard time convincing them that this was not the case. Especially Mr. Olszowski, the trader and banker, insisted on this point. The rebbe—they called him "the Prophet" in Polish—was greatly respected by the Poles, and many town matters were decided in his court. On several occasions during his term as mayor, Mr. Rogowski spoke to "the Prophet." The rebbe was welcoming, he spoke unhurriedly, with measured, restrained gestures. He was about 1.60 meters tall, shorter than his two brothers. Interactions in the rebbe's court were in Yiddish. Rogowski confirmed what I had heard—the townspeople did not want to buy the hallowed wooden beams of the destroyed *beit midrash*, for fear of a malediction.

Rogowski spoke at length and in some excitement about the handling of the cemetery. The Germans began its destruction, but either did not have time to complete it, or changed their plans. In 1953, the city built a wall around it and the *ohel* of the *ẓaddikim* was restored with the help of a rabbi who came from Lodz. The town now maintains the cemetery and employs a custodian for its care. Mr. Rogowski continued his explanations on how all this came about, and the more he talked, the less I understood. Out of courtesy I refrained from quizzing him on this. The truth is, he emphasized, that at first Jews came and wanted to pay the municipality for the cemetery's maintenance, but heaven forbid, he had refused any payment. Other towns, however, received huge amounts. A committee came from the United States and said that the Jews would build the cemetery wall out of their own pocket. In the end, the city decided to put up the wall. I had a hard time separating the wheat from the chaff.

At any rate, when I arrived at the cemetery I met the custodian, an old Pole, who before the war had lived nearby with his sister—from their window, they would look out over the graves. Now he was a lonely widower and lived far from here, working hard for a measly monthly salary. First, I went to the *ohel* of the *ẓaddikim*. The *ohel* was walled up and sealed but the tombstones had been brought out and affixed on the structure's outer wall. The writing is still quite legible. On the right is the stone of Reb Beẓalel Yair, with the inscription below it: "This stone is the tombstone for our honored teacher and rabbi R. Beẓalel Yair, son of our honored teacher and rabbi R. Yeḥiel of blessed memory for the life to come, may his soul be bound in the bundle of life, and was buried on Wednesday, 27 of Adar 5694 [1934]. We cannot describe him, for so he decreed in his holy Will."

The tombstone of Reb Yeraḥmiel Israel Isaac, the author of *Yismaḥ Yisroel*, who died in 1910, and the stone of his brother, Reb Shmuel Ẓvi, who died in

Tombstone of the third Rebbe of Aleksander, R. Shmuel Ẓvi. The bottom slab reads: "We cannot describe him, for so he decreed in his holy Will not to be described by any epithet"

1924, repeat the same formulaic statement "We cannot describe him" etc. In the middle, between the sons, is the tombstone of the Old Rebbe their father, Yeḥiel Dancyger, who died in 1894, and it is from this stone that the formula is taken—the injunction not to describe the *ẓaddikim* by any epithet. Between the stone of Reb Yeraḥmiel Israel and that of his father there is a blank space, perhaps intended for the grave of the last rebbe who perished in Treblinka.

The whole rectangle, eleven square meters, was built from the thick wall that used to surround the *ohel* and is surfaced with cement, covered with a roof that allows rainwater runoff. Inside the sealed structure there are eighteen graves of family members of the *ẓaddikim,* so the custodian said.

From him I learned that the Germans had taken out many gravestones from this cemetery for paving Aleksandrow's streets. In addition, "hooligans" had stolen stones. For this reason there is a vacant area between the *ohel* of the *ẓaddikim* and a large grave, built of cement and lacking an inscription. Here, the custodian told me, is buried "the greatest prophet of the Jews," by which I assume he meant the grave of the *ẓaddik,* Reb Heynekh of Aleksander. A bit further on, another empty area. However, there are no weeds, thick bushes, or garbage. Twice a year the area is mowed, also for fear of fire, as some years ago a fire that broke out here damaged one of the nearby houses. In another place, at the edge of the cemetery, across from the main gate, there is a grave for thirty men and one woman murdered by the Germans in 1939. The inscription reads, "Here the Jews dug the grave and here they were killed." Only one Jew escaped, the custodian said, released by a bribe of silver or gold. We walked among the visible graves and over the many that had sunk and disappeared into the ground, their stones uprooted.

The custodian told me terrible things about the Nazi killings and the Polish "hooligans" rampaging against the Jews. His sister had fled to Warsaw with her husband and children. There, for two years, she had hidden a Jewish woman and her twelve-year-old son. In one of the war's final months, a neighbor informed on her. The Germans came and shot his sister, the Jewish woman, and the boy. His sister's husband and children were not with her at that time, and so were saved.

I left by the gate I had entered. The second, smaller gate, remained as it had been on the day of the *hillulah*. I had come to the cemetery by cab from the tram station and returned there in a ten-minute walk through clean streets, bordered by small houses, surrounded by neat gardens—the former German neighborhood. I recalled the verse "My spirit is broken, my days are extinguished, the grave is ready for me." These slayings, the evil that had made use of tools created by the most wonderful, rational, scientific technology, in order to consummate a nightmare—death trains galloping on the tracks of European culture and its achievements—one simply cannot reconcile oneself to this, never!

Jews had always lived precariously in the cities and towns on the banks of the Vistula (Wisła), the Viliya and the Dniester[10] rivers. Most of them, whether Ḥasidim or *mitnagdim*, God fearing or secular, simple folk or well-educated, had beamed God's light to the distant diasporas. In the *shtetl* of Aleksander, their light had broken through and even reached the Gentiles.

I went to see what remained of the rebbe's court. I already knew that the great *beit midrash* had been dismantled and destroyed. In its place I found a vegetable garden and a row of trees leading to the house that had formerly been the home of the rebbe's family. The house stood there as I remembered it. It is now a boarding school. The director of the boarding school could not tell me anything about the history of the house; he had only arrived in Aleksander five years previously. I walked through the building's two stories, the first consisting of seven rooms, the second of ten, each room with a large window. Behind this house was a new, three-storied school. I looked for the house to which the Ḥasidim, exiting from the *beit midrash*, went to receive the rebbe's "sholem" greeting. This too was still standing, to the right of the rebbe's home, close to the *beit midrash*, a one-story building, containing eight rooms and one spacious room at the entrance, a sort of hall. At the door of this room, Father and I had waited to be received by the rebbe. In that room, I had taken my leave of him. Now the house was a retirement home.

In the street, near the garden and the access to these buildings, on the way to the town's central square, I saw several shops: a kiosk, flower and fruit stands, and vendors of odds and ends. I spoke with a few sales women and customers, choosing, of course, the elderly. Some told me that they were afraid to speak to a stranger since there were "strange types" here who might think that we were discussing the current situation in Poland. In Aleksander too, the Solidarity labor union had held a demonstration in the summer and the police had been heavy-handed. One old carpenter was candid and unafraid. He had known the rebbe's household, and had worked for them from time to time. He too confirmed: The Poles indeed did not want to buy the beams of the *beit midrash*, and "swiping" "German property" from under the Germans' nose meant certain death. Two old women told me that they had formerly worked in Goldberg's hose factory, one from the age of twelve until a long time after her marriage—those were the good days. Today there were only shortages and long queues, and no decent compensation for one's labor. Strict control was exercised over even the smallest businesses.

The town's synagogue at the street corner, which had been built in the days of the *Yismaḥ Yisroel*, was destroyed. There is now a small public garden and behind it, on the other side of the road, where the *shtibel* used to be, a wide street stretches out, Red Army Street.

So, with my own eyes I saw, and from my conversations and readings I received confirmation that indeed most of the physical and cultural edifices of Poland's Jews were burnt and destroyed: schools, *yeshivot*, synagogues, hospitals, charity organizations, community centers. Libraries, museums, and archives were looted. Everything that had been alive and vibrant in the Jewish world had vanished, everything that had excited the heart and expanded the mind—the vision, the acts of charity and grace, the ethics aspiring to sanctity and purity—all perished and gone.

I stood again on Aleksander's main square, near the tram, and pondered the ruination of its sanctity and glory, feeling the loss of "those gone, and no longer with us." Should one not claim from the Polish government compensation for the private property, for "the silver cup of our kiddush?" At least, I felt, it should shoulder responsibility for maintaining and making accessible Jewish cemeteries and archives, without exacting high payments from Jewish institutions in America or from the State of Israel. When I inquired at the Lodz municipal archive why its Jewish division did not have documentation sorted by family name—everything there was arranged by ghetto addresses (does anyone know where his parents or relatives lived in the ghetto, when no letters ever came out of there?)—they replied, "This is how we received the files from the Jewish committee. The Jews could have put money at our disposal to organize the files for the convenience of the inquirers, but we, we are unable to do anything." The insolence of heirs!

It is inevitable that the dead be forgotten. How can one remember the dead, whose children and grandchildren perished with them, unnaturally, and all they have, at best, are distant family remnants, dispersed throughout the world? How can they be remembered if their existence was not implanted into living hearts—to continue its growth as the memory of yesterday opening unto the future?

TRAIN CHAT ON BRIBERY AND ON HOLINESS

On the train to Zdunska Wola, I traveled with a middle-aged woman, accompanied by her son and daughter, an army major, and an elegant, heavyset gentleman. I learned that the latter owned a chain of restaurants including one in Zdunska Wola. He earnestly assured me that in his restaurant one could eat far more cheaply not only than in any hotel but also in any other restaurant.

The woman complained about the difficulty in obtaining products. She buys sausage and delicacies for the doctor who treats her daughter, ill with bone tuberculosis. Just a short time ago the child was released from hospital, and they traveled to Lodz to see the doctor. She said how difficult it had been to get him to deign to treat her child. His wife-secretary told her outright that if she wanted to speed up the girl's admission to surgery she had better bring chocolate, sausage, and other treats. Moreover, before the surgery she had to bring the doctor dollars. Since a series of operations was required, the doctor received a huge amount of money, she said.

"Medical care is free in Poland," I remarked.

"But without bribes, you can't get to a good doctor and to surgery."

"And if you were to report this case to the authorities?"

"They would only laugh and shrug their shoulders. My husband has access to government officials, but it's no use."

The major wanted to divert the conversation to a different topic: Zdunska Wola is proud today of her illustrious son, Maximilian Kolbe, who that very week was about to be canonized by the Vatican. The boy, who sat across from me next to his mother, said softly, "He is my Grandpa's brother, my name is Piotrek Kolbe."

Yes, the papers were full of stories about the Franciscan Father Kolbe, a native of Zdunska Wola, who, as a prisoner in Auschwitz, gave his life to save another Pole, a father of children whom the Germans were about to send to his death. Here was a saint, an exemplar of Christian love, a "martyr-witness" of the faith, tortured and abused, like Jesus, who saved humanity when he accepted suffering and death to atone for its sins, so announced the sermons published in the papers and the many masses said for him in the churches. Five thousand Poles, escorted by a distinguished government delegation, made pilgrimage to Rome to participate in the canonization ceremony of the "Martyr of Auschwitz." The Holy Father, John Paul II, formerly Bishop of Cracow, Karol Wojtyła, crowned Zdunska Wola's son as a saint in St. Peter's Square, near the apostle's tomb. The following Sunday the ceremony would be broadcast on Polish TV to warm hearts, to elevate spirits. During these days of hardship and depression, this was a ray of light to all the nation's sons and, as the Polish people saw it, to all the nations of the world.

Far be it from me to begrudge the saint his fame. But I could not help feeling some reservation about the humanity and ethics he had exercised while he was still a free man. Kolbe, as I read in a German newspaper, used to edit a Franciscan journal whose platform in matters of faith and policy toward the neighboring people, Germans and Russians, as well as in its attitude to the Jews, echoed the same narrow-minded, unimaginative and intolerant position then commonly prevailing in the ranks of the popular Polish Catholic priesthood. Even at the beginning of the war he still wrote about the Jews not without odium. Naturally, in Poland, one could not breathe a word about this. On my first day in Wroclaw I saw multitudes crowding at church doors, and I listened to some of the sermons about the heroic and saintly Pole who had walked in the footsteps of Jesus. Incidentally, the name Maximilian Kolbe indicates, I believe, German ("Swabian") extraction.

I could not help thinking of stories from the Holocaust literature, documenting how Jews—friends, relatives, or non-relatives—sacrificed their lives to save others. Famous[11] is the incident that occurred in the town of Włodawa: when the SS searched for the Rebbe of Radzyn, a young man came forward and declared that *he* was the rebbe. He wished to redeem the rebbe's life with his own, similarly to Kolbe's act. The Nazis discovered his intention to "cheat" them, and after finding the rebbe, killed them both. As will be recalled from

Chapter 13, this was the town—"Narrow and crowded and wider than any width"—that Yiẓḥak Katzenelson described as a symbol of Jewish sanctity and ethics. In Jewish habitations throughout Poland there were no few Kolbes: Who remembers them? I do not wish to minimize Maximilian Kolbe's deed. I am dust under the feet of saints, be they of Abraham's covenant or not.

IN THE CITY OF THE SAINT—AND SAINTS

Truly agitated by fear and love, I stepped out of the train station of Zdunska Wola. Fittingly, its dimensions were still modest. Many fine filaments, cherished bonds of childhood, bound me to this town, the home of my ancestors, my mother, uncles and aunts and their families. This is where as a child my heart opened to the world. In this town, I felt "at home," more than in Lodz. Some of my poems were composed here. During a visit there for one of the big weddings of the Strykowski family (my mother's family, as mentioned in Chapter 14), in which the entire large extended family celebrated together, I wrote the poem *Joy* (*Gil*), which was published in the respectable Hebrew journal *Ha-olam* (September 1928), next to works by A. A. Kabak, Yakov Steinberg, and other well known writers. At this last wedding in Poland that I attended, I felt the power of family love. Granduncle Yidl Maroko was its senior member, and he was shown no less respect than that bestowed upon the town's rabbi.

I confess that when I recently found the poem *Joy* in one of my well-worn files, I could not understand what had prompted this exuberance, Until, that is, I recalled that wedding—the occasion when I composed it. However, already in those days, joy was shadowed by the darkness moving ineluctably closer.

The main streets had not changed their names, just as their directions to the neighboring towns had not changed—Lasek Street, Szadek Street, Sieradz Street. To all appearances, everything remained as it had been. But a Jewish face was nowhere to be seen.

I was told that the town had grown and its population, apparently including the neighboring suburbs and villages, had now reached 40,000—all Poles. Not only have the Jews vanished, but the large German community, the pioneers of the town's textile industry, were all gone. Only the names of a few houses, Fuchs and Schulz, bear witness to their former presence. From the trees of the Fuchs garden I would pick apples and pears in my childhood. They stood next to the fence of Grandmother's house, and their branches hung out into our garden—a temptation for any small thief. I saw that a few trees were still standing. The neighbors, even the oldest among them, had little information about the family of my uncle Beresz, the former residents of the house on 28 Sieradz Street. I had better luck when I walked as far as the end of the street, formerly on the outskirts of town, to the home of my uncle Mordekhai Mendel Strykowski and his wife, Aunt Basia. The wooden house had been replaced by a new two-story brick house, but an old lady I questioned there, cried excitedly, "Basia, Basia! Of course, I knew her. I would go in and out of her shop."

She led me to a yard, the back of which borders on an open field. I immediately recognized the place. Here I would sometimes keep an eye on an unruly calf for which I would receive a liter of milk from its mother.

The stone houses nearby were just as they had been. The old woman told me that here, on this street, the Nazis had shot my uncle and his son-in-law on the first day of their entry into the town. Reports I have read differed concerning the location of the murder and its circumstances, but this is of no importance.

A younger woman that I met in the yard told me that in her childhood she would enter my aunt's shop, a sort of general store, a few times a day and played with her girls. One of them grew up to become a beauty. "Yes, your uncle's family were good and friendly neighbors, well-liked by everyone."

However, based on the history of Zdunska Wola's Jews, such amicable neighborly relations were as difficult to find as the Christian love preached by the priests in Kolbe's town. Testimonies relate that looting of Jewish shops and homes began immediately following the departure of the Polish authorities from the town, led by the rabble of the *Volksdeutsche*, abetted by Poles. When the occupation army entered, Jews who had some property, factories and shops were the first victims of abuse, and my uncle and cousin were among the first to be killed. Could my girl cousins, among them that beauty, have escaped? They knew Polish, knew their surroundings and its inhabitants, but who would dare hide them? I recalled Yiẓḥak Zuckerman's well-known words: "In Poland, to save one Jew, a hundred righteous people (*ẓaddikim*) were required, but for informing and extraditing, one evil person sufficed."

Before their deportation to labor or extermination camps once the local ghetto was demolished in August 1942, the Jews of Zdunska Wola were prey to harassment and killings by the Nazis. I passed by the market square, "Liberty Square," where the hangings and killings of Jews had taken place. In nearby Staszic Square, Jews were hanged on Purim, March 1942. Shlomo Żelichowski and his fellows were hanged on Shavu'ot, May 1942. I stood next to the house of Dr. Yakov Lemberg, the physician, head of the Zionists and a longtime community leader, who was appointed by the Nazis as the head of the ghetto administration, the "Elder of the Jews." Despite some reservations I have read concerning this, I am convinced that he was a leader and community functionary worthy of honorable remembrance, a man of fine personal qualities who suffered the torment of leading a Jewish community in those days of terror. When the ghetto was liquidated, the Nazis, headed by Hans Biebow, the German in charge of administering the Lodz Ghetto, demanded that he make the *selekzia* in Zdunska Wola with the Nazis, and that he collaborate with them once he was brought to the Lodz Ghetto, where most of those fit for work had been transferred. He declined both demands.

The first *selekzia* took place in Staszic Square. The second, the main one, in the cemetery, lasted two days, during which a few dozen Jews were killed. Those fit for work were transported to the Lodz Ghetto in trains that crawled along for two whole days, but most of the population, about 8,000 souls, were transferred to the Chelmno death camp. Some reports say that a few hundred Jews were taken to a wood near the town of Warta where they were shot and their bodies burned. On the last days of August 1942, before Rosh Hashanah, the fine community of Zdunska Wola came to an end. Before the departure of the train, loaded mostly with able-bodied young men, Biebow pulled Dr. Lemberg out of the wagon and drove him—perhaps to the cemetery, possibly to a nearby forest—where, it is said, he was shot and buried.

When I stood in the cemetery in front of individual and mass graves, I took the prayerbook out of my pocket. I wanted to say *Kaddish* and *El male raḥamim*. But my throat choked. I knew that I would be unable to contain myself. I just scanned the letters. Had I started reciting the *Kaddish* aloud, I would have broken down, and, overcome, I would have been unable to continue the trip. I had to reach Breslau-Wroclaw that afternoon. From the cemetery, through the town's streets, I headed back to the train station.

Formerly, a Friday like this was a busy market day. Now, however, I saw nothing of the plenty that I remembered from the old days. A little honey, a little cheese, a little milk, some baskets and crates of fruit and vegetables. It was just a caricature of a former Polish agricultural marketplace.

On Sieradz Street, the Great Synagogue used to stand, and next to it the *beit midrash*. These had been demolished and burned. In their stead, I found some houses and gardens and the restaurant of my acquaintance from the train. Only one old man was able to say something about the destruction: Immediately after the town's occupation, the following day, the Nazis threw in grenades and burned houses and even obliged the Jews to clear away the debris. Not far from the market and the houses built on the former synagogue and *beit midrash*, there is a church where Kolbe used to pray in his youth when he resided here. Now his family members attend it. For the following Sunday, a celebratory mass was scheduled in memory of Zdunska Wola's most illustrious son, the new saint. I felt it a strange coincidence that I should have arrived in my town, this "precious cornerstone" of my childhood memories, precisely at this time of its great celebration.

Other children were playing in our yards, supplanting yesterday's reality, emptying it. In his *Elegy on Jewish Towns*[12] (written in Warsaw in 1947), Antoni Słonimski mourned:

> Those towns are no longer, they've passed like shadows,
> And these shadows will fall between our words ...

Indeed a thick shadow devours our words and disrupts them. But very strange to me is the end of that stanza:

> Before two nations, nourished by the sufferings of centuries,
> Will approach each other fraternally, and again unite.

I do not fathom his meaning.

IN WROCLAW, FORMERLY BRESLAU

Without border controls this time I passed onto former German soil to Breslau, Silesia's capital, now the Polish city of Wroclaw. Again I had a sensation of *déja vu*—I had already made this journey in the past, stopping at the same stations, arriving at the same city. The first time I had approached it, with anticipation and apprehension, was in the autumn of 1928.

By astonishing coincidence, sitting in the train I read that the approaching winter was expected to arrive early and to be exceptionally severe, similar only to the winter of 1928. The paper explained: "The winter of 1928 was extremely cold, with lots of snow and frost, and it set in early. The farmers knew this was in store by the behavior of the bees, which had become that autumn, beginning in September, very aggressive." And now, wrote the reporter, the stinging of the bees is again showing us the weather we can expect.

Silesia and Breslau—an entire population was uprooted from here and replaced by another ethnic group. Political science teaches that the use of violence is the most common "natural means" in international relations, and that the state has a lawful monopoly of the use of violence within its borders. The state is the sole mandated employer of violence, and its struggle with other states is always over the rights of dominion. Sociologists like Ludwig

Gumplowicz and Franz Oppenheimer taught that every group seeks to satisfy its needs, not through work and trade, but by conquest, and that the essence of conquest is the conquest of territory, which, until our era, was the chief source of wealth. Through conquest states were established and populations exploited or expelled, exterminated or acculturated. The accumulation of wealth in the hands of the few is not the fruit of their talents, but of their conquests. Property does not have a tendency to accumulate all by itself, and wealth is not the reward of industrious, talented workers, as the liberal or Marxist schools believed. Max Weber thought that the state assumes the right to monopolize violence also in its relations with other countries, and goes out to conquer and expand its lawful right to use violence.

"Every state is founded on force," Trotsky declared during the peace negotiations at Brest-Litovsk in 1918. In the former Breslau, which had numbered before World War II about six hundred thousand Germans, the ascendant group had been the conquering *Junkers*, the Prussian landowners (although less so than in East Prussia). In post-World War II Wroclaw, one could clearly see the results of territorial conquest, exchange of populations, and the expulsion of the losers. In exchange for ceding certain regions of Lithuania and the Ukraine to Russia, the Poles were permitted to annex parts of Germany and to transfer to Silesia the Polish population of the ceded Ukrainian Galicia. Thus, all of Silesia is now inhabited by Poles, as though a stolen entity—the duchy ruled by the Polish Piast dynasty until the end of the seventeenth century—has been returned to its rightful owner.

Wroclaw today, with its approximately half a million Polish inhabitants, is the country's fourth largest city. Heavily damaged in World War II, the city has been resurrected from rubble with great talent and industry. In its center is the beautifully restored main square with its late Gothic town hall. The medieval cathedral has also been restored, as well as many other Renaissance and Baroque buildings. I was glad to see the familiar old central train station and its surrounding buildings still there, unchanged. However, the Panorama Hotel was new, and some streets appeared new, or their appearance had changed.

JOYLESS FESTIVAL OF JOY; IN FRONT OF THE JEWISH THEOLOGICAL SEMINARY

On the afternoon of my arrival, there was not much time to look around. I hurried to the synagogue in the former Wallstrasse. I knew the place well: The Orthodox synagogue named The White Stork (Zum Weissen Storch), a spacious and attractive building, stood in an inner courtyard. I used to come there occasionally on Saturdays to pray and to hear sermons by rabbis Moses Hoffmann and Max Simonsohn. The prayers used to be led by cantor Weiss, a learned scholar, with a tremendous bass voice. Now the building stood abandoned. It had not been torched on the "Night of the Broken Glass," unlike the ornate liberal synagogue, probably because it was enclosed all around by inhabited buildings. It is not in use now. Prayers are held in a small hall in a wing on the left side.

I got there early, even before the afternoon prayer, and had time to introduce myself and to speak with a few of the attendees, about fifteen tired-looking old Jews, remnants of the horror. The leader of Breslau's community, where about 2,000 Jews had congregated after the Holocaust, was Mr. Moshe Finkelstein, who also served as representative of all the other communities in Poland in dealings with the Polish government. Most of the Jews in this prayer hall originated from Lvov, Tarnopol, and other cities in Galicia. Only one of the participants was from Vilnius.

From Mr. Finkelstein I learned a few things about the Jews of Breslau and the entire region today. The community members live on pensions and

Perished in Theresienstadt—the loving, childless couple, Eugen and Recha Perle, who used to host out-of-town rabbinic students in their home on Wallstrasse 8, next to the White Stork Synagogue

only a handful work in any kind of remunerative employment. A few young people take part in a Communist club. There is also a Jewish kindergarten.

I was told that thanks to Mr. Finkelstein's endeavors, the Polish radio had broadcasted that year before the Days of Awe old recordings of cantorial pieces sung by Yossele Rosenblatt and Moshe Koussevitzky, a real treat for the Jewish audience. It was the first time they had heard them.

Sad indeed were the *hakafot*[13]on that night of *Simḥat Torah,* as the verses of comfort and rejoicing were chanted. I recalled Breslau and its Jews in its holy days and festivals. In the building in front of the synagogue, facing the street, I would frequently dine on Friday nights at the table of a lovely couple, the uncle and aunt of my future wife. Indeed, it was there I met the young woman who married me.

It was hard to sing, "We will be glad and rejoice in His salvation."[14] From the depth of my heart, the cry went out: "Helper of the weak, please deliver us!"[15] Please deliver the sons of this last generation of the Polish exile. Their number did not even suffice for the seven traditional *hakafot.* We made do with less.

As I was leaving the prayer hall, a tall man, younger than the rest of my new acquaintances, Julian M., accompanied me. From our conversation I learned

The girl who married me, Flora Perle

that he was the son of a famous teacher from Lvov, had enlisted as a young man in the Russian army, had been wounded several times, participated in the conquest of Berlin, and had been decorated with a number of medals for valor and other honors. Here before me stood a hero of World War II who, though he had endured much hardship and suffering, still looked full of energy and love of life—on his good days. He confessed that he also had days of weakness and depression. He was a bachelor, living on a pension and various discounts and benefits. Some family survivors lived in Israel, but his only sister and her children were living in Wroclaw.

However, I did not learn all these details at once. I was in a hurry to get to the end of the street, to Wallstrasse 14, to the building that used to house the Jewish Theological Seminary, where I had pursued the academic study of Jewish history and culture and the classical sources of Judaism.

Jewish Theological Seminary building, Breslau

The building was dark and locked, hermetically shuttered, blocked-up, a phantom monument. Julian and I went around it a couple of times. Now it belonged to the government or the army, and served as a depot, though all the houses around it were residential. I told Julian about the famous institution that had formerly occupied this building.

The Jewish Theological Seminary in Breslau was founded in 1854. Its first head was Rabbi Zacharias Frankel, author of an *Introduction to the Mishnah* and other works, who also taught there, followed by instructors such as the historians Heinrich Ẓvi Graetz and Markus Mordekhai Brann. Its graduates included scholars like Moritz Güdemann, David Kaufmann, Hermann Cohen, and additional outstanding rabbis from Germany and other countries. In my day it was an institution of modest size (about 60 students altogether; 28 entered with me that year—the largest freshman class in the institution's history), but very prestigious and significant. Standing in front of the locked gate I recalled the classrooms on the ground floor, the library and synagogue on the top floor, and, in the middle floor, the apartments of two of our lecturers, Professor Guttmann and Dr. Rabin.

The four leading lecturers were renowned scholars: Yeḥiel Michal Hacohen Guttmann, the Talmud instructor, was one of the great experts in his field,

Diese Karte ersetzt auch den sonst zur Erlangung von Fahrpreisermäßigung erforderlichen Personalausweis.

Jüdisch-theologisches Seminar Breslau
(Fränkel'sche Stiftung.)

Ausweiskarte
(Nur gültig mit der angehängten zweiten Hälfte)
für

stud. theol.
inscribiert
aus
(Wohnort der Eltern)

Das Dozenten-Kollegium
Z. Z. Vorsitzender
...chrift des Inhabers

Gültig nur mit der angehängten ersten Hälfte und für das durch Abstempelung bezeichnete Halbjahr

Student ID from Jewish theological seminary

author of *Key to the Talmud* (*Mafteaḥ ha-Talmud, Clavis Talmudi*) and other important books in Hebrew and German. He fought publicly in German law courts to defend the Talmudic literature from attacks by anti-Semitic "scholars," who intentionally distorted and garbled the texts in order to reduce them to preposterous nonsense, all for the sake of maligning Judaism and Jews. Professor Guttmann managed to flee to Budapest, where he died during the war years (1942).

Yiẓḥak (Isaak) Heinemann taught medieval Jewish philosophy, as well as the exegetical methods of homiletic literature (*aggadah*), in comparison to Hellenistic interpretation methods. Despite his deafness he was a superb lecturer and teacher who enchanted us with his wisdom. He translated the writings of Philo of Alexandria and the Stoic authors from Greek to German and edited the *Monatsschrift*, the leading journal of the Science of Judaism in Germany, which had been founded by Zacharias Frankel and Graetz. Heinemann settled in Ereẓ Israel, where he continued his leading research at the Hebrew University in Jerusalem.

With profound expertise and much wit, Israel Rabin taught Jewish history, as well as the Bible and its exegesis. His studies dealt with the Jewish

Prof. Isaak Heinemann (1876–1957)

communities of Silesia. He also wrote an important study on biblical interpretation in the light of moderate, conservative critical theory. He too succeeded in reaching Ereẓ Israel. I devoted to him a comprehensive essay in an anthology that portrays the leading Jewish scholars in Western Europe before the Holocaust.[16] It was a joy to be his guest on Sabbaths and Festivals. His home on the Seminary's second floor was a meeting place for his colleagues and students and many acquaintances. People from Western and Eastern Europe met there in an atmosphere of Torah and wisdom and relaxed hospitality.

Albert Lewkowitz taught modern Jewish philosophy, pedagogy and the psychology of education. His comprehensive book on Judaism and the intellectual movements of the nineteenth century *Das Judentum und die geistigen Strömungen des 19. Jahrhunderts* (1935) contains much valuable information and thought. I had the good fortune of being able to assist him when he settled in Haifa, and eventually invited him to teach philosophy at the Teachers' Training College which I directed there.

The Seminary students studied concurrently at the University of Breslau, and each pursued his subject of choice: philosophy, history, or Semitic languages and similar topics that would assist a rabbi and a scholar. That university still stands on the banks of the Oder River—an elegant, monumental Baroque building. My alma mater has not lost its beauty, although the halls, the classrooms, the elaborate entrance, the wide corridors in which we used to stroll during the breaks, are now somewhat neglected. I was surprised to see that the statue of the young fencer, mounted on the fountain in front of the building, now faces a memorial plaque in honor of Polish rebels killed ... in 1963. The names are of students from the University of Lvov who revolted against the Russian government in that year of Polish insurgence. The former University of Breslau is now primarily the former University of Lvov: Very soon the professors who were uprooted from their homes in Galicia, the lately arrived exiles, will educate here a generation of Wroclaw-born scholars who will seek to meld the old with the new.

On April 1, 1933, the day the Nazis imposed a boycott on Jewish shops and businesses, I left Breslau and Germany, headed for Ereẓ Israel. The last things I saw of the new government's practices were Jewish shops, lawyer's offices and doctors' clinics, all smeared with Stars of David, in the center of which, in large letters, stood the word *Jude*. "Pure Aryans" were warned not to patronize these businesses. For good measure, the authorities placed S. A. thugs on guard to prevent entry and to heap invectives on any who dared disobey. However, based on what I could see, I felt on that day that the crowds did not accept the boycott with much enthusiasm. The reaction was more one of stupefaction. Germans were not used to a public display of such an anti-Jewish attitude in a country living by the "rule of law." The customers also knew that in many Jewish shops, especially in the large department stores, prices were often lower than in the "pure Aryan" shops. In addition, of course, many people were attached to doctors and lawyers of their choosing. After a while, however, the populace accepted the decree—the initial delegitimization of Jewish livelihoods, one of the first steps in the eradication of "non-Aryans," on the road to the "Final Solution."

Many German Jews deluded themselves that those early acts were just some temporary dysfunction, a demagogic subterfuge that would surely fail, a bad dream bound to dissipate like fog. When I completed my university studies in Breslau, before the boycott, I did a bit of research into the situation in Germany, and at the beginning of the year, just before Hitler came to power, I published the results of my inquiry in the main newspaper of the Social-Democrats.[17] I did not follow wishful dreams and reached some hard conclusions. What I saw on the day of my departure from Germany's horror reinforced them.

MARTIAL LAW

The following day I wandered about town. The large-scale enterprise of reconstruction, restoration, and new construction that I saw before me filled me with admiration. I walked along the old familiar streets with an open notepad in my hand. Some streets I could not find, especially in the area of the former Königsplatz, where entire houses and streets had been razed. I looked for the Street of the Sword, Schwertstrasse, where my wife's parents had lived, but it was the sword of the authorities that nearly got me there. I stood next to a house that I thought was close to that street, and wrote its name down in my notepad. All of a sudden, two uniform wearers jumped at me. "Don't you know that this place is off limits? Dokumenty!" they barked. I heard later that this expression for a request to show one's papers had been introduced by the Russians. When one goes out on the street, one needs to carry not just one card, but several documents. And what was I writing in my notepad? Didn't I know that martial law was in effect? I tried to justify myself, that I had seen no sign prohibiting approach to the place. A sign indeed existed, but was at some distance. The American passport seemed to have made some impression; they looked it over, and finally returned it. One of the cops stated that he could do unpleasant things with my passport, such as detaining it. I replied, "Why would he do this to a tourist who has come a long distance to look for the home where his wife was born, and he brings to Poland foreign currency?" I was very nervous that they might scrutinize my notepad scribbled in Hebrew. Luckily, they let me go in peace. Here on Wroclaw's streets I got a taste, just a whiff, of the terror of totalitarian regimes.

To all appearances, the Poles have attained their centuries-old heart's desire. Here in Silesia the House of Piast and its dynasty of kings and ministers, the fathers of the Polish state, had once ruled. Here were the "roots," the Poles' initial holdings, to which they had always wished to return and to own. From conversations with Julian and others in Wroclaw I got the impression that the feeling of national solidarity really surged when multitudes of Polish settlers moved to Silesia and its capital Breslau-Wroclaw. However, the "geographic compensation" exacted by this return to Silesia was tied up with the sorrow of exile from what had been eastern Poland and with the feeling that the "historic justice" had been accomplished by Stalin's fiat, and not as an act of courage and wisdom by the Polish nation. The Poles, in a tragic history decreed by their geopolitical position between two formidable enemies, and by leaders ill equipped to adapt to the exigencies of reality, have more than once been disappointed and misled in their national enthusiasm.

In Wroclaw, much more than in Lodz, I felt the population's frustrations, expressed in depression and protest. Indeed, the day following my departure a demonstration parade against government moves to ban the Solidarity trade union got underway. The taxi driver, the hotel workers, the university professors, like people in the street, expressed their discontent with the government and its actions, in fact—their great anger and desire for change. True, in all these conversations I heard a deep anxiety lest the Russians intervene, yet many got up their courage to act.

Through the good offices of a professor from the University of Illinois whom I had met at the hotel, I was invited to an informal gathering with some twenty lecturers at the Wroclaw University. The subject discussed was the U.S. support for the Polish government. Most, although not all agreed that President Reagan had done well to cancel the most favored nation status for Polish exports to the United States. In view of the fact that the Polish state already owed the U.S. 28 billion dollars, the U.S. had determined that Poland not be given any further loans and assistance as long as it remained under General Jaruzelski's rule. I listened with astonishment at the sharp words I heard levelled against the Communist regime and against the Russians, who were pressuring Jaruzelski to put an end to Solidarity. The meeting was not public, but it s tenor testified to a degree of free speech that had prevailed there before the imposition of martial law.

Officially, Poland has a number of political organizations and parties and at first I was impressed by the diversity of newspapers, seemingly indicative of the existence of heterogeneous political movements. However, I quickly realized, as I had assumed from the beginning, especially in these days of martial law, that the Polish Communist Party apparatus controlled all spheres of society, economy, army and police, the bureaucracy and academia; it could not tolerate the potential emergence of a democratic opposition party such as Solidarity.

The country was seething. It was clear to me that before long the entire edifice would be shaken to its foundations. The Solidarity movement's flyer that I saw in Wroclaw protested against the abolition of the free worker's union by the decision of the "generals' regime of truncheons," with which the Sejm had cowardly complied, like a mere rubber stamp. The struggle would continue. The watchwords at the top of the page were God, honor, homeland, liberty, and independence. The signatories included the movement's head in the Wroclaw province.

"Why are they meddling in the affairs of the State of Israel and its actions in Lebanon!" shouted the cab driver who drove me around town. "Those hypocrites! What are they doing to *our* country?" His outspoken words against his government were not necessarily a complimentary reflection on mine. The press was spreading all the vilifications of the official Polish propaganda about the war in Lebanon. Granted, it also reported with horror about the murder that occurred in the synagogue in Rome on that last evening of Sukkot, when I visited the Stork Synagogue, but compared it to the acts of the Israeli army in Lebanon and to the deeds of the Nazis in Auschwitz. I understood that the comparison to Auschwitz appears frequently in the Polish media, whenever Jews are injured or inflict injury on others.

In Wroclaw, as in the other Polish towns I visited, the streets were rather quiet. There was no buzz of teenagers milling about, nor the ferment of trade or the clamor of construction. People seemed withdrawn, walking hunched and fearful of any interference by the authorities. The streets lacked aesthetics: no illuminated window shops showing colorful wares, no eye-catching advertising signs, few goods in the shops and the markets—indifferent to the would-be buyer. Everything looked bland. Speech was muted, as though vocal cords were silenced, and everywhere the lowered heads of those seeming to accept their fate in submission—so different from Poland's pre-war streets, and certainly from the former Jewish street. However, perhaps I am only voicing here the impressions of a passing visitor who observes every fault.

One of the professors asked me, "Do you know of Poland's demoralization shortly before the war, and especially, during the war years? It spread throughout society like a vicious infection. Theft, informing, prostitution, and murder, each man's hand at the other's throat, and not only against the Jews, among ourselves too. People abandoned all restraint in lawless thuggery and bloody violence. They knew that the Germans would not touch them. On the contrary, they put themselves at the service of the Nazis for all manner of despicable errands. Later, when the state was re-established, there came a moral and patriotic revival. Slowly, life returned to its course. Hope grew in the early days of Gomułka. Lately, all the rays of light have concentrated on the Solidarity movement. Now that it has been outlawed, we again feel helpless, dispirited." He used an apt Polish expression for despondency and despair.

Julian preferred talking about Israel to discussing present-day Poland. He also returned to his own past, even though it was "terribly hard." In long conversations, he told me his life story. He was sixteen years old when he enlisted in the Red Army, after he and his father the professor were sent from Tarnopol to inner Russia. He suffered no anti-Semitism from the Russians. He mentioned the medals he had received, but did not speak of his heroic exploits. The Polish army recognized both his medals and rank so that he was considered a retired Polish officer and received a pension and benefits. In Israel, he believed, he would be unable to make a decent living at his age and with his disability.

Julian surprised me with his extreme views about Zionism—in favor of Israel's sovereignty over all the territory of Ereẓ Israel. Israel's victory over its enemies restored his faith in the existence of God. During the war and the horrors of the Holocaust, he had lost the faith he had received in his father's home and even after the victory over the Nazis, he did not believe that God's hand had worked this great deed, but rather that it was the actions of the nations. God had left the land, or He was hiding and keeping silent; in either case, faith in Him was useless. Now Julian believed that indeed God had left the countries of our *galut*, but had come to dwell in Ereẓ Israel. There His hand had been supreme. Israel's victories in the Six Day War, in the Yom Kippur War and now, in Lebanon, enabled him to stand up straight. Many Jews, indeed all Jews, he assured me, barring a few die-hard Communists, were proud of the Israel Defense Force's campaigns. Many Poles too, in contrast to the official propaganda about the Zionist imperialist aggressions, admired its triumphs. Here they knew how to read between the lines of a newspaper and form an accurate evaluation. His main tenet: Be strong and do not put your trust in the *goyim*.

THE SOLIDARITY MOVEMENT AND THE ECONOMIC-POLITICAL STRUGGLE

Even before my visit to Poland the leaders of the Solidarity movement were being persecuted and arrested. Lech Wałęsa was imprisoned. That same week of my visit, on October 8, the Sejm passed the Trade Unions Act whereby Solidarity was officially outlawed. Before, during, and following that week the media persisted with warnings about the perils of the Solidarity movement—not that it was the cause of the country's economic and social crisis, but that it had certainly aggravated it with a political rift. I listened to the concluding speeches of General Jaruzelski, his ministers and members of the Sejm. Thanks to my hotel TV, I now saw most of Poland's leaders and heard their views. Speeches that I did not catch on TV I read on the front pages of the following day's newspapers.

Solidarity's arguments were not heard. Its leaders were in prison or internment camps and reporters and intellectuals who had opposed the government were not allowed to air their views or worse—their views were perverted and falsified. In the name of the ideal of "democratic centralism," it was permissible to cover up political processes and conceal reality under ideological veils. However, that same week the veils were lifted, at least some of them, and brutal authoritarianism revelled.

It should be noted that the Solidarity movement grew mainly in the port cities and in the towns abandoned by the Germans. There new Polish immigrants had settled, a young and toughened populace which had not yet found itself. It seemed as though Solidarity endowed this populace with a new identity; at any rate, it helped unite them for local and nationwide action. Solidarity emerged as a "renaissance" movement aimed at reviving a productive and democratic Poland, and within a short time it succeeded in bringing together the masses—factory workers and liberal professionals, artists and professors. To raise living standards, it envisaged reorganizing production through "self-management" and participation in governance, which would increase both output and the worker's dignity.

However, the movement acted with restraint, so I was told, in most of its moves, and was especially careful not to challenge four principles that were the pillars of the Communist regime. The cruel suppression of the attempted revolts in Hungary, East Germany, and Czechoslovakia, had taught the Poles to be wary, and not to do away with (a) **nationalization**. Solidarity limited itself to target the excessive bureaucratization of state institutions that created shortages in primary materials and essential goods.

The movement never challenged (b) the **principle of the Warsaw Pact**, that is, the principle that Poland was tied to the Soviet Union and the other Eastern Bloc states in an unbreakable alliance. However, as in its culture Poland saw itself as a Western state, the movement also brought to the fore strong anti-Russia currents. Polish patriots had a long, complicated, and bitter reckoning with their Russian conquerors-liberators, going all the way back to Poland's first partition (1772). The Poles with whom I spoke saw Soviet Russia as the continuation of despotic Tsarism.

I heard, however, that had East Germany meddled in the conflict between Solidarity and Jaruzelski's government, and had its soldiers breached the state's frontiers, the Poles would have fought fiercely. What the Germans perpetrated here is not forgotten. Solidarity was indeed a national-patriotic movement (under whose aegis some anti-Semitic tropes were also voiced). The national anthem was frequently sung at its meetings. Its programmatic declarations omitted the concept "socialism" and its associated slogans. On May Day, they honored the memory of the Warsaw Uprising of 1944—the revolt of the patriots and fighters of the national, non-Communist Home Army whose leaders were arrested and some shot by the Red Army for "anti-Soviet activities."

In addition, the movement did not demand abolition of the (c) **principle of censorship**, for fear that if censorship were abolished, unbridled criticism of Russia would surge, as had happened in the Prague Spring (1968), and a Russian invasion would be inevitable. Nor did it contest the principle of (d) **the Communist Party's rule**, making do with a demand for trade union participation in government and representation in its subordinate institutions beyond the ranks of Party-appointed officials; in other words, it demanded limiting political appointments and a measure of "self-management" in plants. It also demanded the secret ballot in Party congresses. These requests and demands were accompanied by strikes and demonstrations that really paralyzed the Party in the winter of 1980. The impression was that most of its members were actually rooting for Solidarity. Its heads, apparently, took fright; the sacred ideal of "democratic centralism" was in peril. However, Russia's pressure induced them not to yield.

A tangle of social, economic and political problems were being debated, with strikes, demonstrations and protest parades on the one hand, and arrests, tear gas, and water cannons on the other. The Trade Unions Act enacted by the Sejm on October 8, 1982 adopted in some of its formulations the language of the renewal movement, but threw out its core. The struggle for the existence of Solidarity in the week of my visit led me to believe that Poland was indeed the weakest link in the Soviet iron chain. How would all this turn out? The shipyards in the port cities and the large factories and mines in Silesia had concentrations of tens of thousands of workers. With the evident shortages in goods and commodities, it would be foolish to expect domestic peace. It did not seem to me that the Poles, eighty percent of whom had expressed their support of Solidarity just a year or so ago, would long remain a silent majority. Facing them was the oppressive apparatus of state, with the menace of potential Russian intervention in the background, and not many were as yet prepared to risk their lives in decisive action. Close to my departure from Poland, strikes broke out again in a number of cities, such as Gdansk, Szczecin, and Wroclaw.

Where did Polish Jews stand in these matters? Among the remnants of Jewish Communists, so I heard, many supported Solidarity, and the movement even had several important Jewish leaders in Lodz, Warsaw and Wroclaw. However, a number of prominent Jews or people of Jewish descent also stood on the other side of the barricade. On TV, I saw Jerzy Urban, the government spokesman and, some say, General Jaruzelski's speechwriter. He is the grandson of Yeshayahu Uger, founder and first editor of the *Lodzer Tageblatt*, formerly the most popular Jewish newspaper in our city.

RETURN TO WARSAW

The week I spent in Poland, I read about two books that dealt with the help that Poles gave to Jews during the war, especially in the ghettos. At about that time, the book by Tadeusz Bednarczyk *Duty is Stronger than Death* (*Obowiązek silniejszy od śmierci*) appeared in Warsaw, wherein the author named hundreds of helpers, praised principally the actions undertaken by priests, and discussed at length the help given, at enormous personal risk, to Warsaw Ghetto Jews, also in arms supply and military organization. Bednarczyk was a senior officer in the Polish underground and active in preparing the Warsaw Ghetto uprising. It is difficult for me to form a clear opinion on this matter. I accept Yiẓḥak Ẓuckerman's statement quoted earlier: To save the life of one Jew it took one hundred good Poles from among the Righteous of the Nation, and to hand over a Jew only one treacherous Pole was required. About this situation—rescue of Jews by Poles on the one hand and informing on them on the other—I had read in the stories of Jerzy Andrzejewski's *Holy Week* (*Wielki Tydzień*, 1945), the week of the Warsaw Ghetto Uprising. The Polish media tend to report a great deal about the help and rescue. In Wroclaw, I saw a street named Ghetto Heroes. A similar name has been given to a street in Lodz.

Poet Jerzy Ficowski (1924–2006)

I was much moved to read in a literary magazine that Yiẓḥak Katzenelson's *Song of the Murdered Jewish People* was about to be published in Polish, translated by Jerzy Ficowski. I later learned that this translator was one of the righteous of the Polish nation, a powerfully expressive poet and writer who showed a love of Jews both in his own poetry and in his translations. He dedicated the above translation "to our Jewish brothers in Poland on the 40th anniversary of their battle in the Warsaw Ghetto." In his collection of poems *A Reading of Ashes* (*Odczytanie popiołów*), he identifies himself as "their unburned brother."[18]

Even though the papers denounced Israel's campaign in Lebanon, the two lieutenant colonels in my train compartment on the way back to Warsaw were very satisfied with the IDF's standards and performance. However, they cut this conversation short and did not return to the subject. They were far more interested in the Polish army's participation in the celebrations marking 300 years since the victory of King Jan Sobieski over the Turks. The battle of Kahlenberg, which saved Vienna from the prolonged and dangerous Turkish siege, was "a decisive event in the history of European culture and of the entire Christian world," where the Poles again showed the world that they were "the shield of Christianity and Western civilization." The newspapers had already announced the arrival of a high-level Austrian delegation. In the works: a parade-procession of Polish cavalry and artillery units reenacting Jan Sobieski's campaign along the entire historic route. The officers discussed various logistical and provisioning problems.

In the long conversation which started up and broke off periodically, as is normal among passengers during a journey, the chief recurring themes were consumer goods, appliances and travel: how one acquired goods, food, clothing and machines, their prices, and where and how one traveled. They calculated the price of my vest and of the shoes on my feet and concluded that each item would cost an entire monthly salary, or more, of a worker in Poland. They spoke of economic crime in Poland, of tax evasion, speculators, and smugglers. They were the ones responsible for the shortage of shoes or of coffee in government stores. Ah well, not the Jews this time. One of the women taking part in the conversation said she had just returned from Hungary, and praised the food and the abundance there. My fellow travelers were also worried about the widespread drunkenness and growing drug abuse.

IN THE HEART OF THE WARSAW GHETTO—THE HEART OF THE HOLOCAUST

At the end of the long train ride, I arrived back in Warsaw and at the Hotel Europa. After a rather expensive dinner—an orchestra played, couples danced—I went out into the city streets. However, there were not many lights. The following day I had another look at the large, beautiful metropolis Warsaw had become. Most of its buildings were destroyed in the war, especially during the Polish uprising at the end of July 1944, when Poles attempted to preempt the Red Army's advance in order to liberate their capital themselves. For weeks the Germans bombed and burned, turning the streets into mounds of rubble, until the insurgents surrendered. Only then did the Russians, who stood by and watched the horrific spectacle at a distance of fifteen kilometers, finally begin the liberating assault.

More than one third of Warsaw's former total population had been Jews: 350,000 souls, the largest Jewish community in Europe (the second largest was Vienna, the third—Lodz), a center of vibrant, tumultuous life. Today, only some 600 members are registered in the community's office. It is generally assumed that there are about 2,000 Jews, but that most of them maintain no ties with any Jewish organization.

I stood in the large piazza—formerly the anguished, diseased ghetto. Here the ghetto fighters fought and here they fell. Around the piazza the streets that had once hummed with Jewish life branch out: Mila, Niska, Zamenhof, Karmelicka, Dzielna, and the famous Nalewki nearby. Under the occupation, the Nazis packed the entire Jewish population of Warsaw and of many neighboring towns into a fenced off area that was not more than the twentieth part of the city.

I walked up the three steps in the memorial circle, made of red stones, and read the inscription on the marble slab. The dedicatory words appear in three languages: Polish, Yiddish and Hebrew, "For those who fell in an unprecedented and heroic struggle for the dignity and freedom of the Jewish people, for a free Poland, and for the liberation of mankind." In Yiddish, "Di gefallene in dem bayshpilozen heldishen kamf fer koved un frayhayt fun Yiddishen folk, fer a fraye Poylin, fer di bafrayung fun mensh."

New buildings surround the piazza. Trees and shrubs have been planted around a stone wall where the large bronze monument for the ghetto fighters has been placed: several prominent figures, an old man and young fighters, women and children, children with big, intelligent eyes. Eight wide steps lead up to the monument created by the sculptor Nathan Rapoport, a copy of which stands in the Yad Vashem Holocaust memorial in Jerusalem. The more one looks at it and discerns the details of the horrific drama it describes, the greater its impact. The inscription is short and simple, "The Jewish people to its fighters-martyrs."

Not far from here, on a large central street named for the uprising's commander Mordekhai Anielewicz stands his life-size monument. The residents of the adjacent streets crisscross the piazza, passing by the monuments without drawing near. On this lovely autumn morning life flows in its channels, pursuing its lawful course. Flowerbeds surround the place that had once seethed and erupted with the desperate, proud revolt of the last Jews in Poland.

There are still some relics in Warsaw of the life that is no more: the Jewish Social and Cultural Association in Poland, the Esther Kaminski State Jewish Theater, and the Jewish Historical Institute in the Polish Academy of Sciences, which has a rich archive of the history of Jews in Poland.

There is even a Yiddish weekly published in Warsaw, *The People's Voice* (*Folks Shtimme*). In two to three thousand copies, the Jewish "people" in Poland make their voice heard. A large portion of the copies is sent abroad. In April 1983, in commemoration of the Warsaw Ghetto Uprising, forty years after the event, a meticulously restored synagogue, the Nożyk, was inaugurated at a dignified ceremony, in the presence of Jewish delegations from Israel and the diaspora and the heads of the Polish government.

I confess that I learned these last points from newspapers and books. I myself wandered through the streets of Warsaw in the formerly overcrowded Jewish neighborhoods, and stood alone in front of the memorial monuments—to contemplate the sights of the Holocaust and remember the souls of the fighters-martyrs. Here the history of Jews on Polish soil ended. A fabric of life and creativity stretching back over a thousand years, a history that reached its highest intensity between the two world wars, terminated here.

Formerly, preachers in Poland would use the Talmudic tale of Rabbah bar bar Hana[19] to warn: The gigantic fish, on whose back a mound of sand has accumulated so that it looks like dry land, would one day flip over, and those who thought that they had reached peace and prosperity would suddenly find themselves swept away in vicious waters. This is how we had formerly lived in Poland—on the sandy back of just such a fish.

CHAPTER 16

Poland's Five Great Changes—and One Fixation

Summary of the fundamental changes—economic, demographic, and cultural—in post WWII Poland, as seen in 1982. One old trait, however, remains unchanged.

From what I saw, from conversations with people, and from reading before and after the trip, I learned that five major transformations have fundamentally changed Poland from the time I left it, more precisely—from the end of World War II.

The first transformation was the **move from an agricultural, largely backward country to a predominantly industrialized**—although, one might say, still backward—**country**. So much so that Polish agriculture no longer meets the needs of the population and import of cereals and animal fodder is required. The village too has changed its appearance. Near the spacious, nicely furnished homes, one sees today storage areas and garages housing a variety of farm machinery and even private cars. I recalled the thatched roofs of peasant houses of former days. No comparison.

The cities have grown; many factories have been built in the suburbs and with them new housing complexes for the workers. These apartments are more spacious than former city tenements, but supply does not keep up with demand. My acquaintance Leon told me in his room on Skladowa Street in Lodz that he too had signed up for a flat, but the waiting period could be ten or more years, even twenty.

Industrial plants, trade, and banking are all nationalized—officially owned by the workers, but in practice governed by the regime and its bureaucrats. Only small shops and kiosks are in private hands; indeed, I saw quite a few kiosks and various vendors' stands, perhaps no fewer than in the past. Formerly, beggars, Jews and non-Jews, were a common sight on city streets. While beggars have disappeared from the streets, I did see quite a few drunkards on Piotrkowska,

Lodz's main street, and I read warnings in the press about the spread of alcoholism stemming from workers' frustration with their tedious work.

By law, everyone is obliged to work, and indeed, I saw no idlers and unemployed people hanging around. However, about a third of the work force, I was told, does not show up on the job due to "work-related" illness. The low motivation to work in the government-run economy causes neglect and waste of public assets and resources. People talked to me quite a bit about the black market, where dollars or dollar equivalents will buy you anything.

The second transformation is **ethnic-national**. I could see it wherever I turned. Except for a few tourists in the hotels, largely from Communist countries, you do not see other nationalities in this country. Lodz no longer has German or Jewish neighborhoods, nor are there any Ukrainians or Belarusians. All the minorities are gone. I had left a Poland of twenty million Poles and ten million minority ethnics, and now the population is a monolithic forty million Poles, the largest nation in the Eastern Bloc, barring the Russians. The dream of anti-Semitic patriots, the persecutors of Jews and all other ethnicities, is fulfilled: an independent and free Poland—"for Poles only."

This ethnic transformation entailed a **geographic transformation**—the expulsion of Germans from Silesia and other districts, and the expulsion of the Poles from the eastern regions, areas transferred to the Ukrainian or Belarusian Soviet Republics. These exchanges were rapid and brutal. Poland gained some and lost some, and it is not for me to calculate its net balance. Poland received the German territories "*Deutsche rein*," cleansed of Germans, except for those who acculturated among the Poles or continued living among them as German "marranos." The Russians were not about to relinquish the territories they had seized after the Molotov-Ribbentrop pact, but the Poles, apparently, received satisfactory compensation.

I did not hear in my conversations resentment about the territories taken from Poland, though I did hear quite a bit of anger at the Russians. No need to go back as far as Russia's role in the partitions of Poland. Poles have not forgotten the Katyn massacre (1940), when the Russians brutally killed off the cream of the Polish officer corps. Notwithstanding Russian denials, every Pole believes this. Nor do the Poles forget what the Russians did to their country and its citizens before, during, and after the conquest.

Poles are suspicious of any pan-Slavic ideology, which they view as a smokescreen for Russian dominance. Many of them reject the Soviet-Communist ideology. They believe that Russia exploits their country's resources and its work force, and compensates them only stingily with oil and raw materials. In their eyes, Poland is not yet independent and free. This sentiment increased, of course, in the months when the government fought ferociously and cunningly against Solidarity.

The fourth major transformation I saw in Poland was the **catholicization** of the country. Not that Poland was not Catholic previously, but before World War II there were also Russian Orthodox, Greek Orthodox, Unitarians, Lutherans, Calvinists, and of course, Jews. Today a population that is 95 percent Catholic is served by over 17,000 priests, whereas a mere handful of clergy of other denominations remains. The Church has risen to a degree of prestige and importance as in no other Communist country. The great festival processions, the pilgrimages to Częstochowa and other important shrines have become mass demonstrations.

In my wanderings in the streets of Lodz, I entered the church on Freedom Square (Plac Wolności) to find, on a regular weekday, several dozen worshippers. For mass, hundreds attended. Granted, this church is in the city center. On my first day in Wroclaw, the day of Kolbe's canonization, the churches were filled to the rafters, with a large crowd outside listening to the sermons. The visit of Pope John Paul II aroused enormous rejoicing and enthusiasm, and not only among the devout. Clearly, Polish nationalism—antagonistic to Russian Orthodoxy and to German Protestantism—impels the Poles to coalesce around the Catholic Church with greater devotion than do all other believers in Europe. However, we see that with all their love and admiration for the Pope, the Poles do not widely accept his views on divorce and abortion. It seems, then, that the Catholic Church in Poland serves its believers both as a bastion for the individuation of the Polish nation, for distinguishing its identity, and as the ram's horns with which to gore Communism. The Church truly expresses the "Polish way of life," in keeping with the national tradition. Otherwise, it is difficult to explain the unparalleled prominence and prestige it is accorded in Poland.

The Catholic attitude toward the Jews is a painful chapter unto itself. A few believers—Righteous among the Nations—rescued Jews and stood by them, among whom some Catholic priests are also numbered. However, the prejudices inculcated down the ages by the Church were largely responsible for the Poles' hostility during the days of the great annihilation, and afterward. It is not by chance that the Final Solution was carried out on Polish soil, and that *after the war* more Jews were uprooted from here than from Bulgaria or Romania, more even than from Germany. Our reckoning with the Catholic Church is bitter and stark.

Finally, the fifth transformation—**education**. I arrived in Poland at the opening of the new academic year in the institutions of higher learning. Some 400,000 students streamed to the universities, technical colleges, teachers' training colleges, and the various institutions for the arts, management, and other professions. Many come from the villages and small towns. New universities were built after the war, such as the one in Lodz; in my day, more than half the population was still illiterate and only one popular, unaccredited university had just opened. Today, most Poles are high school graduates, and many pursue higher learning. The high schools now teach, besides Polish and Russian, another foreign language—French or English. Thanks to compulsory and free schooling, there are many Polish scientists and scholars. The country's culture, its institutions of higher learning, its research institutes, newspapers, theaters, its entire worldview, all give the impression of being products of Western Enlightenment. Indeed, the Poles with whom I spoke seemed uncomfortable to hear their country labeled Communist.

Five changes, then—industrial, ethnic, geographic, religious, and educational—have transformed Poland. Many old problems have been solved or improved, and new ones have arisen—social, economic, and cultural. Especially acute are the challenges facing personal and corporate freedom.

One cannot complete the portrait of this country without noting one additional amazing fact, a fact that is not a transformation, rather, a deformity that has not yet been removed, a sort of enduring disfigurement of Poland.

Anti-Semitism is still a distinctive hallmark of this country. Behold this miracle: hatred of Jews in the absence of Jews!

Initially, the shared disaster of Nazi occupation unified all Polish citizens, so I was told, but only during the first days of terror. Soon thereafter, the old "Endak" anti-Jewish spirit of the Christian-Democratic Party, which had governed Poland before the war, returned. At the end of the war, after Poland was emptied of Jews, opposition to anti-Semitism prevailed, part of casting off the Nazi regime and its race ideology. However, after a relatively short period, and especially after the Six Day War, anti-Semitic policy became the official party line. Even the few thousand Jews that had remained in Poland after the pogroms in the town of Kielce (1946) were compelled to leave this country of blood. Previously, Nazi ideology had fertilized Poland's anti-Semitic soil; today it is Communist propaganda that feeds it.

Anti-Semitism without Jews, or almost without Jews! Of what importance are those tiny, impoverished communities, the remnants of three and a half million in former "crown-adorned Poland?"[1] The image of the monstrous Jew inculcated by the Church, by Nazism and Communism is still operative, now rolled together into the modern anti-Semitic version, mainly called anti-Zionism, and anti the State of Israel.

This is the party line, and most of it is of Soviet import, which drastically reduces its credibility among Poles. Still, the fact remains that with every mishap that occurs anti-Semitic, anti-Zionist, and anti-Israel arguments are served up to discredit the regime's enemies and defend its actions. A terrible spectacle of a country with no Jews, which continues to hate the Jews that are no more—a propaganda-fabricated demonization concocted by a reactionary regime.

This frightening spectacle of spiritual inertia, manipulated by the politicians, reminds me of an image used by Julian Tuwim, the great Jewish-Polish poet, when news of the scope of the Holocaust reached him in New York in 1944. He then composed a manifesto titled "We, Polish Jews ..." and this is how he ends this manifesto-dirge: "An enormous and ever-growing skeleton stands over Europe. The flame of dangerous anger glistens from its eye sockets, and its fingers have curled into a bony fist. And He, our Leader and Dictator, will instruct us in our rights and our demands."[2] I have difficulty grasping the sense of his last sentence, but I have no doubt that the horrible skeleton is the specter of the Jew, as the Poles, in their evil spirit,[3] in their terrified heart, in their nightmare dream, still see him: a Jew aflame in dangerous fury, a fire that is never extinguished.

Notes

CHAPTER 1

1. Wladyslaw Grabski (1874–1938) was a political economist and prime minister of Poland (1920, 1923–25), who reorganized Poland's monetary and financial system after World War I. In 1924 he implemented decrees that imposed heavy taxation on middle class traders and industrialists, a sales tax, and nationalization of certain industries (tobacco, liquor), all areas in which Jews were disproportionately represented. These measures accelerated the impoverishment of Polish Jews in the 1920s and drove the fourth *aliyah*, also known as "Grabski's *aliyah*."
2. It was customary among simple, God-fearing Jews to wrap their sick child in a prayer shawl and pace the floor praying. The idea being that the power of all the prayers ever said under that *tallit* would intensify prayers for the child's healing.
3. Polish Aleksandrow, a small town south of Lodz, today a city suburb.
4. Thomas Mann, *Essays of Three Decades*, trans. H. T. Lowe-Porter (New York: Alfred Knopf, 1947), 100.
5. Galicia—the region between Central and Eastern Europe, between modern Poland and the Ukraine, with Cracow in the west and Lvov in the east as its most important cities. The First Partition of Poland (1772) handed this area to Austria, hence a strong Germanic influence in the region during the nineteenth century.
6. Shabbetai Ẓvi—a self-proclaimed seventeenth century messiah, whose message sparked strong Jewish religious revival throughout the Ottoman Empire and Europe, and commensurate disappointment when he converted to Islam under the Sultan's pressure. An offshoot of the Sabbatean movement, the Frankists, followers of Jacob Frank (1726–91), mainly in Poland, formed a subversive mystical movement. Eventually they converted to Catholicism.
7. Polish Gora Kalwaria.
8. *Ḥaredi(m)* (Hebrew)—strict adherents to the pre-Enlightenment, pre-Emancipation and pre-Zionist form of European rabbinic or Ḥasidic Judaism.
9. Mizraḥi—a modern Orthodox, pro-Zionist religious-political movement, which developed and spread after World War I.
10. The part of Poland under Russian control, as outlined at the Congress of Vienna (1815).
11. Majer Balaban, *Die Judenstadt von Lublin* (1919); *Żydowskie miasto w Lublinie* (1919). Free translation.
12. Po-lin—a formerly popular pun on the literal Hebrew meaning of these syllables, signifying "here rest," or "here sleep," i.e., an indication of the permanence of Jewish habitation in Poland.
13. The three national poets of Polish Romantic literature, known as the three bards, were Adam Mickiewicz (1798–1855), Julius Słowacki (1809–1849) and Zygmunt Krasiński (1812–1859). They were viewed as prophets or seers, who not only voiced Polish national sentiments but also foresaw the nation's future.

14. See Chapter 11 on the study of Polish literature in the Hebrew high school. [Author's note]
15. *Hillulah* (Hebrew)—anniversary of a saintly man's death, especially that of a Ḥasidic rebbe (a *ẓaddik*), celebrated by his devotees as a joyful event.

CHAPTER 2

1. Polish Warka.
2. The reference appears to be to Reb Mordekhai Menaḥem Mendel Kalisz (1819–1868), known as the Silent Rebbe. However, he could not have been the rebbe toward whom the author's grandfather was headed in the snow, since the latter died in 1892, long after that rebbe's death. It seems that stories of different journeys are conflated here.
3. Ḥaim Naḥman Bialik, "At Dusk's Last Glimmering," *Im dimdumei haḥamah*, 1902, free translation.
4. Rabbi Yaakov Yiẓḥak Halevy Horowitz (?–1815), earned his appellation as "Seer" thanks to extraordinary visual powers. He introduced into Ḥasidism the veneration of the rebbe as master, as though he were an exalted prince.
5. Rabbi Yaakov Yiẓḥak of Pshedborzh (1765–1813), later of Pshyscha (Przysucha), was initially a disciple of the Seer of Lublin. He later rebelled and insisted that Ḥasidism needed to be based on Torah study, not only on piety. His appellation "Holy Yood" was a reference to his writings, all of which had the word *ha-Yehudi* (Yood, Jew) in their titles.
6. Rabbi Simḥa Bunim (1765–1827), disciple of the Holy Yood, and his successor in Pshyscha. Credited with "saving *Ḥasidut* from spiritual stagnation by elevating it into a movement of non-conformist young scholars who detested pose and pride, superficiality and mechanical ritualism." Milton Aron, *Ideas and Ideals of the Ḥasidim* (New York, Citadel Press, 1969), 240.
7. Rabbi Menaḥem Mendel Morgenstern (1788–1859), a close disciple of Rabbi Simḥa Bunim and one of Ḥasidism's most influential figures. He wished "to transform *Ḥasidut* from a mass movement into a kind of order of the spiritual elite." Ibid. 252.
8. See note 2.
9. *Tish*, or *tisch* (Yiddish: table)—the gathering of Ḥasidim around their rebbe, where food (often only symbolic morsels from the rebbe's plate) is served, with Torah-talk, songs and prayers. Considered an event of great holiness in Ḥasidism.

CHAPTER 3

1. In theologian Rudolf Otto's (1869–1927) vocabulary in *The Idea of the Holy*.
2. Science of Judaism (*Wissenschaft des Judentums*)—a nineteenth century intellectual effort, centered in Germany, to study Jewish history, literature and culture using critical, scientific methods.

CHAPTER 4

1. An unfriendly gesture toward observant Jews, who normally kept their heads covered.
2. *Ha-zefirah* (*Ha-Tsfira, Ha-tzefira*, morning in Hebrew) was an influential Hebrew language newspaper published in Poland in 1862 and then, with interruptions in the years 1874–1931.

It was the first Hebrew paper with an emphasis on the sciences. Its founder and first editor was Ḥaim Zelig Słonimski, grandfather of the Polish poet Antoni Słonimski.

3. *Ha-olam*—the central organ of the World Zionist Organization, published as a weekly from 1907 to 1950.
4. *Ketuvim*—a Hebrew weekly for culture, literature and the arts, initiated by H. N. Bialik and published in Tel Aviv from 1926 to 1933.
5. *Davar*—the influential daily newspaper of the Labor Party in Mandatory Palestine and later in the State of Israel (1925–1996).
6. Yeḥiel Rosenzweig, (Jechiel Rozencwajg), 1895–1943, thus thirteen years older than the author. He was murdered in Treblinka following the Warsaw Ghetto uprising in 1943.
7. Policies formulated by Russian Zionists at a meeting held in Helsingfors (Helsinki) in December 1906, following the pogroms in Russia.
8. Gruenbaum (1879–1970) continued an active public life during and after the Holocaust and was one of the signatories of Israel's Declaration of Independence (1948).
9. Tarbut (Hebrew: culture)—a Zionist-supported network of secular, Hebrew-language schools in Poland, Romania and Lithuania, which operated primarily between the world wars. By 1939, it enrolled in its approximately 270 institutions about 25 percent of all students enrolled in Jewish schools in Poland, and nine percent of Poland's entire Jewish student population. (from Wikipedia)
10. Simon Dubnow (1860–1941)—historian who rejected assimilation, but viewed Zionism as a pipedream. His alternative: Jewish autonomism, a form of self-rule within the Jewish diaspora. Dubnow was murdered by the Nazis in Riga.

CHAPTER 5

1. These young Ḥasidim were inspired by the dynamic Rebbe of Ger, Avraham Mordekhai Alter (1866–1948, succeeded his father in 1905), who, almost uniquely among the Ḥasidic rebbes of his time, realized the importance of political and cultural activism in counteracting Jewish and non-Jewish secular influences. This included the foundation of a political party, Agudat Israel, a youth movement, a worker's movement, a daily paper, schools, and non-Zionist support of settlement in Ereẓ Israel. The party he founded, the oldest party in name and agenda in Israeli politics, continues to be very influential to this day.
2. A. Z. Aescoli [Eshkoli], *Kehilat Lodz: ir ve-em be-Yisrael* [The Lodz Community: A Jewish Mother-City], Jerusalem: Ha-Maḥlaka le'inyanei ha-no'ar shel ha-Histadrut ha-Ẓionit [Youth Section of the Zionist Organization], 1947, p. 107. Aharon Ze'ev Aescoly (1901–1948) emerged from a *shtibel* of Aleksander Ḥasidim in Lodz to study at the rabbinical seminary in Berlin and then at the Sorbonne in Paris, where he wrote about Ḥasidism and about the messianic movements. He acquired a reputation as an important and multifaceted scholar. [Author's note]
3. Habima Theater—The first Hebrew speaking theater, founded in Bialystok in 1912. In 1926, the theater toured Europe and the United States, to great acclaim. The company settled in Ereẓ Israel in 1931. In Israel today it carries the epithet of "National Theater."
4. Joint Distribution Committee (JDC)—a U.S.-based Jewish philanthropic aid organization, founded in 1914 and still active today. In the wake of World War I, the Joint was particularly instrumental in rebuilding devastated Jewish communities in Eastern Europe and in Ottoman Palestine.

5. About the Yiddish press, and especially about *Haynt*, its history and policy, contributors and authors, see Ḥaim Finkelstein, *Haynt, a Tsaytung bay Yidn, 1908–1939* (Tel Aviv: Perets Publishers, 1978). [Now on the web, *Today: A Jewish Newspaper*, 1908–1939].
On literary life in Poland, and in Lodz in particular, between the two wars, see:
Shlomo Schweitzer, *Polish Jewry*, Year Book 2 (Tel Aviv: World Federation of Polish Jews, 1968). Isaiah Trunk, *Antologye fun der Yiddisher proze in Poyln: Tsvishn beyde velt milkhomes (1914–1939)* [Anthology of Yiddish Prose in Poland: Between the Two World Wars 1914–1939], (Buenos Aires: Tsentral Farband far Poylishe Yidn in Argentina, 1949). Ḥaim Leib Fuchs (Fox), *Lodzh shel Mayle dos yidishe gaystiḳe un derhoybene lodzh, 100 yor yidishe un oykh hebreishe literatur un kultur in lodzh un in di arumiḳe shtet un shtetlekh* [Lodz on High, the Jewish Spiritual and Elevated Lodz, 100 Years of Yiddish and also Hebrew literature and Culture in Lodz and in the Surrounding Cities and Towns] (Tel Aviv: Perets Publishers, 1972). [Author's notes]
6. Israel (Yisroel) Rabon (1900–1941) grew up in Balut and spent most of the interwar years in Lodz as a writer. After the Germans invaded Poland in September 1939, he escaped to Vilnius and was shot in Ponar. His second, unfinished novel from 1934 was titled *Balut: roman fun a forshṭoṭ* [Balut: Novel of an Urban Neighborhood], where he pictured the degenerate life of the working district.
7. *Ha-sneh*—a literary monthly that appeared in Warsaw in 1929, edited by the poet Yaakov Cahan.
8. Israel Lichtenstein (1883–1933)—Bund activist and educator who specialized in the education of blind and deaf children. He edited Bundist magazines, from 1926 the weekly *Lodzer Weker* and participated in the Lodz City Council.
9. Leib Holenderski, a Lodz City Councilman and a leader of the Po'aley Zion (labor Zionist organization), died in the Dachau concentration camp, 1940, aged 55.
10. Lucjan Dobroszycki, ed., *The Chronicle of the Lodz Ghetto, 1941–1944* (New Haven: Yale University Press, 1984).
11. Much has been written about the Lodz ghetto and about Rumkowski. As I was not confined there, I cannot speak of it and perhaps do not have the right to do so. See: Yisroel Tabaksblat, *Khurbn Lodzh, 6 yor natsi-gehenem [The Destruction of Lodz, Six Years of Nazi Hell*] (Buenos Aires, 1946), and Isaiah Trunk, *Łodz Ghetto: a History*, translated and edited by Robert Moses Shapiro, published in association with the United States Holocaust Memorial Museum (Bloomington, IN: Indiana University Press, 2006). [Author's note]

CHAPTER 6

1. *Maggid*—an itinerant popular preacher. Dov Ber ben Avraham of Mezeritch (died 1772), was a disciple of Ḥasidism's founder, the Ba'al Shem Tov, and was chosen as his successor to lead the early movement.
2. Elimelekh Weisblum (1717–1787) of Lizhensk (Lezajsk in Polish)—one of the founders of Ḥasidism, a close associate of the *maggid* of Mezeritch.
3. Yeḥezkel ben Yehuda HaLevi Landau (1713–1793) was an influential authority in Jewish law. His best-known work *Noda Biyehudah* ("Known in Judah") consists of responsa that were much esteemed for their logic and independence.

4. See Chapter 2, note 2.
5. The *Sefer ha-Zohar* [*Book of Splendor* or *Radiance*] is the foundational work of Kabbalah, Jewish mysticism.
6. Reformed Ḥeder (Hebrew: ḥeder metukan)—Founded at the end of the nineteenth century, in the aftermath of the *haskalah* movement and the spread of Zionism in Eastern Europe, these institutions adopted some modern pedagogical concepts, and incorporated subjects besides Talmud learning (or allocated time for the pupils to learn such subjects at other institutions).
7. *Yismaḥ Yisroel*, volume 2, end of the book of Deuteronomy, pages 198–199.
8. Ibid, page 179.

CHAPTER 7

1. Regarding the statistics, see also Chapter 15, note 9.
2. Ḥanokh Heynekh HaKohen Levin (1798–1870), served as Rebbe of Aleksander from 1866 until his death.
3. Yiẓḥak Heynekh Sonenberg, *A Zer Sheyne Vunderlekhe Geshikhte fun R. Heynekh meAleksander* (Lodz:1926).
4. Ohel (Hebrew: tent)—refers to a small masonry structure built around a grave as a sign of the prominence of the deceased, especially of Ḥasidic rebbe*s*.
5. Yeḥiel Lerer (1910–1943) was a Yiddish poet, deported from the Warsaw ghetto to Treblinka. *Beit Aba* was translated from Yiddish into Hebrew by S. Meltzer (Tel Aviv: Am Oved Publishers, 1946).
6. In the interwar period, there were approximately 200 Jews in Burzenin.
7. *El maleh raḥamim* ("God full of Mercy")—a prayer for the soul of the departed, recited at the graveside during the burial service and at memorial services.
8. *Haẓur tamim po'alo* ("He is the Rock, his works are perfect") from Deuteronomy 32:4.
9. *Mikva'ot* ("Pools of Water")—Tractate of the *Mishnah* dealing with laws pertaining to the building and maintenance of a ritual bath.
10. *Kaddish* (Aramaic: *holy*) is a hymn of praises to God, used in the synagogue liturgy to separate between sections of the service. The *Kaddish deRabbanan* ("the rabbis' *kaddish*") is used after any part of the service that includes extracts from the Mishnah or Talmud. Mourners say *Kaddish* to show that despite their loss they still praise God.
11. Menashe Freiman, *Tif'eret Yisrael* (Lodz: 1931; second edition, Bnei Brak: 1974). [Author's note]
12. *Yiḥudim* ("Unifications") is a form of meditation in Jewish mysticism, whereby certain supernal elements are unified through one's mystical devotions.
13. *Dveikut* (Hebrew: clinging, adherence)—in Jewish mysticism (Kabbalah and Ḥasidism), intense concentration on communion, or unification, with the divine.

CHAPTER 8

1. AdMoR—acronym for **Ad**onenu, **M**orenu, **VeR**abbenu, (Hebrew: "Our Master, Our Teacher, and Our Rabbi"). This honorific title is usually reserved for heads of Ḥasidic dynasties, and is followed by the name of the town where they preside, or where the dynasty founders presided.

2. Max Weber, "The Three Types of Legitimate Rule," trans. Hans Gerth, in *Berkeley Publications in Society and Institutions* 4, no. 11–1:(1958) 1. Weber also refers to the three types of legitimate rule in his 1919 essay "Politik als Beruf," ("Politics as a Vocation"), which Shmueli translated into Hebrew, *Ha-politika be-torat mikẓo'a* (Jerusalem and Tel Aviv: Shocken, 1962). See also Efraim Shmueli, "The 'Pariah People' and its 'Charismatic Leadership'—A Reevaluation of Max Weber's 'Ancient Judaism.'" *Proceedings of the American Academy of Jewish Research* XXXVI (1968): 167–247.
3. Published in 1934, appeared in English as *Salvation*, trans. Willa and Edwin Muir (New York: Putnam, 1951).
4. Yisrael Yeraḥmiel Yiẓḥak Dancyger (*Yismaḥ Yisroel*) in a letter to his nephew upon the latter's *bar-miẓvah*. See Menashe Freiman, *Tif'eret Yisrael* (Lodz:1931), Chapter 5, 104.
5. Ibid. 10.
6. *Sheyne Yidn* (Yiddish: handsome Jews)—prosperous, respectable Jews, an expression often used sarcastically.
7. Israel Joshua Singer (1893–1944, New York)—Yiddish novelist, older brother of Isaac Bashevis Singer. *The Brothers Ashkenazi* first appeared in Poland, in Yiddish, then in the U.S., in English, in 1936, where it became a New York Times Best Seller.
8. Władysław Stanisław Reymont (1867–1925)—Nobel Prize in Literature (1924). His best-known work is the four-volume novel *Chłopi* (*The Peasants*). *Land of Promise* (1898) is a social panorama of the city of Lodz during the industrial revolution.
9. Roman Dmowski (1864–1939)—Polish politician, co-founder and chief ideologue of the National Democracy (ND, in Polish Endecja) movement. He opposed Jozef Piłsudski's vision of a multinational Poland, preferring the marginalization of ethnic minorities in order to enhance Polish nationalism.
10. *Shmone Esre* (Hebrew: eighteen)—The central prayer of Jewish services, counting eighteen benedictions.
11. To procreate.
12. Reminiscent of "It is an ill wind that blows nobody any good."
13. From the *piyut* (liturgical poem) *Emet ve-Emunah* in the prayer book, a reference to the miracles of the Ten Plagues in the land of Ḥam (Egypt).
14. *Shivḥei ha-Besht (In Praise of Baal Shem Tov)*, *Adat ẓaddikim* (Lvov: 1865), *Qehal Ḥasidim* (Lvov: 1966), or *Shivḥei Ẓaddikim* and *Keter Shem Tov*. [Author's note]
15. In the Bible, the word *peta'*, *peti'a'* (surprise, wonder) is close to *peẓi'a'* (wound), and frequently appears in conjunction with the word *shever* (break). [Author's note] The author expanded on the philosophy of wonder in *Pli'a va-ḥashiva be-olam mada'i-tekhnologi* [*Wondering and Thinking in a Techno-Scientific World*], (Jerusalem: The Bialik Institute, 1985).
16. Pereẓ Smolenskin (1885–1842)—a Russian-born Zionist and Hebrew writer, founded in Vienna a Hebrew literary journal *Ha-shaḥar*, which became a platform for *haskalah* writers.
17. Yizḥak Erter (1792–1851)—Galicia-born satirist, excommunicated for his *haskalah* leanings by Rabbi Jacob Orenstein, grandfather of Dr. Braude (see chapter 10).
18. Yehuda Leib Gordon (YaLaG) (1830–1892) often used biblical and historical themes and protagonists in his polemical poems. His most well-known verse appeared in his 1866 poem *Hakiẓa 'ami* (*Awake my People*), "Be a man when you go out and a Jew in your home," which encapsulates the movement's call on Jews to abandon their isolation from surrounding cultures while remaining committed to their own faith.
19. YaLaG, in the narrative poem *Between the Lions' Teeth*, about the fall of Jerusalem to the Romans.

20. YaLaG, in the narrative poem *Ẓedekiah in the Prison House,* about the fall of the Judean kingdom to the Babylonians, quotes Exodus 19:6, God's injunction to His people: "And ye shall be unto me a kingdom of priests, and an holy nation."
21. *Josippon*—historical narrative in Hebrew, of anonymous authorship (presumably from tenth century southern Italy), describing the period of the Second Temple, the wars of the Jews against the Romans, ending with the fall of the last fortress Massada.
22. The Ten Martyrs—ten Sages martyred by the Romans in the period after the destruction of the Second Temple.
23. Betar fortress—the last Judean stronghold in the Bar Kokhba revolt to fall to the Romans in 135 CE.
24. The Great Assembly, or *Synod,* in Jewish tradition, was an assembly of 120 scribes, sages, and prophets, active from the early Second Temple Period to the early Hellenistic period (mid-fourth century BCE) and credited with finalizing the canon of the Hebrew Bible, and various synagogue prayers and rituals.
25. Shmuel (Samuel) of Neharde'a in Babylonia, second century CE, insisted that the source of disease should be sought not in the Evil Eye, but in noxious influence exercised by the air and the climate.
26. *Birkhei Yosef* (Livorno, 1774), *Yoreh De'a,* section 336.
27. *Yismaḥ Yisroel* on *Ki tavo.*
28. Solomon Luria (1510–1573) was one of the great *poskim* (decisors) and teachers of his time. He is known for his *halakhic* work *Yam shel Shlomo,* and his Talmudic commentary *Ḥokhmat Shlomo.* Luria is also referred to as *Maharshal,* or *Rashal.*
29. *Yam shel Shlomo,* chapter Kol Bassar, paragraph 12.
30. Tobias Cohn, or Kohn, (1652–1729) a physician in Poland, author of an encyclopedic book *Ma'asseh Toviya* (*Work of Tobias*), published in Venice, 1707, and frequently reprinted.

CHAPTER 9

1. The *tallit katan* (Hebrew: small *tallit*)—a garment worn by Jewish men either under or over one's clothing. It is a poncho-like garment with a hole for the head and special twined and knotted fringes attached to its four corners.
2. *Mussar* (Hebrew: Ethics)—A movement that developed in nineteenth-century Lithuania, dedicated to furthering ethical discipline. The movement's founding is attributed to Rabbi Yisrael Lipkin Salanter (1810–1883).
3. As R. Ḥanina bar Ḥama expounded in the *midrash* (for example Pesikta derav Kahana 12, 25): "At Sinai the Holy One blessed be He, appeared to them with many faces, with a threatening face, with a severe face, with an angry face, with a joyous face, with a laughing face, with a friendly face ... And even though you see all these various forms—'I am the Lord thy God.'" In other words, despite the multiplicity of God's appearances, each of which is different according to the grasp of each individual, God is always one, and always the same that appeared to His people at Sinai. [Author's note]
4. Especially in: Efraim Shmueli, *Morasha u-ma'avak basifrut u-vahagut,* [The Struggle for Continuity in Hebrew Poetry and Philosophy] (Tel Aviv: Yaḥdav Publishers, 1978); *Sheva Tarbuyot Yisrael* (Tel Aviv: Yaḥdav Publishers, 1980) and in an abridged version *Seven Jewish Cultures: A Reinterpretation of Jewish Culture and Thought,* translated and edited by Gila Shmueli (Cambridge: Cambridge University Press, 1990); *Pli'a va-ḥashiva be-olam*

mada'i-tekhnology,[Wondering and Thinking in a Techno-Scientific World] (Jerusalem: Bialik Institute, 1985).

5. The author here uses the terminology he elaborated in *Seven Jewish Cultures*, where he identified in Jewish history seven distinct successive cultures, or frameworks of thought and experience, in which the meaning of Jewish life is always re-interpreted. The cultures in his periodization are the biblical, the Talmudic, the Poetic-Philosophic, the Mystical (with Ḥasidism as its late offshoot), the Rabbinic, the culture of the Emancipation, and the National-Israeli culture.
6. Paul Tillich, *Systematic Theology*, Volume I (Chicago: University of Chicago Press, 1951). In Tillich's words, God is "das was uns absolut angeht."

CHAPTER 10

1. The Hit'aḥdut (Hebrew: union) movement arose in1920 as a union between the Po'el Ha-ẓa'ir party in Ereẓ Israel and the right wing of the Ẓe'irei Ẓion in western Galicia—national, socialist and anti-Marxist.
2. For a recent evaluation, see Natalia Aleksiun, "Marcus Braude and the Making of the Future Jewish Elite in Poland," in *A Romantic Polish-Jew—Rabbi Osjasz Thon from Various Perspectives*, edited by Michal Galas, Shoshana Ronen, Studies in Jewish Civilization in Poland, (Cracow: Jagiellonian University Press, 2015), pp. 151–167.
3. See its history and details, and especially about the high schools founded by Dr. Braude, in the articles and books by Arie Tartakower and Haim Ormian and other educators, who took part in the establishment of these institutions and followed their development. [Author's note]
4. Only in 1926, Shlomo Bodzinger, a Lodz industrialist and Aleksander Ḥasid, entered the Senate. [Author's note]

CHAPTER 11

1. Ḥovevei Ẓion (Lovers of Zion)—individuals and organizations in the Czarist Russian Empire, who responded to the 1881 and subsequent pogroms by promoting Jewish immigration to Ereẓ Israel. Considered the precursors of modern Zionism.
2. Shmuel (Samuel) Tchernowitz (1879–1929)—Hebrew journalist and editor, one of the first modern correspondents of the Hebrew press. *Ha-Ẓefirah* published his monograph on the Benei Moshe Society, which was later published as a book, *Benei Moshe u-Tekufatam* (1914). Brother of Chaim Tchernowitz.
3. Only some years later did Dubnow's history books appear in German, then in Hebrew. His book *Essays on Old and New Judaism* was translated into Hebrew by Avraham Levinson in 1937. [Author's note].
4. Moshe Schoenfeld (1911–1965)—emigrated to Ereẓ Israel in 1932, became a leader in the youth and kibbutz settlement activities of the Agudat Israel (ultra-Orthodox) party.
5. Ozer Ḥuldai (1907–1969)—father of Tel Aviv mayor Ron Ḥuldai.
6. Shlomo Szpan (1898–1962)—teacher and school supervisor, author, poet and translator. Emigrated to Ereẓ Israel in 1923. Member of the Hebrew Language Academy, translated classical Greek literature into Hebrew.

7. Nathan Eck (Ekron), *Ha-to'im be-darkhei ha-mavet, Havai ve-hagut biyemei ha-kilayon, Wandering on the Roads of Death, Life and Thoughts in the Days of Destruction,* (Jerusalem: Yad Va-Shem, 1960).
8. Mordecai Ze'ev Feierberg (1874–1899)—Published several short stories, encouraged by Aḥad Ha'am, among which "The Shadows," which relates the night-time ruminations of a solitary adolescent narrator in the shadowy, crumbling, abandoned *beit midrash.*
9. Nathan Eck, *Sho'at hayehudim be-europa* (*Holocaust of the Jews of Europe*) (Jerusalem: Yad Vashem and Kibbutz Hame'uḥad, 1975).
10. The instructor-educator in charge of the class, a more responsible charge than that of "home room" teacher in the American system.
11. Hugo Bergmann (1883–1975)—Prague-born philosopher at the Hebrew University in Jerusalem and the university's first rector from 1935–1938.
12. Ben-Zion Rappaport (1884–1942)—high school teacher in Cracow, a self-taught scholar on medieval and general (mainly German) philosophy and on the methodology of scientific inquiry, subjects on which he published two books before the war. His last book *Teva va-ru'aḥ: meḥkarim filosofiim (Nature and Spirit: Philosophical Inquiries)* (Jerusalem: Bialik Institute, 1953) is based on a manuscript he tossed out of the train that deported him to Belzec death camp. A Polish peasant, who found the notebook in a field, delivered it after the war to Jews who brought it to print in Israel.
13. Op. cit., Page 78.
14. E. Shmueli, "Dyokano shel historyon le'umi—bimlot 60 shanah lemoto shel Y. N. Simḥoni" (Portrait of a National Historian—on the Sixtieth Anniversary of the Death of Y. N. Simḥoni), *Kivunim—Ktav 'et le-yahadut u-leẓionut,* no. 31 (May 1986): 37–62.
15. Salo Wittmayer Baron (1895–1989)—received rabbinical ordination at the Jewish Theological Seminary in Vienna and three doctorate degrees (in philosophy, political science, and law) from the University of Vienna. Began teaching at the Jewish Teachers College in Vienna in 1926, but was persuaded to move to New York to teach at the Jewish Institute of Religion by Rabbi Stephen S. Wise. Baron's appointment as Professor of Jewish History, Literature and Institutions at Columbia University in 1929 is considered to mark the beginning of the scholarly study of Jewish History in an American university. His major work: *A Social and Religious History of the Jews* (18 vols., 2d ed. 1952–1983).
16. The author translated Mahler's Yiddish manuscript on the history of the Karaites: Raphael Mahler, *Hakara'im* (Tel Aviv: Sifriyat Hapo'alim, 1949).
17. Davar—the Labor Party daily newspaper in Mandatory Palestine and later Israel, founded in 1925, shut down in 1996.
18. *To jest Oświeçim!* (Warsaw, 1945), 106 pp. English translation by Joseph Leftwich, *This Was Oswiecim. The Story of a Murder Camp* (London: 1946) 86 pp. Also in Yiddish, *Oshvyentshim* (*Auschwitz*) (Buenos Aires: 1950), 223 pp. [Author's note]
19. It is worth mentioning here briefly one of the most distinguished of this last generation of young scholars on Polish soil, a friend of Friedman—Ringelblum.

    Emanuel Ringelblum (born in Buczacz, now Ukraine, in 1900) studied history at the University of Warsaw with historians Marceli Handelsman and Yitzhak Schiper. His dissertation (1927) on *Jewish life in Warsaw in the Middle Ages,* published in 1932, provided a new picture of medieval Jewish occupations—traders, artisans, physicians, and landowners. Ringelblum believed that the productivization of Polish Jews, helped by cooperatives and banks, was possible. In 1926–29, he published a collection *Yunge Historiker* (*Young Historians*) under his editorship and that of Raphael Mahler, and later—*Bletter far Geshikhte* (1934,

1938), where important new research on the Jews of Warsaw, Lublin, Płock and Kutno, first appeared.

Ringelblum specialized in the history of Jews in the eighteenth century, and, in his books from 1923 and 1934, he described the situation of the Jews prior to the partition of Poland, as well as their participation in Kościuszko's uprising. He discovered that there were many Jewish farmers who took part in the defense of Warsaw during this uprising, and that among the defenders there were Jewish soldiers. Some of his studies described Jewish artisanry and the beginnings of Jewish industry in Poland. He also gathered information about beggars in the eighteenth century.

In the Warsaw ghetto, he founded a clandestine archive, which collected data about Nazi atrocities from all over Poland. Meetings among the researchers, evaluators, leaders and writers who worked on the archive were camouflaged as *oneg Shabbat* ['Sabbath delight' get-togethers]. Based on the information gathered, Ringelblum composed memoranda and sent reports abroad. After the suppression of the uprising and the destruction of the Warsaw ghetto, he succeeded in slipping with his family to the Aryan section of Warsaw, but fell into the hands of the Gestapo in March 1944. Even though his book on the relations between Jews and Poles during the war opens with thanks to the Poles, who twice saved him from the Nazis, and although he was thus ostensibly a living testimony of Polish aid to Jews, his words about the Poles are not all praise. His book shows the extent of the cruelty, greed and murderous malevolence of many Poles. (See E. Ringelblum, *Polish-Jewish Relations during the Second World War* (New York: 1976, edited by J. Kermish and S. Krakowski). In general, he agrees with Mordechai Tenenbaum, a hero of the Białystok ghetto uprising, that for a Jew there was no place in Poland free of hatred and murder, or, at the very least, free of blackmail and theft. (See Ringelblum, *Kesovim fun geto*, 2 volumes, Warsaw, 1961–1963.) [Author's note]

20. Dr. Wilhelm Fallek (1887–1941)—a teacher in the First Boys Hebrew High School down the street, published in 1931 a book in Polish on the influence of the Bible on Polish literature. His intention was to bring this literature closer to the Jewish student, to make him see it as not entirely alien to the spirit of Judaism. [Author's note]
21. Moses Hadas, trans., *The Basic Works of Cicero* (New York: The Modern Library, 1951), 163.
22. Ibid, page 168.
23. Tacitus, *The Annals*, ed. E. H. Blakeney, tr. Arthur Murphy, (New York, E. P. Dutton; London: J. M. Dent & Sons, 1908), Vol. 1, 498–502.
24. E. Shmueli, *Anshei Ha-Renaissance* (*Men of the Renaissance: The Rise of the Bourgeois World and First Crisis in Modern Society*), in two volumes (Tel Aviv: Massada, 1949), second edition, 1968.
25. Seneca, *Moral Letters to Lucilius*, (*Epistulae morales ad Lucilium*), Letter 44—On Philosophy and Pedigrees, translated by Richard Mott Gummere, digital Loeb Classical Library.
26. Ibid.
27. See Chapter 1, note 14.
28. In Heine's well-known words about the Bible for the Jews.
29. The famous motto of Theodor Herzl's *Altneuland*, 1902.
30. Yehuda Halevi, *The Selected poems of Yehuda Halevi*, annotated and translated by Hillel Halkin, 2011, published by Nextbook Inc., p. 21.
31. Adam Mickiewicz, *Pan Tadeusz, or The Last Foray in Lithuania, a Story of Life among Polish Gentlefolk in the Years 1811 and 1812*, in Twelve Books, trans. George Rapall Noyes (London and Toronto: J. M. Dent & Sons Ltd, 1917).

32. This memoir was written when Poland was under the Communist dictatorship of General Wojciech Jaruzelski (1981–1989).
33. Dov Ber Bolochower (1723–1805)—a Jewish scholar and leader of the Bolechow community, wrote a memoir that contains many economic and social details of eighteenth century Eastern European Jewish life. The autobiographical part of *Zichronoth R. Dov Ber Me 'Bolechow* was translated from Hebrew into Yiddish and English, and published by Marc Wischnitzer in Berlin, 1922.
34. *Majufes*—Yiddish pronunciation of Hebrew *ma yafit* (how beautiful you are), a verse from Song of Songs 7:7, which appears at the head of a liturgical poem sung in honor of the Sabbath on Friday nights. The title of this *piyut* received in Polish the meaning of a Jewish song or dance, where the Jew appears in a ridiculous, degrading light.
35. Council of Four Lands—a central body of Jewish delegates from four parts of Poland, which functioned from the second half of the sixteenth century to 1764. The delegates met to discuss matters of importance to the Jewish community, mainly levying the taxes exacted by the rulers, later also representing their communities before the rulers.
36. This is a free translation from the Hebrew, as given by the author, who, presumably, translated it from the Polish text presented by Balaban.
37. Spoken to friend and wealthy patron Ksawery Branicki, another Polish émigré in France.
38. Juliusz Slowacki, *Kordian* (Act III, scene 4), written in 1833 in rhymed Alexandrines. The following citation is a very free rendition, based on the author's Hebrew. However, there exists an English translation of *Kordian* by Gerard T. Kapolka, published by The Green Lantern Press in 2011.
39. UN approval of a partition plan for Mandatory Palestine to establish two separate independent states, one for Arabs, one for Jews.
40. Uri Zvi Greenberg (1896–1981)—an Israeli poet, noted and therefore often sidelined for his Revisionist (i.e. a follower of Jabotinsky's nationalistic stance) views, including support of violent opposition to the British Mandatory government in Erez Israel during the 1930s and 1940s. He believed that the Holocaust was a 'tragic but almost inevitable outcome of Jewish indifference to their destiny.' As early as 1923, Greenberg "envisioned and warned of the destruction of European Jewry." [Wikipedia]
41. Avraham Shlonsky (1900–1973)—an Israeli poet, satirist and editor, leader of the anti-Bialik rebels in Hebrew poetry, noted for his mastery of the Hebrew language and for striking, often witty linguistic innovations.
42. *Massada* by Yiẓḥak Lamdan (1899–1954), a stirring epic poem, both dramatic and lyrical, became an instant "classic" among Zionist-oriented, activist, *aliyah*-bound youth when it appeared in 1927, and remained influential for decades, well after the establishment of the State of Israel. In 1934, Lamdan founded in Tel Aviv a journal for literature and culture, *Gilyonot*, and invited the young author to its cadre of regular contributors, offering him a platform for his early essays. Lamdan and the author remained friends until the former's premature death. The author devoted a comprehensive biographical-critical essay to Lamdan's work in his *Morasha u-ma'avak ba-shirah uva-hagut* (*The Struggle for Continuity in Hebrew Poetry and Philosophy*), (Tel Aviv: Yaḥdav Publishers, 1978).
43. Julian Tuwim, "Wiersze o państwie," 1935.
44. Translated by Anthony Polonsky, "Julian Tuwim – Confronting Antisemitism in Poland," in *The Individual in History: Essays in Honor of Jehuda Reinharz*, ed. ChaeRan Y. Freeze et al. (Waltham, MA: Brandeis University Press, 2015), 388.
45. Titled *Murzyn warszawski* (*Warsaw Negro*).

46. "He also refused to permit the staging of his prewar play *Murzyn warszawski* because of its harsh depictions of Jews." Eugenia Prokop-Janiec in the Online Edition of the YIVO Encyclopedia of Jews in Eastern Europe.
47. In the 1905 poem *Akhen gam zeh mussar elohim* (*Indeed this too is God's rebuke*).
48. Arie Tartakower, *Ḥurban o hitḥadshut* (*Destruction or Renewal?*), *Ha-olam*, 18–22, 1928. [Author's note].
49. This strange, symbolic story of Anhelli, the man-angel who suffered and died for Poland, is narrated in Old Testament style. It deals with the sufferings of the oppressed Poles and with the country's ultimate destiny.
50. The following text was published in the Israeli daily *Yedi'ot Aḥaronot*, on July 1, 1962, a year after the death of Israel Schumacher. [Author's note]
51. Popular Yiddish song, first published in 1901, by M. M. Warshawsky (1848–1907), about a rabbi teaching his young *ḥeder* pupils the Hebrew alphabet.
52. Avrom Reyzen (Abraham Reisen, or Raisin) (1876–1953)—a Yiddish writer, poet and editor. This poem was first published in 1902 in the *Yiddishe Folkszeitung* (Cracow), no. 24. Trans. Henry Greenfield, Joseph Friedlander, comp. The Standard Book of Jewish Verse, 1917.
53. A Yiddish cabaret song from the 1920s about a wagon driver who does not care much about getting his passengers to their destinations, but is hurrying to an inn, where he drinks, gambles, and loses his money, horse and wagon, to return home to his wife with only the whip.
54. In the 1963 newspaper eulogy, the author amplified his high school reminiscences with a brief valuation of Schumacher's later professional and national standing:

"Armed with laughter, satire and grotesque ridicule, he traversed the Jewish world, back and forth, probing deeply into the crowds' wellsprings of laughter, and draining them to the ultimate teardrop hidden in their depth, in a sort of clownery of seriousness.

A comic actor *sui generis*, one who tickled the intelligentsia no less than the commoner, he would, in a boyish game, tilt his mirrors to one or the other side, and immediately all the distortions in our lives, its vanities, its passing and permanent nonsense, would be reflected in them.

He began his way on the Yiddish comedy stage in his hometown Lodz, with his colleague Shimon Dzigan, with whom he appeared throughout most of his life as the famous "Dzigan and Schumacher" duo. In Warsaw, he gained fame, and thereafter, night after night, Jewish theaters throughout Poland thundered with hilarity. The crowds shook with heartened, salutary, back straightening laughter; his humor came as a draft of life in the furious pre-Holocaust period, the period of the rule of the generals and its "mild" anti-Semitism—economic boycott, ghetto benches in university classrooms, and unbridled Jew-hatred elsewhere. During the war, he was in Russia. Prison, concentration and labor camps. Then back to Poland, the murdered Jewish Poland, ransacked of its multitudes. For a while, he wished to raise the spirits of the Jewish remnants there. Then he moved to Paris, from there—to America, and eventually to Israel. From here, he would travel to the United States and Latin America. His home was the Jewish Yiddish speaking multitudes, their griefs and their joys.

The Jewish world responded with cheers, poured on him a bounty of fame and love, saw in him the emissary of the witty, healing Jewish humor.

Toward the end of his life, after he parted from his colleague Dzigan, he turned to tragic drama, to the nation's tragedy, to the truth that had been latent in him from the beginning.

In his short life, he knew many vicissitudes. He was 53 at his death."

CHAPTER 12

1. See below, note 6.
2. This museum and archive in Kibbutz Loḥamei Ha-geta'ot is dedicated to the legacy of the Holocaust and of the ghetto fighters, and, specifically, to the spiritual legacy of Yiẓḥak Katzenelson. It published Katzenelson's works with Ha-kibbutz Ha-me'uchad Publishers, culminating in 1988 in a five-volume complete Hebrew edition.
3. For a poet, a critical difference between the two accents is not only the pronunciation, which would affect the rhyme, but the word stress, which affects the rhythm. Ashkenazi Hebrew usually places the stress on a word's first or second syllable, whereas in the Sephardic version, the accent usually falls on the last. Thus, an Ashkenazi would greet a fellow Jew with '**Sho**-lem al'**eikh**-em, while a Sephardi would say Sha-'**lom** alei-'**khem**.
4. David Frishman (or Frischmann, 1859–1922)—a Hebrew and Yiddish literary critic, editor, writer, poet, and translator, who aspired to create a modern Jewish literature unconnected to the burning issues of Jewish civic and communal life. "He envisioned an elitist, refined Hebrew literature that could parallel the achievements of classic works of Western literature. He was skeptical about the value of Jewish cultural heritage and believed that the development of taste and aesthetic sensitivity was the key to a modern Jewish renaissance." (YIVO Encyclopedia of Jews in Eastern Europe website).
5. Katzenelson translated Heinrich Heine's *Buch der Lieder* (*The Book of Songs*) into Hebrew, 1923.
6. See Efraim Shmueli, *Beit Yisrael u-medinat Yisrael* (*The House of Israel and the State of Israel*), Yavneh, 1966, page 35. The author is mainly referring to the three major modern-era responses to the problems of Jewish existence—Jewish liberalism, the national movement (spearheaded by political and practical Zionism), and Jewish socialism—and to the institutions, organs, and creative talents that each produced to achieve its goals. The proliferation of diverse parties and associations described in Chapter 3, testifies to the multiplicity of problems that preoccupied the Jewish public at the time. These rendered difficult any clear orientation for a public that was just beginning to take its first steps in the arena of political organization.
7. H. N. Bialik, *Shiratenu ha-ẓe'irah*, (*Our Young Poetry*), 1907.
8. Y. H. Brenner, *Kol kitvei Y. H. Brenner* (Collected Works) (Tel Aviv: Ha-kibbutz Ha-me'uchad and Dvir, 1960), Vol. II, 248, essay titled "Me-hirhurei koreh" (Reflections of a Reader).
9. In the terminology of modern literary criticism theory, one may say that young Katzenelson inclined toward the Symbolist movement of his day, which distanced itself from topics of public concern, opposed realistic or scientific interpretation of art, and placed a heavy emphasis on poetry's resonance, its vitality and atmosphere, more than on thought. Poetry's role was not to teach, but to arouse, astound, and delight. [Author's note].
10. Shaul Tchernichovsky, *Al Ha-dam, Klil Sonnetot*, number XV, 1923.

CHAPTER 13

1. Dror—A Zionist Labor oriented movement, whose leaders, having escaped from Nazi- to Russian-occupied Poland, decided to infiltrate back into several ghettos, in order to continue Jewish-Zionist education work, of which the best known is the underground *gymnasia* in the Warsaw Ghetto.
2. Yiẓḥak Katzenelson, *Ketavim Aḥaronim*, 3rd ed. (Tel Aviv: Ha-kibbutz ha-me'uchad Publishers and the Ghetto Fighter's House, 1969), p. 32.

3. Katzenelson, op. cit., 20.
4. The *Song about Shloyme Żelichowski* and *The Song of the Radzyner*, as well as *The Song of the Murdered Jewish People*, were translated from Yiddish into Hebrew by M. Z. Wolfowski and were published in Katzenelson's *Collected Works*, Volume V (Last Works), 1947, 1956, and 1988, Ha-kibbutz ha-me'uchad Publishers and the Ghetto Fighter's House. [Author's note] An English translation of the first two mentioned above is available on the Poetry in Hell website: Yiddish Poetry in the Ringelblum Archives, Translated by Sarah Traister Moskovitz.
5. Katzenelson, op. cit., V, 265.
6. Ibid., 64.
7. Recently, some literary critics have begun paying serious attention to these works. Yeḥiel Szeintuch, for example, published a comprehensive and fascinating article, "The Individual and the Collective in *The Song of Shlomo Zelichowski.*" See the anthology *Gal'ed*, Volume 6. [Author's note]
8. Katzenelson, op. cit., 5.
9. Katzenelson, op. cit., Plays, 183.
10. Katzenelson, op. cit., 1972 edition, 16.
11. Katzenelson, op. cit., 155.
12. Ibid., 43.
13. It may seem strange that the author here questions what the poet did *not* write. However, he maintained that during the Holocaust, many turned to reflect upon the Binding of Isaac in an attempt to derive a contemporary lesson from this central symbol. The Holocaust appeared as one great binding-sacrifice of the entire Jewish people. The last Rebbe of Aleksander, Reb Yiẓḥak Menaḥem Mendel Dancyger, who perished in Treblinka, thought about this too, and the Ḥasidim who later collected his sermons and reflections entitled the work *Akedat Yiẓḥak*, the Binding of Isaac. Thus, it could be expected that Katzenelson would write about this symbol, especially as "we know how much a Jew identifies with the person after whom he is named." E. Shmueli, "Kiddush ha-shem biyemei ha-shoah," in *Sefer ha-yovel likhevod maran* R. Yosef Dov Soloveichik, 1987, 1200.
14. "Another planet," or "planet Auschwitz"—expression coined by survivor and author Yehiel De-Nur (1909–2001), also known by his pen name Ka-Tsetnik 135633, in his evidence at the Eichmann trial in 1961.
15. Rabbi Yiẓḥak Nissenbaum (1868–1942)—Zionist religious leader of the Mizraḥi movement, who declared during the Holocaust that the imperative of the hour was to preserve ("sanctify") life, rather than martyrdom to sanctify God's name.
16. Translated by Hillel Halkin in *The Complex Greatness of the Jewish National Poet, Part One,* Ḥayyim Naḥman Bialik. Jewish Chronicle/Heritage Images/Getty Images. AUG 29, 2017.
17. Dov Sadan, *Avnei Gader*, (Ramat Gan: Massada, 1970), 54. [Author's note]
18. Katzenelson, op. cit., 92.
19. Psalm 77:3—"Ezkera elohim ve'ehemaia" (I remembered God, and was troubled) is also the title of an eighth century penitential poem, recited on the close of the Yom Kippur liturgy, lamenting the destruction of Jerusalem and the nation's suffering in exile. Here, the poet substituted the city for God.
20. Katzenelson, op. cit., 163.
21. Katzenelson, op. cit., 156.
22. The author made no comment on Canto V.
23. Eck, op. cit., 209.
24. Katzenelson, op. cit., 108.

25. Katzenelson, op. cit., pp. 140–141.
26. In Hebrew—*aviv ha-'iv'im*, a similar sound, but a contrast of meanings.

CHAPTER 14

1. An early version of this chapter appeared in a Hebrew anthology devoted to the Jewish community of Zdunska Wola, published in 1966.
2. This feud was described by Y. Y. Trunk in *Poyln Zikhroines un Bilder*, Vol. 3, Chapter 3, 19–24. There is no indication whether this is the material the author read.
3. *Nathan the Wise*—a play by the German dramatist and philosopher Gotthold Ephraim Lessing (1729–1781). Set in Jerusalem at the time of Third Crusade, it makes a plea for religious tolerance among Christians, Moslems and Jews.
4. The memoir by Isaac Neuman *The Narrow Bridge: Beyond the Holocaust* (Champaign, IL: University of Illinois Press, 2000) contains a chapter devoted to this uncle, Mendel Strykowski, with whom the young Neuman had studied Torah in Zdunska Wola in the 1930s. Besides describing R. Mendel's fine qualities and wisdom, Neuman revealed an interesting biographical detail:

   "He had been in the German army during World War I and toward its end was taken prisoner in Russia and sent to Siberia. For four years his family heard nothing of him. Then, one day in early 1922, a shabbily dressed stranger, bearded and thin, arrived in Zdunska Wola and entered Reb Mendel's store. A seven-year-old girl stood behind the cash register. The stranger greeted the little girl. She looked at the poor starving Jew and immediately took some change from the cash register to offer him. The stranger began to cry. Thinking she had not given him enough, she dug out some more change and offered that. When he did not leave, she called to her mother in the back room to bring the stranger some food. Her mother looked at the stranger and screamed. It was her husband, Reb Mendel . . . What had kept him alive as a prisoner, he told them, was the hope of seeing his family again and seeing how his daughter was being taught things of the spirit."

   This almost fable-like account confirms the author's testimony about the generosity and spirit of *ẓedakah* that prevailed in his mother's family. Puzzling, however, that he never mentioned his uncle's military service and long captivity. Surely, it would have been a subject of anxious discussion in the family in his childhood and early adolescence?
5. "He is despised and rejected of men . . . Surely he hath borne our griefs, and carried our sorrows . . ." etc.
6. See Chapter 11, note 42.

CHAPTER 15

1. "Kiddush ha-Shem bi-yemei ha-sho'ah" in *Sefer Yovel in Honor of R. Yosef Dov Halevi Soloveitchik*, (Jerusalem: the Rav Kook Institute, 1984), Vol. 2. [Author's note]
2. *Beit Yisrael u-Medinat Yisrael, Ha-ẓibbur ha-yehudi be-America, iyunim bi-tmurot u-vemegamot*, (Tel Aviv: Yavneh Publishers and the College of Jewish Studies, Cleveland, Ohio, 1966).
3. This poem is from Katzenelson's *Vittel Diary*. Omitted here is the author's allusion to a famous short poem by Avraham Shlonsky, *Storm* (*Sufa*), which ends with the words "you have become a multitude of sobs" (*at hayit le-alfei yevava*), a painful twist on the beautiful blessing given to our biblical matriarch Rebecca: "May you become a mother of multitudes" (*hayi le-alfei revava*).

4. Excerpts from "For this Now is Weeping" (*Ki zeh khevar bekhi*), in Uri Ẓvi Greenberg, *Reḥovot ha-nahar* (Tel Aviv: Shocken Publishing House Ltd, 1951), 80. This long poem echoes the tradition of medieval Hebrew poetry by its use of an insistent monorhyme ending with the "noo" sound of the possessive plural form—our—hence the editor-translator's attempt at least partially to reproduce this peculiarity.
5. See Avraham Yehuda Brzezinski, *Rabbi Eliyahu Haim Meisel z"l—Ha-rav be-Lodz* (Tel Aviv: 56/1955). [Author's note]
6. It is a pleasure and a duty to note that at the turn of the twenty-first century the situation here changed dramatically for the better thanks to the initiative and efforts of certain local residents, notably Dr. Kamila Klauzinska and the Yachad Group, Prof. Daniel Wagner from Israel, and descendants of Zdunska Wola residents around the world.
7. Elazar ben Kalir (aka Ha-kalir, sixth-seventh century CE) in the acrostic *piyut* beginning with the words "A nation firm [in its faith] as a rampart" *(Ohm ani ḥomah),* recited as part of the *hoshana* ("please save") liturgy, which evokes the Sukkot Festival service as it was performed in the Temple in Jerusalem.
8. From another *piyut* of Ha-kalir from the *hoshana* liturgy—*Le-ma'an eytan,* in which God is petitioned to help us for the sake of, or because of the merit of, great individuals in Jewish history.
9. According to the Wikipedia Hebrew entry for Aleksandrow, in 1939 there were 3,500 Jews living there, about one third of the population. This number is pretty close to the statistics for 1921, which the author cites in Chapter 7. However, if Mr. Rogowski's numbers for 1939 were accurate, it seems that the relative number of Jews to non-Jews had changed dramatically, i.e., far fewer Jews, relatively speaking, than two decades earlier.
10. Rivers flowing through Poland, Lithuania and the Ukraine-Moldova, respectively, denoting the area of dense Jewish settlement in Eastern Europe.
11. Cited by Yehoshu'a Aibeshits in *Bi-kedushah uvi-gevurah* (Tel Aviv: 1975). [Author's note]
12. English translation in *Stranger in Our Midst: Images of the Jew in Polish Literature*, ed. Harold B. Segel, (Ithaca: Cornell University Press, 1996).
13. *Hakafot* (Hebrew: circling)—the tradition on Sukkot of circling the reader's platform in the synagogue with the Four Species on each of the seven days of the Festival. On the eighth day, Simḥat Torah, the custom is to take the Torah scrolls out of the ark and to circle the reader's platform and parade throughout the synagogue seven times or more with singing and dancing. The *Piyut* chanted is *Elohei ha-ruḥot* (*God of the Spirits*).
14. Isaiah 25:9, recited when the Ark is opened for the *hakafot.*
15. Words recited in the sixth *hakafah.*
16. Federbush, Shimon (ed), *Ḥokhmat yisrael bema'arav europa* (*Jewish studies in Western Europe*), (Jerusalem-Tel Aviv: Ogen Publishing with M. Neuman Publishers, 1958). This volume also contains contributions profiling Prof. Y. M. Ha-Cohen Guttmann and Prof. Y. Heinemann, by D. S. Levinger and E. E. Urbach, respectively.
17. The editor was unable to locate this publication through the internet. However, the German Jewish students' journal *Der Jüdische Student* reprinted it in its December 1932 (Brochure 11) issue: Ephraim Szmulewicz, *Zum geistigen Gesicht des Nationalsozialismus* (The Intellectual Visage of National Socialism), 308–311. Based on his readings of Nazi ideologues, the author concluded that war in Europe was inevitable and that the Jewish future was dire.
18. Jerzy Ficowski (1924–2006). In 1986, with the publication of *A Reading of Ashes* in a bibliophilic dual language Hebrew-Polish edition *Kriat Efer-mikleh,* trans. Shalom Lindenbaum, (Tel Aviv: Gazit, 1985), Ficowski was awarded the Ka-Tsetnik Prize, at a ceremony held at the residence of the President of Israel in Jerusalem. Ficowski reacted:

"When I finally finished writing the poems of *A Reading of Ashes*, and they were published in London, in 1979, I wrote then that my biggest dream was that these poems would one day be translated into Hebrew and Yiddish, so that they would thus speak in the language of the people whose murdered sons and daughters they came to lament . . ." (From Hebrew Wikipedia). Denied a passport by the Polish regime, the poet was prevented from travelling to Israel to receive the prize in person. His wife represented him at the ceremony in Jerusalem.

19. Babylonian Talmud, Tractate Bava Batra 73b: "Once, while on a ship, we came to a gigantic fish at rest, which we supposed to be an island, since there was sand on its back, in which grass was growing. We therefore landed, made a fire, and cooked our meal. But when the fish felt the heat he rolled over, and we would have drowned had not the ship been near." This tale is retold in the first voyage of Sinbad the Sailor in the *One Thousand and One Nights*.

CHAPTER 16

1. In Hebrew: *Polin ha-ma'atirah*—a take-off on the biblical "crown-wearing Tyre" (Is. 23:8).
2. This English translation by Krystyna Piórkowska, republished on the internet, is from Kunert, A. K (ed.), Polacy-Zydzi / Polen-Juden / Poles-Jews, 1939–1945: Wybor Zrodel / Quellenauswahl / Selection of Documents (English, German and Polish Edition), published by Rada Ochrony Pamieci Walk i Meczenstwa, Instytut Dziedzictwa Narodowego, Oficyna Wydawnicza Rytm, Warsaw, 2001.
3. The author here used the biblical expression *ru'aḥ ra'ah*, evil spirit, or madness, as in 1 Samuel, 16:14–15, which describes the madness-torment that descended upon the tragic King Saul: "The Lord's spirit left Saul, and an evil spirit sent by the Lord tormented him." In Polish: "Duch zły od Pana."

Glossary

All words in Hebrew, unless otherwise indicated

ADMOR, admorim	acronym for **Ad**onenu, **Mo**renu ve**R**abenu (our master, our teacher and our rabbi), honorific title for a Ḥasidic rebbe.
Aggadah	the homiletic, non-legal segments of the Talmud, consisting of legends, anecdotes, and diverse narratives.
Ahavat Yisrael	love of one's fellow Jews, and by extension of every person.
Akademieh (Yiddish)	public function, event, ceremony.
Aliyah	(coming up) refers here to historic waves of Jewish immigration to the Land of Israel, or to the immigration there of an individual.
Avrekh(im)	recently married young man, often still living at his parents-in-law's expense in order to devote himself to Torah study, before assuming the responsibility of providing for his family.
Ba'al mofet	miracle worker.
Baal Shem Tov	(one with a good reputation, often rendered in English as Master of the Good Name), or the acronym **BESHT**—name given to the mystic Rabbi Israel ben Eliezer (c. 1698–1760), regarded as the founder of Ḥasidism.
Beit din	rabbinic court.
Beit midrash	house of Talmudic Jewish learning, adjacent to the synagogue.
Dayan(im)	judge(s) in a rabbinic court.
Derekh ereẓ	the way of the world, worldly occupation, also good manners.

Dveikut	(clinging, adherence) in Jewish mysticism, intense concentration on communion, or unification, with the divine.
Dybbuk	in Jewish folklore, the soul of a dead person that takes possession of a live host. The term became widely known through S. Ansky's popular play *The Dybbuk*, first performed in Warsaw in 1920.
El maleh raḥamim	"God full of Mercy," the prayer for the soul of the deceased to ascend to heaven, recited at the graveside during burial and memorial services.
Epikores	(from the Greek philosopher Epicurus) a heretic.
Ereẓ Israel, or Yisrael	Land of Israel, the name used by Jews to designate their homeland.
Gabbai	person responsible for the smooth running of a synagogue (beadle, sexton, or warden). In Ḥasidism, the term usually refers to the rebbe's secretary or personal assistant.
Gemarah	see Talmud.
Goy(im)	a people or nation, including the people of Israel. With the advent of Christianity, the term generally designated non-Jews, both nations and individuals, i.e., "gentiles."
Gvir	a town's rich man.
Gymnasia, gymnasium	term borrowed from Greek for a Central European high school.
Haggadah	text recited at the Seder table on Passover eve, containing a narrative of the Exodus.
Ḥallah	traditionally a braided white flour bread eaten on the Sabbath and Festival Days.
Halakhah, halakhic	the collective body of Jewish religious law.
Ḥaluẓ(im)	pioneer(s) preparing for settlement in the Land of Israel, or already settled there.
Ḥaredi(m)	ultra-Orthodox adherents to the pre-Zionist, pre-Enlightenment and pre-Emancipation form of European rabbinic Judaism.

Ḥasidism, Ḥasidut	a pietistic Jewish revival movement that arose in eighteenth century western Ukraine as a reaction against an elitist, scholarly rabbinic leadership. Founded by the Ba'al Shem Tov and his disciples. Today considered a sub-group of the ultra-Orthodox (Ḥaredi) camp.
Haskalah	an intellectual movement (c. 1770–1881) in Russia and parts of Eastern Europe that strove for cultural and moral Jewish renewal, concurrently with integration of Jews in their surrounding societies.
Ḥeder	one-room school located in the teacher's home, where children, aged three to twelve or thirteen, spent the entire day studying the essential Jewish religious texts.
Ḥerem	ban placed on a Jewish community member by the congregation's leaders, similar to the Catholic excommunication.
Hillulah	anniversary of a ẓaddik's death, celebrated at the court by his devotees as a joyful event.
HY"D (Hashem yikom damam)	may God avenge their blood, a tag designating individuals who were killed as a result of anti-Jewish violence.
'Iluy	prodigy, a natural genius in textual (usually Talmudic) study.
Kabbalah	a tradition of Jewish mysticism, originating in medieval Spain, Ḥasidism being one of its late offshoots.
Kaddish	a hymn of praises about God (in Aramaic), which separates sections of the liturgy. The term often refers specifically to the reciting of the kaddish by a mourner, whereby the mourners declare that despite their loss, they still praise God.
Kapota	(from French capote) long black coat, traditionally of silk, worn by Ḥasidim on Sabbaths and Holy Days.
Ketubah	Jewish marriage contract.
Kever avot	grave of one's ancestors.
Kiddush	blessing recited over wine or grape juice to sanctify the Sabbath and Holy Days.
Kippah	skullcap.
Klal Yisrael	all of Israel, the Jewish people.

Klipot	peels, or husks, represent the evil or impure spiritual forces in Jewish mysticism.
Kvittel, kvitlach (Yiddish)	petitionary note handed to the rebbe, or placed on a ẓaddik's tombstone, or in the Western Wall.
Leḥayim	(To life) the traditional Jewish toast over a glass of wine or liquor.
Litvaks	Jews from the former Grand Duchy of Lithuania. The term usually refers to the traditional, more cerebral Talmud-focused rabbinic Orthodoxy, which predated, and opposed, Ḥasidism, hence known also as mitnagdim (opponents).
Luftmentsh(n) (Yiddish)	person living on air, impractical at earning a living.
Maggid	an itinerant preacher, skilled at instruction of moral and religious conduct through captivating interpretation of biblical texts.
Maror	bitter herb eaten at the Seder table on Passover eve.
Maskil(im)	"enlightened", critical, having imbibed secular learning, a product of the Haskalah movement.
Matmid	a persistent, unflagging person, traditionally an epithet of praise for a Talmudic scholar.
Maẓẓah	unleavened Passover bread.
Mazal tov, mazel tov	good luck.
Mezuzah	a piece of parchment bearing the prayer "Hear O Israel," placed inside a decorative case, and affixed on the doorpost(s) of a Jewish home.
Midrash	a traditional (compiled between c. 400 and 1200 CE) form of biblical exegesis, generally imaginative and homiletic in character. The term refers both to the method and to the body of such texts.
Mikveh	traditional ritual bath facility.
Minyan	minimum quorum of ten adult Jewish men required for communal prayer.
Mitnagdim	see Litvaks.
Mishnah(yot)	see Talmud

Mishneh Torah	Maimonides' codification of the Halakhah (c. 1170–1180 CE)
Miẓvah (miẓvot)	religious commandment.
Mohel	a Jew trained in performing the circumcision of a male infant.
Nakhes (Yiddish)	gratification, satisfaction, especially the kind derived by parents from their children.
Niggun	tune, melody, refers in Hasidism to tunes used in religious songs or prayers, using biblical verses, or without lyrics. Here, the author uses the term in its Yiddish intonation to indicate the soulful, hard to define essence of the old tradition.
Ohel	tent, a small masonry structure built around a grave as a sign of the prominence of the deceased, especially of Ḥasidic rebbes.
Pidyon(ot)	money given to a ẓaddik in order to mitigate a spiritual judgment hanging over a person, such as ill health.
Pilpul	method of studying the Talmud through intense textual analysis in attempts to either explain conceptual differences between various rulings or to reconcile any apparent contradictions. The term is sometimes used derogatorily, to indicate exaggerated hairsplitting.
Posek (poskim)	decisor, or legal scholar, who determines the position of the Halakhah, where it is unclear or indecisive, on a given question.
Piyut(im)	from Greek for poem, a post-biblical liturgical work chanted or recited during services.
Psukei dezimra	prescribed chapters from the Book of Psalms recited in the morning prayer service.
Rebbe	rabbi, spiritual leader of a Ḥasidic group of followers.
Responsum, responsa (Latin)	rabbinic written responses to specific, practical questions addressed to them by congregants, also the literary body of such rulings given by the poskim.
Rosh Hashanah	festival marking the beginning of the Jewish new year.
Rosh ḥodesh	first day of the lunar month.

Se'udat miẓvah	obligatory festive meal, such as on a bar miẓvah, a wedding, a circumcision.
Shaḥarit	morning prayer service.
Shavu'ot	Pentecost, festival celebrating the giving of the Torah on Mt. Sinai.
Sheyne Yidn (Yiddish)	beautiful Jews, refers to distinguished community members, who serve as models of good conduct, or who pretend to such status.
Shiddukh	matrimonial match, traditionally arranged by a matchmaker.
Shirayim	food leftovers from the rebbe's plate, distributed to the Ḥasidim at a Tish.
Shiv'a	customary seven days of mourning for the dead.
Shlom bayit	domestic peace, family harmony.
Sholem, shalom	peace, greeting.
Shtetl (Yiddish)	small town in Eastern Europe that often had a sizable Jewish population.
Shtibel, shtiblachs (Yiddish)	small prayer-room.
Si'ata dishemaya (Aramaic)	Heaven's help, a wish for good luck.
Siddur	the Jewish daily prayer book.
Shtreimel (Yiddish)	traditional Jewish hat, usually made of fur.
Simḥat Torah	rejoicing with/of the Torah, the holiday that celebrates the conclusion of the annual cycle of public Torah readings and the beginning of a new cycle. It follows immediately after Sukkot.
Sukkah	a temporary hut, decorated inside and topped with branches, where men are required to take their meals during the weeklong festival of Sukkot.
Tachlit, tachlis	purpose, aim, practical aspect of a matter.
Tallit	prayer shawl.

Tallit katan	small tallit, a poncho-like garment worn by Jewish men, generally under one's clothing, with special twined and knotted fringes attached to its four corners.
Shulḥan Arukh	the most widely consulted compilation of Jewish law (Halakhah), authored by Joseph Karo in 1563.
Talmud	A body of Jewish opinions and teachings on legal, ritual, ethical and other matters, considered the primary source of Jewish religious law (Halakhah). It is composed of the Mishnah at its core (corpus sealed c. 200 CE), and the Gemarah as the commentary on the Mishnah (corpus sealed c. 500 CE). The words Gemarah and Talmud are often used interchangeably.
Talmud Torah	religious school for impoverished boys offering an elementary education in Hebrew, Bible and Talmud. Whereas the ḥeder was private, the Talmud Torah was supported by the community.
Tashlikh	ritual performed at a large, natural body of flowing water on the afternoon of Rosh Hashanah, during which the worshipers symbolically throw their sins into the water.
Tefillin	phylacteries.
Tikkun	fixing, mending, rectification.
Tish, Tisch (Yiddish)	the gathering of Ḥasidim around their rebbe, where food (often only symbolic morsels from the rebbe's plate) is served, with Torah-talk, songs and prayers. Considered an event of great holiness in Ḥasidism.
Tosafot	halakhic additions by Jewish medieval commentators to Rashi's commentary on the Talmud.
Volksdeutsche (German)	Nazi term for people of German origins who did not hold German citizenship and lived as ethnic minorities in other countries.
Yeshiva	Jewish institution of advanced learning for men that focuses on the study of traditional religious texts, primarily the Talmud and other Halakhic texts.

Yiḥudim	("unifications") a form of meditation in Jewish mysticism, whereby certain supernal elements are unified through one's mystical devotions.
Zekhut or zechus avot	a belief that a Jew may hope for blessing in this world, or reward in the next, by virtue of the great merit of Israel's ancestors, or of the person's own parents.
Ẓaddik(im)	(righteous one) a title generally given to personalities considered saintly, such as a Ḥasidic spiritual master or rebbe.
Ẓedakah	righteousness, commonly used to signify charity in the sense of an ethical obligation.
Zemirot	liturgical songs, usually sung on the Sabbath and Festival Days.

About the Author—Efraim Shmueli (1908–1988)

Born in Lodz, Poland, attended the Jewish Theological Seminary in Breslau, Germany and concomitantly the Friedrich Wilhelm University of Breslau (1928–30, 1931–32), with an interlude at the University of Frankfurt (1930–31). Studied in Frankfurt under Paul Tillich, Karl Mannheim, Max Horkheimer, Martin Buber, and in Breslau under Richard Hoenigswald, Siegfried Marck, and Eugen Kuehnemann. Ph.D. dissertation on Hegel's concept of individuality: "Individualism and Structure of Society in Hegel's Ethics and Social Philosophy" (published 1936).

Emigrated to Mandatory Palestine-Ereẓ Yisrael in 1933, settling in Haifa, where he married Flora Perle of Breslau and had two daughters. In parallel with his teaching career in local high schools, at a teacher's training college, and at the Haifa College (precursor of Haifa University), he studied and wrote on the topics that most keenly engaged him: the enigma of Jewish continuity and creativity, faith and heresy, political science and society notably in Renaissance Europe, and philosophical issues. Was a Visiting Professor at the Chicago College of Jewish Studies (1951–52), the Detroit College of Jewish Studies (1954–56), and the Cleveland College of Jewish Studies (1963–67). The extended periods in the U.S. gave him an opportunity to reflect also on the largest diaspora Jewish community. From 1967–76 he was Professor of Philosophy at the Cleveland State University in Cleveland, Ohio. Lectured extensively in Israel, the U.S., Canada, and Latin America. Upon retirement from Cleveland State University (1976), served until his death as an Adjunct Professor of Philosophy at Haifa University.

For six decades, published in papers and journals, mainly in Hebrew, also a number of papers in English on various philosophical problems. Among his books (in Hebrew, unless otherwise indicated):

History of the Jewish People in Modern Times, 7 volumes, published between 1941 and 1957.

Tradition and Revolution, 1942.

Cervantes, a Critical Analysis of Don Quixote, 1952.

Men of the Renaissance—The Rise of the Bourgeois World and its First Crisis, 2 volumes, 1948, 1952.

Life and Philosophy of Giordano Bruno, 1952.

Faith and Heresy—An Essay on Leon da Modena and Uriel da Costa, 1962.

Don Isaac Abravanel and the Expulsion of the Jews from Spain, 1963.

Assimilation, Identity and the Impact of the Jewish State—Studies in American Jewry, 1966.

The Struggle for Continuity in Hebrew Poetry and Philosophy, 1978.

Seven Jewish Cultures: A Reinterpretation of Jewish History and Thought, 1980 (appeared in English, 1990).

Crossroads of Modern Thought—Studies in Spinoza, Hegel, Marx, Husserl and Mannheim, 1984 (self-published collection of papers in English).

Homo Angustus: Studies in Literature, Existentialism and Philosophy of Hermeneutics, 1985.

Wondering and Thinking in a Techno-Scientific World, 1985.

With the Last Generation of Jews in Poland, 1986.

Judaism between Authority and Inspiration, Studies of Legitimation and Modernization in Jewish History and Contemporary Thought, 1988 (published posthumously).

Translations into Hebrew:

Thomas More, *Utopia* (from Latin), with introduction and notes, 1946

Machiavelli, *Political Writings* (from Italian), with introduction and notes, 1948.

Raphael Mahler, *The Karaites* (from Yiddish), 1949.

Spinoza, *Correspondence* (From Latin), with introduction and notes, 1963.

Max Weber, *Politics as a Vocation* (from German), with introduction and notes, 1961.

Thomas Coenen, *Vain Hopes of the Jews as Revealed in the Figure of Sabbatai Zevi* (from Dutch, with Arthur Lagawier), introduction and notes by Yosef Kaplan, 1998 (appeared posthumously).

List of Photographs

The author as a *ḥeder* boy, c. five years old 3
Colonel Berek Joselewicz wearing Duchy of Warsaw mounted riflemen uniform, painted by Juliusz Fortunat Kossak (1824–1899). Public Domain. 10
Father Mordekhai Dovid Szmulewicz, Lodz, 1937, 50 years old 17
The author at age 18 22
Lodz skyline (YIVO Institute for Jewish Research) 26
Newsstand in Lodz, 1930s (YIVO Institute for Jewish Research) 28
Yeḥiel Rosenzweig, teacher and poet (Wikipedia) 30
Naḥum Sokolov in the 1920s (Wikipedia) 31
Yizhak Gruenbaum (National Library of Israel, courtesy of Bitmuna, Miriam and Leib Klotz Collection) 33
Ze'ev Vladimir Jabotinsky in World War I uniform of the British Jewish battalion (Wikimedia) 36
Funeral of Rabbi Majsel, Lodz, 1912 (YIVO Institute for Jewish Research) 44
Old houses in Baluty (Courtesy of the Ghetto Fighters' House—Itzhak Katzenelson Holocaust and Jewish Resistance Heritage Museum) 49
A Jewish hand-weaver at his loom in Baluty, 1920–30. (YIVO Institute for Jewish Research, courtesy of the Forward Association) 51
A Baluty street merchant selling geese. (YIVO Institute for Jewish Research) 54
Yiẓḥak Menaḥem Dancyiger (1880–1943), fourth ADMOR of Aleksander (1923–1943) walking with his sons and student in the spa of Marienbad, 1937 (Wikipedia) 72
The *ohel* ("tent") structure sheltering the graves of the rebbes of Aleksander and their families. (Courtesy of Monika Czechowicz) 79

Yiẓḥak Menaḥem Dancyger (1880–1943), fourth and last rebbe of Aleksander, only 63 at his death in Treblinka. 105
The Reform Synagogue in Lodz. LYIVO archives 124
Dr. Markus Braude, 1926, charcoal drawing by Marek Szwarc (Courtesy of the Ghetto Fighters' House—Itzhak Katzenelson Holocaust and Jewish Resistance Heritage Museum) 126
A student in the Hebrew gymnasia, aged 18 133
Aḥad Ha'am (Wikipedia) 134
Historian Dr. Philip Friedman (Yiddish Leksikon) 145
Poet Adam Mickiewicz - anonymous 19th century drawing 155
Julian Tuwim (pastel on paper, 1929) by Stanisław Ignacy Witkiewicz Witkacy). Warsaw National Museum 159
Bust of Saul Rieger, 1930s–1940s, by Max (Mordechai) Farbmann, Photo © The Israel Museum, Jerusalem 161
The young Yizhak Katzenelson in an advertising postcard (Courtesy of the Ghetto Fighters' House—Itzhak Katzenelson Holocaust and Jewish Resistance Heritage Museum) 177
The poet in his prime (Courtesy of the Ghetto Fighters' House—Itzhak Katzenelson Holocaust and Jewish Resistance Heritage Museum) 192
"This night, a night of horrors … and a first, first night of redemption." Katzenelson's address to the Hebrew teachers in the Warsaw Ghetto, Passover, 1942 210
Rabbi Lajzer Lipszyc in *Stulcie miasta Zdunska-Woli 1825–1925*, edited by Ludwik Wicher 218
Wola's town crier in *Stulcie miasta Zdunska-Woli 1825–1925*, 1925, edited by Ludwik Wicher 221
Mother Frajda Szmulewicz, nee Strykowska 225
Lodz central train station, 1930, (Lodz State Archive) 235
Skladowa 34, as it looked in 2015 (Courtesy of Ewelina Rudnicka) 238
Poznanski family mausoleum, Lodz Jewish cemetery (Courtesy of Monika Czechowicz) 242
Tombstone of Rabbi Eliezer Lipszyc at the Zdunska Wola cemetery. Courtesy Dr. Kamila Klauzinska and Prof. Ada Yonath 245
Tombstone of the third Rebbe of Aleksander (Courtesy of Monika Czechowicz) 248

Eugen and Recha Perle 258
Flora Perle Shmueli 259
Jewish Theological Seminary building, Breslau-Wroclaw (Wikipedia) 260
Student ID from Jewish Theological Seminary, Breslau 261
Prof. Isaak Heinemann (1876–1957), Wikipedia by Mendilitikin 262
Poet Jerzy Ficowski, Photo: Bartosz Pietrzak / mat. press releases 271

Index

Abarbanel, Isaac, 212
Aescoly (Eshkoli), A. Z. , 50, 283n2
Agnon, S. Y., 185, 244
Aḥad Ha'am (Asher Ginzberg), 35, 127–28, 132–38, 151, 184, 189, 289n8
Aibeshits, Yehoshu'a, 296n11
Akiba, Rabbi, 97, 203
Aleksander rebbes. See Dancyger dynasty
Aleksiun, Natalia, 288n2
Alter, Avraham Mordekhai (Fourth Rebbe of Ger), 228, 283n1
Alter, Simcha Bunim (Sixth Rebbe of Ger), 109
Alter, Yehuda Arieh Leibele (Third Rebbe of Ger), 40
Amiel, Moshe Avigdor, 35
Andrzejewski, Jerzy, 232, 270
Anielewicz, Mordekhai, 273
Anisfeld, Emanuel, 139–43, 150
Asch, Sholem, 31, 86, 116
Assaf, Michael, 170
Azulai, Ḥaim Yosef David (the ḤIDA), 99

Baal Shem Tov (BESHT), 86, 88, 95, 156, 299
Balaban, Majer, 9, 156, 281n11, 291n36
Barash, Asher, 185
Baron, Salo Wittmayer, 144, 289n15
Bartel, Kazimierz, 34
Bar-Yehuda, Penina (Gleicher-Strauch), 154, 158
Bednarczyk, Tadeusz, 270
Ben-Ẓion, S., 185, 289n12
Berdichevsky (Berdyczewski), Micha Joseph, 185–87
Bergmann, Hugo, 141, 289n11
Bergson, Henri, 142
Berkman, Yiẓḥak, 173
Berkowitz, Y. D., 185
Bialer, Tuvia, 94
Bialik, Ḥaim Naḥman, 13, 31, 137, 158, 161, 167, 173–74, 179–181, 183–86, 189–91, 202, 211, 282n3, 283n4
Biebow, Hans, 255
Bodzinger, Shlomo, 45, 94, 288n4
Bolochower, Ber, 156, 291n33
Bonhardt, Simḥa Bunim of Pshyscha ("Holy Yood"), 14, 80
Brandstetter, Michael, 114–15
Brandstetter, Mordekhai David, 115
Branicki, Ksawery, 291
Brann, Markus Mordekhai, 261
Braude, Markus Mordekhai, xvii, 30, 37–38, 68, 114, 117, 125–30, 144, 167, 169–170, 240, 286n17, 288n3
Braude, Natalia (Buber), 96, 131
Braverman, Jonah, 96, 133
Brenner, Y. H., 184–86, 211, 293n8
Broderzon, Moshe, 169

Brodt, Shmuel, 35, 167
Bromberg-Bitkowski, Sigmund, 114
Brzezinski, Avraham Yehuda, 296n5
Buber, Martin, 307
Bzoza, Hanoch, 119

Cahan, Ya'akov, 137, 179, 185, 284n7
Chajes, Ẓvi Hirsch Pereẓ, 32, 136
Cicero, 151
Citrinowski, Yeḥiel, 173
Cohen, Asher (Oskar Kohn), 94
Cohen, Hermann, 261
Cohen, Leibele, 40
Cohn (Kohn), Tobias, 100, 287n30
Copernicus, Nicolaus, 14

Dancyger dynasty, 24, 73–74
Dancyger, Avraham Ḥaim, 75
Dancyger, Beẓalel Yair, 20–21, 24, 40, 58, 77–78, 247
Dancyger, Shmuel Ẓvi Hirsch (Tif'eret Shmuel), 19–20, 23–24, 45, 62, 69, 71, 76, 83, 98, 247–48
Dancyger, Shneur Zalman, 24
Dancyger, Shraga Feivel (of Radom), 24, 33, 75
Dancyger, Yakov Simḥa Bunim, 75
Dancyger, Yeḥiel (the "Old Rebbe"), 18–19, 23–24, 75, 78–84, 86, 90, 110, 248
Dancyger, Yeraḥmiel Yisroel Yiẓḥak (Yismaḥ Yisroel), xvii, 18–19, 21, 24, 61, 68, 71, 86–94, 106, 247–48, 285n7, 286n4
Dancyger, Yisroel Zvi Yair, 24
Dancyger, Yiẓhak Menaḥem Mendel (Akedat Yiẓhak), 20, 24, 69, 71–73, 75, 98, 105, 104–111, 201, 228, 294n13
Delmedigo, Joseph Solomon, 14
De-Nur, Yeḥiel (Ka-Tsetnik), 294n14
Dinur, Ben-Ẓion, 9
Dmowski, Roman, 89, 286n9
Dobroszycki, Lucjan, 284n10
Dostoyevsky, Fyodor, 220
Dubnow, Simon, 37, 134–35, 146, 283n10, 288n3
Dzigan, Shimon, 149, 292n54

Eck (Ekron), Nathan, 96, 132–34, 136–39, 142–43, 157, 196, 207, 289n7, 289n9
Einstein, Albert, 31, 139
Eizman, Jacob, 76
Ellenberg, Shmaryahu, 115
Englard, Shabtai, 42
Erter, Yiẓḥak, 96, 125, 129, 286n17

Fallek, Wilhelm, 290n20
Farbstein, Joshua Heschel, 36
Federbush, Shimon, 296n16
Feierberg, Mordecai Ze'ev, 138, 289n8
Feiner, Yossele, 42
Fichman, Yaakov, 172, 176, 178, 185
Ficowski, Jerzy, 271, 296n18
Finkelstein, Ḥaim, 284n5
Finkelstein, Moshe, 258–59
Foner, Meir, 174–75
Frankel, Zacharias, 261–62
Frank, Jacob, 281n6
Frankists, 7, 9, 156, 281n6
Freilich (Frejlich), Moshe, 46, 149–51, 153–54, 168
Freiman, Menashe, 285n11
Frenkel, Yirmiyahu, 35
Friedman, Philip (Filip), xi, 122, 144–48, 289n19
Frishman (Frischmann), David, 182,184, 293n4
Frishman, Yeshayahu, 148
Froyem Lejzer (Efraim Elazar), 50, 56
Fuchs (Fox), Ḥaim Leib, 253, 284n5

Gans, David, 14
Galileo Galilei, 14, 139
Gelerter, Menaḥem, 170
Gnessin, Uri Nissan, 185
Goethe, Johann Wolfgang von, 23, 219
Goldman, Avraham Moshe, 60–64, 104
Gomułka, Władysław, 267
Gordon, Jeremiah, 224
Gordon, Y. L. (YaLaG), 96, 174, 286nn18–20
Grabski, Władysław, 1, 53, 281n1
Graetz, Heinrich Ẓvi, 146, 261–62, 146
Greenberg, Uri Ẓvi , 158, 179, 237, 291n40, 296n4
Grimm Brothers, 97
Grobart (Graubart), Yehuda Leib, 35
Gruenbaum, Yiẓḥak, 31–35, 167, 283n8
Güdemann, Moritz, 261
Gumplowicz, Ludwig, 257
Guttmann, Yeḥiel Michal Hacohen, 261–62, 296n16

Halevi, Yehuda, 155, 290n29
Halkin, Hillel, 290n30, 294n16
Handelsman, Marceli, 289n19
Ḥanina bar Ḥama, 287n3
Hauptmann, Gerhart, 179
Hecht, Shabtai, 42
Heftman, Joseph, 172
Hegel, Georg Wilhelm Friedrich, 23, 307
Heine, Heinrich, 154, 183, 219, 290n27
Heinemann, Yiẓḥak (Isaak), 262, 296n16
Herzl, Theodore, 29, 127, 131, 133, 168
Hitler, Adolf, 35, 147, 193, 195, 197, 204, 227, 232, 264
Hoenigswald, Richard, 307
Hoffmann, Moses, 258
Holenderski, Leib, 50, 284n9
Horkheimer, Max, 307
Horowitz, Yaakov Yiẓḥak Halevy ("Seer of Lublin"), 14, 282n4
Ḥuldai (Obzhensky), Ozer, 136, 288n5
Ḥuldai, Ron, 288n5

Ibn Gabirol, Solomon, 144

Jabotinsky, Vladimir Ze'ev, 31, 36, 128,167, 291n40
Jaruzelski, Wojciech, 265, 268, 270, 291n32
John Paul II, 252, 277
Joselewicz, Berek, 9–10
Joselewicz, Joseph, 9
Josephus Flavius, 144
Joshua ben Korḥa, 193

Kabak, A. A., 253
Kahn, Israel, 45
Kahn, Lazar, 29
Kalir (ha-Kalir), Elazar ben, 296n7
Kalisz, Mordekhai Menaḥem Mendel (the "Silent Rebbe"), 13, 15, 63, 82, 282n2
Kamieniecki (Kamenetzky), A. S., 146
Katzenelson, Jacob Benjamin, 174, 189
Katzenelson, Yiẓḥak, x, xviii, 29, 128, 138, 172–207, 210, 212, 231, 233, 253, 271, 293n2, 293n5, 293n9, 294n13, 295n3
Katzenelson, Ẓvi, 196
Katznelson, Berl, 182
Kaufmann, David, 261
Klausner, Joseph, 180
Klauzinska, Kamila, xv, 296n6
Kleinman, Moshe, 137
Kolbe, Maximilian, 251–55, 277
Konstadt, Herman, 242–43
Korczak, Janusz, 207
Kosciuszko, Tadeusz, 9, 43, 290n19
Koussevitzky, Moshe, 259
Kowalski, Yehudah Leib, 35
Krasiński, Zygmunt, 167, 281n13

Kroy, Ẓvi, 29
Kuehnemann, Eugen, 307

Lamdan, Yiẓḥak, 158, 225, 291n42
Landau, Yeḥezkel ben Yehuda HaLevi (Noda Biyehudah), 63, 284n3
Leiner, Shmuel Shlomo. See Radzyner Rebbe
Lemberg, Yakov, 254–55
Lenin, Vladimir, 1
Lerer, Yeḥiel, 76, 285n5
Lessing, Gotthold Ephraim, 219, 295n3
Levin, Ḥanock Heynekh HaKohen of Aleksander, 74–75, 248, 285n2
Levin, Yiẓḥak-Meir, 167
Levinger, D. S., 296n16
Levy Yiẓḥak of Berditchev, 23
Lewkowitz, Albert, 263
Lichtenstein, Israel, 37, 50, 284n8
Lipszyc (Liebszyc), Eliezer (Lajzer), xv,77, 217, 244–45
Lubetkin, Ẓivia, 207
Ludendorff, Erich, 219
Luria, Solomon (RaSHaL), 287n28

Maeterlinck, Maurice, 176, 179
Mahler, Raphael, 145, 289n16, 289n19
Maimonides, 63, 67, 99, 216
Makower family, 42
Mann, Thomas, 6, 281n4
Mannheim, Karl, 307
Maroko, Avraham Mordekhai, 106, 229
Marck, Siegfried, 307
Maroko, Mordekhai David, 77–78, 87
Maroko, Yidl, 15, 77–78, 92, 229, 253
Maroko, Yosef Eliezer, 229
Meisel (Majsel), Eliyahu Ḥaim 44, 56, 242
Meltzer, Shimshon, 10, 285n5
Mendele the Book Peddler (Mendele Mocher Sforim, born Sholem Yankev Abramovich), ix, 40, 116,137, 174, 184, 191, 211, 220
Mezeritch, Dov Ber ben Avraham, maggid of, 61, 284n1
Mickiewicz, Adam, 9, 155–57, 167, 281n13
Mincberg, Leib, 241
Mintz, Benjamin, 39
Moreino, Ze'ev, 243
Morgenstern (fellow student), 136
Morgenstern, Menaḥem Mendel of Kotzk, 14, 216, 246, 282n7
Mukdoni, A., 29

Napoleon Bonaparte, 9, 155
Neuman, Isaac, 295n4
Nissenbaum, Yiẓḥak, 35, 201, 294n15

Oberbaum, Simḥa, 42
Obzhensky (Ḥuldai), Ozer, 136
Ochocki, Jan Duklan, 156
Olshanski, Teofil, 48
Olszowski, Mr., 246–47
Oppenheimer, Franz, 257
Orenstein, Jacob Meshulam, 125, 129, 286n17
Ormian, Ḥaim, 115, 288n3
Otto, Rudolf, 282n1

Pabianice, rebbe, 72, 109, 216
Pacanowski (Gavish), Shmuel, 136
Peretz, Y. L., 47, 173, 188, 211
Perle, Eugen and Recha, 258
Perle, Flora, 259, 307
Perlman, Avraham, 114
Piłsudksi, Jozef, 34, 48, 55, 158, 227, 286n9
Platau, Stashek (Shlomo), 139
Popper, Karl, 142
Poznański, Israel Kalmanowicz, 239, 242–43

Prilutzky, Noah, 37, 47, 167
Prokop-Janiec, Eugenia, 292n46
Prussak, Avraham, 50
Prywes, Moshe, 162

Rabbah bar bar Hana, 274
Rabbinowicz, Shaul Pinchas, 146
Rabin, Israel, 261–62
Rabinowicz, Rabbi Yaakov Yiẓḥak ("Holy Yood"), 14, 282nn5–6
Rabinowitz, Yaakov, 185
Rabon, Israel, 50, 284n6
Radzyner Rebbe (Leiner, Shmuel Shlomo), 196, 198, 200, 202–4, 207, 252
Rapoport, Nathan, 273
Rappaport, Ben-Ẓion, 141–42, 289n12
Reagan, Ronald, 265
Reich, Leon, 34, 167
Reymont, Władysław Stanisław, 89, 232, 245, 286n8
Reyzen (Reisen, Raisin), Avrom (Abraham), 41, 292n52
Rieger, Eliezer, 162
Rieger, Elisheva, 162
Rieger, Shaul, 114–15, 119, 161–62, 165–66
Ringelblum, Emanuel, 145, 289n19
Rogowy, Avraham Mordekhai, 39
Rogowski, Stefan, 245–47, 296n9
Rosenblat, Uri, 45
Rosenblatt, Yossele, 259
Rosenzweig, Yeḥiel (Jechiel Rozencwajg), 29–30, 172, 283n6
Rothschild, Edmond de, 31
Rumkowski, Mordekhai Ḥaim, 58, 147, 226, 284n11
Russ, Moshe Neḥemia, 42

Sadan, Dov, 202, 294n17
Salanter, Yisrael Lipkin, 287n2
Samuel, Herbert, 31
Savitzky (Saviv), Aharon, 135, 165
Schiper (Schipper), Dr. Yiẓḥak (Ignacy), 167, 289n19
Schlosser, Ichi Meir, 66
Schnitzler, Arthur, 179
Schoenfeld, Moshe, 135, 288n4
Scholem Aleichem, 163, 215, 220
Schumacher (Szumacher), Israel, 149, 166- 69, 292n50, 292n54
Schweitzer, Shlomo, 284n5
Seneca, 152–54
Shabbetai Ẓvi, 7, 281n6
Shapiro, Ḥaim, 33
Shlonsky, Avraham,158, 179, 291n41, 295n3
Shmuel, Talmudic sage, 99, 287n25
Shmueli, Efraim, 286n2, 287nn4–5, 289n14, 290n24, 293n6, 297n17, 307
Shneur, Zalman, 24, 137, 179, 185
Shofman, Gershon, 179, 185
Silberstein, Markus, 94, 107, 243
Silberzweig, Zalman, 38
Simḥoni, Jacob Naftali, 144, 146, 289n14
Simonsohn, Max, 258
Singer, Isaac Bashevis, 286n7
Singer, Israel Joshua, 89, 286n7
Singer, Yiẓḥak Meir, 71, 77
Skwarczynska, Stefania, 118
Słonimski, Antoni, 158, 160, 256, 283n2
Słonimski, Zelig, 160, 283n2, 291n45, 292n46
Słowacki, Juliusz, 10, 29, 157, 166–67 166, 167, 281n13, 291n38
Smolenskin, Pereẓ, 96, 115, 286n16
Sokolov, Naḥum, 31–32, 167
Sonenberg, Yiẓḥak Heynekh, 75, 285n3
Spiro, Hanna, 119
Starkiewicz, Leon, 118
Steinberg, Yakov, 179, 185, 253
Strykower, Efraim Fishel, 61

Strykowski, Beresz, 219, 222, 225, 254
Strykowski, Fiszel Leib, 222
Strykowski, Mendel, 222–23, 230, 254, 295n4
Sussman, Ezra, 209
Szeintuch, Yeḥiel, 294n7
Szmulewicz, Elimelekh, 175–76
Szmulewicz, Ephraim (Fiszel Leib). See Shmueli, Efraim
Szmulewicz, Frajda (mother), 18, 58, 225, 230
Szmulewicz, Mordekhai Dovid (father), 17, 27, 38, 58, 64, 68–69, 98, 100, 107, 217, 230
Szmulewicz, Moses, 18, 50
Szmulewicz, Yaakov, 176
Steiger (Szteiger), Shlomo (Stanislaw), 47–49
Szpan, Shlomo, 136, 288n6
Szwarc (Schwartz), Marek, 126

Tabaksblat, Yisroel, 284n11
Tabenkin, Yiẓḥak, 182
Tacitus, 151–53
Tartakower, Arie, 129, 165, 170, 288n3, 292n48
Tchernichovsky, Sha'ul, 137, 158, 167, 173, 184–85, 188, 211
Tchernowitz, Chaim, 288n2
Tchernowitz, Shmuel, 133, 288n2
Tenenbaum, Mordechai, 290n19
Thon, Joshua, 167
Tillich, Paul, 112, 288n6, 307
Traister Moskovitz, Sarah, 294n4
Treistman (Trajstman), Eliezer Lajb 44
Trotsky, Leon, 1, 257
Trunk, Isaiah (Y. Y.), 284n5, 284n11, 295n2
Turkow, Mark, 8
Tuwim, Julian, 10, 118, 158–60, 279, 291nn43–44
Tyberg, Rebbe Yehuda Moshe (Emunat Moshe), 24, 69, 77, 83

Uger, Yeshayahu, 45, 270
Urbach, E. E., 296n16
Urban, Jerzy, 270, 296n16

Wagner, Daniel, 296n6
Wałęsa, Lech, 268
Weber, Max, 85–86, 226, 257, 286n2
Weingarten, Yeraḥmiel, 176
Weinryb, Bernard Dov, 145
Weisblum, Elimelech of Lizhensk, 61, 284n2
Weiss, cantor, 258
Weizmann, Chaim, 31, 135
Wiener, Moshe Aharon, 224
Wilson, Woodrow, 2
Wise, Stephen S., 289n15
Wiślicki, Khayim Yankev, 27, 61, 63, 94, 114
Włoszczower, Mordekhai, 42
Woidislawski, Itche Meir, 42
Wojciechowski, Stanisław, 47
Wojdysławski, Yankev, 94
Woler, Mendel, 42
Wyspiański, Stanisław, 157–58

Yismaḥ Yisroel. See Dancyger, Reb Yeraḥmiel Yisroel Yiẓḥak
Yonath, Ada, xv

Żelichowski, Shloyme, 195–96, 200, 203, 254
Zerubavel, Yaakov, 35, 167
Zlotnik, Yehudah Leib (Y. H. Avida), 35, 167
Zuckerman (Cukierman), Yiẓḥak, 193, 197, 199, 207, 254, 270

www.ingramcontent.com/pod-product-compliance
Lightning Source LLC
Chambersburg PA
CBHW020235170426
43202CB00008B/94
9781644695982